OSKAR von *RIESEMANN*
MOUSSORGSKY

MOUSSORGSKY

O S K A R V O N R I E S E M A N N

Translated from the German by
PAUL ENGLAND

DOVER PUBLICATIONS, INC.
New York

This Dover edition, first published in 1971, is an unabridged republication, with minor corrections, of the English translation originally published by Alfred A. Knopf, New York, in 1929. The original German work was published by the Drei Masken Verlag, Munich, in 1926 with the title *Modest Petrowitsch Mussorgski.*

International Standard Book Number: 0-486-22496-1
Library of Congress Catalog Card Number: 78-138388

Manufactured in the United States of America
Dover Publications Inc.
180 Varick Street
New York, N.Y. 10014

PREFACE

IT WAS originally intended that Volume II of the "*Mono-graphien zur Russischen Musik*" should contain separate accounts of the life and work of the four, or, if we are to include César Cui, the five, Russian composers whose combined artistic activities comprise what used to be known as the New Russian School—a not altogether appropriate description, since an Old Russian School never existed. In addition to Moussorgsky the school includes Rimsky-Korsakov, Borodin, and Balakirev. But the predominant and ever-growing importance of the composer of *Boris Godounov*, the stamp of originality which marks his work, in spite of its unquestionable and deep-rooted affinities with that of his predecessors, and, last but not least, the interest attaching to the stark tragedy of his life—all these things pointed to the necessity of assigning to Moussorgsky a place apart in any literary treatment of the subject. This course is made possible by the surprising richness of material available for the purpose; and the result is that the life of Moussorgsky, instead of being confined to four or five chapters, now fills the whole of Volume II of the monographs. This has meant the relegation of the other members of the New Russian School to Volume III, and a not inconsiderable extension of the original limits of the whole work. We feel sure that no further apology for this decision is necessary, especially in Germany, where the name of Moussorgsky is by this time familiar to all who are interested in music.

It is not easy to write books on Russian music when all access to the national libraries and archives is barred, a fact that will account for many of the deficiences in the present work, of which no one is more fully aware than the author. The amount of printed material for a history of Russian music to be found in the libraries of Germany, never large, is gradually diminishing, while books that, ten years ago, it was easy to purchase have since become bibliographical rarities beyond one's reach. The work on these monographs was begun in Russia, and it would have been impossible for the author to continue it in Germany had it not been for the unexpected help and assistance afforded him from a quarter where, in view of the political events of recent years, he could scarcely have hoped to find it. Inspired by a keen interest in the common cause, and by a most generous impulse of self-sacrifice, for which the writer can never be sufficiently grateful, some of his Russian colleagues placed at his disposal not only some of the rarest publications bearing on the subject, but also a great number of otherwise inaccessible manuscripts. Thanks are due in the first place to Dr. Andreas Rimsky-Korsakov, the son of the composer, and successor to V. Stassov as head of the musical department of the Imperial Public Library in Leningrad, without whose aid the work on the monographs must have come to a standstill. With a courteous readiness that never flagged, with inexhaustible patience and an energy that overcame all obstacles, he helped me, by word and deed, to bring my life of Moussorgsky to a conclusion; indeed, it is no exaggeration to describe him as part author of this volume, and I desire here to place on record my deep sense of the debt I owe him. I should like next to make grateful mention of the late composer Sergei Liapoussov, the friend and pupil of Balakirev, as also of the eminent writer on music Igor Glebov, of Leningrad, and of Professor Alexander Moser, of Moscow, to whom I am severally indebted for valuable contributions to my material.

In accordance with the principles laid down in Volume I of this series, it is the biographical element that is chiefly emphasized in the volume before us, since it is only through the life of an artist that his work can be fully interpreted. This is especially true of a nature so strong and so intensely sensitive as that of Moussorgsky, with whom every actual experience was transmuted into an artistic impression. The recognition of this fact is essential to a proper appreciation of the work of the composer. It is for this reason that, as in the previous volume, I have introduced so many contemporary documents illustrative of the various episodes, and more especially Moussorgsky's own letters, of which a great number have fortunately been preserved; these reflect the mental attitude of the writer in a manner that, however peculiar, is invaluable, and it is on them that the biographical portion of this book is founded.

Several notable studies of Moussorgsky have appeared in Russia in recent years, which the present writer has naturally not been able to ignore, and which have often influenced his judgment considerably in certain directions. The most noteworthy of them are the very valuable essays, "*Boris Godounov*," by A. Rimsky-Korsakov, "Moussorgsky," by Professor J. Lapshin, and "*Khovanstchina* and its Two Authors," by V. Karatigin—all of which appeared in a special "Moussorgsky" volume (Nos. 5, 6) of the excellent Russian publication *Contemporary Musicians* (Leningrad, 1917), edited by A. Rimsky-Korsakov, but since, unfortunately, discontinued—and also the intelligent

ix

appreciation of Moussorgsky by Igor Glebov in his *Symphonic Studies* (Leningrad, 1922). The new and interesting views on Moussorgsky's work put forward in these writings have often led to conclusions of decisive importance.

Any attempt to trace the development of style in Russian music, especially in Russian opera, or to make any deep research into the contributing psychological causes, would have far exceeded the proper limits of my present task—such inquiries must be reserved for a special work. These independent monographs on Russian music are intended to be regarded as raw material, so to speak, with which a writer must make himself familiar before it is possible to use them as a foundation for critical researches of a general character; consequently only a limited space has been devoted to general criticism in the present volume, where it seemed better to confine oneself to such mere allusions as might apply to the special case of Moussorgsky.

In conclusion let me say that my work on the present volume has been made substantially lighter by the generous and unselfish assistance afforded me by the publishers of Moussorgsky's works; it is my pleasant duty to express my sincere gratitude before all to Mr. W. Bessel, of Paris, for his stimulating encouragement in my task, as well as to Messrs. Breitkopf and Härtel, and the firm of M. P. Belaiev in Leipzig.

OSKAR VON RIESEMANN

*Gaienhofen on the Bodensee
(Lake of Constance),
October 1925*

CONTENTS

MOUSSORGSKY

HOUSEHOLDRY

EARLY YEARS
1839 — 56

IN THE Toropetz district of the Government of Pskov, not far from Shishitza, a station on the Windau-Rybinsk railway, lies the village of Karevo, in former times the property of an estate of the same name; since the middle of the seventeenth century this estate, with many of the neighbouring domains, farms, and villages, had been in the possession of the Moussorgsky family.

Like most families of the old Russian nobility, the Moussorgskys traced their descent back to Rurik, the semi-legendary Varangian prince who, in the year 862 was invited by the Slavonic tribes of the north of Europe to rule over their country, which, "though wide and rich, was without law or order." In the oldest genealogical record of the Russian nobility—the "Satin Book" or "Barchatnaia Kniga" as it is called—we find the direct ancestor of the Moussorgskys, Prince Yuri Feodorovitch, a descendant of Rurik in the fifteenth degree. Alexander Yurievitch, the son of Prince Yuri of Smolensk, dropped the title of Prince: be called himself "Monastir"—i.e., Monastery—and became the founder of the Monastirev family, which became extinct in the nineteenth century. His grandson, Roman Vassilievitch Monastirev, named "Moussorga"—i.e., the "Foul-mouthed"—is the founder of the Moussorgsky family, who in former times wrote their name Moussorgskoi, Mousserskoi, or Moussorsky. The Moussorgskys were never very numerous; they never attained to political importance or to a leading position at the tsarist courts of Moscow and Petersburg. Nevertheless there seem to have been some brave Moussorgskys in the army of the Moscow tsars; the "Archer" Michael Ivanovitch Moussorgsky, who took part in the war against Poland in the years 1654–6, was rewarded by the Tsar Alexei Michailovitch in the year 1670 with extensive possessions in the Government of Pskov; to these his grandson Grigori Grigorievitch added still further territory in the Toropetz district of the same Government, including the estate of Karevo on the lake of Shishzo. For a time the Moussorgskys were now great landowners; the composer's father, Peter Alexeievitch, in the year 1851 still owned ten thousand desiatines (eleven thousand hectares) in the Government of Pskov, and a hundred and fifty desiatines in that of Yaroslav. For several generations the Moussorgskys had intermarried with many of the noble families of Russia, and particularly, as is so usual with the country nobility, with those of their own and the neighbouring governments; amongst their nearest relations we find the families of Voronzov-Velyaninov, Koslov, Arbusov, Golenistchev-Kutúsov, Rodsyanko, and others. Peter Alexeievitch Moussorgsky, the composer's father, was the illegitimate son of Alexei Grigorievitch Moussorgsky, an officer in the Preobrazhensky Guard regiment. After the birth of the child the father married the mother, who was a serf, Irene Georgievna Yegorovna by name, and their son was made legitimate in the year 1820 by ukase of the Senate; though it was not till thirteen years after his death (1865) that his name was entered on the roll of the nobility of the Government of Pskov.

From the picturesque point of view the neighbourhood of Karevo can have little charm for the pampered eye of the inhabitant of western Europe. Far as the eye can reach, fields and meadows, lofty, impenetrable forests, give an air of monotony to the landscape here, as in the whole of the "Sarmatian Plain"; nevertheless its melancholy and yet

4

suggestive atmosphere makes an infinitely alluring and unique appeal to a sympathetic soul that can rightly understand the mysterious and intimate language in which Nature here speaks to us. Not without reason do the Russians love their land above all earthly things and prefer a simple birch wood beside some freshly ploughed field to all the glories of the most luxuriant landscape; with them the love of country is a part of their being, a physical sensation of community with their native land. In these vast solitudes the cords that Nature weaves to bind mortals to herself are of quite extraordinary strength and toughness; men will languish, and even die, when those cords are roughly severed.

Variety is introduced into the landscape around Karevo by two lakes, which lie close together; one of them, called Shishitza (from "*shishzo*," the old word for "broth"), belonged to the estate. Its banks are overgrown with primeval pines and other trees, the home of game and other wild creatures in such abundance as could scarcely be found in Europe outside the dense forests of Russia. It can easily be imagined how the waters of the lake and the branches of the century-old oaks that surrounded it have always whispered and murmured many a tale and legend of their country's dark and troubled past.

One of these told how, at the time of the Streltzy risings, that gloomy and terrible period of Russian history just before the advent of Peter the Great, from which Moussorgsky has taken the plot of his *Khovanstchina*, a messenger on horseback who was sent by one of the rebel bands to rouse the Streltzy of Toropetz to some perhaps decisive battle with the young Tsar Peter was drowned in the waters of the angry lake.

Many are the storms that have swept over the domain of Karevo and its inhabitants. Of the house itself at the time of the Revolution in 1917 only one wing remained—built of wood, like most country-houses in Russia; today probably

5

even that has disappeared. The main body of the building had been pulled down at an earlier date, when the property was sold by auction. One of the later tenants, a wealthy fishery-owner, attracted to Karevo by the abundant harvest of fish in the lake, built himself a new residence on another site; thus we no longer know what the house looked like in which one of the most gifted composers of the nineteenth century first saw the light—for it was here at Karevo that Modest Petrovitch Moussorgsky was born, on the 16th (28th) of March 1839.

*   *   *

The first ten years of Moussorgsky's life were spent on his father's estate, under the protecting care of his parents. The materials for a reliable account of this period of his life and the youthful years that followed are very scanty; chief among them is an autobiographical sketch written by Moussorgsky shortly before his death, to which frequent reference will be made.

The life led by the Moussorgsky family in Karevo was of the comfortable character, and on the patriarchal lines usual among the great landed proprietors before the liberation of the serfs. The days passed in leisurely succession; almost each day had its fixed duties, hallowed by tradition, indoors or out, in cellar and store-room, and its no less strictly defined agricultural labours on arable land or pasture, in meadow and in forest. The only variety was afforded by the numerous feast days of the Russian calendar, which were always kept with the greatest devotion by the rural and village population and afforded a welcome opportunity for all sorts of excesses in eating and drinking. The same may be said of the not too frequent exchange of visits with friends and neighbours. Moussorgsky, in later years, immortalized the spirit of Russian hospitality in one of his songs: "The Banquet" (words by Koltzov).

6

Moussorgsky's father, as was customary at that time, had spent some years in the service of the State, and had been an official of the Senate in Petersburg; but while still comparatively young, he had retired altogether into the country to undertake the personal management of his extensive estates. He is said to have been exceptionally musical. His wife, the composer's mother, was a Tchirikov by birth, and, like himself, belonged to the country gentry of the Pskov Government. She is described by her relations as a lady of highly romantic tendencies, rather *exaltée*, and sentimental; nevertheless she was a model wife and mother. In her youth she was very fond of writing poetry, but, as her verses did not rise above the ordinary amateur level, they are not likely to be dragged from their obscure repose in her diaries and the albums of her various female acquaintances.

There can be no doubt that it was from his mother, whom he came to love so dearly, that Moussorgsky got his "cheerful nature" as well as his "taste for story-telling," while his musical gifts were an inheritance from his father.

Modest Moussorgsky was the youngest of four brothers, of whom the two eldest died very young; the only companion of his boyhood was his brother Filaret, his senior by three years, who survived him many years.

Very early, almost with the first manifestation of conscious existence, Moussorgsky was swayed by a deep love of the Russian character and the Russian people. As we have seen, his grandmother on his father's side had been a serf, and, in consequence, the pure unadulterated blood of the Russian peasantry mingled in his veins with the blue blood of his ancestors, the aristocratic "Rurikovitchi"—i.e., descendants of Rurik. The blend was a good one. It was probably to his peasant ancestry that Moussorgsky owed that astonishing power of identifying himself with the subtlest emotions of the soul of the Russian people, of which

7

he gave proof time after time in his compositions, during the later part of his career.

One of the few pieces of information that we possess concerning Moussorgsky's childhood occurs in a letter from his brother Filaret to Vladimir Stassov, the Petersburg art-critic. We read: "In boyhood and youth, as well as in his later years, my brother Modest had a special predilection for everything connected with the people and the peasantry. Even the Russian moujik was a human being in his eyes." This last remark need not astonish us. In Moussorgsky's younger days the system of serfdom, with all its abuses, still obtained in Russia. The Russian peasant, according to the prevailing notion, was a chattel, or at best a beast of burden, to be bought and sold like a sack of corn or a cart-horse. No one troubled about his inner life, or about any attempts he might make to express his emotions. As to a soul—that luxury of the higher classes—it was simply assumed that the peasant had none; the whole wide and fruitful field of the psychology of the Russian peasantry still remained entirely unexplored. Moussorgsky's attitude, the infinitely loving solicitude with which he sought after the human element in the soul of the Russian peasant, was by no means such a matter of course at that time as it appears to be today.

Moussorgsky loved the Russian people, not merely as a picturesque object that one enjoys painting, but still keeps at least at arm's length—he loved them with the passionate love of a kindred soul that can feel for the sorrows of others. In later life he even thought seriously for a time of "going to the people," as the Russian phrase well describes it, like the Russian Socialists of the eighteen-sixties, the "Narodniki" as they are called (from "*narod*," the people), or his later contemporary among the ranks of writers and philosophers Leo Tolstoy. In a letter to Stassov, of June 16 and 22, 1872, he writes: "Now suppose your Moussorianin were to go on a tramp through Russia, our dear motherland, ploughing up the black earth—not the reclaimed tracts, already fertilized—no! the virgin soil for me, that no man has touched! It is the people I mean—I long not merely to get to know them, but to be *admitted to their brotherhood!*"

The artist was, of course, always alert in Moussorgsky's nature, and there were times when this desire to utilize the full artistic possibilities of the peasant class of the people assumed almost the form of a hallucination. We can trace the working of some overpowering artistic inspiration in the following passage from a letter to the painter Ilia Riepin (June 13, 1875): "It is *the people* I want to depict; sleeping or waking, eating or drinking, I have them constantly in my mind's eye—again and again they rise before me, in all their reality, huge, unvarnished, with no tinsel trappings! How rich a treasure awaits the composer in the speech of the people—so long, that is, as any corner of the land remains to which the railway has not penetrated—what inexhaustible possibilities of getting at their real life! A true artist who should dig deep enough would indeed have cause to dance for joy at the results!"

The ties that, as time went on, were destined to bind the artist and his own people so inseparably together were already forming in his earliest years; among the numerous serfs who, after the good old Russian custom, were lodged in the mansion at Karevo in patriarchal fashion, the boy probably had many good friends who served later on as models for the characters introduced into his works. First and foremost among them would naturally be the nurse— *niania*—that indispensable piece of furniture to be found in every Russian family of the better class. As is well known, the Russian Nanny's appointment is for life—only death can part her from her nursling. In her eyes the child committed to her charge never grows up, is never able to look after himself, but needs her help and her blessing at every

9

step on life's rough way; she will lavish the same tender care upon him at fifty as she did when he was five. Today, unfortunately, this touching type, this living heirloom of every ancestral home, has almost entirely disappeared. Pushkin, in his *Eugen Onegin*, long ago raised an imperishable literary monument to her honour, while Moussorgsky, in the world of music, has given us another, worthy to stand beside it. The reference, of course, is to his enchanting song-cycle *The Nursery*, and the unique scene in the second act of *Boris Godounov* between the children and their *niania*, or "*mamka*" (mammy) as she is sometimes called.

We have it on Moussorgsky's own authority that it was to his *niania* that he owed his earliest artistic impressions. In his autobiographical sketch he tells us: "Thrown so much in my nurse's society, I soon became familiar with all the Russian fairy-tales, with the result that, child as I was, I often could not sleep at night. The acquaintance thus formed with the spirit of the people and their modes of life furnished the chief incentive to my earliest improvisations on the pianoforte, even before I knew the most elementary rules of piano-playing." The abnormal sensibility of his nervous system, which at this early age robbed the boy Moussorgsky of his sleep and made him so extraordinarily receptive of artistic impressions may well have been the origin of those frequent attacks in later life and of the final complete loss of emotional self-control, which led to so early and tragic an end.

Moussorgsky, however, unlike Pushkin, has made little direct artistic use of the varied and many-coloured scenes in the Russian fairyland that his nurse unveiled before him. The story told by the nurse in *Boris Godounov*, and the fantastic figures that the child in the song "Child and Nurse" sees pass before him, are the only artistic result of those childish recollections that in other ways bore such fruit in the boy's imagination. Moussorgsky made no use in his

operas either of the fairy-tales, or of the *biliny*, the legends
and popular epics of his country; this wide and promising
field he left to Rimsky-Korsakov, who became the real musical interpreter of fairy-tales for the Russian stage, while
Moussorgsky confined himself to the realistic side of Russian life, in which he never failed to find some new subject
rich in artistic opportunities.

It need hardly be said that Moussorgsky was a musical
prodigy, as nearly all great musicians have been, in so far
as he showed signs of extraordinary powers in early youth.
Fortunately not all parents are so short-sighted as to force
their children's precocious talents or make material profit
out of them. In Moussorgsky's case, of course, the question
never arose; in the days of his youth, musical ability, a taste
for art, were regarded by people of his class as agreeable
social accomplishments, but certainly not as serious indications of exceptional endowments that might influence the
whole career of those to whom they had been given. The boy
Moussorgsky, who, to use his own words, began to improvise
in his own way on the piano before he knew how to play,
received his first piano-lessons from his mother, who was
soon superseded by a German governess—at that time almost as indispensable a fixture in the houses of the Russian
nobility as the *niania*. The boy's progress was, as we might
expect, astonishing; when only seven years old he could play
the smaller pieces of Liszt, and at the age of nine, at an
evening party in his parents' house, he played a concerto
by Field (whose Moscow reputation was just then spreading
throughout Russia) and earned well-merited praise for his
performance.

These surprising proofs of his talent decided Moussorgsky's father, who, though not a performer himself,
worshipped music, to give his son a more elaborate musical
education than was possible in the country, but nothing,

11

of course, that could be called "professional" training—for a young aristocrat, that would hardly have been becoming.

* * *

In August 1849, at the beginning of the scholastic year, Peter Alexeievitch Moussorgsky took his two sons to Petersburg, where they were entered at the school of SS. Peter and Paul. The lads brought little learning with them from their country home, beyond the ability to converse fluently in three languages. In the education of young people of good family in Russia at that time, nothing was considered so essential as a good knowledge of foreign languages. A perfect mastery of French was indispensable for admission to the salons of the best society in Petersburg, where it was practically the only language spoken; German ran it close, out of compliment to the many German princes and princesses who have sat in succession on the throne of Russia; important, too, in this respect was the influence of the nobility of the Baltic provinces, who occupied most of the appointments at court. Moreover, in accordance with a long-standing Russian tradition, which survived until quite recently, three important personages in every community had to be German—the doctor, the apothecary, and the school-teacher—since only Germans were to be relied upon (in Russian estimation) for the conscientiousness which is essential to these professions, and in which Russians felt their countrymen to be lacking. The German governess already referred to had, of course, taken pains to give the young Moussorgskys a good elementary knowledge of German; and it was probably the considerations just mentioned that induced the father to place his sons in a German academy. The school of SS. Peter and Paul was a German classical gymnasium, beyond question the best-conducted secondary school in Petersburg at that time. Here Moussorgsky laid the foundation of his knowledge of Latin and quickly perfected himself in German. The instruction in most of the subjects was given in German, and the pupils spoke German among themselves, so that Moussorgsky soon became a perfect master of the language. He had already adopted French as his second mother-tongue and spoke it not merely fluently, but with some pretensions to a more than ordinary elegance of expression. For a long time he used it by preference in ordinary conversation, for Russian was slow in taking its place in the salons of Petersburg. When, later on, Moussorgsky went more and more deeply into the study of the real Russia, until it became the sole object of his thoughts and feelings and artistic activities, he became ever more and more absorbed in the spirit of the Russian language, which gradually revealed to him all its beauties and its hidden treasures. The deeper he delved in this field, the stranger and more fascinating were the archaic turns of expression that he brought to light, especially when, in preparation for his *Khovanstchina*, he devoted himself to researches into the sectarian disputes of Old Russia, and pored for months over the old chronicles in the monasteries of Moscow. His letters give a lively idea of his diction at that time, interwoven as it is, not only with scraps of French and German, but also with all sorts of crabbed expressions from the ecclesiastical Russian of the Middle Ages.

Moussorgsky remained only two years at the school; he then passed into an army training establishment, for it was inevitable that, as the younger son of a noble house, he should adopt the career of an officer. This establishment, kept by a certain Komarov, was situated near the barracks of the Ismailov Infantry regiment, in order that the pupils might become acquainted with the best traditions of military drill from the first, by personal observation. So for a time Moussorgsky, this visionary enthusiast for freedom, this interpreter of men's souls, had to march up and down the barrack

13

yard to the beat of the drum, and stand at attention, his hands by his sides.

Komarov's establishment was looked upon as the stepping-stone to the Guards' Cadet Academy, at which Moussorgsky was entered in August 1852. Of his life during the four years that he remained there, little is known. In his autobiographical sketch Moussorgsky states that he was "distinguished by special kindness on the part of the Emperor Nicholas I," but he tells us nothing further of the form assumed by the first and only Imperial favour that was ever granted him. According to his brother Filaret, Moussorgsky was extraordinarily quick at learning and made good progress, while, as his reports show, he was always among the first students of his class. He was on good terms with his comrades, who liked him and many of whom introduced him to their family circles. All his spare time was devoted to reading; he read a great deal, especially historical works, and he devoured the German philosophers with much enthusiasm, but little discrimination.

Young Moussorgsky's musical training was entrusted to a certain Anton Herke. Herke, who was considered one of the best pianists and teachers in Petersburg, was himself a pupil of Adolf Henselt, who had come to Petersburg in 1838 and, owing to his great success as a pianist, especially in court circles, had settled there permanently. Moussorgsky's lessons from Herke were probably intended to be merely a preparation for a more advanced course under Henselt, but this never came off. Herke's musical quality is put plainly before us in a criticism by Alexander Serov that has come down to us. Writing of a concert in which Beethoven's Choral Fantasia was given, he says: "The piano part was played by Anton Herke, whose virtuosity is justly appreciated in Petersburg. He discharged his exceedingly difficult task in a truly masterly manner and with extraordinary accuracy; but to breathe the spirit of high poetry into a performance on

14

the piano, that indeed is a gift granted to only too few among mortals." From these remarks it seems highly probable that Moussorgsky got little poetical enlightenment from Herke's instruction—not that he needed to receive what was already latent in him. In any case he rapidly acquired from his teacher the foundations of a sound technique. Moussorgsky in his autobiography tells us that, when only twelve years old, at a private concert in one of the aristocratic salons of Petersburg, he made such a sensation by his playing of a rondo by Herz that Herke, who was a stern critic, rewarded him with a copy of Beethoven's Sonata in A flat, which the young genius must have enjoyed far more than Herz's rondo. Although Herke apparently approved of the boy's attempts at composition—he helped him to publish his first piece for the piano—unfortunately he had not sufficient insight to take a little trouble over the general musical training of his little self-taught pupil; as the composer's brother Filaret expressly testifies, he never gave him even the rudiments of musical theory, to say nothing of a knowledge of harmony, which Moussorgsky would certainly have mastered with perfect ease, and so spared himself much labour and vexation in later life. Herke seems to have been interested exclusively in the piano-playing of his young pupil, which was indeed so remarkable that, by the unanimous verdict of his professional contemporaries, he might, with serious application to this branch of music, have rivalled even the great Anton Rubinstein. Moussorgsky's lessons with Herke were continued until he had finished his military schooling, though with much less assiduity in the last two years than at first. Instead of playing himself, Moussorgsky now merely attended the lessons that Herke gave to the children of General Sutthov, the director of the Cadet School. Excellent as was the result of Herke's teaching on the fingers of his pupil, its effect on his mentality was less happy; in this respect Moussorgsky derived greater

15

benefit from his intercourse with another of his teachers, the divinity master of the Academy.

For this man, "little Father" Krupsky, Moussorgsky conceived, as he tells us, a romantic affection and used to visit him frequently, not only for religious conversation, but also in order to become initiated, under his guidance, into the old Church music of Russia, Byzantine and Catholic alike, and even, as we find in a special note in the French edition of the autobiography, the chorales of the Lutheran Church. We gather from this that Father Krupsky, unlike most of his class, was a very tolerant man, at any rate in questions of Church music. One finds here and there among priests of the Russian Church some who, breaking away from a narrow-minded orthodoxy, show a wise and kindly understanding of the convictions of all who seek after God earnestly, however tortuous their paths. Father Krupsky seems to have been one of these. It is thoroughly characteristic of young Moussorgsky's whole nature that this was the teacher to whom he felt himself particularly drawn. The grounding he received from Father Krupsky was doubtless of the greatest importance for the exact knowledge and profound understanding of the essence and spirit of Russian Church music that the composer displayed later on in many of his works, great and small.

With regard to attempts at composition during this first period of his schooling there is hardly anything to record. His first piece for the piano was written at the age of thirteen; it was a polka, to which the young composer gave the name "Porte-Ensigne Polka (Ensign's Polka)," and which he dedicated to his new comrades of the Cadet School; his teacher, Herke, was so pleased with it that he arranged to have it published by Bernard of Petersburg. The piece was printed "greatly to the composer's annoyance," as Moussorgsky writes to Madame Ludmilla Shestakova, Glinka's sister, when drawing up a list of his works at her request.

His cause of complaint no longer exists, however, as the piece has disappeared and there is little reason to suppose, especially since the Revolution of 1917, that it may still be found in any family archives. The loss of the polka is not to be deplored, if one may judge of its quality by another pianoforte piece of Moussorgsky's composed about the same time, and still in existence. It is called "*Souvenir d'enfance*"; the manuscript, which is in the Public Library at Petersburg, bears the inscription "*dedié à son ami Nikolas Obolensky,*" and the date "16 October 1857," when the musician was eighteen years old; but we shall not be far wrong in assuming that the piece was written much earlier. It is a perfectly harmless composition, half barcarole, half Cracovienne, in rather slow tempo; in any case, there is no trace of "the lion's claw" in it.

That Moussorgsky's musical ambition had already a very different goal in sight is clear from the circumstance that, unencumbered by any technical knowledge, with all the energy of youthful audacity, he began to compose an opera to a libretto that he had himself compiled from Victor Hugo's romance *Han d'Islande.* "Nothing came of it—it was impossible that anything should—for the composer was seventeen years old," writes Moussorgsky in the catalogue of his works already referred to. Of such of the music as was completed nothing has survived, unless Moussorgsky, according to his practice later on, may have incorporated some of it in other compositions; of this, however, we cannot be certain.

Moussorgsky left the Cadet School in 1856; in accordance with the family tradition, he was entered on the roll of the Preobrazhensky Guards, in which his grandfather and many others of his ancestors had served. This regiment traced its origin back to the Young Guard formed by Peter the Great when a boy, from his playfellows, the "Potieshny" as they were called, to whom Moussorgsky towards the end of his life raised so striking a memorial in *Khovanstchina.*

17

II

MILITARY SERVICE

1856 – 60

IN THE autumn of 1856 a remarkable meeting took place in a military hospital far on the outskirts of the city, on what is called the "Viborg side." In the guard-room a young military doctor, second house-surgeon of the infirmary, and a still younger new-fledged Ensign of the Guards, on duty as officer in command of the guard, found themselves together. As both were bored to death, they got into conversation and struck up an acquaintance. The doctor was Alexander Borodin, the officer was Moussorgsky. Neither could have foreseen that they would soon encounter each other again on a very different plane and shine side by side as stars of the first magnitude in the firmament of Russian music; neither had at the time the least intention of adopting music as a career and exchanging hospital and guard-room for the concert hall and the theatre.

Borodin has an entertaining account of the meeting in a letter to Stassov, which is given in every life of Moussorgsky; so lively and convincing is his portrait of the young composer that it may find a place here. He writes: "There was something absolutely boyish about Moussorgsky at that time; he was very elegant and looked like a lieutenant in a picture-book; his uniform was spick and span, his small feet were turned neatly outwards, his hair curled and scented with the utmost care; his exquisitely manicured hands might have served as a model for a 'grand seigneur.' His manners were elegant and aristocratic and he spoke with a slight nasal twang, employing a large number of French expressions,

18

sometimes a little *recherché*. He was not without a touch of foppery, kept well within bounds, but unmistakable. His good breeding and courtesy were conspicuous. All the ladies smiled upon him. That same evening we were both invited to dine with the head surgeon of the hospital, who had a grown-up daughter and frequently gave parties, to which the doctors and officers on duty were always invited. Moussorgsky sat down to the piano and played, very sweetly and pleasingly, with some affected movements of the hands, pieces from *Traviata* and *Trovatore*, while his hearers stood round and murmured in chorus: 'Charming! Delicious!' I met Moussorgsky three or four times like this—that is, on duty at the hospital or at the head surgeon's evenings; later on I lost sight of him for some time, as the parties came to an end and I joined the Military Medical Academy as assistant professor of chemistry."

It is difficult to recognize Moussorgsky, the creator of *Boris Godounov* and *Khovanstchina*, in Borodin's description; the sketch of his outward appearance is probably correct, indeed it tallies with a portrait of the composer in the uniform of the Preobrazhensky regiment, taken at the time, and still extant; but it is naturally impossible that a mere casual meeting could have revealed to Borodin the young officer's inner nature. In any case, it would be wrong to draw conclusions as to Moussorgsky's musical taste at the time from the description of his performances on the piano—what will a young man not do to please a company of pretty women? We may supplement Borodin's account by the oral testimony of some of Moussorgsky's regimental comrades, given in Stassov's life of the composer; from these we learn that Moussorgsky did not at that time share the musical taste of his contemporaries, who, without exception, naturally worshipped at the fashionable shrine of Italian opera. On the contrary, he was always trying to convert them to something better by playing selections from Mozart's *Don Giovanni*,

19

which he had got to know probably through Herke and which he extolled as the only "true and genuine music." It required no little independence of judgment to set oneself up in this way against the prevailing standards of the time, but in this quality Moussorgsky certainly was not wanting, nor in the courage to stand up for his opinion at all times and in all circumstances, to enforce it in the face of all cavils, and never to make the least concession where art was concerned. To form a right idea and a proper appreciation of Moussorgsky and the whole beginning of the "neo-Russian school" it is necessary to have some conception of what the musical life of Petersburg was like at that period. To refute any possible charge of partiality, I shall call as evidence not the testimony of any of those later valiant champions of reform, of whom Moussorgsky was the most impatient and the most passionate representative, but the positive statement of a musician whom one certainly cannot credit with any particularly progressive sympathies, nor with any desire to quarrel with his opponents. Anton Rubinstein writes in his autobiography: "Russian opera was at that time (the fifties of the last century), and for some considerable period afterwards, discredited. I wrote my operas to Italian and German texts, just because the Russian theatre was no friend of opera, and because there was practically no musical culture among educated Russian society—there were only a number of dilettanti whose judgment in music was short-sighted and warped, and who demanded that every art, and especially music, should conform to their own amateurish standards. The melodies of the operas of that time—works by Pacini, Rossini, Bellini, and all the rest of them—were regarded as musical masterpieces that, for grace, beauty, and profundity, could never be surpassed. People were simply unable to see musical beauty anywhere but in this thin, easily flowing stream of melody, the interest of which was only occasionally heightened by the orchestral accompaniment, for the most part intolerably monotonous and stereotyped. Music was not asked to fulfil any serious task—in short, society was still in the primitive stage of its musical development."

It is obvious from this that Moussorgsky had no choice but *Traviata* and *Trovatore* with which to gratify the admiring ladies who crowded round him. Fortunately Fate had other views for Moussorgsky than to let him become the musical darling of the ladies of Petersburg.

*   *   *

Very soon after his entrance into the great world, so to speak, in the winter of 1856–7, something occurred that was destined to influence the whole development of his personality and the direction of his creative talent—he was introduced by one of his regimental comrades into the house of the composer Alexander Dargomizhky.

Dargomizhky was, at that time, beyond question the most important musical personality of the older generation in Petersburg. Glinka, deeply disappointed at the reception by the Petersburg public, and in particular by the influential musical circle described above, of his fine opera *Russlan*, had turned his back upon Petersburg and migrated to Berlin, where, in conjunction with Siegfried Dehn, the librarian of the Royal Musical Library, he applied himself to contrapuntal studies and endeavoured to solve the riddle of the harmonic basis of Russian folk-song and the cantilenas of the Russian liturgy. He died in Berlin in February 1857.

Dargomizhky, who was also a living proof of the saying that a prophet has no honour in his own country, had retired in disgust from the official musical world of Petersburg. A considerable landed proprietor, he was sufficiently endowed with this world's goods. He used to spend the winter in the capital, where he lived the life of a grand seigneur, troubling himself little about the good public, who bowed before the fashionable musical idol, Italian opera, and ignored the other music, of the home-made Russian variety. Dargomizhky consoled himself with a small circle of sympathizers whom he gathered round him. Once a week he had musical evenings in his house, at which, as he writes in one of his letters, "Russian music was performed, simply, naturally, and without any striving after effect—in a word, as our departed friend Michael Ivanovitch [Glinka] loved to have it done."

Russian music, to tell the truth, did not exist at that time in any great quantity; it consisted almost exclusively of works by Glinka and Dargomizhky himself, together with those of some of their amateur supporters, Prince Kastrioto-Skanderbek, Sokolov, etc. Some contemporary memoirs have preserved delightful and attractive descriptions of these musical evenings. Dargomizhky himself is the central figure, surrounded by a crowd of graceful young lady singers, whom he taught free of charge and with whom he was so infatuated that he used to declare that he would never have become a composer had there been no lady singers in the world. We have also his father, a stiff old aristocrat, who kept jealous watch to see that strict silence was maintained during the performances, and at the slightest noise would come down upon the offender with a loud "Sh!" The composer's sisters, too, were always present, the one old-maidish, despotic, and keenly critical, the other young and pretty, with a graceful way of handling the harp. The musical performances were generally good, even distinguished, for Dargomizhky spent much time in getting them up and conducted them in person. Such was the circle into which the seventeen-year-old Moussorgsky was introduced. He used often to say in later life, as Stassov tells us, that his real musical existence dated from this time. Nevertheless Dargomizhky, who was then still himself in the stage of development—his mature works *Russalka* and *The Stone Guest* were not yet written—had at first no marked influence upon Moussorgsky; of the surprising progress he was soon to reveal in his *Stone Guest*, which established him at once as the spiritual leader of the "young Russian" movement in music, there were at that time no signs.

In Dargomizhky's house Moussorgsky made the acquaintance of César Cui, and soon afterwards of Mili Balakirev—two events that were of historic importance for the development of Russian music, and for Moussorgsky a turning-point in his career.

Both of these new friends, Cui and Balakirev, were some years older than Moussorgsky; Cui was twenty-two, Balakirev twenty-one. With Cui, who in his early days in Vilna had already had some lessons in composition from Moniuszko, Moussorgsky at once struck up an intimate friendship. The elder man's superiority in matters of music was not so very great and was certainly never paraded. Moreover the two young people, apart from their musical sympathies, had certain other interests in common. Cui, too, was an officer; he was in an artillery regiment, and, unlike his unpractical young friend, attained to high distinction in his profession —when he retired he was a General, and regular Professor of Fortification at the Nikolai Academy of the Great General Staff. No doubt the two young lieutenants in their friendly talks had more to say about counterpoint and chords of six-four than about the construction of redoubts and garrison discipline. They were fond of playing duets on the piano, especially the symphonies of Schumann, which were new to Moussorgsky and made a deep impression on him. Naturally they showed each other their own compositions, and it is characteristic of both that Moussorgsky from the very first thought more highly of Cui's work than the latter ever did of Moussorgsky's.

Very different from this picture is the impression we get of Moussorgsky's relations with Balakirev.

Mili Balakirev had come to Petersburg in the previous

year—i.e., in December 1855. Up to that date he had lived in the remotest depths of Russia, first in Nizhni Novgorod, then on the estate of the wealthy Russian magnate and patron of art, N. D. Ulibishev, whose life of Mozart was much talked about in its time. Here Balakirev had found opportunity to make himself a sound practical musician in every branch of the art; when only fifteen years old, he used regularly to conduct Ulibishev's private orchestra, which was on so large a scale that it was capable of performing the first four symphonies of Beethoven. Balakirev is probably the purest example of a self-taught composer of the first rank to be found in the history of music; with the exception of ten piano-lessons from Dubuc, the Moscow professor, he never had any kind of musical instruction whatever. One of his first acquaintances in Petersburg was Glinka, the object of his musical idolatry, to whom his patron Ulibishev introduced him. Glinka, of course, at once perceived the extraordinary quality of Balakirev's talent, and after listening to some of the young musician's compositions, among which was a brilliant fantasia on themes from the elder man's own opera *A Life for the Tsar*, he predicted for him a brilliant musical career—a prophecy that for some time received only a modest fulfilment. The fact that the great Glinka, immediately before he left his ungrateful country for ever, should have imparted this musical papal benediction, so to speak, to the aspiring composer, naturally invested Balakirev with a quite peculiar halo in the eyes of young admirers and adherents, who soon gathered round him. Not that Balakirev needed this circumstance to assert his unlimited authority over the young musicians of his circle. Rimsky-Korsakov, in his *My Musical Life*, maintains that Balakirev at that period exercised a sort of "magnetic or spiritualistic" power, which no one in close contact with him could resist. "One obeyed him without questioning, so amazing was the compelling magic of his personality. A young man with wonderfully restless eyes, which flashed fire, a small neatly trimmed beard, and a peculiarly incisive, authoritative, unvarnished way of talking—ready at any time to give a fine and technically perfect improvisation at the piano, able to play everything he knew from memory, to memorize any new work, after a bare hearing, he could not fail to cast a unique spell. Although he cordially recognized the smallest sign of talent in others, he could not help feeling his own superiority, which the others were quite ready to acknowledge. His influence on those around him knew no limits."

Small wonder, then, if Moussorgsky, too, at first submitted to the musical domination of Balakirev. He soon asked the elder man to give him regular musical instruction— the very earliest letter from Moussorgsky to Balakirev that has been preserved (dated December 16, 1857) speaks of a "lesson." Balakirev agreed to his request, all the more readily as he naturally recognized at once the brilliant musical gifts of the young officer; the lessons, however, were not very regular, since anything like strict application was an impossibility to this ardent young enthusiast, as he himself freely acknowledged. In an account of his relations with the composer of *Boris*, which he wrote at Stassov's request after Moussorgsky's death, we read: "As I am no theorist, I could not give Moussorgsky instruction in harmony (as Rimsky-Korsakov, for instance, now teaches it), so I confined myself to explaining the different forms of composition; with this object we played through all Beethoven's symphonies and many of the works of Schumann, Schubert, Glinka, and others, as piano duets. I pointed out the technical structure of these compositions as we went through them, and got him to analyse the various musical forms. So far as I remember, there were few actual professional lessons; these came to an end, for one reason or another, and were succeeded by friendly exchange of opinions."

What this "exchange of opinions" amounted to we gather from other contemporary witnesses, especially from Rimsky-Korsakov's *My Musical Life,* already mentioned, which gives us so many illuminating and characteristic glimpses of that interesting period of Russian musical history. Rimsky-Korsakov, it is true, joined the Balakirev circle some years later, in the winter of 1861, when he was merely a newly-fledged, seventeen-year-old midshipman of the Russian fleet; but one can feel certain that the methods that Balakirev employed with him were the same as those he had used in the musical training of Moussorgsky.

"Balakirev, who not only had never gone through a regular course of harmony and counterpoint, but had never even touched on them, apparently did not see the necessity for such studies. A distinguished pianist, an excellent reader at sight, with an astounding power of improvisation, endowed by nature with a feeling for correct harmony and part-writing, he possessed the technique of composition in no ordinary degree—part of this was born in him, part had been acquired by his own practical experience. Counterpoint, sense of form, a knowledge of orchestration—everything, in short, that a composer needs—he had at his fingers' ends; all these had been further developed by an extensive course of musical reading and his extraordinary power of memory, which was faultless and unfailing. This is one of the most important foundations of sound musical criticism, and as a critic, especially of technique, Balakirev was astounding. He was aware, as if by instinct, of every technical defect, of every imperfection, however insignificant, in the form. When we youngsters played over our attempts at composition to him, he would at once detect every fault in harmonization, form, modulation, etc., and without further reflection would illustrate the mistakes on the piano, while he showed us how to alter—i.e., to improve—the offending passage. In most cases he would praise, say the first four bars of a work, and reject the next eight as a failure—he would commend the beginning of a melody, blame the rest of it, and then go on to praise the transition to the next phrase, and so on. No work was ever considered and judged as an æsthetic whole. In accordance with this method Balakirev generally introduced new works to his circle only in fragmentary fashion; first he would play the conclusion, then the beginning, then the middle of a piece, a plan that made the oddest impression on listeners from outside who happened to be present. He always made his pupils show him the first germs of a proposed new composition, if it were only the first four or eight bars; he would begin his criticism, and show how the sketch might be improved—would praise the first two bars, find fault with the next two, would turn them into ridicule and do his best to disgust the composer. He set little value on rapid work or a large output, but always required that a composition should be subjected to frequent revision and recasting; with the result that the creative process, under the controlling influence of self-criticism, was often endlessly drawn out. His despotic nature demanded that the composition in hand should be refashioned in exact correspondence to his own hints and suggestions; so other men's compositions often contained whole passages that were the work of Balakirev and not of the alleged composer. As he himself had never gone through a strict course of training, he denied that it was necessary for others to do so; he thought that a composer did not need any preparatory studies—all he had to do was just to compose, to create, and to get experience from his own works."

Well may Rimsky-Korsakov question whether this method, which Balakirev followed with all his young friends and pupils alike, was the right one. It is an easy matter to impart a really sound foundation of technical knowledge to any pupil of marked ability, provided one follows a definite course. One or two years' regular work at the development of technique, a few systematic exercises in free composition and instrumentation, would have sufficed to give the young musicians what they spent half their life, if not the whole of it, in acquiring. Balakirev made the mistake of exalting to a principle a method that had given such astounding results in himself, thanks to the happy conjunction of his peculiar and independent talent with exceptionally favourable opportunities for self-instruction. Balakirev maintained the fallacy that preliminary studies in theory and technical exercises could be in a great measure replaced by æsthetic reactions and practical work at composition. He was like certain teachers of swimming who, with hardly any preliminaries, push their confiding pupils into the water and throw them the rope only after the poor floundering creatures have swallowed so much water that they are in danger of going under. A few people, it is true, have really learnt to swim in this way; but one must not take the exception for the rule, since most people under these conditions lose not only their breath, but their desire for any further instruction.

Moussorgsky had to suffer all his life long for the defects and omissions in Balakirev's peculiar system of training. Like the poor swimmer, he was pitched at once into the deep and rocky stream of the sonata form, where he splashed about in fairly helpless fashion, as we learn from a letter to Balakirev (February 25, 1858): "I must confess, to my very great shame, that the *allegro* is not yet ready—so I must do as you bid me, however much it goes against the grain, and write to excuse myself for having not yet finished the beastly thing."

Still, this method of Balakirev's undoubtedly had its good points; it may be solely due to this that the peculiar talent of the composer of *Khovanstchina* was allowed to develop so freely and to bear blossoms of such unexampled originality. At the same time there is no doubt that a firm foundation of technical knowledge would have spared him many of the sufferings and torments of his later years—sufferings that, though he refused to acknowledge their existence, made harder and darker yet his difficult and thorny path.

The musical intercourse between the two was not confined to the lessons and the intimate "exchange of ideas"; every Saturday there was a musical evening at Balakirev's house, where all his young friends and pupils assembled together, with a few others who shared his artistic ideals. These gatherings, according to Rimsky-Korsakov, were stimulating in the highest degree—Balakirev turned them into a sort of "seminary of practical musical anatomy." The masterpieces of music that particularly interested him, or that he considered specially instructive for some reason or other, were dissected, their structure, down to the finest tissue, laid bare, analysed, and appreciated. Balakirev would play through the symphonies of Schumann, Beethoven's quartets, etc., either alone or as duets with Moussorgsky; often, too, the latter, who, in addition to an agreeable baritone voice, possessed, according to the unanimous testimony of his contemporaries, an inimitable talent for interpretation, would sing scenes from Glinka's *Russlan*, and similar pieces. Their taste, as a whole, was mostly for Schumann and the later quartets of Beethoven and Glinka. The first eight symphonies of Beethoven were only partially approved; the ninth, on the other hand, was regarded as the highest achievement in instrumental music. Mendelssohn, whom Moussorgsky preferred to speak of as Mendel, was not a favourite, except for a few works, such as the *Midsummer Night's Dream* and *Hebrides* overtures, and the finale of the octet; indeed, Balakirev had even undertaken an organized campaign in the press against the composer of the *Songs without Words*; these were the latest craze in Petersburg just then, and Balakirev thought them dangerous, as likely to have a weakening effect upon the musical tendencies of the time. Mozart and Haydn were considered too simple and out of date—alas for youthful folly!—but we must remember that

29

we have to do with a lot of hot-headed young artists, from seventeen to twenty-two, with modernist tendencies. Bach was looked upon as a musical fossil, a cold mathematician, a sort of composing-machine; Handel, on the contrary, was admired as a force. They had no high opinion of Chopin; many of his works were pleasing, but they failed to find a deeper meaning in them; they liked best some of his mazurkas. Berlioz, whose works were just beginning to make their way in Russia, was highly esteemed. Liszt, on the other hand, was not accepted at first; his music was considered theatrical, insincere, showy, sometimes in the nature of a caricature. Wagner had not yet begun to be talked about. Glinka was the object of their idolatry; Dargomizhky had a certain reputation, especially for the recitative in his *Russalka,* and some of his songs ("The Paladin," "An Oriental Air"); his three orchestral fantasies they regarded with wonder as a sort of curious jest; but, generally speaking, he was not allowed at first to have any really great talent and they laughed at the manifestations of his artistic ambition. Rubinstein they held in the greatest esteem, but only as a pianist; as a composer he was thought to be wholly devoid of taste or talent. Serov's *Judith* had not yet appeared, so that he did not count as a composer at that time.

From all this we can form a clear idea of the lines on which Balakirev laboured to develop the taste of his musical disciples. His ideas were progressive and national through and through; most of his disciples of that period, though not all, actually followed him along that path and remained faithful to it.

The members of the Balakirev circle did not confine themselves at their meetings to musical performances; they made themselves acquainted at the same time with the literary productions of the day; heated discussions arose, and questions were propounded on matters of abstract æsthetics and general artistic interest. Moussorgsky, who had a decided talent for acting and declamation, gave good assistance in the reading of dramatic works; Rimsky-Korsakov recalls how on one occasion he heard Moussorgsky read Kukolnik's tragedy *Prince Kholmsky* to the accompaniment of Glinka's incidental music. But the circle also contained other representatives of literature, ancient and modern, chief among them, as "literary adviser" to the circle, being Vladimir Stassov, the writer on art and later librarian to the Imperial Public Library in Petersburg. In his early years Stassov had been a close friend of Alexander Serov, from whom he gradually became estranged, owing to his inability to share in the latter's pronounced sympathies with the art of western Europe, and his ardent enthusiasm for Wagner. Stassov, on the other hand, was a convinced adherent of the Slavophil movement, which was at that time gaining ground in Russian political and literary circles and to which he devoted not only his enormous store of almost universal knowledge, but also his exceedingly powerful, energetic, and fiery personality and his brilliant gifts as an author. He at once recognized the great importance of the Balakirev circle for the development of a national, or pan-Slavonic, artistic culture and took an active part henceforth, as a staunch and valiant champion, in promoting the artistic ideas that originated among them, as well as the practical realization of these in the form of musical and operatic creations. From the first he attached himself most closely to Moussorgsky, of whose predominant importance among his artistic companions he had never any doubt. He stood by Moussorgsky's side with unfailing fidelity during the whole of the latter's thorny career; it was not till just at the close that he found himself unable to accompany him farther along the lonely road he had chosen; his friendship, and his literary collaboration no less, were of the very highest importance to the composer of *Boris Godounov* and *Khovanstchina*. We shall have much to say of it in this volume.

The musical meetings of the Balakirev circle occasionally took place at Cui's, where they could play double duets on his two pianos, Moussorgsky providing the necessary arrangements of Berlioz's "Queen Mab" and "Capulet's Feast," Balakirev's *King Lear*, etc. In this way Balakirev managed, by a proper distribution of his forces, to combine the useful with the agreeable. The executants of these double duets were generally Balakirev, Moussorgsky, Cui, and Dmitri Stassov—a brother of Vladimir Stassov, a distinguished pianist, and afterwards director of the Imperial Russian Musical Society—occasionally, also, Filaret Moussorgsky, the composer's brother.

Moussorgsky's regard for Balakirev did not depend only on the fact that he found in him an experienced musician and a reliable guide in artistic matters, from whom he had much to learn; he conceived a real liking for him as a man, and, as his letters show us, he did not hesitate to reveal to him the most intimate secrets of the emotional side of his nature. This attitude towards his friend, who was only a few years his senior, is shown by Moussorgsky in a letter to Balakirev, of October 18, 1859. He writes:

"As to what I think of you, I must review our relations from the beginning of our acquaintance. From the very first I recognized your superiority; in all our discussions I was struck by the clearness of your thought and the tenacity of your opinions. At times I felt vexed with myself and with you that it should be so, but I had to bow to the truth. I now see plainly that it was only my vanity which made me so obstinate in all our differences of opinion, as well as in my personal relations to you. Again—you know the former excessive gentleness of my nature, which did me so much harm with people who were not worthy of it—and yet, as soon as my *amour-propre* was wounded, all my pride awoke. So I began to analyse the people around me—I made rapid progress and was always on my guard. Still, I have never overlooked the least fault on my part in the matter of right and wrong. I am greatly indebted to you, Mili, for my changed attitude towards men and women—you have awakened me out of a deep sleep.—Later on I came to understand you thoroughly and to feel cordially drawn towards you, as I always found in you an echo of my own thoughts—sometimes, indeed, the germ from which they sprang. Our latest intercourse has brought your personality so near to mine that I have come to place absolute trust in you. The role of Pasha *à la* Dargo[mizhky] is so petty and worthless that I can never imagine you wishing to assume it—besides, it would not suit you at all."

In spite of this last assurance we can discern in Moussorgsky's letters to Balakirev certain signs of the respect felt by a younger man for his senior—a slight embarrassment and lack of ease, such as we display in the presence of people whom we reverence and of whose kindly notice we feel not quite worthy, although we look forward to it and would not throw it away for any consideration. There are traces of this attitude in passages like the following: "My letters, I fear, do not give you much pleasure in any case, as I am not accustomed to write about serious things, and I soon put people off with my nonsense" (August 13, 1858). Again: "Forgive me for rambling on like this, but my head is turning round—I have just come off parade at the palace" (January 7, 1858)—and there are many similar passages.

Moussorgsky, as we know from the story of his childhood, was of a peculiarly sensitive nature, far too open to impressions, whether external or internal. In his youth he showed a decided leaning to mysticism; this disappeared altogether in later years, at least in his personal attitude towards metaphysical questions, although these would seriously exercise him from time to time. It was just in the last years of his life that his dramatic instinct led him to become, in his opera *Khovanstchina*, the musical historian of religious mysticism in Russia. As a young man he was keenly interested in all questions relating to a supernatural world beyond our own. It is by no mere chance that we find him, at the age of nineteen, translating in hot haste Lavater's letters on the state of the soul after death, a subject that particularly appealed to him. In writing to inform Balakirev of what he is doing he adds, with a hint of apology: "Besides, it is a subject that has always transported me to the land of dreams." His tendency to introspection, with all its attendant religious and moral scruples, brought on acute nervous attacks, which, though they always ran a more or less favourable course, were naturally not without their influence on the young composer's sensitive temperament. The causes of this abnormal sensitiveness—whether they were hereditary or not—are naturally only matter for speculation; so also is the connexion between these strange attacks in early life and the complete collapse of his will-power towards the end, with all its tragic consequences.

The first mention we find of a nervous breakdown is in a letter of Moussorgsky to Balakirev (October 19, 1859). "Dear Mili," he writes, "you reproach me with two peculiarities that you assume to be present in me. I will begin with the first, the mysticism, or, as you rightly express it, the mystic strain in my nature. Two years ago, as you know, I was in the grip of a terrible illness, which attacked me with extraordinary violence while I was staying in the country. The cause of this was mysticism, aggravated by cynical thoughts about the Deity; it got much worse after I came to Petersburg. I managed to conceal it from you, but you must have noticed its effects upon my music. I suffered greatly and became fearfully sensitive—even morbidly so. Then —either as the result of distractions, or thanks to the fact that I gave myself up to fantastic reveries, which held me captive for a long time—my mysticism began gradually to disappear, and when my reason had gained the upper hand,

34

I took steps to get rid of it altogether. I have made a great effort of late to conquer the thing, and fortunately I have succeeded. At present I have put mysticism far from me—I hope for ever, since it is incompatible with a healthy, intellectual, and moral development."

Moussorgsky's rejoicings over his recovery were, unfortunately, premature—the old state of nervous excitement and irritability soon returned. Again he feels compelled to acquaint Balakirev with his psychic condition, which now gives him grave anxiety. Nearly a whole year elapses before he can inform his friend that he believes himself to be finally cured of his mysticism. But a letter written in the interval has been preserved, and is of the greatest psychological interest; it gives us an insight into the soul of the creator of *Boris* and at the same time fills us with astonishment that one so young should be able to pass so calm, so objective a judgment on his own morbid condition. The letter is dated February 10, 1860: "Thank God, I seem to be making some recovery from my heavy, heavy suffering, moral and physical. You remember, Mili, how, two years ago, we were walking down Garden Street together—you were going home—it was summertime. We had just been reading *Manfred*—I was so wildly excited by the sufferings of that lofty spirit that I cried out: 'How I wish I were Manfred!'—I was quite a child at the time, remember!—Fate thought fit, apparently, to grant my wish—I became Manfred for the time, literally —my spirit slew my flesh! Now I must have recourse to every kind of antidote. Dearest Mili, I know you are fond of me—then for God's sake keep a tight rein on me when we are talking together, and don't let me kick over the traces! For the time being, too, I must give up all my musical activities and avoid every kind of work that tries the brain, if I am to get better. My rule must be: 'Everything must be done for the material cure, even at the expense of the moral.' The reasons for my nervous excitability are clear to me now. It is

35

not only the result of my illness, which was merely contributory, so to speak—the chief causes are as follows: youth, an immoderate capacity for enthusiasm, a strong, unconquerable desire for omniscience, exaggerated introspection, and an idealism that even went so far as to take the dream for the reality. I see now that, at the age of twenty, the physical side of me is not sufficiently developed to keep pace with my forced moral growth. My illness accounts for the check in my physical development—the moral force in me has stifled it. We must now come to its assistance; distractions—yet as much rest as possible—gymnastics, cold baths—these must be my salvation."

That the young Moussorgsky was right to limit his musical activities for a time is evident from another passage of the same letter, in which he describes the impression made on him by the music of a certain ballet that he had just heard—it is clear that not the strongest nerves could stand such a strain. After abusing the "frightful" quality of the ballet and calling the composer, Puni, a "Scythian," Moussorgsky writes: "Nevertheless the ballet made a remarkable impression on me—I was very nearly ill in the theatre. When I got home and went to bed, I was at once assailed by painful dreams, by hallucinations so sweet, yet terrible, so intoxicating, that to die in such a state would have seemed an easy thing. That, fortunately, was the end of my sufferings; I now feel much better—at any rate I am perfectly calm." At the end of this letter he says: "Mili, I feel as if I had awakened from a heavy dream." But again this feeling of being cured at last was only a delusion—for nearly a whole year Moussorgsky suffered from this morbid condition of the nerves. This is plain from a letter he wrote from Petersburg (September 26, 1860) to Balakirev, who was then staying in Nizhni Novgorod, where his home was. "My illness lasted till August and it was only by recourse to long periods of intermission that I was able to go on with my music. All those

36

months from May to August my brain felt weakened and overworked. . . . You, Mili, will be delighted at the change that has taken place in me, for, no doubt, it is very apparent in my compositions. My brain is now strong again and has returned to the sphere of realities—the fire of youth has grown cold, everything has settled down, there is no more talk of mysticism. . . . Thank God, Mili, I have completely recovered."

It was in this year that Moussorgsky, as he himself tells us, decided on the particular direction of his musical career—a choice that was soon to make him one of the most prominent representatives of the school of realism in art. Stassov's assumption that this highly important event took place five years later is therefore incorrect—at the end of the letter just quoted, Moussorgsky declares with unmistakable clearness: *"A new period of my musical life has now begun."*

This internal reaction that finally decided Moussorgsky's artistic and intellectual development had been preceded not long before by a no less important change in his outward circumstances. In the spring of 1859 Moussorgsky had retired from military service. His decision to lay aside the uniform that he had worn for not quite three years had been already taken in the previous summer. Stassov tells us that he had often discussed the matter with Moussorgsky at that time and had done all he could to dissuade his friend from his purpose, but Moussorgsky continued deaf to all arguments. In vain did Stassov quote the example of Lermontov, who had remained an officer of hussars to the day of his death (an early death, it is true) and had become a great poet in spite of all the parades and other military duties. "But I am not Lermontov," Moussorgsky would object. "He, I dare say, found it possible to combine the one thing with the other, but for me it is not possible. The service hinders me from working as I should like to do." What finally decided Moussorgsky was, no doubt, the fact that in the summer of 1859 he was to be exchanged into the battalion of sharpshooters attached to his regiment, then on garrison duty at Tsarskaia Slavianka, a tiny place not far from Petersburg. That meant not only a separation from Balakirev, Dargomizhky, Cui, and everything in Petersburg that had become dear to him, but, above all, the absolute impossibility of any sort of serious musical study. Moussorgsky had no opposition to fear from his family; his father had died in 1853, his brother Filaret was living in the country, at Karevo, and farming the ancestral estates, which had been left to himself and his brother jointly, so that he had certainly no interest in advising Modest's continuance in his present costly career. As for his mother, she was only too happy to be able to keep her beloved son with her in Petersburg. Accordingly this important step in Moussorgsky's life was accomplished without friction of any kind.

Instead of accompanying the sharpshooters to Tsarskaia Slavianka, Moussorgsky was now able, in the summer of 1859, to fulfil his long-cherished desire of seeing Moscow. His interest in the old city of the tsars, which was to play so important a part in his dramatic output as the scene of his two great works for the stage, *Boris Godounov* and *Khovanstchina*, increased with his growing interest in Russian realism and the history of his country. Balakirev had been in Moscow the year before; in answer to a letter of his from that city Moussorgsky writes: "Your description of the Kremlin, Mili, has plunged me deep in thought; moreover, thanks to you, these five minutes of wistful reverie have given me unspeakable delight." The opportunity for visiting Moscow arose from a visit that he paid in the May of this year to his Petersburg friends, the Shilovskys, on their estate of Glebovo, not far from the old city, where he was destined to spend several summers later on. Madame Shilovsky, a daughter of Verderevsky, the civil governor of Siberia at that time, was a very well-known figure in the musical circles of Petersburg. She was known as an amateur singer and was a constant attendant at musical evenings at Dargomizhky's. Her contemporaries (Youri Arnold, Stassov, etc.) praise her fine mezzo-soprano voice, which only lacked proper training, and the rather gipsy-like fire of her singing, but are far more enthusiastic over her great beauty and her piquant personality, which was dangerous to most men with whom she came in contact. Her husband, Shilovsky, belonged to one of the most aristocratic regiments of the Guards in Petersburg, besides being one of the richest of the country nobility in the Government of Moscow; later he acquired a certain literary reputation as the author of the libretto of Tchaikovsky's *Eugen Onegin*. The style of living in the Shilovsky mansion was unusually magnificent, even for a Russian nobleman. All through the summer Shilovsky gave operatic performances in his private theatre, in order to give his wife an opportunity to try her powers upon the stage. Orchestra and chorus (where Shilovsky's own private chapel choir was not sufficient) and certain extra soloists were enrolled from Moscow. The direction of these performances was generally in the hands of K. N. Liadov, the musical director of the Petersburg opera, who was a friend of the family.

Moussorgsky, who was just then struggling with severe nervous trouble, came to Glebovo in May in search of recovery, and found it. The luxurious surroundings and the tender, unobtrusive thoughtfulness of his host and hostess, who always let their guests do exactly as they pleased, had a most beneficial effect upon his excited state. "Everything here," he writes to Balakirev, "is just as it should be—he must be devilishly rich, this Shilovsky!" (May 12, 1859.) A performance of *A Life for the Tsar*, with the lady of the house as Vania, was planned for the summer, and Moussorgsky helped Shilovsky's choir master to rehearse the choruses; the rest of the performers came from Petersburg—"*tutta la compagnia,*" as Moussorgsky writes—i.e., Dargomizhky and most of the singers who formed the personnel of his house concerts.

From Glebovo, Moussorgsky went to Moscow to see the Kremlin, that goal of his "wistful reveries." Scarcely anyone can have seen that sight without carrying away an ineffaceable impression; small wonder, then, if the impression made on Moussorgsky's sensitive nature amounted almost to an hallucination. A letter to Balakirev of June 23, 1859 bears witness to the feelings with which the ancient city of the tsars inspired him. He writes: "Mili, at last it has been granted me to gaze on Jericho—I will describe my impressions for your benefit. As I approached the city, I at once noticed a very remarkable thing—from the belfries and domes of the churches was wafted a breath of the olden time, long since gone by. The Red Gate is striking and pleased me greatly. Then nothing of any note till you come to the Kremlin, the wonderful Kremlin! An involuntary feeling of awe and reverence came upon me as I approached . . . here indeed is the hallowed past! The Church of Vassili Blashenny (Basil the Blessed) gave me a very agreeable but strange sensation—I expected any moment to see a Boyar go by in long coat and high fur cap."

Moussorgsky visited all the other sights of Moscow in a proper spirit of reverence; in passing through the Spassky Gate, which leads through the wall of the Kremlin (on which, as is well known, three *troikas* can drive abreast), he took off his hat like all the passers-by—a national custom that pleased him greatly. In the old palace of the tsars his admiration was especially aroused by the picturesque and striking Granovitaia Palata, the banqueting-hall in which, among other events, the trial of the enlightened Patriarch Nikon took place. In the noble Archangelsky Cathedral he spent much time among the tombs of all the famous men—some heroes, some criminals—who, before the coming of Peter the Great, had occupied the Imperial throne of Russia—there they lie, all those brilliant or sinister figures of Russia's history in ages past, the legendary hero Dmitri Donskoi side by side with Boris Godounov, Ivan the Terrible with the murdered Tsarevitch Dmitri, and so on. The thought of Glinka's opera *A Life for the Tsar* made him pause where the Romanovs are buried. Next he ascended to the bell tower called Ivan Veliki (Ivan the Great), to enjoy the indiscribable beauty of the view over the city and the great plain of Moscow. In spite of its name, the tower is known to have been built by Boris Godounov in order to give employment to his people in a time of scarcity.

Again the sensations begotten by the Kremlin awaken something like hallucination in Moussorgsky's brain. "One thing more," he writes. "In the museum stands a stage-coach that belonged to the Tsar Alexei Michailovitch, a stupendous thing, of foreign workmanship. On the back seat they have placed an arm-chair, a sort of *porte-chaise*. As I looked in, I thought I saw the figure of the old Tsar Alexei, issuing his commands to the voivodes whom he is sending to Little Russia."

The general impressions he received from "Little Mother Moscow" are summed up by the twenty-year-old Moussorgsky in the following pregnant words, which, in a sense, contain the program and the explanation of the whole of his later artistic activities: "Moscow certainly transported me to another world, the world of the past—a world that, though it was full of horrors, still, I know not why, attracts me strongly. I will tell you something—hitherto I have been a cosmopolitan, but now I feel a certain change at work; everything that is Russian is becoming near and dear to me . . . I believe I am now beginning really to love my country."

The memories that Moussorgsky took back with him to the banks of the Neva had in them some precious germs of art which found a congenial and fruitful soil in the Petersburg of 1860; and springing up in luxuriant abundance, yielded the rich harvest that we see in the songs and operas that he has bequeathed to his own country and to all the world.

So far—i.e., up to 1860—Moussorgsky's achievements as a composer were certainly still very slight. As an officer in Petersburg he had lived the ordinary life of a young officer with a comfortable income—parties, theatres, all the usual diversions in which his comrades shared, alternated with the discharge of his military duties. In such an existence he had naturally few leisure hours to devote to music—although, as he writes to Balakirev (June 8, 1858), he would "awfully like to be a decent composer," he was very far from following any systematic course of study. Balakirev's dangerous principle that one learns most by learning nothing, appealed to him, because it encouraged the easy-going disposition common to all young people, and it is naturally more flattering to youthful vanity to write sonatas and symphonies than to do exercises in harmony. And so we find Moussorgsky in 1858 actually engaged in writing two sonatas at the same time. The one in E flat was written in the country, where he was staying for his brother's wedding, and dedicated to the newly-married pair; he copied out and sent the principal themes in a letter to Balakirev, but there is nothing remarkable in them. The other sonata, in F sharp minor ("quite simple," he calls it), was begun after his return to Petersburg in the autumn. Both sonatas have disappeared and we need not mourn their loss. On the other hand, a sonata for pianoforte duet, or rather an *allegro* movement in C major, written in 1860, has survived, though it has not yet been published. The manuscript of the piece, which was most probably designed for orchestra, is in the possession of Madame N. N. Rimsky-Korsakov, the wife of the composer. The most remarkable thing about it is a few words written on it; over the date December 8, 1860 we read in the composer's handwriting: "I have got married"; he used here a form of the verb "to marry" that in Russian can only apply to the female sex—its exact meaning is: "I have given myself as a wife"—so that the phrase, whether we consider the meaning or the form, is merely nonsense.

Another still unpublished piece, written a few months later (March 14, 1862), is a short piece for orchestra, "*Alla Marcia Notturna*," which bears the inscription: "An attempt at orchestration—for Wednesday's lesson." The manuscript is in the Public Library in Petersburg. It is not clear who was to give Moussorgsky that "Wednesday lesson" on instrumentation; Balakirev expressly declared in Stassov's presence that he had no knowledge of this composition, which is quite unimportant, both in subject and in orchestration; as Dargomizhky, too, is out of the question, Moussorgsky must have had a few lessons from some other teacher, of whom nothing is known.

We have also two instrumental scherzos, written in 1858. Balakirev was especially devoted to this form of composition; not only did he delight in writing scherzos himself, but he used to recommend this form to his pupils and followers as being particularly instructive. One of Moussorgsky's scherzos, in B flat, was arranged for orchestra later on, with help from Balakirev, and performed in 1860 at one of the first series of symphony concerts given by the Imperial Russian Musical Society under the direction of Anton Rubinstein. A notice of this concert written by A. Serov has been preserved; it is interesting not only as being the first printed criticism of work by Moussorgsky, but also as the only criticism of the composer ever written by Serov, who later on threw the whole weight of his personality into the fight against the artistic movement represented by the Balakirev circle. This first effort of Moussorgsky, which gave little promise of what was to come, was hailed by Serov with kindly encouragement. He writes: "Still more satisfactory was the

43

warm reception given by the public to the Russian composer A. P. [*sic*] Moussorgsky, who made his debut with a capital (though much too short) orchestral piece, a scherzo in B flat. This has certainly not the interest of the scherzo by C. Cui heard so recently; still it shows decided talent on the part of the young composer, now at the beginning of his career. It is worthy of note that this symphonic fragment, the work of an unknown composer, placed as it was by the side of a work by a famous *maestro*, not only lost nothing, but actually gained by comparison." The work of the *maestro* referred to was the *Struensee* music of Meyerbeer. The other scherzo, in C sharp minor, was also probably intended for the orchestra, but Moussorgsky never scored it; neither of them was printed in the composer's lifetime.

A sketch written at that time—*Schamyl's March*—has survived in the form of a pianoforte arrangement. Moussorgsky always sympathized warmly with all revolutionary leaders—he felt that he was himself called to do for music what they had accomplished in the sphere of politics. Schamyl had supported the freedom of the mountain tribes of the Caucasus against the Tsar's Governor, Prince Bariatinsky, to whom he surrendered on August 25, 1859, after many years of resistance. Moussorgsky's *March* was a sort of cantata (with Georgian text) for chorus, with tenor and bass solos—but he never got further than the first sketch; the manuscript is in the possession of V. Y. Belsky, the librettist of Rimsky-Korsakov, who probably gave it to him; it is still unpublished.

Two small pieces for piano complete the list of instrumental compositions of this period. One is known under the title "A Child's Jest"—it was known originally as "A Child's Scherzo," at least this is how Moussorgsky calls it in a letter to Balakirev, September 26, 1860. Stassov is mistaken in supposing that the piece was written in 1859; on the manuscript, which is in the possession of M. D. Calvocoressi, the date is given as May 28, 1860. It was not published till 1873, so we may assume that it underwent some revision before printing; otherwise the correctness of the writing would be amazing, considering what we know of the composer's limited acquaintance with composition at the time. The piece is essentially a harmless piece of drawing-room music, in the style of an étude, and might just as well have been written by Stephen Heller as by Moussorgsky. The other piece, from the year 1859, is of greater significance to the composer's biography, though in itself it is just such another school-room piece; it is called "*Impromptu passionné*," and sounds like an agreeable, if rather clumsy, imitation of Schumann. On a copy of the original manuscript, in the possession of Bessel, the publisher, Rimsky-Korsakov has written: "What a number of mistakes and misconceptions!" He did wisely in deciding not to edit it for publication. But what is really interesting about the piece is the subtitle that Moussorgsky gave it: "To the memory of Beltov and Liuba." These are the hero and heroine of Alexander Hertzen's romance *Who is to blame?* which made an enormous sensation in Petersburg society at that time. Beltov belongs to that type which occurs so frequently in Russian literature, "the one who is not wanted"; he is disappointed with life and with himself, until Liuba, by her avowal of love and the kiss she gives him, enlightens him as to the meaning of his existence, which, however, can never find its fulfilment, for Liuba belongs to another man, who is his best friend. In this scene of the kiss Moussorgsky found the inspiration for the little piece; it is dedicated to Nadeshda Petrovna Opotchinina, the sister of one of the friends he had made at Dargomizhky's musical evenings. This musical avowal, as it were, lets us into a secret to which we shall return as occasion offers. It is in any case significant that Moussorgsky, at the age of nineteen, should have chosen this theme for his "*Impromptu passionné*."

Two other pieces for piano, "*Prélude*" and "*Menuet*

monstre," which Stassov mentions together with the "*Im-promptu*" as belonging to this time, are lost.

Until a short time ago the songs composed by Moussorg-sky in the year 1857–60, of which he speaks in his letters, were thought to be lost, with one exception. It was not till 1909, twenty-seven years after the composer's death, that news came from Paris of the finding of a Moussorgsky manu-script containing seventeen of the composer's early songs, and an arrangement for two voices of an Italian romance, L. Gordigiani's "*Ogni sabbato avrete il lume accesso*." Of the seventeen songs in the Paris manuscript (bequeathed by Charles Malherbe, the writer on music, to the library of the Paris Conservatoire) six belong to the years 1857–60. Of these, as we have said, only one, "Ah, only tell me why!" was already known; it had been printed during the compos-er's lifetime, in the year 1867; as a composition it is pleasing and refined, though in no way characteristic of the later Moussorgsky. The voice part is written on the folk-song model. The words are ascribed in the Paris manuscript to Pushkin, but this is an error, as no such poem is to be found in his works; it is not known who wrote the verses that Mous-sorgsky sought to pass off under the name of Pushkin—pos-sibly they were his own. The influence of Russian folk-music is still more clearly indicated in another of the Paris songs, "Where art thou, my star?" These verses, purely popular in style, are also probably the work of Moussorgsky, who was just seventeen years old when he wrote the song. Neverthe-less, of the six songs written at this time the palm must be awarded to this one. The restful melody, with its fine curve, flows on in the Phrygian mode (F sharp minor with the E natural), which is so frequently found in Russian folk-songs. In later years Moussorgsky wrote a companion piece to this song in the "*Dumka*," sung by the Párobok in the posthu-mous opera *The Fair at Sorótchintzy*; here too the fine me-lodic curves are built up on the Phrygian mode. Another of

these six songs has the subtitle: "A musical narration," and
gives a mournful impression of a midnight burial. A finer
ear will not fail to notice a certain Schubertian strain running through this composition; Moussorgsky here introduces for the first time that wavering between major and
minor that he was to employ with such subtle effect later on;
here the alternation of E flat major with E flat minor produces a sort of harmonic chiaroscuro, which has a quite peculiar charm. The words of this song—the first line is:
"Sadly the leaves are sighing"—are from a poem by Pleshtcheiev, with extensive alterations. From the very beginning
of his career Moussorgsky never had any scruples when dealing with the text of other people's verses; all must be subordi-
nated to the demands of the music; whether it was by Pushkin,
or some bungling amateur, he would alter the poem to suit his
own artistic ends. In setting a lyric he never considered himself as the interpreter of another's thoughts and feelings,
but regarded the poet as a mere assistant, whose business it
was to help him to the attainment of his own musical ends,
which lay farther beneath the surface and seemed to him of
greater importance than the actual words. People have
blamed Moussorgsky severely for this arbitrary treatment of
the poetical text, especially in the case of *Boris*, but not always with justice, as we shall see when we go further into
the question.

Of the other three songs two are settings of poems by
Koltzov. It was no mere accident that Moussorgsky, even in
his youth, had been strongly attracted to this author; Koltzov was the first Russian poet to establish a connexion between the popular songs of his country and the poetry of
the literary class. In his youth he had kept the sheep and
driven the cows to pasture, and even after he had been removed, by a patron's hand, from his rustic surroundings
and established in the literary circle of Moscow, he still succeeded, as no Russian poet had yet done, in sounding the

47

true note of the folk-song. It has been said, and rightly, of
his poems that they cannot be recited, but only sung to the
balalaika. It is significant of the direction which Moussorgsky's artistic development was to take that he early showed
so decided a preference for Koltzov's poems as subjects for
musical setting. One of the two is a lively drinking song—
"Capriccio," the composer named it—which storms along
to the clinking of glasses and clatter of dishes, delightfully
imitated in the accompaniment; we may conclude from the
piano part that it was probably intended for orchestral treatment. The other song, "I have castles to spare," begins with
an effective *allegro*, but has a plaintive ending: riches are no
cure for heart-ache. In this song, although Moussorgsky is
still far from that mastery of expression which marks his
later work, he is already sufficiently an artist to produce
some striking effects with the still crude material at his command. After the "Star," with its folk-song quality, this song
is the best of the series. The weakest is the last, one of the
few love-songs Moussorgsky ever wrote—these may be count-
ed on the fingers of one hand, and all are more or less failures.
Even the youth of twenty could not find real expression and
convincing phrases for the "language of love." Finding that
in this particular field he could not get beyond the limit of
conventional sentiment, in later years he stubbornly refused
to compose for any words of what is called a lyric character;
the reasons for this we shall discuss later on. The song in question—"What mean the words of love?" to words by an unimportant poet called Amossov—is dedicated to Madame
M. W. Shilovskaia, the châtelaine at Glebovo, and may be
taken as a *pièce d'occasion*, sent in gratitude for hospitality
received. The surprising thing in these songs is that in them
alone of all Moussorgsky's compositions we find clear traces
of the influence of Mendelssohn, with whom, except in this
instance, he had absolutely nothing in common. Probably

certain chance-remembered phrases still rang in his ears, without his troubling to think from where they came.

All the songs in the Paris manuscript have carefully written dedications; among them we find the names of Mesdames Grünberg and Sinaide Burtzeva, the singers, of M. Mikeshin, the sculptor, who designed the Katharina Monument and other similar works in Petersburg, of Plato Borispaletz, the artist, and friend of Glinka and Dargomizhky, whose portraits he painted, etc. From these names we can form an idea of the sort of society in which Moussorgsky moved at that time. Of the other songs in the Paris manuscript, belonging to a later period, we shall speak in the proper place.

In addition to these instrumental and vocal compositions Moussorgsky, in 1858–60, made several experiments in writing for the stage. Ever since his first amateurish attempts at composition he had been irresistibly drawn to this field, in which he was destined later to reap his richest laurels. After the failure of his first essay with *Han d'Islande* he was not soon induced to venture on another actual opera, but preferred to try his hand at writing incidental music for plays, taking as his models probably Glinka's music to Kukolnik's drama *Prince Kholmsky* and Balakirev's music to *King Lear*. In 1852 appeared the first Russian translation of the *Œdipus* of Sophocles, by Shestakov, and for this Moussorgsky undertook to write all the incidental music. Several numbers were actually completed; in his letter to Balakirev he mentions the overture and several choruses, among them an *allegro* in E flat, introduced by an *andante* in B flat minor, which, as Moussorgsky expressed it, was to be his "farewell to mysticism"; this chorus was introduced later into *Salambo*. Stassov claims to have seen several numbers of the *Œdipus* music and to have heard Moussorgsky play them on the piano. Besides the chorus alluded to, the only number that has survived is a fine chorus in F minor for the Eu-

menides in the temple scene, just before the entrance of
Œdipus, the concluding movement of which ("Ye gods, have
pity!"), in F major (Lydian mode), is particularly effective. Judging from this specimen, we have every reason to
regret the loss of the remainder.

To 1860 must also be assigned the first tentative sketch
of a work to which Moussorgsky was always returning, after
longer or shorter intervals, but to which he never succeeded
in giving the final form—a task reserved for Rimsky-Korsakov after Moussorgsky's death; I refer to the well-known
symphonic poem now called *A Night on the Bare Mountain.*
Originally (i.e., in 1860), as we learn from a letter of the
composer to Balakirev (September 26), this piece was intended as incidental music to Baron Mengden's drama *The
Witches.* It was to represent a regular witches' sabbath, interspersed with a few intermezzos, the appearance of various
wizards, a solemn march for all the hellish crew, and a scene
depicting the triumph of Beelzebub, whom Mengden represents as the lord and master of the festival. Moussorgsky fell
in love with the subject, and looked forward to a success;
nevertheless, at the time nothing more was heard of this work,
which has since gone through many remarkable and un-
looked-for changes in the passage of years.

Of a sacred chorus "*Vladiko dnei moïch* (Lord of my
days)" also mentioned in the same letter to Balakirev, no
trace has survived. With a mention of the many pianoforte
arrangements made by Moussorgsky at this period, mostly
for the use of the Balakirev circle, the record of his musical
activities in his early student days, while he was still an officer, is complete. The first piece he arranged for piano duet
was Balakirev's "Russian Overture"; he seems to have been
very proud of his own work, for he writes to the composer
(September 20, 1859) : "Mili, the four-handed arrangement
of your overture is finished, and I am much pleased with it;
the orchestral *tutti* are all quite successful, the complicated

50

passages in imitation are all quite easy to play; in short, everything is as it should be." Balakirev, however, seems to have been of a different opinion, for in a subsequent letter Moussorgsky writes (December 25, 1860): "Don't be too vexed about the overture—don't forget it was my first attempt of the kind." Rimsky-Korsakov mentions in *My Musical Life* that when the Balakirev circle met at Cui's, arrangements for eight hands by Moussorgsky of several orchestral pieces by Berlioz ("Queen Mab," "Capulet's Feast") and by Balakirev (*King Lear*) were performed.

Though Moussorgsky's output in the matter of composition in his early years was nothing very remarkable for either quantity or quality, one cannot call it wholly worthless; side by side with so much that is quite amateurish, we find a few comparative successes—e.g., some of the songs ("Ah, only tell me why!" "Where art thou, my star?" "I have castles to spare"), the temple scene from *Œdipus*, and the B flat Scherzo.

The fact that Moussorgsky was such an easy convert to Balakirev's anarchical principles of education and found so little difficulty in assimilating the artistic theories founded on them shows how deeply he was imbued with the characteristics of his race. The Slavs, and especially the Russians, are and always have been disposed to rely on direct inspiration and natural technical brilliancy rather than on the acquisition of fundamental knowledge and the power won by hard work; this applies not only to music, but to the other arts, to literature, and even to science. Although this principle seems extremely risky if taken as a general rule, still we must admit that, in every field, there have been exceptional individuals who have justified it by their achievements, and of these Moussorgsky is one of the most convincing examples.

The alteration in his way of living brought about by his retirement from military service, together with his conversion from mysticism to realism, had a favourable result—if we may believe Borodin's account—on Moussorgsky's outward appearance as well as on his inner nature. Borodin met him again in the autumn of 1859 at the house of a certain professor at the Military Academy of Medicine, who was the friend of both. He tells us: "Moussorgsky had already left the service. He had grown much more manly and rather stouter in appearance; every trace of military smartness had disappeared. The distinction in his dress and manner was the same as before, but not the slightest hint of dandyism remained. We were introduced, but at once recognized each other, and recalled our first meeting in the hospital. Moussorgsky told me he had left the service in order to devote himself entirely to music, as it was impossible to combine the two. Our conversation then turned involuntarily to music. I was at that time an enthusiastic admirer of Mendelssohn— of Schumann I knew hardly anything. Moussorgsky, on the other hand, was now a friend of Balakirev, and already on the track of all sorts of new tendencies in music, of which I had no conception. When the company saw what we had in common, they proposed that we should play duets—and the A minor symphony of Mendelssohn into the bargain. Moussorgsky turned up his nose a little, but consented, only begging that he might be excused from the *andante*, which, he said, had nothing of the symphony about it, but was just a "Song without Words" or some such thing arranged for orchestra —so we played the first movement and the scherzo. Then Moussorgsky began to rave about the symphonies of Schumann, of which I was quite ignorant; so he sat down to the piano and played some fragments of the E flat symphony from memory. When he came to the middle movement, he stopped, with this remark: 'Now, this is where the musical mathematics begin.' It was all new and delightful to me. Seeing how interested I was, he played quite a number of pieces, all of which were new to me. It came out that he was a composer himself; as I naturally expressed the peculiar interest I felt at this discovery, he gave me some idea on the piano of a scherzo he had written—I think it was the one in B flat. When he came to the trio, he hissed through his teeth: 'Now here is something in the oriental style!' I was absolutely amazed at the strange new elements in his music. I cannot say that it pleased me at first, though I was greatly impressed by the novelty of it, but the longer I listened, the more I came to enjoy it. I confess that at first I did not take seriously Moussorgsky's assurance that he meant to devote himself entirely to music—I thought it just a harmless piece of swagger—but after hearing the Scherzo I hesitated: was I to believe him or not? . . . "

Moussorgsky certainly entered upon his career with a firm step and quiet mind—never once did he look back. Fortunately he had no foreboding of the thorny path that lay before him, nor was he yet conscious of his goal. But when once he had shaken off his tendency to mysticism, he was no longer in doubt as to the direction he had to take—it was to lead him to the realization of those mighty artistic conceptions the outlines of which took ever clearer shape in the course of the next few years.

III
STORM AND STRESS
1860 – 5

IN READING the lives of celebrated men, and of most of the great artists, we usually find that their path through life winds upward in proportion to the recognition which, despite the opposition of their contemporaries, comes to them at last. From the wild life of Bohemia to the well-ordered existence of a comfortable prosperity—that is the regular course. We must expect to find numerous obstructions and deflections from the straight path, but it is seldom that these are so powerful as to convert the established rule into its exact opposite. Yet in the case of Moussorgsky this is what actually happened; born into the high life of the aristocracy, he sank, in the course of a comparatively short existence, almost to the lowest depths of the underworld. Why was this? What were the causes that gave so tragic a turn to his fate? Was it his own fault, or another's—weakness of character, or the force of circumstances? To these questions there can be no uncertain answer. The tragic story of Moussorgsky's life shows us how a lofty nature, nobly planned, inspired by nothing but the kindliest and justest impulses of humanity and the purest artistic ambition, can, under the pin-pricks of petty material and moral worries, and the blows and buffets of fortune—almost continuous but for one short interval —collapse entirely and be left to lie helpless in the dust. When we look for Moussorgsky's own share of the blame, we find that it consists only in his utter unfitness for the struggles for existence—not from weakness, but from his inca-

54

pacity to learn those tricks of fence that others used against him, and in his helplessness to parry or elude the blows of fate. He was a fighter who understood only how to attack; he could not defend or take cover. Neither in art nor in life did he ever give way by a hair's breadth or make the slightest concession in matters of conscience; to the very last he stood up as the dauntless champion of whatever seemed to him right and true and of good report—and of course he was bound to fall. It is a heart-breaking spectacle and makes one rage against the methods of our social system, which always breaks down when it has to deal with exceptional cases.

During the period of his military service in Petersburg Moussorgsky lived part of the time with his mother, and part with his elder brother. The establishment in Petersburg was conducted in the same patriarchal fashion as the country-house at Karevo; the proverbial Russian hospitality was practised in fullest measure—"the *samovar* on the table was never cold," as the Russian expression has it. Unfortunately we possess no detailed contemporary portrait of Moussorgsky's mother. Stassov tells us, from his personal observation, that not only did Moussorgsky cling to his mother with a childlike devotion, but a bond of real friendship grew up between mother and son; the latter's correspondence with Balakirev gives us some illuminating glimpses of this admirable woman and of the tender motherly care she lavished on both of her sons. We read how she would open the door and call out to Modinka (a customary pet name for Modest) to wish Balakirev good health, as that was the best thing in life; or how she would sit and practise "Miller's Boy" (a card-game) with great diligence in order to be able to beat Balakirev, who was particularly good at it. These letters give one the impression that Moussorgsky was still able to enjoy to the full the blessings of a peaceful and comfortable family life; his leaving the army naturally made no alteration in his domestic habits, but merely confirmed them, since the prospective composer had now more time in which to enjoy the comforts of home to his heart's content.

His spare time was now, of course, to be devoted to special musical study—but now, as before, this got no further than the friendly exchange of letters with Balakirev. True, there was a good deal of composition going on meanwhile, but as to any regular studies or exercises, we hear only of good intentions, but nothing of their fulfilment. In a letter written on the first day of the Christmas holidays, 1860, we read: "Thanks, Mili, for letting me off the writing of another scherzo, all the more as I am just now in no mood for anything so playful, but incline rather to a solemn *andante*. I shall work at part-writing, beginning with something in three parts. I intend to accomplish something really worth while. It is a wholesome discipline for me to remember that my harmonies gave you the impression of a badly mixed salad! That must not be!" But in spite of this very sensible resolution, Moussorgsky never really wavered for a moment in his contemptuous opinion of anything like scholarship. In a letter that Moussorgsky wrote to his young teacher a year later—he was twenty-three at the time—he gives most amusing expression to these opinions. For the better understanding, not only of this letter, but also of the condition of music in Petersburg at that time, some preliminary remarks are necessary.

In opposition to the Musical Society, wholly German in its sympathies, which owed its origin to Anton Rubinstein, together with its classes for instruction, which in 1862 came to be known as the Conservatoire, Balakirev and G. Y. Lomakin, the excellent conductor of Count Sheremetiev's church choir, started in the same year the Musical Free School for choral singing. Both institutions organized symphony concerts, the former with Rubinstein as conductor, the latter conducted by Balakirev, with Lomakin for choral works. According to one of the articles of its constitution, each concert of the Musical Society was bound to include at least one work by a Russian composer in its program. This condition, however, was but loosely adhered to, and it was the concerts of the Musical Free School that actually became the stronghold of Russian music—so long, that is, as these concerts continued. For the inevitable naturally happened; the concerts of the Free School could not hold out against the all-powerful Musical Society, which had the Court and the whole of the so-called high society of Petersburg behind it, and moreover received a large State subsidy, while the Free School had absolutely no funds, and its public consisted of members of the small community of admirers of Russian music, drawn chiefly from the impecunious literary circles.

On April 28, 1862 Moussorgsky writes as follows to Balakirev from the country, where news had been received of the opening of the Musical Free School and the success of the first two concerts: "I bid you hail, and may the new-born school flourish and prosper! . . . I am far from maintaining that all learning means obscurantism; at the same time I find the free and unforced development of natural aptitude, which is sure to be radically fresh and sound, incomparably more sympathetic than any scholastic or (*cela revient au même*) academic training. . . . Just think of all the rubbish these professors cram into the heads of the young disciples, and of how the pupils' heads must ache before they are competent to sift the chaff from the wheat—i.e., to throw away whatsoever is valueless and keep the essential. One is irresistibly reminded of the conversation between Mephistopheles and the innocent Freshman. With what fiendish cunning does the Devil terrify the wretched youth with every sort of foolish doctrine, whether antediluvian or 'up to date'! A true professor indeed—only more honest than ours, for he frightens his pupils away—they lead them on! I have a definite purpose in dwelling on all this, and will now pass from

57

schools of philosophy to schools of music. In Piter [Petersburg] they have lately set up two music schools, side by side, which are the exact opposite of each other in character; the one is—just a den of professors; the other a free association of human beings whose object is to discover certain fundamental principles of their art, on which they can all agree. In the one place Zaremba and Tupinstein ['*tupo*' in Russian means 'stupid'], clad in their anti-musical professorial togas, cram pupils with every sort of rubbish, and so infect them from the very first. The unfortunate pupils see before them, not human beings, but two saints on pillars, holding some sort of silly scribble in their hands, which they say contains the rules of music. Tupinstein is a dullard by nature, so he is merely doing his duty in imparting his dullness to others. Not so Zaremba—a cunning fellow, that—just the man to clap true art into a strait jacket. Having attained to the dignity of Doctor—he is really more like a cobbler in a pedagogue's night-cap—he is not so childish and simple as to base his views and his counsels on musical logic or æsthetics. Not he—he has been taught the rules! That is the lymph with which he inoculates all the poor fools of music students against any possibility of acquiring a knowledge of music in a natural way.—Down on your knees to Mendel!—that is Zaremba's way of salvation. Mendel is God and Zaremba is his prophet! As for Aunty Helen [the Grand Duchess Helène Pavlovna, formerly Princess of Sachsen-Altenburg, the chief patron of the Russian Musical Society], I suppose she cannot live to the age of Methuselah—she is but a temporary affliction. . . . In the other school we have you and Gaschenka ['Gabriel' Lomakin]. What more is there to say? You are a genius, and consequently all that is bold and free and strong comes natural to you. It is such men that humanity needs. So here is all success and a prosperous future to your good work! Once more I say: 'Hail to the newly born!' "

The relations between the leading musicians in Petersburg being what they were, it is clear that no *rapprochement* between Moussorgsky and the Russian Musical Society was possible. Dmitri Stassov, one of the first acting directors or supervisors of the society, endeavoured for a while to act as go-between, but soon gave up the thankless task. Only once did he succeed in getting a work of Moussorgsky's performed by the society—this was the B flat Scherzo mentioned in the previous chapter. A proposal to perform the chorus from the temple scene in *Œdipus* fell through in consequence of the exceedingly undiplomatic behaviour of the composer; writing to Balakirev on the subject (November 9, 1860), he says: "I was at Stassov's today. With regard to my chorus, the committee, he told me, had come to the following decision: if I found at rehearsal that my work could safely be sung in public, the performance would take place. An instinct of self-preservation made me tell Stassov that the chorus was to be sung *agitato,* and as it was very short, it would need to be preceded by a short *andante* in order to make the *agitato* more effective; and so I requested him to give my chorus back to me. Does this imbecile society suppose that it can teach me? I have my chorus back, and am heartily glad that a collision with Rubinstein has thus been averted. *Basta!* I have had quite enough of the Musical Society."

But the Musical Society had also had enough of the high-handed composer. So long as Rubinstein was at the head of affairs and continued to conduct the symphony concerts, never again did the name of Moussorgsky appear on their program. The chorus from *Œdipus* was first performed by the conductor of the Marie Theatre, K. N. Liadov, in 1861, at a Russian concert, together with some other short compositions of the young Russian school.

In spite of the doubtless good intentions with which Moussorgsky began his musical studies, he showed little zeal in carrying them on, and his success was small in proportion, so far as regular practical work at harmony and counterpoint went. In default of the sort of teacher who understands how to make the driest stuff always fresh and palatable, an impetuous nature like Moussorgsky's could not be expected to savour it for long. Whether he ever looked into the matter is doubtful—it is certain that he never understood it. This particular kind of study never tended to raise the value of musical science in his estimation, since his creative spirit was hampered rather than helped by the rules of composition, which he must have known, though he never mastered them. His output during the years 1861–2 was very small; this, as well as his slackness in the matter of study, may possibly have been due to other causes arising from events of the time quite apart from his musical life. The year 1861 yields one composition only; but, fortunately, what is lacking in quantity is made up in quality, for the "Intermezzo *in modo classico*" is undoubtedly among the most pleasing of Moussorgsky's instrumental works. The piece was originally written for piano, and was scored for orchestra later on by the composer (in 1867) and in an entirely new arrangement by Rimsky-Korsakov in 1883. In connexion with this piece, with its mighty leading theme, recalling the spirit of Bach's organ toccatas, and its enchantingly graceful trio, Stassov tells a characteristic anecdote that describes, in a most convincing manner, how a musical idea was engendered in the composer's mind. Moussorgsky confessed to his friend that the piece had a secret "program" and, in spite of the pompous title "*in modo classico*," was imbued through and through with the spirit of Russian nationalism. The impulse to write it came from a scene of Russian country life, apparently insignificant in itself, but which, as sometimes happens, sank deep into his memory. In the winter of 1861 Moussorgsky spent some time on the family estate, in the Government of Pskov. One fine day—it was holiday time—while the sun shone brightly over the glittering wastes of snow, he saw a gang of peasant lads walking over the plain, and having some difficulty in getting through the deeper drifts; every minute some of them would sink in and had then laboriously to extract themselves from the snow. "The effect," said Moussorgsky, "was charming and picturesque, gay and serious at the same time. Suddenly in the distance a crowd of young women appeared, singing and laughing as they came along the shining way. The picture at once took musical shape in my imagination; quite unexpectedly the first melody was born, with its vigorous up-and-down Bach-like movement, and the merry, laughing women were transformed into the theme that I afterwards used for the middle part, or trio—and all *in modo classico,* in keeping with my musical activities at that time. And that is how the 'Intermezzo' came to be written." Everyone who knows the piece must own that no more charming "program" could be imagined for it; its history is a perfect example of how visual impressions are transformed into musical ideas.

Moussorgsky spent the January of 1861 in Moscow, where he had gone to visit his friends the Shilovskys—at least he gives their house as his address, and his letters to Balakirev hint at no other reason for his stay in the "White City." We learn indeed that he had a very happy time in Moscow, surrounded by quite a crowd of young students and musicians, whom he would "move to tears" by his rendering of Schumann's Sonata in F sharp minor, Beethoven's Quartet in F, and particularly of Schubert's C major symphony; while their evenings were spent in talks and discussions about "history, politics, chemistry, art—in short, whatever happens to come along." "These people," he writes (January 13, 1861), "form a sort of coterie in Moscow; as you know, those who are really good for anything always keep to themselves, and it is well it should be so." Nevertheless his association with "these people" drew forth a reproof

from Balakirev for moving in such "limited surroundings";
Moussorgsky's reply to his stern mentor was as follows (January 19): "As to the passage in which you are pleased to
take me to task for preferring the company of 'limited personalities,' I have only one answer to make: tell me who are
your associates, and I will tell you who you are—so the logical consequence of your remark is that I, too, must be
'limited.' "

With the official musical circles in Moscow Moussorgsky had as little sympathy as with those in Petersburg. A
Conservatoire had been established in Moscow at the same
time as the one in Petersburg, and actually by the brother of
Anton Rubinstein—Nikolai—who had also attracted a number of German professors, Laub, Albrecht, Hubert, etc., to
the new institution. Moussorgsky avoided it; he writes on
January 16: "I have not been to the German Ministry of
Music they have established here, not even to the Saturday
concert—the program did not attract me. Nikolai Rubinstein is a worthy relation of Anton—he lets his home-made
Moscow pianists play Chopin—*pièces de salon*—the height
of absurdity!"

Moussorgsky did not neglect his own work altogether
amidst the social pleasures of Moscow. Certainly his health
seems once more to have been far from satisfactory, as we may
conclude from the following passage in the letter quoted
above: "I seem to be all right again. If only God will grant
me good health—then you'll see how I can write! Only I get
tired so quickly—no, no, composing is no light work—however, cold water is a help." This apparently self-prescribed
cold-water cure so far succeeded that he was even able to plan
the sketch of a symphony; it was to be in D major, with an
Andante in F sharp minor and a Scherzo in B. He worked
at the two middle sections while in Moscow, and apparently
with success, for he is able to write to Balakirev: "The Scherzo
is finished; I have now only the second trio to do, and am

working at it. The Scherzo is quite a big affair, in the real symphonic style; I am dedicating it, the whole symphony in fact, to the members of our Wednesday Musical Circle." Next day he writes: "I have arranged the Scherzo for piano duet—all very proper and correct, and particularly easy to play. I hope to submit it to our tribunal some Wednesday soon." Neither the Scherzo nor any other movement of the symphony has been preserved, nor does any member of the Balakirev "tribunal" mention it.

It is in one of these letters from Moscow that we find the first hint of impatience on Moussorgsky's part under his friend's fatherly admonitions. Balakirev was only a few years his senior and as Moussorgsky's development progressed, this inequality wore away—and as his belief in his own powers increased, his faith in the absolute artistic superiority of his friend began, though slowly, to disappear. Balakirev, it appears, had not only reproached Moussorgsky with his liking for the society of "limited personalities," but also warned him against being "swamped" in the musical conditions of Moscow. To this, Moussorgsky replied: "As to the prospect of my being swamped and having to be pulled out of the swamp, I will merely say this: if I really have genius, I shall not be 'swamped'—least of all while my mental activities are being stimulated; but if you think that this is not so, why trouble to come to the rescue of a useless nonentity? One thing I am sure of—your letter was the offspring of that peevish mood of yours, which rests on a false assumption; it is time you ceased to treat me as a child who must be held in leading-strings for fear he should fall. That is my answer to your cross and hasty letter, Mili—but, I thank you for it, all the same."

Shortly after Moussorgsky's return to Petersburg, at the beginning of February, an event occurred of the greatest importance for his future, bringing fatal consequences in its train. On February 19, 1861 the liberator Tsar, Alexan-

63

der II, issued his ukase by which serfdom in Russia was abolished. The passing of this measure of State diverted the political and economical destinies of the whole Empire into entirely new channels. For the lesser gentry of the smaller country estates it meant ruin, almost without exception. The Moussorgsky family, although their property had shrunk somewhat after the father's death, and the principal estate had been let to others, had still something to fall back upon; but under the new conditions the threatened crash could not long be averted. So long as the mother was alive, they managed, by dint of heavy pecuniary sacrifices and with the help of the most risky, even desperate financial transactions, to preserve at least a part of the estate, but the position grew worse year by year. The great house in Petersburg had to be given up; the mother went back to live at Karevo, the country-seat. In his letters we find Moussorgsky constantly pleading that he has no time, as "our affairs" require his attention. Now we find him interviewing various people on business, running round to all sorts of brokers, appearing before the magistrates, at another time called upon to make some important decision in the absence of his brother. In short, the old peaceful, pleasant life is gone beyond recall; in its place we find unrest, excitement, business worries, and cares of every kind. Small wonder, then, that in such circumstances Moussorgsky's musical activities came to a complete standstill. The list of his compositions shows that with the exception of the "Intermezzo" he wrote nothing at all during 1861, 1862, and the first half of 1863. Almost continuous journeys between Petersburg and Karevo, and thence to the town of Toropetz, where the greater part of the business seems to have been transacted, took up nearly the whole of his time. His permanent residence, so far as he can be said to have had one, after his mother's retirement to the country in 1862, was in the house of his brother Filaret, now married and settled in Petersburg. In a letter of Moussorgsky to Cé-

sar Cui, written from Toropetz about this time, we have a
graphic but scarcely cheerful description of his feelings and
of the conditions then prevalent in the country and the provincial towns of Russia. Among other things he writes: "It
is all so tedious, dreary, annoying—one can hardly describe
it. What have we done that our agent should play us such a
dirty trick over the property? I had intended to do some decent work—instead of which, if you please, I am perpetually
making investigations, giving information, running round
from one police court to another! If my mother were not in
Toropetz, these fools here would drive me quite crazy—it is
only on her account that I stay on; it makes her so happy to
have me with her, and I am glad to be able to give her the
pleasure. But oh! these neighbours of ours, the farmers!—
these 'planters,' rather! They are very proud of the club they
have opened in the little town, and meet there almost every
evening to play *radau*. The proceedings generally open with
a speech, followed by some sort of general announcements
for the benefit of these 'gentlemen,' and nearly always end
in such an uproar that one feels inclined to send for the police. . . . All this goes on in an aristocratic club, and these
are the gentry with whom one has to associate; and day after
day they bore you with tales of their 'lost rights' and 'total
ruin'—nothing but howling and gnashing of teeth, and
noisy scenes. . . . True, there are some young fellows who
are rather more decent—the 'young fools,' as they are called
—but one hardly ever sees them, as it is they who negotiate
with the peasants, and consequently they spend most of their
time in travelling. And this is the fetid atmosphere in which
I, poor sinner, have to live and breathe! It can hardly be said
to be good for the artistic part of one—a man has enough to
do to prevent the stink from hanging about and choking him
—what chance has music in such circumstances as these?"

Among these "young fools," filled as they were with abstract ideals, who were in favour of the disastrous measure

for the abolition of serfdom, and whose sympathy actually hastened the day of its arrival, we must certainly reckon Moussorgsky. The opportunity to "throw in his lot with the people" seemed to have arrived—and his idealistic efforts met with the usual reward.

In spite of the "fetid atmosphere" that he had to breathe in the summer of 1863, Moussorgsky's muse was not altogether silent; at the end of his letter to Cui, quoted above, we find the following: "Some days ago I came across a short poem by Goethe; I was delighted with it and hastened to set it to music. I could not expect to succeed with anything big just now, as all my thoughts (thanks to the agent) revolve around the police station and similar things—still one can try one's hand at trifles. The poem comes from *Wilhelm Meister*, I believe—it is about a beggar, and a beggar might certainly sing my music without any pangs of conscience—at least in my opinion." The poem in question is the Harper's Song: "*An die Türen will ich schleichen*"—the fact that he turns the poor harper into a beggar must be put down to the composer's ignorance of German literature. The music seems to have been written to the original German text; in any case Goethe's words go to it quite as well as the successful Russian translation—anonymous, but most probably by the composer himself. This was the last German poem that he set to music, with the exception of some verses by Heine. "The Harper's Song" belongs unquestionably to Moussorgsky's finest contributions to vocal music; the bold "atonality" of the ending was something quite unheard of at that time (1863); the song is written in E flat minor; while the major third, G flat-B flat, is sustained in the middle parts, the bass (in the lower octave) enters, on the unaccented part of the bar, with another third, C flat-E flat. The impressionistic effect of this idea, in a composition that is otherwise quite simple in its harmonic structure, is very striking; as a French critic remarks, one seems to hear soft footsteps dying away in the distance. The "trifles" referred to in the letter to Cui include two other songs, also written in the summer of 1863, one of which by no means deserved the contemptuous description given by the composer. It is actually rather a *scena* than a song, being a vigorous and dramatic rendering of King Saul's farewell before the battle, from the poem by Byron in the *Hebrew Melodies*. This fine composition, which in some particulars—e.g., the fanfares at the beginning and in the middle—already foreshadows the future composer of *Boris* and *Khovanstchina*, is one of the few songs of Moussorgsky that were very popular with Russian singers during his lifetime; given by a singer with a good voice and a gift for dramatic expression, it makes a powerful impression. "King Saul" is dedicated to A. P. Opotchinin, for whom, both as a singer and as a man, Moussorgsky cherished an ever-increasing admiration. The last of the three songs belonging to the summer of 1863 is a "Love-song," dedicated to Opotchinin's sister Nadeshda; it is just as poor in invention and feeble in expression as the love-song mentioned in the previous chapter. The text is by Kourotchkin, a Russian author of no importance, and begins: "We parted coldly from each other." How far Moussorgsky's rare lyric outbursts were the result of his own personal experience must remain a matter of conjecture, on which we shall touch at greater length in a later chapter.

Of these three songs only one, "King Saul," was printed during the composer's lifetime, and that not till 1871, eight years after it had been written; the other two were brought to light on the discovery of the Paris manuscript. The Paris version of "King Saul" differs considerably—and not to the advantage of the work—from the first edition of 1871; in that year Moussorgsky had probably taken the piano accompaniment in hand—either alone, or with the help of Rimsky-Korsakov, with whom he shared rooms at that time—and submitted it to a thorough and very beneficial revision, before sending it to press. The Paris version reveals certain striking blemishes, which only the strangest conception of music could regard as special "flashes of genius"—a view that unfortunately has found favour with a certain class of critics.

In dealing with these songs we have slightly anticipated the sequence of events; let us return to the correspondence with Balakirev, which in 1862—a year absolutely barren of musical activity—is particularly rich in interesting sidelights on the development of Moussorgsky's personality.

At the beginning of the spring of 1862 he had escaped for a time from the official atmosphere of Petersburg, with its boards, peasant councils, and agricultural banks, and was living in the country, in the Government of Pskov, on the Volok estate, belonging to a family named Kushelev, with whom he was intimate. The particular object of his visit to this house is not known, nor the reason why he did not go to his own home if he needed country air; his letters from Volok throw no light on the question; but, generally speaking, these letters contain so much of interest that one is tempted to give them in full, despite their length. One reason that drove him to the country appears to have been the recurrence of a slight nervous depression. His first letter to Balakirev from Volok is dated March 11, and is as follows:

"*I am writing the* andante.

"I am very comfortable here, in good health at present, and in relatively good spirits; I am leading the life of a decent, respectable person, going to bed at eleven and getting up at eight, and I find it very good for me. It is still snowing here, with wind and frost—I am impatient for the spring, in order to begin the cure. It is time to be sensible—I have played the fool long enough; now I must settle down to a definite task, but that can only be done when one is in a normal state of mind; so long as the fever is in one's veins, one can only indulge one's fancies, and that is merely to squander one's powers senselessly and to no purpose.

"What about your concert engagements? Is the archpriest Dubinstein ['*dubina*' is Russian for an unmannerly clown] plotting your destruction? Write and tell me all about it! Has Korsik [Rimsky-Korsakov] finished his scherzo, and is it a success? It is sure to be! Do let me know—these things interest me enormously.

"A change of scene and a new way of living have a very refreshing effect; one views the past in a clear light and can make a bold attempt to estimate the value of what has been done. I now see that, if I have not absolutely shirked my task, still, thanks to my truly Russian laziness, I have devilishly little to show in the way of achievement. Although I have no very great faith in my talent, I cannot doubt that I possess a certain amount; so it is my intention to set to work *to the very best of my ability*—at the same time I am looking for some other way of making myself useful. Moreover I have discovered a certain tendency in myself, that becomes ever more apparent—something very like instability or excessive softness—what you used to call 'doughiness.' I have just begun to realize it, and it worries me, for dough takes the impression of dirty fingers just as much as of clean ones. In any case I am resolved to rid myself of it—I find it too troublesome. It is all the more tiresome now that I propose to settle down to something sensible. Don't suppose that this letter is my *andante*, as you well might from the general tone of it, and the underlining at the beginning! In my finale the second theme still hangs fire—the wretched thing simply *won't* come! Perhaps the spring will help matters."

The *andante* and finale in question probably belong to the Sonata in D major (possibly another form of the symphony he had intended to write), to which he refers again in his next letter from Volok, but of which no trace has been found. The mention of some "useful employment" which he had in view shows us that Moussorgsky was beginning to realize that in the future, owing to his altered circumstances, he might be compelled to earn a living by his own exertions, an anticipation which, alas! was shortly to be fulfilled.

Moussorgsky's next letter from Volok contains a passage in which he gives his impressions, amusingly contrasted, of the French and the Germans—based partly on a French work on natural philosophy that he happened to be reading, partly on his acquaintance with the German tutor of the family with which he was living. The letter is dated March 31, 1862.

" . . . The *andante* is finished; I am writing the *allegro* of the finale; the spring, I believe, will see the beginning of the real birth-pangs, and then I must prepare for the *accouchement*. At present a sonatina in D is on the way—I have already begun the Scherzo in B minor. The first *allegro* and the scherzo of the Beethoven quartet are finished—I intend to get it done in time for our next season. That is the sum total of my musical activities. I am well and my brain is all right. I find it easy to work.

"While the children of my good landlady are industriously climpering on the keyboard, striking all sorts of chords, possible and impossible (they call it 'music-lessons'! It certainly interferes sadly with *my* music!), I am reading a very interesting work, on nature in general and human nature in particular. The book is called: *De la philosophie de la nature*; one is agreeably surprised to find that it contains no trace of that narrow spirit which admits within its pale only the initiated who are familiar with the terminology and dogmas of the various secret societies of philosophers. This book was written by a man who knows his subject thoroughly and is able to present his thoughts in clear, straightforward fashion. . . . After the Revolution, when France was swarming with bigoted Catholics and other tyrants calling themselves dictators and presidents, the book was condemned and burnt. O Frenchmen! O republicans! As usual, most of the copies were saved before the idiotic sentence could be carried out. Thanks to the approach of spring, which makes the roads impassable, I am confined to the four walls of my *petit réduit*, with a hot-blooded Prussian to keep me company; he is tutor to my hostess's children, a remarkably energetic and capable fellow, with a clear and well-developed understanding. His Spartan nature is a great help to me and I seem to be losing my Attic softness; he drags me out for walks, regardless of the snow-drifts, into which we often sink up to the waist. In his opinion my lethargy is due to sluggish circulation—my constitution requires constant brisking up before it can gain strength. . . .These *promenades monstres* are certainly very beneficial.

"My Prussian plays the piano rather well and has no small musical ability. He entertains me from time to time with the shorter fugues of Bach; my favourite is the one in E, with prelude, which fortunately he plays quite well. The piano is a semitone below pitch, so that the fugue is really played in E flat, which pleases me, for I don't like the key of E.

"I have been sounding my Prussian on all sorts of subjects and I find that we have much in common. I confess I was beginning to entertain very unfavourable opinions of the Germans in Russia, indeed of Germans altogether—not, of course, of their *artists* and *scholars*, who are a race apart. As soon as a German comes to Russia he naturally leaves his *world of beer and Riga cigars* behind him; that is true of all of them, from the departmental directors in the Government to the high priest Dubinstein and the contemptible Karlchen [Karl Schubert, a distinguished 'cello-player, soloist at the Marie Theatre and director of the University Symphony Concerts in Petersburg]. My Prussian has surpassed himself! What do you say to this? The 16th of March was my birthday—I was hardly awake when a poem was brought to me, with a rose pinned to the paper! Poetry and metaphors! I was naturally much pleased with such a delicate act of homage—but how German, how thoroughly German! The verses, too, are not altogether lacking in power; the author is naturally too sensible to liken me to a rose, so they haven't turned out badly. . . . "

It is to be regretted that we do not know the name of this "hot-blooded" and sensible Prussian who contrived such a successful "walking-cure" for Moussorgsky, besides playing Bach's fugues to him; it may possibly have been a certain Herr von Madewais—"my friend Madewais," as Moussorgsky calls him in his autobiography—of whom we shall have more to say when we come to discuss the Paris manuscript.

Moussorgsky seems to have been less anxious about his altered circumstances than were his friends in Petersburg, who apparently proposed to render him substantial assistance, with Balakirev as intermediary; we gather as much from a letter from the composer dated September 24, 1862, when he was living not far from Petersburg, at Minkino, a small property that his brother had bought.

"Your kind proposal," he writes, "is so strongly put that to reject it would be to disappoint the benevolent intentions of my good friends—so much I can see from your manly and warm-hearted letter. Kindness such as this can only be rightly repaid by actions, so I will not waste time on words. If my situation were such that I was actually in want and there was no hope in view, there could be no objection to accepting your offer. As things are, however, I do not feel justified in taking advantage of my friends' unnecessary alarm; that would be deceiving them and I value their regard far too highly to do a thing like that.

"My income is diminished, it is true, but not to the extent of depriving me of all possibility of preserving my independence. Accustomed as I have been to a life of comfort, in some respects even of luxury, I have naturally felt anxious for the future, and it is no wonder if I looked glum—anyone else would probably do the same in similar circumstances. I fully understand the feeling of apprehension expressed in your letter and am convinced that it is quite genuine. It is precisely for this reason that I beg you not to be anxious on my account, and to calm the fears of all those good people who are interesting themselves on my behalf. My present circumstances make such anxiety unnecessary, and it is particularly painful to me, since there is nothing in the world that I detest so much as deceit and treachery. Believe me, my dear Mili, I have had to go very carefully into the question of how I am to make shift with my diminished income—especially as for the past two years I have been living a regular family life among people with whom I was on excellent terms and who from the first rather spoilt me than stood in my way. After most serious consideration and a mathematically exact calculation of my finances I have come to the conclusion that the deficit in my budget will make it impossible for me to take up my residence in Petersburg in September, as I wanted to do—I must wait another month; I shall, however, be able to live fairly comfortably in the city from the beginning of October till April or the beginning of May. So, owing to my straitened circumstances, I shall have to postpone the renewal of intercourse with my friends, though only for one month. That is a good deal, I admit, but I readily make the sacrifice for the sake of the relief it will afford my relations and friends. I think I may take it for granted that all who really love me will prefer to see me leading an independent existence rather than flashing like a meteor across the scene only to make a speedy exit. I hope you will approve of my decision; after all, one month of rural retirement will enable me to enjoy seven months of peace and quiet in the interesting and stimulating atmosphere of the capital. As to employment, I should like to try for some job under Government, as that affords the best security; but I shall have to wait till the New Year, when all the changes are made in the personnel of the various departments. From what I have told you, my dear friend, you can form an idea of my situation, so reassure my friends, and yourself as well; you really must—I adjure you in the name of deception, the worst of all evils, which you must avoid.

"The change in my fortunes had a somewhat depressing effect, but only for a time; thanks to my fairly elastic nature, I have recovered my spirits and hope to stand firm. If I am out of humour, it is not autumn in the country, nor yet my financial difficulties, that is to blame. It is something quite different—I have been suffering from author's spleen! I am really ashamed to confess it, but your tepid appreciation of my *Witches* set up a severe irritation of my artistic *amour-propre*! I am of opinion—always was and always shall be—that the piece in question contains some fairly good music, and what makes it all the more important is the fact that it is my first independent work of any size. But my fit of spleen has passed, as everything passes; I have accepted my fate as a misunderstood composer and have already begun on a new work, for I find the scent of the pine woods particularly inspiring. So, my friend, you can perform my *Witches* or not, just as you please; in any case I refuse to make the slightest alteration, either in the general plan or in the working-out; both are intimately related to the subject of the picture, and the work in it is honest stuff, no shams or imitations. Every composer can recall the mood in which his work had its rise and was thought out, and this feeling—i.e., the recollection of former moods—forms the groundwork of the criticism he passes on his own achievements. I have fulfilled my task as well as I could, within the limits of my powers.—As to the *Witches* I am prepared to make certain alterations in the percussion parts, where I have gone wrong. However, we can talk over the whole

affair some other time; if you have an hour to spare, write
and tell me what you think about it.

"Farewell now, and best thanks for your straightforward letter—it has given me fresh strength and inspiration.
It is indescribably comforting to feel that one is the object
of a friend's regard—that is better than the biggest balance
at the bank. Kind regards to all who love me. . . . "

This letter is extraordinarily characteristic of Moussorgsky, in three ways. First, we notice how he lays it down
as the chief consideration that a man should be self-support-
ing, and not dependent on others for his material existence;
for a spoiled youth of twenty-three, and "his mother's darling," this is by no means the invariable attitude, and we are
compelled to feel the highest respect for the young composer
and prospective government employé. Secondly, we hear
proclaimed in bold *fortissimo* the first article of his moral
and artistic credo, on which the whole of his later life and
all his artistic activities were founded: "Of all evils deception is the worst." An almost morbid love of truth, a passionate hatred of anything like misrepresentation, deceit,
hypocrisy, lying, compromise, permeates all his thoughts and
actions, in life as well as in art. Thirdly—and at the present
crisis of his life this is the most important thing of all—we
find him quietly but firmly throwing off the artistic domination of Balakirev, exercised always with the utmost impatience, though hitherto most patiently endured. Even to pro-
cure a performance of his own work Moussorgsky is no
longer willing to make the slightest concession—henceforth
his own artistic conscience is to be his sole arbiter; in matters
in which he feels himself to be the responsible authority, no
power on earth can move him.

And thus, poorer in the things of this world, but richer
in resolution, in faith in himself and his artistic mission,
Moussorgsky enters upon a new phase of existence; youth
and its dreams are gone for ever; the struggle now begins.

75

IV

THE YEARS OF GROWTH
1865 — 8

WHEN Moussorgsky returned to Petersburg in the autumn
of 1863, after a visit to his mother in the country, an important change took place in his manner of living; instead of
returning to his brother Filaret's residence, he joined with
five other young fellows in sharing a bachelor establishment,
which they called their "Commune." All the members of the
band were drawn from the best society in Petersburg; the
young people were eager for the bonds of a close *camara-
derie* and for an atmosphere intellectually more bracing than
that afforded by the humdrum existence and ordinary dis-
sipations of the *jeunesse dorée* of Petersburg at that time.
Most of them had some sort of special taste, literary or artistic, that they cultivated with ability, zeal, and thoroughness, in a greater or less degree; all were keen on enlarging
the circle of their interests, by means of a constant mutual
exchange of opinions. The names of these young "Commun-
ists" are of no importance, since, with the exception of
Moussorgsky, none of them can lay claim to any special notice. This "Commune" was just one of the many centres of
that "enlightened culture" which characterized the intellectual and artistic life of Petersburg about the middle of the
nineteenth century. The outward forms of this communal
life were particularly pleasant, and well calculated to conjure up a certain sense of spiritual affinity. Each member of
the group had a room of his own, which, except by special
permission, was taboo to all the rest, and this, the principal

law of an unwritten code, was most strictly adhered to. A
common room served them for meals and social gatherings;
here they met in the evening, after work was over, for reading or entertainments, to exchange views on art or literature,
to make music—in short, to cultivate what they called an
"intellectualized sociability." From time to time one might
meet there some distinguished guest from the world of art or
literature, or Moussorgsky would introduce some of his musical friends to the little community. In his autobiography
he mentions among other close acquaintances of that period
a whole row of literary celebrities—Turgeniev, Kotomarov,
the historian, Grigorovitch, the novelist, Kavelin, Pisemsky,
Shevtchenko, the poet of Little Russia, who was shortly
afterwards condemned to exile on account of his inspired
songs dealing with the freedom of Ukrainia, and others. In
his manuscript Dostoievsky's name was also mentioned, but
was erased later; so far as can be ascertained, Moussorgsky
was never personally acquainted with that giant of Russian
literature, with whose art his own had so much in common.

As we have seen, the life of the "Commune" provided
incentives for the most varied activities; in later life Moussorgsky often declared that he reckoned the two years spent
there among the happiest of his life. There was only one
thing to darken his existence. In a letter to Balakirev quoted
above, Moussorgsky expresses his intention to "look around
for some post under Government," and such a post he had
found. In the autumn of 1863 he was appointed an official
in the Engineering Department of the Ministry of Trans-
port. For eighteen long years he had to pull at the traces
in which Russian officialdom dragged the rickety chariot of
State along through the swamps of corruption and the mire
of the blackest obscurantism, to land it finally in the abyss of
the Revolution. Naturally Moussorgsky never got beyond a
subordinate position, since any kind of strenuous effort was
foreign to his nature. "The government official discharges

his duties daily from eleven to four—more than that he does not do"—this fairly represents the view that Moussorgsky took of his ministerial responsibilities. There is a grotesque mingling of tragedy and comedy in the thought of Moussorgsky, the passionate idealist, placed in such a position. Here is a man intensely enthusiastic for every kind of liberty and culture, whose glowing heart endeavoured always to discover the essential truth and the highest meaning in all the deceptive shows of this life, who hated nothing so much as formalism in every shape—yet this born revolutionary is doomed for many long years to sit at his desk, day after day, his heart and head bursting with the noblest musical and artistic inspirations, and instead of confiding these to paper, is compelled to write all sorts of useless reports, or to stand in his blue uniform before his stern chief and receive his orders.

The Russian satirist Saltikov-Shtchedrin in one of his tales gives a sketch of the typical Petersburg *tchinovnik* (government cleık), in which the following occurs: "Do you understand this paper?" asks the head of the department. "No," comes the unhesitating reply, "but that doesn't matter—I can answer it all the same!"

It is certain that Moussorgsky was quite unfitted for this kind of bureaucratic routine, and his career, in consequence, was far from brilliant. When, some years before his death, he got himself transferred from the Ministry of Crown Lands to the Imperial Control, the chief of the department that he was leaving wrote the following surprising remark on the margin of the resignation form: "Granted with pleasure."

During his residence at the "Commune" Moussorgsky seems to have had some idea of trying to find some way of adding to his slender salary as government official. His brother Filaret relates that about that time he set eagerly about making Russian translations of celebrated criminal trials in

France and Germany—Pitaval's *Les Causes célèbres*, and other similar works; we have no information, however, as to whether he found a market for his labours, just as we know nothing of the fate of his earlier translation of Lavater.

His official employment and his translations, together with the vigorous social life of the "Commune," left him little time for musical activities. But even under these unfavourable conditions his muse was not completely silenced; indeed, his stay at the "Commune" witnessed a great step forward in Moussorgsky's musical development, as he now began to apply himself seriously to that species of composition to which he had hitherto given only casual attention, but which nevertheless was soon to become the peculiar field of his artistic exertions; the reference, of course, is to the field of opera, or, rather, of music-drama.

In the early sixties of the last century the fashionable romance of the entire civilized world interested at that time in Latin culture was Flaubert's *Salammbô*. It appeared in 1862 and was the result of the author's travels in Egypt and Syria during the years 1849–50 and a visit to Carthage in 1858, for purposes of study. This remarkable book, with its picturesque, flexible, powerful style, its realistic method of presentment—an absolute novelty at the time—and the really poetical fervour of its diction, naturally made a deep impression on the members of the little "Commune," whom it roused to a lively enthusiasm. Its effect on Moussorgsky was so great that it was weeks before he could shake off its influence; in consequence he determined to write an opera on the subject of Salammbô. What attracted him to Flaubert's romance was not so much the history of Carthage as the simple straightforward, but truly dramatic story of the love-intrigue between Salammbô, Hamilcar's lovely and stately daughter, and her father's deadliest foe, the passionate, foolhardy Mathô, once a Carthaginian slave, but now commander-in-chief of the Libyans, thirsting for love and revenge.

79

Moussorgsky was delighted, moreover, with the abundant opportunities that the plot offered for introducing the crowd
as a lively, bustling element of the action, either all together
or in separate groups—priests, common soldiers, senators,
slaves, Salammbô's women, etc. As a matter of fact, we find
him, as soon as he had made his first outline of the opera,
taking much more interest in the management of masses of
people, and choral *ensemble* in the grand style, than in the
dramatic or lyrical details of the work. Even in these early
sketches we have incontestable proof that Moussorgsky was
a born composer for the stage, a dramatist by the grace of
God. He wrote his own libretti, not from any special conviction, or by adhesion to any recognized æsthetic principle, but
merely because it never occurred to him to suppose that anyone else could shape the dramatic situations to suit him.

All Moussorgsky had to do here was to make an arrangement of the finished literary work that lay before him.
The dramatic situations took shape in his mind simultaneous-
ly with the stage picture—the common experience of every
true dramatist—and the suggestive force that emanated
from them admitted of no questioning. During the period of
artistic creation Moussorgsky was guided solely by his own
imagination and intuition. He sketched his designs rapidly
and with a sure hand and paid no attention whatever to the
suggestions of others; the material on which he happened to
be working seemed to him not sufficiently important in itself to call for any such precaution, whether it was a romance
of Flaubert, or one of Gogol's grotesque sketches, or a
drama by Pushkin. The arbitrary spirit that he showed in
dealing with the work of the great French realist we find
displayed again later in dealing with Pushkin's *Boris Godounov*; when once his creative imagination began to burn, he
recognized no other authority.

Part of the lines of *Salambo* he wrote himself, part
he took just as he found them—that is, when dealing with

a certain situation he would use the verses of any author if they seemed to him to meet the requirements of the moment. Thus for the text of *Salambo* he made use of poems by Heine as well as by the Russian poets, Maïkov, Shukovsky, Poleshaiev, and others.

In this, his first work for the stage, we find Moussorgsky already attaching the greatest importance to the stage-directions, which appear even in the first sketches; it is clear from this that the composer's musical ideas from the very beginning have their rise in and are suggested by the stage picture. From various passages in Flaubert's romance he collected exact descriptions of the appearance and costume of each of the characters in the play, and even of the different groups of people who crowd the stage as chorus. He gives strict directions down to the smallest detail, as to the locality, the architecture of the temple and other buildings, the underground prison, the landscape for the back curtain; every gesture, every movement, every pose is written down. He shows, moreover, a knowledge of the value of the weather in creating a stage effect—what we may call the meteorological element—and understands exactly how this may be expressed and emphasized in the music. Accordingly his sketches for *Salambo* swarm with directions such as the following: "The evening is oppressively warm, with a thunder-storm threatening"; "The people remain motionless, struck by Salambo's beauty and her resolute demeanour"; "The image of Moloch gives out a fiery glow—the red light falls on Eshmun's bronze horse"; "Mathô, chained, in gloomy mood, exhausted by torture, is sitting on a black stone, with bowed head, his coarse grey cloak on the ground beside him; when the priests have finished speaking, he springs erect, then sinks back again on to the stone, and whispers brokenly: 'This is the end!' " The framework of the stage picture is always clearly cut, so as to set off the particular action, and the movements of the actors are exactly indicated.

81

There is no doubt that *Salambo* had a special fascination for Moussorgsky because of its oriental atmosphere. All members of the "neo-Russian" school (which was practically the same as the Balakirev "circle") believed at that time that they had discovered in the East the promised land of music. It was the time when orientalism was beginning to be fashionable in the musical world, but nowhere had it found such idolatrous worshippers as in the four Russian composers Balakirev, Moussorgsky, Rimsky-Korsakov, and Borodin. We have seen already the effect made upon the last-named by his first introduction, through Moussorgsky, to the oriental idiom in music. Moussorgsky had made his first attempt at orientalism in music with the trio in the B flat Scherzo and it seems not to have suited him. In a letter written to his musical confessor, Balakirev, just after the completion of the Scherzo (February 25, 1858) he writes: "I find myself in such a constant state of indolence and languishment that I don't know how I am ever to shake it off. Never again—not for any consideration—will I write oriental music—and all this is owing to your traps and snares."

This resolve, due to a fit of boyish petulance rather than to any serious reflection, was not long adhered to; while working on *Salambo* Moussorgsky again succumbed to the fascination of the Orient.

Moussorgsky never finished his opera *Salambo*, although he got considerably further with it than he had done with *Han d'Islande*; he completed a pianoforte arrangement of some of the big scenes and even made some progress with the instrumentation. But during his "Commune" period his interest in native art, in the broadest sense of the term, developed so rapidly that Africa and its inhabitants gradually lost their charm for him. Nevertheless he was eagerly at work on *Salambo* in 1863, and still more so in 1864; after that the references to it in his correspondence are only very occasional; the last of all is in a letter to Balakirev (April 20,

1866), in which he mentions a "War-song of the Libyans—chorus for men's voices, on a theme you know, with a variation in the Georgian style." This chorus has not survived, nor can I find any trace of it among the composer's papers; Stassov thinks that it was resuscitated later in the choral work, for mixed voices, *Joshua*, a contention that is incapable of proof, though the markedly oriental character of this chorus, with its two themes in the Dorian minor—so common in Georgian melodies—would make it seem very probable. On the other hand, Rimsky-Korsakov, in *My Musical Life*, tells us that Moussorgsky got the principal theme of this chorus from hearing a Jewish family, in whose house he was living, sing it during a celebration of the Feast of Tabernacles. Shortly before this the opera, which had been laid aside for more than a year, was increased by yet another number, with this description: "The priestesses comfort Salambo and clothe her in wedding garments"; the manuscript bears the date February 8, 1866.

In the arrangement for piano, which contains hints for scoring, Moussorgsky has left us three complete scenes of the opera—the second scene of Act II, the first of Act III, and the first of Act IV.

The first of these takes place in the temple of the goddess Tanit (Astarte); the beautiful virgin, Salambo, princess of Carthage, daughter of the all-powerful Suffete Hamilcar, entreats the goddess "to kindle in her breast the fire of holy love." The maiden, "whose soul goes out in prayer, like the perfume of flowers in wine," adorns the altar of Tanit with flowers, for "in sweet odours dwell the souls of the immortals." The sacred veil of Tanit (the *zaimph*), which covers the statue of the goddess, is the talisman on the possession of which depend the greatness and the glory of Carthage. Salambo lies down on the couch at the foot of the altar, to keep watch over the *zaimph*. Mathô, the young Libyan General, guided by the slave Spendius, steals into the temple in order to steal the sacred mantle and thus ensure victory for his own nation. Salambo wakes from sleep, but all her prayers and entreaties fail to turn the daring youth from his purpose, although he loves Salambo and she in turn has long worshipped him at a distance. Mathô snatches the mantle from the statue and makes his escape, pursued by Salambo's curse; the act closes with the excitement of the people, who rush on from all sides. The lively action of the scene, and the feeling of tense expectation it produces, are sufficient guarantee of its effectiveness on the stage—nevertheless it had to wait fifty years before its worth was proved.

Similarly the first scene of the third act contains all the elements required for a striking theatrical effect. We are present at a sacrifice to Moloch; in the forecourt of a temple, on a lofty plinth, approached by steps, rises a colossal brazen statue of the god, surrounded by the Carthaginian priests. From huge piles of logs the flames arise; their fiery glow lights up the gigantic image, into whose jaws innocent children are to be thrown as a propitiatory offering. The combination of three choruses effectually prevents any flagging of the dramatic interest; the priests bow down before the god, the children and their mothers are weeping and wailing, while the people beseech their fearful deity, in return for the bloody sacrifice, to destroy the enemy even now at the gates of Carthage and to scatter their bones to the four winds. When the frenzy of the supplicants has reached its height, Salambo advances and announces to the people that she herself will penetrate to the Libyan camp and bring back the stolen *zaimph* from Mathô's tent. Her honour, her life, seem but a small price to pay when the destiny of her city and of her people is at stake. This whole scene is worked up to a dramatic climax with quite extraordinary power.

The first scene of Act IV shows us Mathô a prisoner and in chains, thanks to the treachery of a Libyan slave. He has a lengthy monologue, expressive of his longing for Salambo and his thoughts on the death that awaits him; enter the priests in procession, accompanied by four Pentarchs, who pronounce the death-sentence on Mathô—here we have the verses of Heine referred to above. This is as far as Moussorgsky got with the composition of *Salambo*, except for the "Song of the Balearic Islander," mentioned elsewhere.

It is probable that any other composer would have been most strongly attracted by the heavily sensuous atmosphere (characteristically African) of the scene in Mathô's tent in which Salambo gets possession of the *zaimph* by the sacrifice of her virginity. But Moussorgsky was proof against such allurement—the erotic, even in its unusual manifestations, had no interest for him. It would seem reasonable to conclude that this marked dislike for giving artistic expression to feelings by which the whole world is kept in place, and which usually take precedence of all other sources of musical inspiration, must have been deeply rooted in the composer's inner nature.

While working at this opera Moussorgsky decided to change its title to *The Libyan*—"and rightly, too," says Stassov, "since the chief figure, on whom the whole of the action depends, is Mathô the Libyan, certainly not Salambo, who is cast for the rather passive role usually allotted to the amorous heroine of opera."

In turning the story of *Salammbô* into an opera libretto Moussorgsky was able to demonstrate his dramatic ability in devising effective scenes and providing them with suitable music; but one side of his manifold artistic personality was scarcely brought into play—his incomparable power of revealing through his music the inner workings of the soul. The characters in *Salambo* are not nearly so sharply drawn as are the manifold types and figures to be found in his later works for the stage; they are not creatures of flesh and blood, they lack those countless individual traits, so finely observed, so cleverly embodied in the music, which distinguish every

85

character in *Boris* and more especially in *Khovanstchina*. The dramatis personæ in *Salambo* are just the conventional operatic figures, very far removed from the masterly characterization, the noble actuality of presentment to which Moussorgsky afterwards attained. This is true not only of the separate characters, but also of the various groups that form the chorus. Moussorgsky, who, in his artistic creations as in his life, was always strongly moved in proportion to the truth and sincerity of the feelings he was called upon to express, may have discovered this himself—in consequence he gradually lost all interest in this particular work. "A fine sort of Carthage that would have been!" he remarked later.

The manuscripts of those scenes of *Salambo*—or *The Libyan*—that were completed for piano score are, for the most part, preserved in the Public Library at Petersburg. The music, only a very small part of which has so far been published in its original form, has fortunately escaped the untimely and unmerited fate of being buried, with other manuscripts, in the cupboards of the Moussorgsky archives, the composer himself having duly provided for their resurrection.

In considering the question of this resuscitation of the *Salambo* music we find ourselves faced with an almost incredible circumstance that seems to defy the most elementary laws of artistic creation and musical inspiration. Still, there it is, and we must make the best of it; a great part of the music written for *Salambo* was afterward used by Moussorgsky for other purposes, more especially in a dramatic work that would seem to offer the greatest possible contrast to Flaubert's African romance—the *Boris Godounov* of Pushkin. In one work we have the burning sands of Africa, in the other the frozen snows of Moscow—on one hand the fiery temperament, the inflammable passions of the tropics, on the other the emotions of the Russian, slow to kindle, but impossible to extinguish—here the swift decision of the southern nature, there the tangled complexities of Slav psychology. The contrasts seem even more marked when we examine the way in which Moussorgsky has carried out his adaptations. A few examples may be given: Salambo's invocation of the goddess Tanit is changed into the recitative sung by the dying Boris; the music for Mathô, the slave Spendius, and Salambo, after the *zaimph* has been stolen, is used for the scene in the last act of *Boris*, where the two Jesuit fathers, Tchernikovsky and Lavitzky, are seized by the excited populace; the beginning of the scene of the sacrifice to Moloch reappears in the E flat minor section of Boris's *arioso* in the third act of the opera; and the scene where the Pentarchs pass sentence of death on Mathô furnishes the musical groundwork for the scene of the Council of Boyars in the last act but one of *Boris*; the fact that both these last instances are concerned with a death-sentence may afford some consolation to our musical purists.

Certain portions of *Salambo* were utilized by Moussorgsky in other works—the transformation of the war-song of the Libyans into the chorus *Joshua* has already been mentioned; a chorus of the excited Carthaginian populace becomes a folk-chorus in the opera *The Fair at Sorótchintzy*, after having done duty for a short time in the operatic ballet *Mlada*, which never saw the light.

One thing, however, may confidently be asserted—that no one could detect, by either eye or ear, the African origin of the passages in question—those, for instance, in *Boris*. There is no work in the whole of musical literature where each note corresponds so exactly to the given situation and so helpfully accords with the moods and feelings to be expressed, as in Moussorgsky's *Boris Godounov*; the passages referred to are no exception to the rule; on the contrary, they are constantly confirming it. What, then, follows? A fundamental law of musical æsthetics—"that music may be able to represent the dynamic and kinetic development of a particular sentiment or psychic emotion, but is unable to illustrate it more precisely."

Of course the musical material borrowed from *Salambo* has not been transferred note for note to the other works—much of it was expanded, shortened, recast, or altered in one way or another, though still remaining essentially the same. Only a small part of the *Salambo* music was left unused, and still awaits its resurrection among the Moussorgsky archives in the Petersburg Public Library; included in it are Mathô's pathetic monologue before the delivery of the death-sentence, and the hymn to Tanit, together with the succeeding scene of the theft of the *zaimph*.

The discovery of the Paris manuscript in the year 1909 brought with it a further surprise in connexion with the *Salambo* music; the last number but one of the collection is the "Song of a young Balearic Islander," with the direction "to be sung during the feast in Hamilcar's gardens," the well-known scene with which Flaubert's romance opens. Up to the time of this discovery all that was known of this song was a short fragment found among Moussorgsky's papers, consisting of the first sixteen bars of the accompaniment, with the note: "etc., etc."; and there is a stage-direction that is wanting in the Paris manuscript: "A young Balearic Islander is sitting on a cask; he has metal castanets in his hands, and rocks himself to and fro as he sings." The piece is noteworthy for its oriental colouring, which, while used with great discretion, is very expressive in its simple monotony; its effects are obtained without any persistent use of the chromatic scale and without the perpetual whining of the augmented second.

*　　*　　*

During his residence in the "Commune" Moussorgsky had not been exclusively under the influence of the seductive

Princess of Carthage. Flaubert's oriental romance, with its heavy atmosphere of lust and blood and terror, its fleeting, shimmering forms of fantasy, though it had gratified the theatrical needs of his creative impulse, had not entirely confused his wholesome sense of actuality; his artistic nature was too deeply rooted in his native soil to admit of any permanent estrangement.

At the very time that he was working at *Salambo* he was composing certain songs that have their foundations deep in the life of Russia, or at any rate in the true Russian spirit. The most important of them is the song called "Kallistratus," or, as we find in another manuscript, "Kallistratushka," the customary diminutive of the name. On the manuscript in the Petersburg Public Library is written in Moussorgsky's own hand: "A first attempt at humorous music." To anyone who is not a Russian this description would probably be unintelligible, nor would he find it easy to discover where the humour lies. The words are by Nekrassov, "the poet of the poor, the wretched, and the forsaken." Kallistrat, a young peasant, is thinking of the cradle-song his mother used to sing to him: "Kallistratus, you are born to be happy—free and careless shall your life be," and contrasts these words with the sad reality—his own actual poverty, his wife and children in rags. There is no trace of bitterness in his words—rather, good-humoured irony at his own expense, and a quiet acceptance of his lot. There is no rebellion—merely the usual Slavonic fatalism. Nothing could be less conducive to merriment than "humour" of this kind. The song is a wonderful example of that mood of "smiling through one's tears" which Gogol introduced into Russian literature. In his music Moussorgsky has found the ideal setting for the words; the song expresses a deep and heart-felt sympathy with the poor young peasant, so defenceless in the face of life's betrayals, who calmly accepts his overthrow without railing at either God or man. The

89

music, like the underlying psychology of the words, is genuinely Russian; in style it may be taken as a model for a composition in the folk-song manner. It is easy enough to specify the elements from which this style is evolved, yet the mere insistence on a complete want of symmetry in the rhythm, whether of bar or phrase, or the choice of a strictly diatonic melody in no fixed key, is of little use by itself; other Russian composers employ these devices and yet fail to bring the hearers under the charm of the mood required—this depends not on the elements themselves, but on the spirit that combines and forms them into a complete whole. In a work of art the greatest secret of all is that creative gift for the attainment of which no mere knowledge of the elements, however accurate, is sufficient.

"Kallistratushka" has been preserved in two distinct, though essentially different, versions; one is to be found in the Paris manuscript, the other as a separate manuscript in the Public Library of Petersburg. A companion piece of almost equal worth is a song written to a poem by Koltzov; this also breathes the spirit of genuine Russian folk-song, although the elaborate accompaniment produces an effect that is the very reverse of primitive. The poem, of six lines, like so many specimens of Russian folk-poetry, contains merely a bald statement of facts—the consequences are left to the imagination of the hearer:

> A storm is raging—
> How dark the heavens!
> On earth no light!
> 'Tis long past sunset—
> In mist and terror
> Broodeth the night.

That is all—but see what a grand, what a deeply impressive picture of nature and the soul of man Moussorgsky has made of these simple words! The accompaniment, as in the songs "Kallistratus" and "King Saul," was probably designed in the first place for orchestra—this we may see from the score, which has all the appearance of an arrangement for pianoforte. The leading musical idea of the stormy accompaniment was used again by the composer at a later date in the chorus of the rebel peasants in the last scene of *Boris Godounov*, and it cannot be denied that it is equally appropriate to the raging elements and the unrestrained passions of the mob.

Almost contemporary with these two songs—i.e., from March to May 1864—is another vocal composition of Moussorgsky's that gives some promise of the great distinction he was to obtain later in this field. This is one of his few love-songs, and the last but one that he wrote; the poem is by Pushkin, or, rather, the poetical germ, for the composer has made so free with the poet's lines that only the fundamental idea—the appearance in a dream of the beloved, who gives herself to her unhappy lover—has survived. Moussorgsky calls his song "A Fantasy" in one version, "An Improvisation" in the other—for two completely different versions are in existence. The first edition, of 1871, presents an entirely different appearance from the original form of the song as we find it in the Paris manuscript; a comparison of the two is all in favour of the printed copy. It was this version that Moussorgsky arranged for orchestra in 1868; later Rimsky-Korsakov supplied another orchestral arrangement, which was made, by hook or by crook, to fit Pushkin's original words. This love-song, like the others, was dedicated by Moussorgsky to Nadeshda Opotchinina.

Still another musical number, quite unimportant, dates from the year 1864—an arrangement for two voices of an Italian romance by the Neapolitan composer Luigi Gordigiani, whose songs were much in demand about this time. This duet, *"Ogni Sabbato avrete il lume acceso,"* was first brought to light by the discovery of the Paris manuscript;

91

it has never been published. It is not known for what purpose Moussorgsky undertook this arrangement; the manuscript has a note: *"L'arrangemento è dedicato al signor Vold. Grotscii"*; who this Grotscii (Grodsky) was has not been discovered; he plays no further part in Moussorgsky's life.

*   *   *

At the beginning of 1865 Moussorgsky's mother died. This event, besides making a deep and painful impression on the young composer, who had found his chief moral support in the mother he so dearly loved, also brought with it material consequences of the most serious kind. Hitherto the Moussorgskys had managed to keep up at least the appearance of a comfortable position; on the family estate at Karevo the mother had maintained their former way of living, even though on a more modest scale; in this place, to which he was attached by a thousand memories of his boyhood and early youth, Moussorgsky had spent nearly all his summers, and in the other seasons he was frequently there. The death of his mother put an instant end to all this, the old stately life of the landed proprietor was gone for ever and beyond recall. Karevo came under the hammer; Moussorgsky's connexion with his native soil, with his own acres, was ended; henceforth, wherever he went, he was merely a guest and no longer his own master.

Shortly after his mother's death Moussorgsky paid his first musical tribute to her memory in the song "Prayer," on Lermontov's lovely and tender poem of the same name. This is the first of Moussorgsky's songs in which he turned to practical account the knowledge of Russian Church music that he had gained from Father Krupsky. The purity and austerity of its harmonization lend this song, especially at the beginning, a character of ascetic piety that suits well with the matter of the poem. In the pianoforte accompaniment we find certain harsh passages and false progressions that might easily have been avoided, but that were probably intentional; and it is just these uncouth errors of style in his earlier compositions that are praised by a certain group of the composer's admirers as particularly brilliant flashes of genius. The existence of this song was first made known by the discovery of the Paris manuscript. After this song came two short pieces: *Recollections of Childhood*; the manuscript, now in the Public Library, has the inscription: "I dedicate these pieces to the memory of my darling mother." The writing down of these pieces was never completed—the second breaks off in the middle; both are trifles of no importance, although in each of them we find here and there a turn of expression that suggests the later Moussorgsky. In the first, called "Nanny and I," the narrative form, in the Schumann manner, is happily caught, and there is a thoroughly characteristic touch at the close, where the childish question brings the song (which is in G major) to an end with the interval of an ascending fifth, E to B; one cannot wonder that in an age so accustomed to strict tonality of cadence such liberties as this awakened the profound astonishment and disapproval of the critics, even when otherwise well-disposed. The second piece is called "The First Punishment ("Nanny shuts me up in a dark room)." The struggles of the small offender, who obviously offers a lively resistance, are delightfully described, and in the persistent restlessness of the figure in semiquavers we clearly hear the harsh tones of the scolding Nanny.

In the same category as these *Recollections* may be placed two piano pieces of the same date: "*Duma* (Reverie)," written on a theme by W. Loginov, one of Moussorgsky's comrades at the "Commune," to whom he also dedicated the song "The storms rage"; and "*La Capricieuse*," on a theme by another of his friends, Count L. Heyden. These trifles

93

show no sign of Moussorgsky's personality and are of no importance in the portrayal of his musical development.

Of far greater interest is a vocal composition of this period—it could scarcely be described as a "song"; it is, rather, an experiment in continuous recitative, with piano accompaniment. Though a recitative, it has no dramatic stresses—it might be described as a *parlando,* in somewhat exalted mood. At that time, when *il bel canto* enjoyed an absolute supremacy, such an experiment was naturally a piece of unparalleled audacity; it never got even beyond the innermost circle of Moussorgsky's musical friends. This piece, which contains some knotty passages, one might almost say impertinences, very characteristic of the composer, was not published in his lifetime. The Paris manuscript first brought it to light. It is called "The Outcast"; the author of the words conceals his name under the initials "Iv. G. M."; the poem probably deals with an actual occurrence in the social life of Petersburg at that time. The subject may be summed up in the words of the New Testament: "Let him who is without sin among you cast the first stone." As an experiment in an entirely new treatment of the voice part in a song, it can hardly count as a great artistic achievement— as the Russian proverb says, "the first buckwheat cake is always a failure"—nevertheless it is very significant of the direction that Moussorgsky's genius was henceforth to follow in the field of vocal music; the origins of this new direction, its limitations, and its goal will be fully dealt with in the next chapter.

In the autumn of 1865 Moussorgsky's way of life underwent another far-reaching change. Owing to the many recent blows that Fate had dealt him, his mother's death, the decline of his financial resources, the burden of his official duties, and the unprofitable period spent in the Engineering Department, his nervous system, which was never too robust, became completely undermined—all the signs seemed

94

to point to a breakdown. In a letter to Balakirev, January 16, 1864, we read: "Mili, my nerve trouble is working up again in a most unpleasant manner and I am obliged to watch it very carefully. To ward off a bad attack I intend to stay quietly at home for a time and take a rest, so please don't count on me for *Undine*" (a performance of Lortzing's opera at the Marie Theatre).

Spring and summer brought no improvement in his condition, and in autumn, the beginning of the season, his brother Filaret Petrovitch Moussorgsky was moved to take energetic measures. He writes to Stassov as follows: "In the autumn of 1865 my brother Modest became seriously unwell and it was evident that a frightful illness was impending. Accordingly my wife and I made every possible effort to induce him to leave the 'Commune' and come to live with us. He did not at first take to the idea, for he had got so accustomed to being with his comrades, but he soon fell in once more with the ways of family life."

Moussorgsky lived with his brother and sister-in-law during the rest of 1865, the next two years, and part of 1868, when his brother again went to live in the country, on his small estate of Minkino, not far from Petersburg. In the portion of the letter quoted above, one is struck by the mention of the "frightful illness" that was threatening. Without further information it is not easy to understand what this dark allusion means, but it not improbably refers to one of the first attacks of that truly "frightful" disease to which Moussorgsky was destined to fall a victim in the very prime of manhood.

It is a fact—and not all the lives of great men that ever were written for the edification of the "young person" can alter it—that genius is almost always associated with some so-called "moral defect," which nevertheless leaves the general morale of the man, and his ethical equipment, untouched. Such a man is like a crystal with a crack in it, which, except for the one fine line that runs right through it, remains perfectly pure and clear. The biographer's attempts at concealment, palliation, or whitewashing fail in their object; to tell only half the truth, or to leave it untold, gives rise to worse suspicions, and to false suppositions based on a total lack of comprehension. For this reason it is best to look the fact of Moussorgsky's alcoholism calmly in the face—it can no longer be questioned, still less can it be merely ignored—in this way we shall find it loses much of its repulsiveness. Before we judge, let us try to understand—as we read in the words of Moussorgsky's song "The Outcast (The Lost Soul)":

> Look not on her to despise her,
> Turn not away from her so,
> They are more blessèd and wiser
> Who can forgive, for they know.

INTERMEZZO

IN SPITE of the total want of system in his musical studies—thanks to the peculiar theories of his teacher Balakirev—Moussorgsky's artistic development followed a perfectly straight, one might almost say a compulsory, course. It conducted him to a certain definite goal, an artistic standpoint on which he felt secure and from which alone he, as a creative artist, was able to consider the world. In seeking to characterize the peculiar essence of Moussorgsky's genius, people have had recourse (as they generally do) to a cliché, from which there is no escape whenever his music comes up for discussion. Moussorgsky's "musical realism"—that is the catch-phrase which is found in every article ever written on the subject, and in these two words the writers claim to have given an exact and exhaustive description of Moussorgsky's quality as a composer. But, as with many another catchword applied to exceptional cases, so with this one—we find ourselves compelled to twist it and turn it, pinch or expand it, lop off a bit in one place, add something in another, in order to make it fit the particular instance, and even then the result is never wholly satisfactory.

To the question whether Moussorgsky was a realist in his art, most people will probably be inclined, at the moment, to answer yes. Yet what is such evidence worth? At first sight, nothing—for with a little goodwill it is just as easy to deny as to confirm it, even though, in a certain sense, it seems to be true beyond a doubt.

But first we have to find an answer to another question: What is realism? Thereby it soon becomes evident that it is

97

not easy—nay, that it is impossible—to apply any catch-phrase to all cases with equal success, and consequently we shall begin to feel doubtful as to the right answer to our original question.

If we consult Brockhaus, we find the following: "Realism is the wider sense means the concentration on accepted realities, coupled with a rejection of all ideas or ideals that transcend them; so in art it is the theory that admits of no higher aim than the closest possible correspondence with natural truth."

Was Moussorgsky a realist in this sense? Most certainly not; "correspondence with nature" was never the aim or the goal of his art, but merely the artistic medium for the attainment of the highest, the final, goal of every art, which has at all times and in every place been the same—I mean that sense, hardly capable of definition, of inward purification and exaltation which we experience in the contemplation of every true work of art.

The application of the term "realism" to Moussorgsky seems all the more unfortunate when we consider that it bears a certain connotation of something ordinary, ugly, repulsive, and therefore the very reverse of artistic; we grant that this use of it is incorrect, but it cannot be ignored. In England, for instance, it is widely accepted: the *Encyclopædia Britannica* has the following short and summary definition: "The realist is he who deliberately declines to select his subjects from the beautiful or harmonious, and, more especially, describes ugly things and brings out details of an unsavoury sort." As a definition of this kind would probably have been emphatically rejected by Moussorgsky, it is plain that caution must be exercised in the use of it. Nevertheless it is surprising how frequently one meets with it, especially in French contributions to the discussion on Moussorgsky's art, although the expression "realism" is on the whole not very common in France. Even *La Grande Encyclopédie* states:

"The meaning of the term 'realism' is not perfectly clear," and for this reason gives the preference (though not with reference to Moussorgsky) to the expression *"naturalisme"* (which Zola had introduced into literature and the terminology of æsthetics), because this seems to widen the field of artistic investigation, whereas the term "realism" would seem to narrow it. These considerations might well apply to the art of Moussorgsky. The expression "naturalism" exactly describes one essential peculiarity of his art, in so far as it signifies, especially in the older treatises, the practice of an art purely on the assumption that it is a natural gift, without training, and with no professional knowledge of the "laws" of art and the technique corresponding with them. In this sense Moussorgsky certainly was, beyond all question, a naturalist; but even apart from this narrower meaning of the term, Moussorgsky's art may be called naturalistic, because it starts from the basic proposition that nothing that is natural can be either wrong or inartistic. Moussorgsky himself never spoke of his art as either realistic or naturalistic; he was no friend to scientific categories and definitions, or, indeed to æsthetic labels of any sort—he saw quite plainly his artistic goal and he knew exactly what he wanted. Whether others agreed with him he hardly cared to inquire; he was not in the least interested to know whether his methods for attaining his own aims fitted in nicely with any particular scientific system or not.

In our days the question of the æsthetic foundation for Moussorgsky's artistic theories has lost the charm of novelty. Countless volumes have since been written on realism and naturalism in every field of art, and no final decision has yet been reached on the question of their justification and their æsthetic values; how, indeed, can any question be solved once and for all time when the answer, in the last resort, must still depend upon the personal factor and the taste of the time?

99

Today, at any rate, we may take it for granted, it is a matter of complete indifference whether Moussorgsky's artistic aims and achievements are labelled "realism" or "naturalism" or "*verismo,*" or whether some new expression— "psychologism," shall we say, or something similar?—is found for them. The only thing that matters is that we now know the meaning and the true nature of his artistic endeavours, and we can judge whether his achievements as a composer are in harmony with these.

The age we live in is, generally speaking, more tolerant than Moussorgsky's; certainly more practical, inasmuch as today a work of art is estimated rather by the effect it produces than by the theoretical principles on which it is built, and to which its effect is due. It was not so in Moussorgsky's time. It was precisely around the theoretical basis for the artistic views upheld by him that there raged a battle so embittered that it was often quite impossible to arrive at any true estimate of the actual artistic result. All his life long Moussorgsky was compelled to protect himself against the malignant attacks launched at him from behind the bulwarks of theoretical prejudice, with spears and arrows too often steeped in the poison of envy and ill will. But his efforts were for the most part in vain, and what he suffered in the struggle, not only morally, but also materially, was grievous indeed; there is no doubt that the whole tragic story of his later years was definitely influenced by the apparent hopelessness of this conflict. It is for this reason that these questions, unimportant as they now appear, must occupy a central position in the history of his life.

Moussorgsky's artistic career coincided with an age that neither saw nor wished to see beauty in what actually exists—its endeavour was to fashion beauty according to abstract laws. The artist's task, it was held, was not to draw beauty from nature and her forms, organic or inorganic, but rather to run it into the set mould that reality offered.

Moussorgsky constantly protested with all his energy against the acceptance of such a purely theoretical æstheticism. For him the only source of art was reality in all its outward shows and appearances, but most of all in the loftiest and, if not the most perfect, at least the most various, most complex of its forms, man. He had no wish to build better than nature or to improve on reality. His only ambition was to arouse in others, through the products of his own creative imagination, the same impressions as he himself derived from nature—to the creative genius, he held, nature appeals directly as a work of art, whereas the ordinary mortal must see it through the medium of another man's imagination. The power that can produce a work of art by merely imitating or representing nature without any intention of idealizing is the soul of the artist, which manifests itself in the result; the richer his intellect, the more attractive his soul, the greater and deeper will be the effect of his work. The true artist, in fact, sees nature not as *she* is, but as *he* himself is; and the highest result his art can achieve is so to affect others through the contemplation of his works that they may come to see her through his own eyes.

It has been said of the so-called realistic movement in general, and of Moussorgsky's art in particular, that it is distinguished by the fact that the personality of the artist disappears completely behind the object represented; this shows a total misunderstanding of the essential nature of all art. To copy nature merely for pleasure, to aim at producing as exact an imitation as possible, without any further object in view—this is an amusing exercise that can only be associated with the very first step in the development of any art; in the arena of conscious artistic endeavour, and with strong and genuinely creative natures like Moussorgsky's, there can naturally be no question of such a thing—the artist who is worthy of the name is never a mere duplicating machine. Yet it is precisely this reproach that was raised

against Moussorgsky by the short-sighted critics of his time
—it was always the same old barrel-organ tune of "slavish
and soulless imitation of nature," "mechanical copy of
reality," mere "documents," "photographs," etc. This was all
the more amazing when we consider that about twenty years
before the commencement of Moussorgsky's activities another of the great intellects of Russia, Gogol, had introduced
realism or naturalism into Russian art, or rather literature;
but a long time was to elapse before what was accepted as
right in literature was considered allowable in music. In one
of his masterly *Petersburg Tales* Gogol had even made a
sort of profession of faith with regard to his realistic conception of art; it was intended for the edification of his contemporaries, but unfortunately had no great success. In his
story of "The Portrait" he writes: "If you approach your
object in an indifferent mood, devoid of feeling or real sympathy, it will resolve itself into a hideous piece of actuality,
just as would happen if, in order to understand the secret of
a beautiful human being, you were to take a surgeon's knife
and dissect him—you would soon find yourself confronted
with a loathsome corpse. Why is it that a representation of
nature, of ordinary, everyday nature, by the hand of one
artist seems to glow with so fair a light that, so far from making an ordinary everyday impression, it awakens feelings of
pure delight, and life itself seems now to flow more calmly,
smoothly on—while an equally faithful portrait of nature
by another artist produces an effect that is actually mean,
dirty, and common? Come, come!—it is because here there is
no illumination! It is the same with a landscape—however
beautiful it may be, we feel there is something missing when
there is no sun shining in the heavens."

This "illumination," this sun from heaven that sheds
its beams on art, is the love of the artist for his subject; this
alone it is that can give the work of art a soul, this it is
that awakens in the breast of the beholder the same feelings

that inspire the creative artist in relation to his subject. It is this love which lights up the whole of Moussorgsky's work, and by virtue of which his creations make so ineradicable an impression on unprejudiced hearers that they find themselves irresistibly constrained to share in his emotion.

Another charge constantly levelled at Moussorgsky by stupid and malicious tongues was the same as that brought (as we saw at the beginning of this chapter) against realism in general—that he deliberately chose subjects that were ugly, repulsive, low, and therefore unfit for artistic presentment. It was a favourite saying that Moussorgsky absolutely denied the importance of beauty in art; nothing of course could be more absurd than such a statement, yet his opponents never ceased to repeat it. It is true that Moussorgsky always lays special stress on power of expression as an indispensable factor in the artist's equipment and never ceased to jeer at that superficial "beauty," the mere prettiness of the chocolate-box, which represented the ideas of art of so many people at that time; but this by no means implies that he would have laid it down as a principle that beauty ought to be especially avoided as a subject for artistic representation. Further it may be said that he certainly did not shrink from what is called the ugly, though he would hardly have assented to the dictum of another apostle of naturalism, Auguste Rodin: "The uglier a thing is in nature, the lovelier it is in art." But the principle of the later naturalistic school, that everything which nature offers to man is beautiful from the artist's point of view, and consequently a fit subject for artistic treatment, this he certainly had assimilated quite early in his career. In so doing he found himself in the best company; it was a contemporary of Moussorgsky who said of Goethe: "Goethe is far more concerned with the manner of representation than with the thing presented— he treats a chamber-pot and a tabernacle with an equal tenderness. What delights us in him is that he claims an hon-

103

ourable place for things that are least esteemed. In the muck-heap as well as in the sun Goethe found the world-spirit, and it is this spirit that inspired his utterances." These are the words of Wilhelm von Kügelgen, the painter, and author of *Jugenderinnerungen eines alten Mannes* (*An Old Man's Memories of his Youth*); they occur in a letter to his brother Gerhard (March 28, 1847).

In Russia, as we have said, Gogol, long before Moussorgsky, had given expression to similar ideas; in the tale of "The Portrait," already referred to, we find, for instance, the following passage: "Observe and study all that thou seest and make is serve thy purpose of artistic presentment. But learn in everything to look for the hidden meaning and strive before all else to find the secret of creation; blessed is the elect soul to whom that is granted. For such a one nature no longer holds aught that is unworthy; in his hands that which is least esteemed will be made equal to that which is deemed the mightiest. Even that which merited contempt will do so no more, for the lovely spirit of the creator, though unseen, will shine through it, and what we deemed worthy to be despised will now claim our high regard, since it has passed through the cleansing furnace of his soul."

In the world of literature Gogol was the most conspicuous advocate of these convictions, as we see in his masterly short stories; his innumerable followers and imitators, too, among whom we may count practically all the great Russian writers, have upheld them; but it was Moussorgsky who was destined to be the first to transplant them to the field of music. He was fully conscious of what he was doing, and was never for a moment in doubt as to his artistic aims and endeavours; as evidence of this, quite apart from his works, we may be allowed to introduce here certain passages from his correspondence with V. Stassov. The following is of peculiar interest—it is taken from a letter dated October 18, 1872: "The artistic presentment of beauty alone, to use the word in

104

its material sense, is sheer childishness, only fit for the babes
and sucklings of art. To trace *the finer characteristics of human nature* and of the mass of *mankind,* resolutely to penetrate into these unexplored regions and to conquer them—
that is the mission of the genuine artist. *'To unknown shores'*
must be our cry—fearless through the storms, on, past all
the shallows, *to unknown shores*! Man is a social animal and
must be so; in the masses, just as in each individual, there
are finer features that escape our observation, that no one
yet has touched on; to discover and study them, by reading,
observation, and conjecture, to fasten upon them with one's
innermost powers of perception and thus prepare a new
diet for the nourishment of mortals, a healthy, strengthening food that no one yet has tasted—there's a task for you!
Glorious! Glorious!"

Of all the subjects that reality has to offer for the artist's use it is plain that man, individually or collectively,
was the one in which Moussorgsky was chiefly interested, so
that there are good grounds for calling his art, as Rimsky-
Korsakov does, anthropocentric. In this respect Moussorgsky is closely akin to another of the great Russian intellec-
tuals, Dostoievsky. In that author's diaries there is an
expression with reference to his artistic credo which Moussorgsky might have used, and with equal justification. Dostoievsky writes: "They call me a psychologist—that is not
true; I am merely a realist *in the higher sense*—i.e., my business is to portray *the soul of man in all its profundity.*" It
was this psychological realism to the exploration of which
Moussorgsky too devoted his whole artistic life; as we see
from the letter given above, he was fully conscious of the
role he was called upon to play as pioneer in the world of
music. He would fasten with the greatest enthusiasm on any
expression, wherever he found it, that seemed to support
his own convictions—again we may refer to the letter already
quoted for a highly characteristic instance of this tendency.

105

One would hardly guess the influence that had moved Moussorgsky to that effusion—it was the reading of Darwin. Even in the English natural philosopher he thought he had found confirmation of his own ideas, and the reading of his works spurred him on to explore fresh avenues of thought. "I am reading Darwin," he says in the same letter, "and am enraptured. It is not the power and the clarity of his intellect that chain me to him—with those aspects of his colossal genius I was already familiar in his earlier works. No, it is this that holds me captive: while instructing man as to his origin, Darwin understands exactly (how could he help it?) the sort of animal he has to deal with; accordingly he forces him (without his even noticing it) *into the vice-like grip of his own intellect*, and so mighty is the power of his colossal genius that the conscience not only does not struggle against this act of violence, but on the contrary is aware of nothing but joy and bliss during the process. When a strong and passionately amorous woman clasps her lover tight, he is conscious that he is suffering violence; yet he has no desire whatever to free himself from the embrace, since it is this very violence that makes him 'taste the cup of rapture' and 'sets the young blood boiling.' I am not ashamed of this comparison; however we may twist and turn and coquet with the truth, anyone who has been privileged to experience love in all its full power and majesty *has lived*, and will always be conscious that he *has lived, in the world of beauty*, and will permit no shadow to be cast on the raptures he has known. However; my dear prophet, I know you read Darwin last year in English, so I will shut my mouth—*basta*! Nevertheless I will say something of what I have found in Darwin, when reading 'between the lines,' as it were. This colossus from the shores of the island kingdom is so colossal that we shall find him reflected not only in all the oceans, rivers, and lakes, but very probably in the moon as well, so it is not surprising if the force of his ideas has penetrated even to a Lilliputian

106

person like myself and strengthened and steeled me once for all in my endeavours, which perhaps after all have not been so very Lilliputian—it was little David who slew the giant Goliath! In opposition to the general naïve opinions as to the delicacy and beauty of naked Venuses with their elegant contours, of Cupids and fauns, with or without flutes, with fig-leaves or 'as God made them,' I maintain that the antipathetic (excuse me, I should say 'antique'!) art of the Greeks is rude. We Lilliputians have been taught to believe that the classical school of Italian painting is absolute perfection. In my opinion it is a dead thing, and as repulsive as death itself. In poetry there are two giants, rough Homer and fine Shakspere. In music likewise we have two giants, Beethoven, the thinker, and the super-thinker Berlioz. When to these four giants we add all their generals and aides-de-camp, we get a pleasant company enough. But what has this set of subalterns achieved? They have merely dug a big rut alongside of the paths made by the giants, and little enough progress have they made in so doing. A shocking state of things! And what about our own giants? Glinka and Dargomizhky, Pushkin and Lermontov, Gogol and—well, we can only say Gogol over and over again, for he has no parallel—these are all capable field-marshals who have won great victories in the field of art; but their followers spend their time in manuring the ground of the conquered territories, although it is naturally so fertile that it does not require it—here the Little Russians of the black-earth district show greater wisdom. It is Darwin who has finally confirmed me in what has always been my most cherished theory, but which nevertheless, for some reason or other, I have never ventured to put forward without a certain stupid sense of shame."

Then follows the quotation given above, containing the expression "To unknown shores!" The letter also has a post-script that is not without interest: "Although I am not a woman, I will add a P. S. Riepin's 'Burlaki,' Antokolsky's

'Inquisition'—these are pioneer works that point the way to 'unknown shores,' to undiscovered countries."

It is plain from these remarks that Moussorgsky thoroughly understood the connexion between his own ideas and the new movement just then in full swing in Russia in the field of graphic art. The painters Perov and Ilia Riepin, as well as the sculptor Antokolsky, were fighting for exactly the same ideas in the field of graphic art as Moussorgsky was endeavouring to introduce into music; they met with greater success than he, as the general public, as well as the so-called connoisseurs, were much more ready to accept the new tendencies in sculpture and painting than in music.

To go into the reasons for this would lead us too far—Moussorgsky himself was not a little puzzled over them; he saw the superiority of the graphic arts in this respect, without knowing how to explain it. In a letter to Stassov (July 13, 1872) we find the following disquisition: "What I want to know is this: Antokolsky's 'Ivans' (the Fourth and the Third) and especially his 'Yaroslav,' the 'Burlaky' of Riepin, and—last, not least—the sickly boy in Perov's 'Birdcatcher,' the leading couple in his 'Huntsmen,' as well as his 'Village Procession'—why do all these figure scenes actually live, so that on looking at them one involuntarily thinks: 'That is just how I should like to see them'? And why, in spite of their excellent qualities, is no such life to be found in the latest musical compositions? Why, when listening to them, is one so uncertain of their meaning? Please be so good as to enlighten me, only leave the 'limitations of art' out of the question—I accept them only under strict reservations, for, in the religion of the artist, 'the limitations of art' is another expression for standing still. In short, because one distinguished intellect has failed to find the way to freedom, does it follow that there is no possibility of another intellect, perhaps less distinguished, being able to find it? Where then, are the 'limitations'? . . . "

If ever anyone was justified in questioning the impossibility of breaking down the boundaries not only between the different arts, but also between the different branches of one and the same art, it was Moussorgsky, whose whole artistic output proves how easy it is for an artist of strong and determined temperament to abolish them. His astonishment at the superiority of the graphic arts in the matter of truth of expression appears quite unjustifiable in the presence of his own artistic creations; if his musical portraits and *genre* pictures, many of which were already executed when he wrote the letter given above, are placed side by side with the pictures and statues of Riepin, Antokolsky, and Perov, many of them will be found not only to equal, but to surpass them in truth and directness of expression and in delicacy of observation.

*   *   *

The new school of realism, or naturalism, introduced into Russia in the sixties by Perov, Antokolsky and Riepin in art, and by Moussorgsky in music, had long been anticipated in Russian literature, where it soon found unqualified acceptance. Gogol, as we know, was the first to free himself from the fetters of romance and boldly to plunge into the rough seas of actual life—and this, it may be noted, long before Flaubert, Balzac, and Dickens. It took Gogol a surprisingly short time to win his way to victory, though there were plenty of stick-in-the-mud journalists and unintelligent critics in Petersburg to embitter his existence. On the other hand he found in Vissarion Belinsky—a literary critic of the first importance, well versed in the philosophy, poetry, and art of Germany—a champion who understood his real worth and who fought so valiantly for the cause that he may be said to have prepared the way for the whole of the new naturalistic school. The task was made easier for him by the fact that Russia had the good fortune at that time to pos-

109

sess quite a number of novelists of the first rank. Among them were Hertzen, Turgeniev, Gontcharov, Dostoievsky, and Tolstoy, in whose train followed a whole constellation of lesser talents, sufficient in any case for the production of a complete literature, Aksakov, Grigorovitch, Pisemsky, Sologub, as well as the poets, some of whom have already been mentioned, Koltzov, Nekrassov, Pleshtcheiev, Mey, and others.

The realism of all these poets and men of letters led automatically to the exposure of social evils, and, by a natural connexion, of the shortcomings of the system of government; in this way arose the school of the so-called "indictment of society," of which the most distinguished representative was the satirist Saltikov-Shtchedrin. Nor did they confine themselves to attacking these things merely through the medium of literature—they must proceed to action; a proceeding that, as is well known, nearly cost Dostoievsky and the poet Pleshtcheiev their lives and did in fact result in their being exiled to Siberia for a long period.

As the sort of positive counterpart of this negative current, the portrayal of the life of the people began to assume a predominant place in Russian literature, and naturally every care was taken to represent it in as attractive a light as possible—the people had to be loved, therefore they must be depicted as lovable. A similar interest in village life was stirring at that time all over Europe, though it must be confessed that for the most part the sense of reality was altogether shelved in favour of sentimental exaggeration and lachrymose drivel. Even in Russia the apostles of reality failed to see that they had been converted unawares to romanticism, at least in many of their productions. Even Moussorgsky (as we shall see hereafter) did not escape this unconscious metamorphosis; in dealing with the people the artist endeavoured to bring out that characteristic which Gogol had already praised as the peculiar mark of the Russian people—their feeling of pity and sympathy for all the outcasts of fortune, all the fallen, no matter to what depth of degradation such people may have sunk. This attitude of the *literati*, the poets and the artists, towards the people, naturally led to an ever deeper study of their peculiar nature and underlying principles, which later on took the form of a passionate advocacy of the cause of the peasantry and ended in the demand for the abolition of serfdom, and freedom for all. It was in connexion with this movement that, in the sixties, as we have already seen in a letter of Moussorgsky's, the expression "to go to the people"—i.e., to devote oneself solely to the cause of the peasantry—became a rallying-cry in Russia. In after years this movement was cruelly mocked and derided; nevertheless at the time it aroused the interest of the best elements in Russian society and gave expression to that deep and sure instinct which bore fruit in the noble action of the liberator Tsar.

For the arts this movement had important results, inasmuch as it brought to light the genuine art of the people in the forms in which it still existed among the peasantry, though it had hitherto escaped attention. It led to the formation of some model collections of folk-songs, drew attention to popular iconography, produced a whole series of excellent works on folk-lore, and, finally, provided some of the leading creative spirits of the time, Moussorgsky among them, with new and strengthening food with which to minister to the needs of mankind.

This short excursus into the history of Russian literature was necessary, in order to show in what sort of atmosphere Moussorgsky's art was developed. We see now that the gifted composer was not the completely isolated figure, "fallen from heaven," as it were, that he seems to those who view him from a distance; he was emphatically a child of his age and, as an artist, the product of the influences by which he was surrounded. It is all the more surprising, therefore, that

111

he should be the only one to apply the final conclusions of the intellectual movement of the time to the art of music; and it is even more amazing that he was so little understood —even his champion, V. V. Stassov, could not help him there.

V
THE SONGS

THE YEARS 1866 to 1868, which Moussorgsky spent in the house of his brother and sister-in-law in Petersburg, were not rich in outward events. Fate seems to have been no more lavish in this respect than in any other where he was concerned; for instance, Moussorgsky never travelled beyond the borders of Russia (a circumstance that one might apply symbolically in reference to his art) and it was only shortly before his death that he came to have any extensive knowledge of Russia itself, thanks to a concert tour that took him into the southern provinces and the Crimea; up to that date, with the exception of the two excursions to Moscow already described, his holidays on the ancestral estate in the province of Pskov, and occasional visits to the country-houses of friends and acquaintances, his life was spent exclusively in Petersburg and, through the summer months, in the various bungalow settlements—"*datcha* places" ("*datcha*" being Russian for "summer-house")—in the neighbourhood.

His days were divided between work at his office in the Engineering Department, where he spent his morning and part of the afternoon, and a very lively and ever-growing circle of musical friends, which accounted for nearly all his evenings. There was but little time left for composition— only Sundays, saints'-days, which fortunately are fairly frequent in Russia, and the late afternoons; this is not much, and one can only wonder that Moussorgsky's annual musical output was not even smaller than it was, especially since the process of finally putting into shape and writing down

113

his musical ideas must have required more time with him
than with other composers, owing to his uncertainty in matters of technique.

Moussorgsky made no attempt at any work of importance during the period we are now considering; his interest
in *Salambo* slowly but steadily vanished before the ever-
increasing intellectual enthusiasm for the uplift of "the people," nor did any national or popular subject take its place;
instead he applied himself for the time wholly to the writing
of songs, though the word "song" in the current acceptance
of the term can be used in only a very restricted sense of any
of Moussorgsky's vocal compositions. We may be certain
that it was no part of Moussorgsky's artistic scheme to follow in the steps of other song-writers, and of this we have
clear proof in the twenty songs or so that he wrote between
1866 and 1868; in looking through them we find hardly one
that has any affinity with the great mass of vocal literature.
Furthermore, hardly two among them are like each other.
There was nothing Moussorgsky hated so much as conventional patterns; for him it was a self-evident proposition that
the matter and form of a work of art are so mutually dependent that it is only possible to regard them as two aspects
of one single object, the result of a single conception. It is
the Aristotelean principle in philosophy, applied to art—
every idea demands the form that is proper and essential to
it alone. Two identical forms are possible and permissible
only for two identical ideas. Consequently one will look in
vain in Moussorgsky's songs for anything like a set form
that will do duty on all occasions. Traces of what is pro-
fessionally known as "song form" are found, but very rarely, and then only if the text imperatively demands it, either
through a return to the emotional environment of the first
verse, or a repetition of the opening words. The only rule
that Moussorgsky respected as a guiding musical principle
of his vocal compositions is the repetition of certain char-

114

acteristic musical phrases, wherever the sequence of ideas offers an opportunity, thus carrying out in a measure the idea of the leitmotiv on a very small scale. However freely he handles a form, Moussorgsky never gives the impression of mere caprice—on the contrary, the logic of his procedure is invariably surprising and always carries conviction; the result is that when confronted by even his freest forms we have the feeling that they are musically necessary, that they could not be otherwise than what they are. In the hands of a less gifted musican, or a less profound psychologist, such methods would hardly have succeeded. So far Moussorgsky has not found a single imitator in this direction either in Russia or elsewhere. One is hardly inclined to tolerate more or less unsuccessful attempts in this direction; art that is rooted with every fibre in a really distinct personality, altogether unique and peculiar, can never be imitated.

Moussorgsky's songs are so different one from another that it is impossible to deal with them in any summary fashion—they demand and deserve an entirely individual treatment. Even to classify or group them is no easy matter, except where Moussorgsky himself has arranged them in cycles, a favourite practice of his in later years. But this is not so with the twenty songs belonging to the years 1866–8; most of these show an audacity in the choice of subject which at that time was without precedent in the music of Russia or of any other country; in almost every one he plays on certain strings which, to use his own words, "ordinarily elude the touch, and which no one yet has sounded." A large proportion of them is concerned with the emotional experiences of persons of every possible sort, chosen from the humbler grades of the people, to whom at that time his sympathies chiefly inclined. At the same time he nearly always conforms to the demands of the highest art, in that his figures, while taken from life, are yet typical; one may safely talk of "his" figures, even when the words of the song, as often, were not

115

the work of the composer, for his musical portraiture is always so clear-cut, so unmistakable, that it seems as if that alone gives life to the persons in the poem. As we have seen, Moussorgsky never hesitated for a moment when the situation seemed to demand it, to alter the verses and even the ideas of the poet, so as to bring them into conformity with his own creative impulse. It is always his own temperament, his own conception, not the poet's, that are the decisive factor in the impression which his songs produce.

Those that have the rich and varied emotional life of the Russian peasant for their subject might be classed together as "folk-songs," were it not for the possible misunderstanding to which this might give rise—it might suggest that we have to deal with original words and melodies coming from the people themselves, or with a conscious and consistent imitation of them, adapted to their intelligence; neither view is correct. They are "art-songs" in the highest sense of the term, and require a particularly fine artistic sense for their proper appreciation, only, unlike the popular drawing-room romances of the time, they deal with the emotional experiences of beings who hitherto had not been considered capable of any such feelings as those that now stood suddenly revealed with such impressive force in Moussorgsky's music. The occasional, but always discreet employment or imitation of certain phrases characteristic of folk-song is inevitable in the circumstances, but it is far from having the importance of a stylistic principle.

Another thing to be noted in these songs is the entire absence of all artificiality, of any false or overstrained sentiment; it is precisely by their quiet simplicity of expression that they are able to stir the profoundest depths of artistic sympathy and produce the effect of perfect illusion. Marie Olenine d'Alheim is right when she says in her valuable little work on Moussorgsky (*Les Legs de Moussorgsky*): "All the characters in these songs that Moussorgsky has drawn from

the life of the people, whether they talk seriously or merely
chatter, whether they laugh or weep, are drawn with such
strength and certainty, in all the fresh and changing colours
of nature, that a few bars are sufficient to embody them for
us in almost tangible form. It is only a moment since they
came forward out of the silence, few words have been spoken
since their entry—yet that suffices to stamp them for ever
on our memory."

The whole vast world of Russian serfdom, with its various personalities, its manifold activities, its want and misery,
the intolerable burden of daily life embittered by every con-
ceivable form of degradation, torture, oppression—all this
had hitherto had no existence so far as the world of music
was concerned. The ideal figures in Glinka's operas, as well
as those in Dargomizhky's *Russalka*, were quite remote from
reality, while by the writers of songs the Russian peasant
had up to now been regarded as quite unworthy of attention.
What was one to do with him? His soul, that strange mixture
of kind-heartedness and cunning, simplicity and wisdom,
faithful devotion and servility, blind stupidity and ready
wit, was useless for the purposes of the popular lyric. Moussorgsky, however, who cared little or nothing for popular
demands, takes a bold grasp of Russian folk-life, and behold!
it becomes really interesting, wherever he touches it. The very
first experiment, the "Kallistrat" mentioned in the previous
chapter, was successful, the next even more so. This time he
takes as his subject what the Russians call a *"yurodivy,"* or
"God's creature," one of those harmless half-wits, so common in that country, who wander from village to village,
praying and begging, receiving more kicks than halfpence,
yet generally regarded with a certain amount of reverence.
The song "Fair Sávishna" shows a typical example of these
"God's creatures" in a very unusual situation; it is really a
clumsy declaration of love from one of these poor imbeciles,

117

who is mocked and knocked about by everybody, while all the
time he is consumed with a burning passion for the prettiest
girl in the village.

> Lovely Sávishna,
> Thou, my only light,
> Love me, luckless one,
> Ugly as I am!
> Drive me not away
> As the others do!
> Look but once on me
> In my misery! . . .

The song is written throughout in 5-4 time, as the rhythm of
the words demands; the tempo is fairly quick, and there is
no stop, until it suddenly breaks off quite unexpectedly—
the poor creature realizes in a flash that his awkward wooing is quite hopeless. As the subject for a "song," especially
at that date, the material, we must admit, is oddly chosen.
The words are Moussorgsky's own, as we shall henceforward
find in many of his finest and most original songs. Stassov
relates how Moussorgsky told him that this song, like the
music to the "Intermezzo *in modo classico*," was taken straight
from nature; he watched the scene he has depicted from the
window of the farmhouse in Minkino, and the strange mingling of suppressed passion, shame, and bitterness in the
word of the *yurodivy* as he realizes that, after all, the joys
of love are not for him made an indelible impression on the
composer. Moussorgsky dedicated this song to César Cui;
had he foreseen what an amazing misconception of his art
Cui was afterwards to exhibit, he would probably have altered
his mind. In a discussion of this song and one other ("The
Banquet") in which 5-4 time alternates with 6-4, Cui expresses his deep sympathy with the singer, for whom no
proper breathing-places are provided, and he goes on to
make the almost incredible remark that the evil might easily

118

have been remedied by the insertion of a sixth crotchet, with a pause, into the bar of 5-4!

Rimsky-Korsakov's *My Musical Life* has a not uninteresting remark about the relations of Cui and Balakirev to Moussorgsky. He writes: "Although in the sixties Balakirev and Cui were close friends of Moussorgsky's, and genuinely fond of him, their behaviour had always a certain condescension in it, as of elder men towards a younger, from whom, in spite of his undoubted talent, little was to be expected. It seemed to them that something was lacking in him and that he, more than all the rest, was in need of good advice and critical guidance." We shall see in what an offensive form this senseless attitude of superiority, especially on the part of Cui, was to declare itself later on.

Stassov tells us that the song "Fair Sávishna" made a deep impression from the very first on all the members of the Balakirev circle and was at once accepted as the best thing Moussorgsky had yet done; if this be so, Cui must have been more guarded in his criticism at the time, or Moussorgsky would hardly have dedicated the song to him. Frau Marie Olenine d'Alheim, in the book already mentioned, has a pretty, allegorical fancy in this connexion: "Whenever I sang 'Fair Sávishna' ['*L'Innocent*,' in French], I always imagined myself to be the interpreter of Moussorgsky's, the composer's, feelings; I thought of the man himself, of his life of privation, his loneliness, his glowing love of humanity, and all this helped to put me in the right mood; it seemed to me that he himself was this 'God's creature,' whose deep love for mankind, for whose sake alone he still lived on, was never requited. I have always found that this way of interpreting it met with a ready response; I have never sung the song without being conscious that my audience were deeply moved, though they certainly never guessed that they themselves were cast for the part of 'the fair Sávishna.' "

The manuscript of the song, which Cui gave to the

Nikolai Cadet School, formerly the Guards Cadet Academy, in which Moussorgsky was educated, bears the date September 2, 1866; Stassov, however, thinks it was composed as early as the summer of 1865. "Fair Sávishna" and the song "Ah, only tell me why!" mentioned in a previous chapter, were the first of Moussorgsky's compositions (if we except the "Ensign's Polka") to be published in his lifetime—namely, in 1867, by Johannson in Petersburg.

No less familiar to the public of that day was the mood of the two cradle-songs that Moussorgsky composed at this time: "Poor peasant's son," from Ostrovsky's drama *The Voivode*, and "Yeromoushka's Cradle-song," a setting of a poem by Nekrassov. In both of these songs the very first bars conjure up a picture of a poor interior in which a half-starved woman in dandling her child on her hard knotted hands, and building golden castles in the air for him, a golden future, all riches and glory, while the heavy stifling atmosphere of the smoky room scarcely allows her to breathe. In both songs the scene is built up gradually before our eyes; the first one, more especially, is a masterpiece of intimate *genre*-painting, to which few parallels are to be found in the whole range of music. Wonderful is the heavenly glory of the ending, with its notably bare harmonies, which yet contrive to sound like the music of the spheres. An earlier version of this song, found in the Paris manuscript, is more extensive than the one hitherto known—a whole stanza of four lines is missing in the later copy. Moussorgsky probably omitted them from the first printed edition for fear of the censor, for they give expression to the revolutionary thought that all suffering would disappear when the Tsar became aware of the injustice which everywhere prevailed, and felt ashamed of it. Moussorgsky rightly assumed that, according to the ideas of the Russian censorship of the time, the Tsar ought never to feel ashamed, and so, rather than have any unpleasantness, he left the stanza out. The piano accompaniment of the second version compares favourably with the Paris manuscript in correctness, as many unnecessary octaves have been struck out. This song is dedicated by the composer to the memory of his mother, and "Yeromoushka's Cradle-song" to Dargomizhky, "the great teacher of musical truth," according to the inscription on the original manuscript. The song was composed in 1868, by which time Dargomizhky had given up his earlier musical activities and was devoting himself to other tasks. His musical influence on Moussorgsky was not particularly strong, although the latter whole-heartedly adopted the guiding principle of Dargomizhky's later years: *"Rien n'est beau que le vrai; le vrai seul est aimable* (Nothing is beautiful but truth; only truth is worthy to be loved)."

Yeromoushka also is a child of peasant parents, over whose cradle his mother's never-flagging fancy weaves the most splendid visions.

In "The Banquet" we have a brilliant example of a thoroughly Russian song, set to characteristically Russian music. The words are by Koltzov and, as is usual with this poet, are merely a picture, a fragment of Russian life, without any lyrical trimmings or touches of sentiment; in spite of this, or perhaps because of it, the effect of the quiet handling of the figures is all the finer. The music, with its sturdy, almost epic character, enhances the impression in a remarkable degree; it achieves a quite peculiar charm by the device of alternating bars of five-four (5-4) and six-four (6-4), forming a phrase of eleven crotchets, which is maintained throughout. It is to this rhythm more than to anything else that the song owes its specially Russian—one might almost say Byzantine—colour. It is probable that the charm of these primitive Russian rhythms—a development of the always unfettered and unsymmetrical rhythm of the plainsong of the Church—reveals itself only to the ears of "the faithful," which would account for the fact that "outsiders," such as César Cui, never came under its influence. This would lend a curious confirmation to the opinion which was just then being advanced that "Russia" and "Orthodoxy" were identical. "The Banquet" is dedicated to Ludmilla Ivanovna Shestakova, the devoted sister of Michael Glinka, whose acquaintance Moussorgsky had lately made and who afterwards, in the closing years of his life, was a true and motherly friend to him.

In the song "Gathering Mushrooms" we have a whimsical idea for music; the words, by Mey, show us a young peasant woman picking mushrooms in the forest, when it occurs to her, half in jest, half in earnest, that it will be a good thing to get her good-for-nothing husband out of the way by poisoning him with a dish of toadstools, so that she may be free to devote herself to a fair-haired young peasant who has won her affections. The fresh merry mood of it all is characteristic of the irresponsible, untutored psychology of the Russian peasant. At the close, where the phrase "And the moon will shine on our wedding-night" swells and broadens out with such a fine effect, we actually see the woman stretching out her strong young arms in her longing for love.

In some of the songs of this period Moussorgsky explores a field to which he did not again return until a short time before his death—the peculiar atmosphere of Little Russia, or the Ukraine, as it is called. About that time the poems of the Ukrainian poet Schevtchenko, written in the local dialect, and breathing an ardent love of liberty and fatherland—i.e., of an independent Ukrainia—had attracted great attention in the circles of the Russian "intelligentsia," as a timely expression of the "liberating" movement of the day. Those who held "liberal" views felt bound to show their sympathy with the struggle of the home-rulers in Ukrainia and their poet-spokesman. The attitude of the Government was naturally less sympathetic; not only did they suppress the whole of Schevtchenko's writings, but absolutely forbade the use of the Ukrainian dialect—an order that, as is well known, was only slightly modified after the first Russian revolution, in 1905. In the soul of Moussorgsky, constitutionally inclined to opposition and rebellion, the Ukrainian movement naturally awakened the liveliest sympathy, to which he gave expression in music by setting two pieces out of Schevtchenko's drama *The Haidamaks*. One of these songs, "Gopak," has an irresistible swing about it, besides containing countless delicate touches that a loving scrutiny reveals in ever greater number. A young Cossack woman is whirling in a dance expressive of amorous passion, and pouring out her woes in song, in order to forget the fate that chains her to an old husband whom she does not love.

> Hoi! hop! dance the Gopak!
> I am young, my man is an old Cossack!
> His beard and his sword are rusty red,
> And he never smiles, but he scowls instead!
> Oh, my life is dreary and bare—
> > Hoi! hop! why should I cry?
> > For love is there!
> Go out, my old man, go and drink,
> Then out to the inn in the woods I slink . . .
> > I'll drink, and drink, and drink! . . .
> Then out of the house your wife will stray,
> And a handsome lad will come her way! . . .

The other piece from *The Haidamaks*, "Yarema's Song," written in 1866, was completely recast by the composer in 1879. In view of the censorship this song, which is a wild shout for liberty and independence, could not be published in Russia during the existence of a tsarist government; it was first published after the Revolution of 1917 by Bessel, but not in Russia. Both the melodies in this song, the slow, melancholy introduction, and the stormy *allegro*, breathing out revenge and the thirst for freedom, belong to the loveliest of Moussorgsky's inspirations in the folk-song manner; the Ukrainian element in them is emphasized by the use of the peculiar melodic intervals, the agumented or diminished fourth and sixth. The brilliant effect is further assisted by the pianoforte accompaniment, in which the strong, simple harmonies avoid as far as practicable anything so feeble and "un-Russian" as a chord of the seventh. This song might well serve as a national anthem for the Cossacks of the Ukraine, now that their dream of freedom is fulfilled, had not Moussorgsky written it (as he did the "gopak" also), not to the original words, but to Mey's Russian adaptation.

To this period belongs another Cossack song, "By the Don a garden blooms"; the text is a shortened and slightly altered version of Koltzov's dreamy, yet finely wrought poem, out of which Moussorgsky has made a combination of landscape and *genre*-painting that is quite enchanting; the exquisite melody that forms the chief subject is a musical inspiration of the rarest quality.

Not less novel and surprising than the songs referred to are two typical pictures of the street-life of Petersburg that Moussorgsky embodied in music set to words of his own; one of them, "The Orphan," depicts a beggar-boy, starved and frozen, such as one meets too often in the streets of that city. Who is there who has not seen them, those miserable bundles of rags, generally at the corner of some street in the suburbs, standing often barefoot in the snow, and stretching out their hands, blue with the cold, to the passers-by! "Have pity, kind sir, have pity!" so runs the song. "Pity a poor orphan child, who has no fire to warm him, who weeps and suffers, hungers and freezes, whom no one heeds, save the wind and the snow . . . " ending with a sigh of despair —"Oh, have some pity, good, kind sir!"

Of very different stuff is another of Moussorgsky's studies of low life—in "The Ragamuffin" he gives us a *genre* picture with touches of grotesque humour. The scene he depicts is one of frequent occurrence, especially in provincial towns; an unmannerly urchin is pursuing an old woman in the street with taunts and jeers: "Hallo, granny! Hallo, ducky! How charming you look, you old scarecrow, with your sharp nose and big bleary eyes! . . . " The accompaniment to this unpleasing scene would have made a capital instrumental scherzo; it is full of rhythmical suggestions, one actually sees the young rascal cutting his capers around his unhappy victim, until at last the old woman seizes him by the scruff of the neck and thrashes him soundly. "Oh! Ah! Here, don't hit so hard!" cries the urchin.

One must confess that this is quite an original theme for a song—it and its fellows were naturally excluded for many a long year from the prudish aristocratic salons of Petersburg. Moussorgsky dedicated his "Ragamuffin" to his friend Stassov, who took a special delight in anything that was particularly daring.

"The Ragamuffin" may be classed with Moussorgsky's "comic" songs; his only Russian predecessor in this particular field was Dargomizhky, but the latter's humorous efforts, "The Worm," "His Worship," and so on, strike one as very mild affairs when contrasted with Moussorgsky's piquant musical jokes, in which, as in other branches, he achieved something that has never since been equalled by any Russian composer.

To the songs composed at the time of which we are speaking we must add the following: "The Magpie," "The Goat," and "The Seminarist." "The Magpie" is a combination of two poems by Pushkin:

> At my doorway hops a magpie,
> Very smart in black and white,
> Fluttering, chattering, croaking, crying,
> Just to tell me guests are coming!

The bird reminds the composer of a dancing gipsy, telling fortunes with her pack of cards for the benefit of a lively crowd; the song has a broad vocal melody, in five beats, which is very effective:

> I can sing and I can patter,
> With my cards can tell your fortune!

Moussorgsky calls this song "a musical jest," but that does not fully describe its real nature; we seem to catch mysterious hints of something else, which, despite the jesting background, gives us an uncomfortable feeling.

Moussorgsky describes "The Goat" as "a fable taken from high society"; a delicate young girl is pursued by a shaggy, ugly old billy-goat and seeks refuge in the bushes; soon afterwards we find her following a much older, far more shaggy, and still uglier bridegroom to the altar—" 'Tis a love-match, she says, and she intends to make a model wife! . . . "

This song is dedicated to Borodin, the composer, as "The Orphan" is dedicated to his wife. At that time, the middle of the sixties, Borodin was received as a worthy member of the Balakirev circle. Balakirev had naturally been quick to recognize the extraordinary promise shown by the young physician, who had recently been appointed Lecturer in Organic Chemistry to the Military Medical Academy in Petersburg. With Borodin's election to the Balakirev circle the "Powerful Coterie," as it was called, was complete. The origin of this expression, which we so often meet with, is as follows: In 1866, on the occasion of a performance at Prague of Glinka's *Russlan and Ludmilla*, with Balakirev as conductor, Stassov, in one of the numerous articles he devoted to the cause, speaks of Balakirev as the centre of a "powerful coterie" of young Russian composers with high aims, and inspired by nationalist—that is, pan-Slavonic—ideas. Alexander Serov, a fierce opponent of the new movement and its supporters, seized upon the expression and made fun of it in the Petersburg press, with the result that it quickly became popular and passed into permanent use as a nickname for the Balakirev circle.

In the winter of 1866–7 Serov had followed up his first opera, *Judith*, by the production of *Rogneda*; the attitude of the Balakirev circle was one of strong opposition, which showed itself in the most offensive manner; in fact they made it plain to the composer that they did not take him seriously. Serov revenged himself by violently attacking Balakirev as conductor, composer, and musician; he also started a successful newspaper campaign against Cui, in which his superior knowledge and far greater ability as a writer gave him the victory. Rimsky-Korsakov is of opinion that Serov would not have objected to a reconciliation, or even to an alliance with the "Powerful Coterie," but that all attempts at an understanding were thwarted by Balakirev's wooden obstinacy.

In a letter to Stassov, Borodin thus describes his admission into the "circle" and his impressions of Moussorgsky on that occasion: "At that time (1862) I made Balakirev's acquaintance, and it was at his house that I met Moussorgsky for the third time; we recognized each other at once, of course, and recalled our earlier meetings. I found that Moussorgsky had made extraordinary progress with his music. Balakirev was anxious to make me acquainted at once with the compositions of his circle, and, above all, with the symphony of 'the absent member'—i.e., N. A. Rimsky-Korsakov, who was just then sailing round the world as a midshipman in the Russian fleet. Accordingly the two musicians sat down to the piano, Moussorgsky taking the *primo*, Balakirev the *secondo*. Moussorgsky's playing was quite different from what it had been at our former meetings—I was surprised at the brilliance of his rendering, which was well thought out, strong, and full of energy, as well as by the

127

beauty of the composition. Soon after this we became quite intimate with Moussorgsky." Later on, Borodin too came under the spell of Balakirev, whose artistic ideas he adopted as his own for a long period. Ordinarily he was of a cold disposition, and ardent friendships were not congenial to him; indeed he never became really intimate with any member of the "powerful coterie," not even with Moussorgsky.

But to return to the humorous songs. The most successful figure of comedy to be found in them is undoubtedly the seminarist. The introduction of this delectable type into the realm of song was at least as great a novelty as his discovery of the ragamuffin or of the half-wit in "Fair Sávishna"; he must have met them all in real life, and indeed there was no one in Russia who did not know that pale and lanky youth, grown old before his time, with long hair, unhealthy skin, and spectacled eyes, starving for adventure, who was wont to infest the streets of those provincial towns that owned religious seminaries. Moussorgsky shows him to us first while he is at his Latin, trying to get the exceptions of the third declension into his head.

> *Panis, piscis, crinis, finis,*
> *Ignis, lapis, pulvis, cinis. . . .*

But the Devil leads him astray and, instead of the Latin substantives, the thought of the priest's pretty daughter, Stiosha, keeps coming into his mind:

> He has such a pretty daughter—
> Devil take my soul!
> Cheeks like poppies in the cornfield,
> Eyes like burning coal!
> And her lovely breast
> Never seems to rest,
> Heaving up and down
> Underneath her gown.

No wonder that the thought of all these charms spoils his
enjoyment of the Latin declensions! Moreover, on the feast
of the "pious, upright, and virtuous Mitrodora" it so fell
out that the priest noticed how, during the singing of the
verse from the Psalms, "in the sixth ecclesiastical tone," the
lovesick youth kept looking towards the bench where the
peerless Stiosha sat, "lovelier than e'er before." This led
to a row, and the poor lad complains bitterly that the Superior "had 'blessed' him right and left," boxed his ears
soundly, in fact—

> So the Devil made me flighty
> In the house of the Almighty.

For his punishment he has to "swot up" the exceptions in
nouns ending in "*is*": "*sanguis, unguis, et canalis et canalis
et canalis.* . . . "And so ends this amusing *scena*, which
is irresistibly funny when well done! The knowledge of Russian Church music, of the ecclesiastical modes and their treatment, that Moussorgsky had learnt from Father Krupsky is
here employed in a most unexpected manner—it enables him
to write a highly amusing parody of the real thing; again
and again, even in passages requiring the strongest emphasis, the amorous young man falls, quite unconsciously, into
one or other of the ecclesiastical modes. The words of the
song are, as we should expect, by Moussorgsky himself.

"The Seminarist" made quite a stir among the members
and friends of the Balakirev circle, who urged Moussorgsky
to have it printed. This, however, was not such a simple matter; the Ecclesiastical Censorship discovered "indications of
a blasphemous spirit" in the song and forbade its publication; in consequence it had to be printed abroad. It was published at last in 1870 by the firm of Rahter in Leipzig; but
even then little was gained, as permission either to import
or to circulate the song in Russia was refused. The composer describes the adventures of his "Seminarist" in a let-

ter to Stassov (August 18, 1870), which throws such a light on the conditions in Russia at that time that we give it here.

"Missive sent by the Moussorianin to his dear friend Vladimir Vassilievitch.

"Since, as you know, I am very nervous in the matter of my peculiar brand of literary transgressions, I should never have consented of my own accord to the publication of this damned 'Seminarist.' I consider that you, my dear friend, in conjunction with Ludmilla Ivanovna [1] are responsible for its public appearance—you know how you two, and another good friend (A. P. Op), [2] infected me with your own enthusiasm. I think it my duty, then, to describe for your benefit the adventures of the said 'Seminarist' in the dens of the various *fiery dragons* through which he had to pass. This 'lost son,' as I will call him, first stayed for a short time with the Censor for foreign parts, and finally got held up in the office of the Censorship for home affairs; the song could not be offered for sale because of the seminarist's confession at the end that 'Satan had overthrown him in God's holy temple.' Can you understand what there is in that to object to? Almost daily, before the high altar, the priests assault their deacons, or the deacons their priests, with crucifixes and chalices, or, when filled with the Holy Ghost, indulge in a free fight as a matter of course—are these not to be looked upon as 'temptations of the Devil'? The history of how my 'lost son' came home from Germany, once more by way of the dragon's den, is quite simple. The guardian of our sacred customs discovered that the 'Seminarist' contained some Latin words; consequently, according to his ideas, it must have something to do with *religion*, and so was matter for the Censorship. The pitiful way in which this poor creature tried to stammer out his decision aroused my sympathy; I dropped

[1] L. I. Shestakova, Glinka's sister.
[2] A. P. Opotchinin.

my role of sacrificial lamb for that of mentor and did my
best to damp the holy fire of his zeal by assuring him that
the Latin words were nothing more than some exceptions
to the rules for the declensions and were taken from the
Latin grammar, which, in all probability, had been revised,
tested, swallowed, digested, and approved by the recognized
authorities. But all my arguments were vain—official zeal
is not going to give way to mere considerations of common
sense! So off I go once more to the Censor. He advised me to
lodge a petition (I enclose a copy of my letter). . . . We
shall see what this will lead to. I am sending you, dear friend,
one of the hundred printed copies of the 'Seminarist,' so
please welcome my 'lost son' with paternal indulgence and
affection. I am tired of it all, and herewith part company
with the sole remaining copy of the three that the Censor
in his generosity presented to me. Between ourselves, this incident may be said to mark the first 'baptism of fire' of a
musician, and his getting to close quarters with the authorities. [1] The banning my song 'The Seminarist' may be taken
as a sign that musicians are now beginning gradually to be
raised from the ranks of 'nightingales, wandering minstrels,
and moon-struck gallants' and admitted as members of the
human race. At the same time, even if they were to ban every
single thing I write, I should still go on working as long as
strength lasts, for I am not easily thrown off my balance, and
a prohibition such as this only serves to fan more fiercely
the fire of my enthusiasm.—*Vade retro, Satana!*

"Your most affectionate

"Moussorianin"

Enclosed in this letter was the following interesting
document:

[1] The allusion is to Napoleon III's famous telegram describing how the
young Prince Imperial had his "baptism of fire" in the skirmish at Saar-
brücken that opened the Franco-German War.

(Copy)

To the Committee of the Censorship for Foreign Countries
The Suit of M. P. Moussorgsky

Whereas the Committee of the Inland Censorship have refused permission for the sale of my song "The Seminarist," published in Dresden (?), I venture most respectfully to ask the Committee of the Censorship for Foreign Countries to favour me with ten copies of the composition referred to, for distribution to the following persons:

1. To Ludmilla Ivanovna Shestakova, née Glinka   1 copy
2. To Nadeshda Nikolaievna and Alexandra Nikolaievna Purgold   2 copies
3. To Lieutenant Nikolai Andreievitch Rimsky-Korsakov   1 copy
4. To the Director of the Free School of Music, Mili Alexeievitch Balakirev   1 copy
5. To Professor Vladimir Vassilievitch Nikolsky   1 copy
6. To Professor César Antonovitch Cui, Captain of Engineers   1 copy
7. To Privy Counsellor Vladimir Vassilievitch Stassov   1 copy
8. To Privy Counsellor Vladimir Fedorovitch Purgold   1 copy
9. To Professor and Privy Counsellor Alexander Porfirievitch Borodin   1 copy

             Total   10 copies

Modest Petrovitch Moussorgsky

St. Petersburg, 10 Aug. 1870

The ban upon "The Seminarist" was not removed until many years after the composer's death, when in consequence of the Revolution of 1905 even the iron grip of the "Ecclesiastical Censorship" was relaxed. It was not till the year 1907 that a reprint of the song became possible, and of course any public performance of it had all this time been out of the question. [1]

Among Moussorgsky's humorous songs we must include certain satirical pieces, equally in advance of the taste of the time and naturally not calculated to increase the composer's popularity in those circles that he attacked. Although the importance of these pieces is chiefly a local and contemporary one, they are not altogether without permanent value, on account of the witty character of the music, which is of a kind scarcely to be met with elsewhere. In the first of them, "The Classic," Moussorgsky falls foul of a particular opponent, the old-fashioned composer and critic Famintzin, who was hopelessly entangled in the prejudices of the old school of music:

> I'm clear and simple,
> Modest and honest,
> Always æsthetic,
> Only in places
> Mildly pathetic.

The music follows the lines of Clementi, until the hero of the song is overcome by a wave of indignation against the "noise and uproar and unbridled licence" of "the newfangled ways." He ends with the "mildly pathetic" outburst: "In them I see the grave of all true art!" The song, which is in strictly

---

[1] While this work was in the press, the author heard from Petersburg that the head of the Musical Department of the Public (formerly the Imperial) Library, A. N. Rimsky-Korsakov, had found among the documents acquired during the years of the Revolution a previously unknown composition by Moussorgsky. It is a low-comedy vocal number, the furious "curtain lecture" delivered by a village scold to her faithless husband. The copy is entitled "You drunken old beast!" (from an adventure of Pakhomitch), words and music by M. Moussorgsky, with the date September 22, 1866, at Mili Balakirev's, Benardaky House on the Nevsky Prospekt.

classical three-verse form, ends with a note-for-note repetition of the final passage, "which might have been done by a copyist." This direct attack on the champion of "classical music" was provoked by a critique of Famintzin on Rimsky-Korsakov's symphonic poem *Sadko*; in the middle section of the song, at the mention of "newfangled ways," we have a passing reference to the ocean-motif from *Sadko*.

In another of his musical satires, "The Peep-show" or "The Penny Gaff," Moussorgsky slaughters a whole host of his enemies and opponents at the same time; although the piece belongs to a later period—the manuscript is dated June 15, 1870—it resembles "The Classic" in its subject, and the two songs form a class by themselves. The idea and even the name of "The Peep-show" are taken from Stassov, and Moussorgsky was not slow to seize upon it; he was always ready to respond to the influence of others, more especially that of Stassov. The piece was aimed directly at Serov, whose musical opinions had already roused Stassov to furious opposition, which betrayed him into unfairness and short-sighted violence.

Although it is to be regretted that Moussorgsky consented to become the tool of Stassov's private animosity, compensation is to be found in the way in which he has done his work. His musical satire shows no trace of the bitter venom with which Stassov bespatters Serov; in its place we find plenty of wit and humour and some biting though good-natured derision—the spirit is one of delicate banter rather than coarse insult, and therein lies the merit of the work. Had he employed less tactful methods, the piece might perhaps have inflicted greater pain, but would certainly not have been so amusing. Grouped around Serov, the central figure of these musical waxworks, we see several notabilities of lesser importance, but of undeniable interest. First we have Zaremba, who at that time was director of the "German" Conservatoire founded by Rubinstein and whose hobby was a muddled mixture of mysticism and harmony, calculated rather to alarm than to edify his pupils; Moussorgsky brings him on to a parody of a "classical" Handelian theme. The second figure is that of the dilettante musical critic Rostislav (Count Théophile Tolstoy), a man whose ignorance was equalled only by his presumption, and a blind enthusiast for the Italian school. To a waltz-tune written in the stupidest style of second-rate Italian opera, yet not without a certain charm of wit, he sings the praises of Patti—"Pa-pa-pa-ti-ti-ti-ti-ti"—and her flaxen wig, to which he had once devoted one of his highly fashionable *feuilletons*. Next comes our old friend Famintzin, who, to the tune of one of his own feeble songs, bewails the loss of his innocence—that is, in the public eye—he had just had an encounter with Stassov in which he had come off the loser.

After the preliminaries we have the fanfares out of Serov's *Rogneda*: "Attention! Here comes the Titan! How he blusters and staggers and stumbles! How he races and rages and threatens and fumes! Terrible! Awe-inspiring! See him seated on his little nag from Germany, the Bucephalus of the future, and under his arm a bundle of thunderbolts forged in the printing-house! A big arm-chair for His Genius, else he'll never settle down!" A clap of thunder is heard; "it grows dark, and deep night broods over all." (The words are from *Rogneda*). The Muse Euterpe descends from heaven. By this is meant the Grand Duchess Helène Pavlovna, the patroness of the Russian Musical Society, a cultivated and thoroughly artistic lady, who, as a member of a German royal house, had naturally small sympathy with the newfangled nationalist activities of the "Powerful Coterie." Moussorgsky refers to her elsewhere as "a temporary affliction." Mystic, pigmy, infant, and Titan, prostrate themselves in the dust and sing a hymn of praise to a tune taken from *Rogneda*, with words as follows: "Fair-haired daughter of the skies, muse and goddess ever young! Sprinkle thou our parching

135

plains with Olympus' golden rains! So shall our lyre resound thy praise through ages yet to come."

Unlike most of Moussorgsky's compositions, "The Peep-show" not only had an enormous success among the members of the Balakirev circle, but quickly made its way with the general public; the result, however, was injurious rather than beneficial to the composer's artistic reputation, since a large number of people now came to look upon him as a sort of witty jester, who was not to be taken quite seriously. "The Peep-show" is dedicated to V. V. Stassov, its clever originator, and "The Classic" to Nadeshda Petrovna Opotchinina.

Some years later—in 1874—Moussorgsky (again at Stassov's suggestion) proposed to write yet a third musical satire. It was to be called "The Hill of Nettles" and the scene was a hill-top, on which was seated a crab, as a symbol of retrograde tendencies. This crab stood for the musical critic Herman Laroche, a great friend of P. Y. Tchaikovsky. Laroche, a musician of fine culture, and not without talent, although hampered by an invincible indolence, had attached himself whole-heartedly to the chorus of Moussorgsky's blind detractors, among whom, as we shall see later, Tchaikovsky must also be reckoned. This was all the more distressing to Moussorgsky as Laroche's influence on public musical opinion in both the capital cities was very strong, more especially in Moscow, where he had been appointed Professor of Musical History in N. Rubinstein's newly-established Conservatoire. "The Hill of Nettles" never got further than a fairly developed sketch, which has never been published; the manuscript is in the Public Library at Petersburg.

To the year 1866 belong the two last love-songs that Moussorgsky was to write; like the rest of his compositions in the sentimental vein, they are of no great musical interest; nevertheless they are of some biographical importance, and especially the first of the two. This is a setting of some words

136

by Pleshtcheiev, the unhappy poet who was condemned, like Dostoievsky, to exile in Siberia; it is called "*Maliutka* (Darling)" and begins thus: "Why dost thou eye me now and then with looks so gloomy and unkind?" It is not known to whom the piece is addressed, the name in the dedication being concealed—contrary to Moussorgsky's custom—under the letters L. V. A. This is chronologically the last of the songs in the collection entitled *The Years of My Youth*, which was first brought to light in the so-called Paris manuscript; it had not hitherto been known to exist. The circumstance that this song is dated January 7, 1866, and that the next one, which is not included in *The Years of My Youth*, bears the date April 16 of the same year, leads one to suppose that the Paris manuscript was completed at some date between these two. In Moussorgsky's autobiography we find the following much discussed passage: "Some of the most striking and original of the song-pictures—'Sávishna,' 'The Orphan,' 'The Ragamuffin, 'Gopak'—made a remarkable impression on the composer's friend von Madewais [Madeweiss?], who entrusted them to the keeping of the Strasburg University Library, together with an explanatory letter by the composer." The editor of the autobiography, V. Karenin, supposes that the collection here referred to is the same as the Paris manuscript discovered in 1909; this is an error— in the first place, because not a single one of the songs mentioned by Moussorgsky is to be found in *The Years of My Youth*, and, secondly, because the discoverer of the manuscript, Charles Malherbe, mentions that, in the course of his researches, he had some unpleasant experiences in Russia, which he would not have said if he had found the manuscript in Strasburg. As to von Madewais, the friend mentioned in the autobiography, no information is forthcoming —none of Moussorgsky's musical friends in Petersburg seem to have known him. Perhaps he was that "hot-blooded Prussian" of whom Moussorgsky speaks in his letter to Balakirev given above in Chapter iii; as tutor to the Kushelev family, this person resided permanently in the country, and so would not have been known to the rest of Moussorgsky's acquaintances in Petersburg; he plays no further part in the composer's life.

The last love-song Moussorgsky composed was to Heine's poem: *"Ich wollt', meine Liebe ergösse sich* (I would that my love)"; he set the German words, and shows a fine sense of their rhythmical quality, as may be seen, for example, in his treatment of the last line: *"bis in den tiefsten Traum."* The Russian version—Mey's masterly translation —conforms so exactly to the German text that it can be printed under Moussorgsky's music without altering a single note or word; a similar experiment, as we have seen, had been successful in the case of Goethe's "Harper's Song." The music to Heine's poem, as is usual with Moussorgsky's love-songs, is by no means one of the brightest jewels in his treasury of song; nevertheless it is entitled to a place of honour as the best of its class. It seems to have had some special significance in the composer's private history, though this is matter of conjecture rather than of actual knowledge. This song, like most of his lyrical effusions, is dedicated to Nadeshda Petrovna Opotchinina; the original manuscript, in the Public Library of Petersburg, bears an inscription in the composer's handwriting, after the dedication: "In memory of the sentence you passed upon me."

The question of Moussorgsky's relations with women is one that no previous biographer has ever investigated or even touched upon. It is true that the documents which furnish the material for his life afford hardly any clue to the truth—in his letters to Balakirev and Stassov love-affairs are never mentioned; only once, in a letter to Balakirev, dated January 19, 1861, do we find a passing allusion to such matters: "I will confess," he writes, "that there was a time in my life when I nearly went under—not musically, but morally—however, I succeeded in making my escape. You shall hear some time what it was all about—*it was an affair with a woman.*" But he never refers to the subject again in his letters.

Karatigin, the Russian writer on music, in an article dealing with Moussorgsky's birthplace, states that he had heard from the composer's relations that in his youth he had fallen passionately in love with one of his cousins, who died while quite young, and that a packet of Moussorgsky's letters had been placed in her coffin and buried with her. This, however, is merely a matter of hearsay and naturally beyond the reach of confirmation, as the letters referred to must long ago have turned to dust.

Moussorgsky's undoubted aloofness in the matter of women, noticeable throughout his career, might naturally be explained by a lifelong fidelity to this early love-affair, but there is no evidence of any kind for this romantic supposition; the documents that have come down to us point to only one woman as having played an important part in his life—Nadeshda Petrovna Opotchinina, the sister of the talented interpreter of his songs, and his devoted friend. Even between these two the relations have never been clearly established; nevertheless we may confidently assert that they were united by what the French call "*une amitié amoureuse.*" Evidence of this might be found in the dedication of the "*Impromptu passionné,*" which was inspired by one of the most passionate love-scenes in the romance *Who is to blame?* by Hertzen. Possibly Moussorgsky saw himself reflected in the hero, Beltov—he, too, failed to discover the right way of dealing with women until it was too late. There is no doubt that Moussorgsky was one of those natures that are absolutely incapable of half-measures where their strongest personal feelings, such as love and friendship, are concerned. As with his art, so in his life, when he gave himself, he either gave all he had, without reserve, "without looking round,"

139

as the Russians say—or he gave nothing. What was meant by the "sentence" pronounced upon him by Nadeshda Petrovna, what was the cause of it, or what the consequences, we shall never know. In any case the two remained the closest and most faithful friends, although their relationship may not have taken the form he would have wished. When his brother retired to Minkino, his country-house, in 1868, Moussorgsky went to live with Opotchinin and his sister, and this arrangement continued in undisturbed harmony until the year 1875, when it was abruptly ended by the death of Nadeshda Petrovna. Of Moussorgsky's grief at the loss of his friend we have an affecting proof in a certain unfinished composition, now in the Petersburg Public Library, which was first published in 1912. As with most of Moussorgsky's vocal compositions, it is difficult to say exactly to which category it belongs; briefly, it is a vocal piece with piano accompaniment; it is entitled "Cruel Death," with "An Epitaph" for subtitle. The words, also by Moussorgsky, are just as beautiful and touching as the music: "Even as a greedy vulture plunges its talons into the heart of its victim, so hath Death, the ruthless destroyer, snatched thee, even thee, away!" There follows a description of the dead woman, inspired by the deepest, warmest emotion, but devoid of all lachrymose sentimentalism, ending in these words: "When at my mother's death the cruel blows of fate drove me from home into a cheerless exile, when, weary and embittered by suffering, I knocked at the door of thy pure heart, hesitating and shy, like a frightened child, begging for admission, craving help— No, I cannot—I cannot go on—" Here the manuscript breaks off.

After the death of Mlle Opotchinina no other woman seems to have played an important part in Moussorgsky's life, always excepting his motherly friend Ludmilla Ivanovna Shestakova, of whom we shall have much more to say in the following chapters.

140

But we are anticipating the order of events; for nearly ten years longer Moussorgsky was able to enjoy the faithful friendship of the warm-hearted Nadeshda Petrovna; but in the song *"Ich wollt', meine Liebe ergösse sich"* he bade a final farewell to the composition of love-lyrics.

In the summer of 1866 Moussorgsky gave one more proof, after a long interval, of his oriental proclivities, in the "Hebrew Song," a setting of Mey's poem "Like the flower of the field." It differs essentially from most of his vocal compositions of that period as being one of the few instances in which he recognizes that the beauty of pure music has a certain independent importance of its own. The principal theme is an original Hebrew melody, which Moussorgsky had most probably picked up in the Jewish family from whom he got the subject for his chorus *Joshua*. The simplicity and repose expressed by melody and harmony alike create an almost biblical atmosphere and make the most effective background imaginable for the chaste beauty of Mey's poem. The song is dedicated to his brother and sister-in-law.

*   *   *

Moussorgsky had always been a great lover of children. His feeling for them was perhaps in some way akin to his sympathy with the Russian peasantry; it was always the simple, unspoilt natures that attracted him, for there was nothing he so much detested as falsehood, sham, insincerity, untruthfulness in any form, and with children there was no need to be on his guard against these things. Accordingly he not only loved children for their own sake, but found in the little simple incidents of their innocent lives material for artistic treatment. We have already seen him at work on scenes from childhood—his own—and in 1868 he returns to the same subject, only now he handles it from an entirely different point of view.

141

It is characteristic of Moussorgsky that he always endeavoured to give a concrete form to his artistic impulses. He is never quite at home in the forms of purely instrumental music; his creative fancy can function with perfect freedom only when the sung word provides firm ground for the imaginative faculty to work upon.

Such a direct incentive to musical treatment of this kind presented itself in the following "Song for Children," written by Mey:

> Dainty little rose-bush
> Growing in the garden,
> Basking in the sunshine,
> Blest by every shower!
>
> Dainty little maiden
> Dwelling with her parents,
> Mother's little sunbeam,
> Father's only joy!

Moussorgsky's music is as delicate, one might almost say as fragile, as the poem; there is a particularly charming effect at the end—a chord of the dominant seventh, *pianissimo,* on the weak beat, like a question softly uttered by a child —an astonishing piece of audacity for the year 1868. The song was composed at the beginning of April; on the 26th of that month Moussorgsky wrote the first of his *Scenes from Childhood*—a title almost more appropriate here than for Schumann's well-known pieces. The song is called "With my Nanny" and is dedicated to Dargomizhky, who was delighted with it and earnestly advised Moussorgsky to "go ahead" on the same lines. This, however, the composer was unable to do immediately, since, for the next two years, his other musical projects, which, as we shall see, were matured in 1868, kept him so fully occupied that he was unable to attend to anything else. Only in 1870 did he once more turn his thoughts

142

in this direction; he then wrote four songs that, with the previous one (renamed "Child and Nurse"), he put together in a cycle called *The Nursery,* a title suggested by Stassov. In 1872 he added two more numbers, making seven in all. According to his contemporaries, a few other scenes ("A Child's Fantastic Dream," "Two Quarrelsome Children") were so near completion that Moussorgsky would play them on the piano to his intimate friends, but unfortunately they were never written down. In order to give a general impression of the whole we will run through the entire cycle in order, drawing attention to the incidents in each.

In these seven scenes, the result of incredibly delicate observation, each one seems more gracious and full of charm then its predecessor. No artist has ever seen deeper into the soul of a child or presented all its fine and delicate emotions so sympathetically. The actors in these little scenes are generally the children themselves, talking, relating their adventures, behaving with perfect naturalness; only occasionally does the "nanny" (that indispensable confidante in all Russian nurseries), or, it may be, the mother, join in with words of reproof or affection, as circumstances demand. Moussorgsky's music is a triumph of the "naturalistic" method of expression, by means of which he here obtains entirely new and unexpected effects, which are at the same time entirely charming. Every modulation, every touch of expression, has been studied from nature, to the smallest detail, and yet in every number one catches "the voice of the poet" and sees his eyes light up with a smile of tenderness. It is just this smile that the performance of these trifles is meant to call up on the face of the hearer—nothing further is demanded.

No. 1 is called "Child and Nurse" and describes an ordinary conversation between the two. The child insists upon being told a story about "the werewolf who carries off little children into the forest and gobbles up their tender little white bones." "But, Nanny, does he do that to *all* children or only to those naughty wicked ones who beat their nannies? Or perhaps—no, I'd rather hear the story of the king and queen who live in that lovely castle by the sea! And the King limps so badly, and every time he puts his foot down, a toadstool springs up out of the ground—and the Queen can give such a big sneeze that it breaks the window-panes! After all, Nanny, we won't have the story of the werewolf—it frightens me! Let's have the other, the funny one, eh?" It is marvellous what a perfect little masterpiece Moussorgsky has managed to evolve from this truly innocent material, and in what incredibly lively fashion the little scene runs its course.

In the next piece Misha is put in the corner. "You young rascal!" says the nurse, "where is my knitting? Dear, dear! if he hasn't upset the table, and the whole stocking has come undone! Now, then, off you go into the corner!" "But, Nanny, I haven't done anything, really I haven't! Where's the ball of wool? Why, the cat's got it, and the knitting-needles too, depend upon it!" Then follows an aside, *sotto voce*, from the corner: "Misha is a good boy, a very good boy—but Nanny is old and ugly and she has a dirty nose, and her hair is grey—now Misha is clean and nice to look at. Misha won't love Nanny any more—never no more! There!"

Now comes the "droll story," as Schumann would call it, of the cockchafer: "Mamma, mamma, what do you think has happened to me? I was playing in the avenue, under the big trees, and building a house of leaves, a proper house, just as you make them, with a real roof, you know—and then, all of a sudden, a great big black cockchafer fell right on to the roof! And his wings quivered, like this—and he buzzed and looked me straight in the face! Ugh! How frightened I was! And then he spread out his wings and flew right at me and hit me on the head! And then I ducked down, quite low, and didn't stir, only just took a tiny peep to see what he was doing—and—just listen, mamma!—there he was, fallen on his

144

back, and he didn't buzz any more, but lay quite still—only his wings quivered a little. Tell me, mamma, was he dead, or only pretending? I can't understand it—so odd! He just hit himself against me and then fell down! Tell me, mamma, what does it all mean?"

After this exciting experience, which is described in music no less lively than the words, the child is put to bed, but not before she has sung her doll to rest with a cradle-song, the short and lovely melody of which is now and again interrupted by some particularly sharp admonition to the doll, who refuses to go to sleep.

And now the little one must say its evening prayer, according to the good old custom; all the dear ones are mentioned in turn—father, mother, grandmother, and an interminable list of aunts, uncles, cousins male and female, servants—"and, dear God, bless Aunt Katia, Aunt Natasha, Aunt Nasha and Aunt Sasha, Aunt Olga and Aunt Nadia, and Uncle Petia, and Uncle Kolia, and Uncle Grischa, Uncle Valodia, Vania, Mitia, Petia, Sonia, Dasha, Pasha—I can't remember any more, Nanny!" "Oh, you little stupid, how often have I told you to say: 'and have mercy on my poor little soul'!" "—And have mercy on my poor little soul!"— then, half asleep: "Was that all right, Nanny?"

The last number is the tragic history of the cat who tried to eat the dicky-bird and had actually got his paw inside the cage when a well-directed blow drove him off. The little rogue who tells this shocking story is naturally greatly excited—"Only fancy, mamma! What a naughty cat!"—and Moussorgsky turns it all into music with a quite inimitable vivacity.

The piece before this describes a dashing "Ride on a Hobby-horse," in which the rider naturally comes to grief, but, with mamma to comfort him, sets out again with fresh courage. On the way to Yukki, a summer resort on the coast of Finland, he meets with an old acquaintance: "Hallo, Vassia! you'll come and play with me today, won't you? And mind you come early!"

The last two numbers were printed for the first time in a posthumous edition of *The Nursery*. The original title was *At the Bungalow* and they were dedicated to Dmitri Vassilievitch Stassov and his wife, Polyxena Ivanovna. The Stassov children were among those whom Moussorgsky took for his models when writing these songs; others were his brother Filaret's children, Goga (George) and Tania (Tatiana), and Sasha Cui, the little son of the composer, and it was to these that he dedicated the other numbers of the cycle. It is plain from this that the songs were not meant only for grown-up people; the composer knew quite well that they would please the children best and he repeatedly enjoyed the satisfaction of proving that such was the case. This fact made some amends for the hostile reception of his work in the influential musical circles of Petersburg, where the critical bigwigs felt it their duty to attack even these harmless little pieces with the full force of their uncomprehending hatred. What was left for Moussorgsky but to seek consolation among the "babes and sucklings"? In a letter to Stassov (September 10, 1879) describing his impressions of a concert tour in South Russia, he writes: "In Nikolaiev, Mme Leonova [the singer who accompanied him on tour] took me to visit the dear J.'s, and got me to play and sing *The Nursery* to their children. How those children did enjoy it!—the mother, too, was loud in her praises. We repeated the experiment at Kherson in the B.'s' house, with the same result, the same enthusiasm. Oh, Laroche and Soloviev and Ivanov, with Haller and his gang!"

One of his child models, the eldest daughter of D. V. Stassov, afterwards Mme Varvara Dmitrievna Komarova, in her *Memories of my Childhood* gives so graphic an account of Moussorgsky in those days that an extract from it may well be given here: "My recollection of Moussorgsky dates from when I was seven years old—or, rather, I was seven years old when I began to notice his coming to our house; he had probably been a frequent visitor long before then, though I was unaware of it. But all at once he came into the world of us children—'Moussorianin,' as our elders named him, and as we children soon began to call him, supposing it to be his real name. He came very often to see us, both at our town house and also at the bungalow in Samanilovka, near Pargolovo. As he made himself at home with us quite naturally and never talked to us children in that unreal, artificial way that grown-up people who are friends of the family generally do, we soon took a great fancy to him and ended by looking upon him as quite one of ourselves. My sister Sina and I were particularly impressed by the fact that he invariably greeted us as if we were grown-ups; he would kiss our hands with a 'Good day, young ladies!' or 'Allow me, young ladies!'—strange and astonishing it seemed to us, but very delightful; so we came to talk with him quite freely, as if he had been our own age. My brothers, too, were quite at their ease with him and used to tell him all their little adventures, though the youngest was not yet able to pronounce his name properly, but always said 'Moussolianin,' so that when Moussorgsky came to visit us, he would call out to us children, from some way off: 'Hallo! Here is Moussolianin!' The musical sketches 'Naughty Puss,' 'By Hobby-horse to Yukki,' 'The Dream' (this was one of my sister's tales—so far as I know, it has never been published, and I am not sure whether it exists in manuscript, though the composer often played it to us on the piano), and one more number of the *Scenes from Childhood* were founded on the tales we children told him.

"As I was the eldest, Moussorgsky would often talk to me on serious subjects; for instance, he told me how the stars in the sky were arranged in constellations, and how they all had their special names; he taught me where to find the Great Bear, Cassiopeia, Orion, Canis Major, and Sirius. I remem-

147

ber, too, a talk we had one New Year's Eve, when he explained to me why the next day was New Year's Day and why the feast was kept in winter and not in autumn, for, as the child sees it, New Year begins in autumn, when the family return to town from their country villa, and ends in the spring; as for the summer, that is a thing apart, and beyond all computation!

"Moussorgsky often visited us at our bungalow in Samanilovka, where it was quite customary for him to take part in all the trifling incidents of our daily life; for instance, he was present when our little two-year-old brother, who was being tubbed out of doors, gave a piteous scream and, stark naked as he was, ran off across the sands, to be enticed back only by a promise of strawberries. When we were alone with him, Moussorgsky would often play these little scenes to us on the piano, with the different characters plainly shown; he was fond of teasing the tiny brother, who was always crying out for strawberries."

Many things must have gone to the changing of this sunny-natured lover of little children, who was himself still a child in many ways, into the embittered misanthrope that Moussorgsky became towards the end of his career. Fate certainly left nothing undone to bring this about, but men, too, contributed their share.

*   *   *

During the years 1867–8, in addition to the songs here described, Moussorgsky composed a choral setting, with orchestra, of *The Destruction of Sennacherib*, besides scoring his "Intermezzo *in modo classico*" for full orchestra; in this form he dedicates the piece to his new-made friend A. Borodin. A new arrangement of *The Witches* (or *A Night on the Bare Mountain*) also belongs to this period. This composition seems to have given Moussorgsky no rest; he was always overhauling it and endeavouring to give it a form that

148

would satisfy him and he never succeeded. His idea in 1867
was to make it a fantasia for piano and orchestra; the unfinished manuscript of this attempt is preserved in the Petersburg Public Library.

The choral work *The Destruction of Sennacherib* is a
setting of an extract from Byron's *Hebrew Melodies*, from
which Moussorgsky had already taken the text for his "King
Saul before the Battle." Moussorgsky must have considered
this work a success—and rightly—since he dedicated it to
Balakirev, the man for whom, among all his friends, and all
the musical celebrities of Petersburg, he had always had the
greatest respect. This work, thanks to its vigorous rhythms,
the charm of its oriental colouring, which is unobtrusively
sustained throughout, and the peculiar harmonies, wavering
between major and minor, is highly effective; it was produced
by Balakirev at a concert of the Free School of Music, in
February 1867, a few weeks after the completion of the
score. Later, in the winter of 1873–4, Moussorgsky, probably to gratify some wish of Stassov's, completely recast the
middle section of the chorus "And the angel of death spread
his wings on the blast." Long afterwards, in his life of the
composer, Stassov storms against the earlier form of this
middle section: "Why must we always have a trio, in the
classical manner! And what did he mean by this imitation,
perhaps unintentional, of the choral music of western Europe?" Moussorgsky sent the new arrangement of the chorus
to Stassov on his birthday, January 2, 1874, with the following characteristic letter: "Well, my General, I have found
time to comply with your commands! I embrace you heartily
and wish you all good things! The second version of *Sennacherib* is yours by right, so take it from me! I will not go to
Beethoven for my justification—though he wrote four overtures to *Leonora*—I prefer not to justify myself, not even
by appealing to the example of great men. I am as I am, a
little man like any other, and my justification, in your eyes

149

and in my own, is as follows: You know that our dear Mili Balakirev cracked several bad jokes over the first version of *Sennacherib* and even put Gashenka Lomakin [the chorus master of the Free School of Music] in a position of some embarrassment on the occasion of the concert in the Nobles' Hall, 1867. It was to Balakirev that the first version was dedicated—peace be to its memory! You, my dear friend, have persistently drawn my attention to the faults in the middle section of my work; it was composed under your very eyes, and countless times have we both together earned applause from audiences of the most varied kinds; but weightier than all this is the fact that you have taken a great fancy to it in its second form—that is sufficient honour and glory for me, and that is my whole justification. To you I dedicate my *Sennacherib*, and take pride in so doing."

Stassov must indeed have "taken a great fancy" to this work, for, like a fond mother, he finds excuses even for its faults. With the instrumentation Moussorgsky, still quite inexperienced in this department, was not very successful; at any rate, Rimsky-Korsakov considered it necessary to make a thorough revision for the new edition that was brought out after the composer's death. Stassov, on the other hand, in an absolute ecstasy of admiration, writes: "Perhaps the instrumentation is a little heavy and lies too much in the lower range of the orchestra, but that does not matter in this particular case, where the deep, dense current of the music suggests the low, guttural tones that belong to oriental speech"!

Apart from the songs—which cover a wide range of emotions, from the clumsy amorousness of the *yurodivy* to a child's evening prayer—and the choral and orchestral compositions just mentioned, Moussorgsky had been busy from 1866 to 1868 (especially in the summer of this year) on a work of larger dimensions, which, at the time when it was written, was looked upon as the impudent challenge of a musical eccentric of almost anarchical tendencies. Before

150

dealing with this work, which demands a chapter to itself, a few sketches of life in the Petersburg of that time, as described by contemporary writers, may be given in order to throw some light on the role that Moussorgsky played in it, and to make plain the links that connect his artistic productions with the whole of his musical environment.

VI

FRESH PATHS

FOR ABOUT twenty years after Moussorgsky's death his songs were almost entirely unknown to the musical world of Russia, outside the narrow circle of a few devoted admirers. In seeking to account for this, we must consider first of all that about that time—i.e., the last two decades of the nineteenth century—the interest of the Russian musical public was centred almost exclusively in another star just risen on their horizon, which for a time threw all else into obscurity; this was Tchaikovsky, whose melodies were so much more taking, so much more intelligible, than Moussorgsky's and whose whole conception of art was so much easier to grasp that he quickly attained to a popularity almost without a parallel. To Tchaikovsky's music in itself we have no objection to make—this is not the place to criticize it—we merely refer to it as one of the causes that prevented Moussorgsky's songs from at once becoming widely known in Russia. Indeed, there were many other reasons why this was hardly possible in the composer's lifetime. Songs and "romances" were at that time only for home performance; small intimate concerts of vocal music—"*Liederabende* (evenings of songs)," as they were afterwards called—were absolutely unknown to the musical public of Petersburg in the sixties and seventies of the nineteenth century, while the singers at the big concerts confined themselves for the most part to favourite airs from well-know operas, or such "romances" by Glinka, Dargomizhky, or some talented amateur as appealed exclusively to the taste for *bel canto* and so were within the comprehension of all sections of the public.

But even as music for the domestic circle, Moussorgsky's songs could scarcely be said to count; here, too, it was impossible for them to compete with the "romances," since they set both singer and accompanist a task to which few amateurs were equal; amateur music at that time, especially in the matter of singing, was of a commendably high standard—if we are to believe the testimony of contemporary writers—throughout Russia, and especially in Petersburg, but its activities were strictly limited to Italian opera and the home-grown "romances" written in imitation of it.

Thanks to the high level of vocal training among the representatives of what is called "good society," and also through the absence of any extensive system of concert-giving, music in the home circle acquired an importance that it has never since approached. The numerous small musical circles that were formed, and that met regularly, resembled private concerts, at which the entertainments rose to the level of the best public performances. The program on these occasions was not generally on a very exalted plane, seldom going beyond Bellini, Donizetti, or, at the most, Glinka and Dargomizhky. Still, certain fortunate exceptions were to be found and these, naturally, were all the more highly valued. Mention has already been made of Dargomizhky's "Thursdays," and of the fact that he, not unnaturally, preferred to play and listen to his own compositions on these occasions; here, of course, Moussorgsky very rarely got a chance. Similar meetings were held on Saturday evenings at the house of V. P. Opotchinin and his sister; the brother, we are told, was a man of extraordinary talent, with a wonderful voice, whose remarkable versatility as an artist enabled him to cope successfully with the heaviest demands the Moussorgsky songs might make; a pupil of Tamburini and the famous Lablache, he was an officer by profession and had worked

153

his way up the ladder of promotion to the highest position on the General Staff.

How seriously music was taken in this household is proved by a manuscript in Moussorgsky's writing, dated 1867, that is preserved in the Petersburg Public Library; it contains a whole pile of arrangements of Beethoven's quartets for piano solo and is inscribed: "For the Opotchinin Saturday evenings." It includes the scherzo from the E flat Quartet, Op. 59, No. 2, the *andante* from the Quartet in E major, Op. 59, No. 3, the scherzo and *lento* from the Quartet in F, Op. 135, and parts of the Quartet in C sharp minor, Op. 131—a selection that inspires us with the greatest respect for the high level of taste among the frequenters of these musical meetings.

Regular evenings were also held at the house of the Privy Counsellor Vladimir Feodorovitch Purgold, for whom one of the ten examples of "The Seminarist"—the piece that had been snatched from the jaws of a vigilant censorship—had been intended. These particular gatherings acquired a special importance from the fact that they added two new and very valuable members to the musical circle that surrounded the "Powerful Coterie"; these were the old Counsellor's young nieces, Alexandra and Nadeshda Purgold, whose extraordinary musical ability and high artistic endowments are always mentioned by their contemporaries with extravagant enthusiam. One of the two, Alexandra—afterwards Mme Mollas—sang; the other, Nadeshda, who afterwards married Rimsky-Korsakov, played the piano. Borodin declared that Alexandra's singing had such a stimulating and suggestive effect upon the creative imagination that one felt as if she had an actual share in the composition; she was one of the first women to interpret Moussorgsky's songs with real sympathy. The other sister, Nadeshda Ivanovna, who was composer as well as pianist, had received as complete a professional training as was then to be had; her astonishing

154

faculty for playing from full score excited the greatest admiration, and Moussorgsky went so far as to speak of her as "our dear orchestra." Dargomizhky had made the musical education of the two sisters his own peculiar care, instructing one in singing, the other in counterpoint. Stassov writes of the two sisters as follows: "When, later on, they made the acquaintance of Moussorgsky and the rest of the Balakirev troupe, their artistic development was led to even higher flights, until they became two such artists as had never yet been seen among the musical ladies of Russia. Glinka, like Dargomizhky, was constantly surrounded by a swarm of female singers and pianists, who used to perform the romances and *arias* of both composers, in public as well as in private. Among these ladies were not a few whose talent as performers was beyond question; they had fire, *élan*, genuine feeling, and charm, but not one of them—I speak with some authority, as I have heard all of them, at Glinka's house as well as at Dargomizhky's—came within measurable distance of the Purgold sisters in the matter of real talent and profound musical sensibility."

It would almost seem as if, at that period, there existed a close, if mysterious, connexion between the musician's art and the Russian army and navy; with the names of Alexandra Purgold-Mollas and V. P. Opotchinin we must couple that of a certain General K. N. Veliaminov as one who aspired, not without success, to be known as an interpreter of Moussorgsky's songs. Dargomizhky and Stassov praise his singing highly; on the other hand, Rimsky-Korsakov in *My Musical Life*—the pages of which are sometimes too caustic for quotation—paints a very different picture: "An amusing figure was General Veliaminov; keeping close to the accompanist, with one foot tucked behind him, and always holding a key in his right hand, for some unexplained reason, he would make futile attempts to master Moussorgsky's 'Fair Sávishna.' His breath was always giving out, and in

155

almost every one of those merciless passages of five in the bar he would implore the accompanist to give him time to breathe! After this hurried request he would go on with the song—then once more it would be: 'Do give me time to breathe!' " The author of *My Musical Life*, however, gives a better report of another amateur vocalist who put in an appearance about that time at the Balakirev evenings. This was a certain V. N. Ilinsky, a medical student, of whom he writes: "He astonished us all by his sympathetic and really talented rendering of certain *Lieder*, especially Moussorgsky's humorous songs; 'The Peep-show' and 'The Seminarist' were capitally done—even Moussorgsky was satisfied."

That "even Moussorgsky" is significant, for his contemporaries are unanimous in declaring that Moussorgsky himself displayed a quite unsurpassable excellence in the interpretation of his own songs. He was the possessor of a distinguished dramatic talent, with which, from his earliest years, he had been accustomed to delight his friends; when only nineteen he had won his spurs as an actor in the part of an elderly schoolmaster in Victor Krilov's comedy *Straight to the Point*, which was given at César Cui's on that composer's wedding eve. The year after, in a performance the program of which still exists, he appeared in Gogol's *The Trial* as Proletov, the government clerk; and in the one-act comic opera by Cui that followed, *The Mandarin's Son*, he took the leading part of the Mandarin, Kau-Tsing, in which, according to Stassov's account, he displayed such vivacity, so droll a manner, such humour and skill in song, delivery, pose, gesture, and movement that his performance was received with continuous laughter and applause. Moussorgsky's undoubted dramatic ability, together with his agreeable, if not very strong, baritone voice and his astonishing powers as a pianist, was naturally of the greatest assistance to him in interpreting his own songs.

156

Let two of his contemporaries testify to his abilities. Mme Komarova writes: "Having many opportunties of hearing separate scenes and numbers from this opera [*The Mandarin's Son*], we children soon became familiar with them; we knew what pleased us and what did not and we would even venture to beg 'Moussorianin' or Alexander Porfirievitch [Borodin] to play this or that scene to us. I remember how Borodin once, at my request, played over the Polovetzer choruses and dances from the second act of *Prince Igor*— special favourites of mine—while Moussorgsky would interrupt him from time to time with: 'Now, Professor, do let me play instead of you! What are you doing there with those fat little pullets of yours?' (The allusion was to Borodin's hands, which were plump and very white, but by no means wanting in agility—it was just a friendly jest, which was received with hearty laughter.) Moussorgsky then sang Kontchak's air from the same opera, of which he gave a quite incomparable rendering, in a style peculiarly his own, with special emphasis on single words and phrases. For instance, he gave the line: 'Take the desire of thy heart!' with strangely exaggerated expression, accompanying it with a broad gesture of the hand. I still remember the lofty, truly oriental dignity he infused into the words:

> In strength and power none can with me compare!
> All things around me tremble at my coming!

How incomparably tender was his singing of the lines:

> Yet thou, O Prince, hast never yet
> Bent thy proud head before me . . .

and with what passion did he plead:

> I'd be thy friend and not thy foe . . . !

157

Of all the Kontchaks I ever saw, not one ever approached him in this passage, and to this day I can hear Moussorgsky's voice in:

Take the desire of thy heart!"

V. Stassov, in his life of the composer, writes of Moussorgsky as singer and pianist in the following terms: "The performance of any new songs by Moussorgsky was always a great event; the tragic element in some, and the humorous, even comic, nature of others had a remarkable effect upon his intimates, who, like most men of talent, were all very impressionable. By general request these songs were more frequently given than any others, nor is this to be wondered at, considering the favourable conditions under which they were given. As an accompanist Moussorgsky had no equal, especially when he himself was the singer; his audience were invariably carried away by the unparalleled sincerity, naturalness, elegance, simplicity, and humour that flowed from him in one continuous, inexhaustible stream. . . . He was equally great as reciter, singer, and accompanist; in this respect, as we often agreed, he stood alone—no one else could compare with him. Even an exceptional pianist like Anton Rubinstein was not a match for him on this particular ground; both artists could accompany to perfection the finest songs of Schumann, Schubert, and all the other masterpieces of the idealistic, 'legitimate' European school of music, but Moussorgsky was master in another department, in which neither Rubinstein nor any other musician in Europe could approach him—the music of his own people, and particularly his own profoundly national vocal scenes and sketches, founded on the realistic method of Gogol. Here Moussorgsky reigned alone in a province peculiarly his own and at the same time absolutely new and original, where no other musician could follow him."

Musical gatherings at which the young composers,

158

Moussorgsky amongst them, performed their latest productions, or had them performed with the assistance of the other artists we have mentioned, were held also at the composers' own houses—e.g., at César Cui's, as we have already seen, and later at the house of the newly-married Rimsky-Korsakov. These meetings, which had their origin in the Balakirev circle, gradually extended in ever-widening rings, until they found their way into theatrical society, in the house of the most distinguished actor that Russia has produced—O. A. Petrov, the first Susanin in Glinka's *A Life for the Tsar*. Nor did the movement stop here; Glinka's devoted sister, Ludmilla Shestakova, in whose house he spent the last years of his life previous to his removal to Berlin, watched with lively interest the ripening of the unexpectedly abundant harvest—the productions of the New Russian School—that had sprung from the seed sown by her brother. To several of these young composers she acted as a faithful friend and mother, and especially to Moussorgsky, who found in her sympathy one of the most precious of earthly compensations vouchsafed to him by Fate for the many misfortunes he had to endure. Quite a number of his songs were heard for the first time at this lady's house; of her friendly relations with the composer of *Boris*, we shall speak more fully in another place.

Yet another rendezvous for these musical evenings was the residence of V. Stassov. In nearly all the musical projects of the Balakirev circle Stassov had always taken a more or less active part, as literary adviser; we shall see shortly what an extraordinary influence he was to exert, in this capacity, on Moussorgsky's later work. At all the meetings of the Balakirev circle, from the very beginning, Stassov's presence, as either host or guest, had been indispensable. Rimsky-Korsakov in *My Musical Life* naturally cannot resist the temptation to have a sly dig at Stassov, though in this case, strange to say, he tempers it with a touch of genuine appreciation: "At all our gatherings V. Stassov's presence was absolutely indispensable; if he was not there, all felt that something was wanting. It was his custom, when anything was being played, to pretend not to listen, and to talk in a loud voice all the while to the man next to him; this did not prevent him, however, from breaking out, now and again, into enthusiastic cries of 'Splendid! Incomparable!' etc."

It was not till 1866 that Rimsky-Korsakov returned to Petersburg after his tour round the world and resumed his place in the Balakirev circle; he brought with him his first symphony, which naturally made a great sensation. The beginning of his friendship with Moussorgsky dates from this period. Like Borodin, he was unable to resist the attractive personality of the man who wrote *The Nursery*. Although he confesses as much in *My Musical Life,* he does not refrain from some caustic criticism of his new-found friend, for whom at that time he had a sincere affection. "During the season of 1866–7," he writes, "I struck up a close friendship with Moussorgsky. He was living at that time in his married brother's residence near the Kashin Bridge, where I frequently visited him. He played me several fragments of his opera *Salambo*, which roused my warm enthusiasm; it was at this time too, I fancy, that he showed me his fantasia for piano and orchestra, 'Midsummer Eve,' written under the influence of Liszt's *'Danse Macabre.'* I remember also his playing of the beautiful Hebrew choruses, *The Destruction of Sennacherib* and *Joshua,* and his songs—which found no favour with either Balakirev or Cui—including 'Kallistrat' and that fine fantasy 'Night,' with Pushkin's words. In 'Kallistrat' we find the first hint of that realistic method that Moussorgsky was soon to adopt, while in 'Night' he still exhibits the idealistic side of his talent, which later on he deliberately trampled in the mud [!], though he was glad enough on occasions to avail himself of the accumulated musical resources that he owed to its cultivation in former years.

. . . His compositions in this latter style are wanting in two respects—elegance of form and perfect clearness in the working-out of his ideas, defects due to his absolute ignorance of both harmony and counterpoint. We see here the influence of Balakirev and his circle, who first held these branches of musical science up to mockery and later declared that Moussorgsky was incapable of acquiring them [!]; as a result Moussorgsky went without them all his life, and consoled himself with making a sort of virtue of his ignorance and jeering at the technical proficiency of others as merely old-fashioned convention. But when he got hold of some charming simple idea, what splendid use he made of it, in spite of his prejudices! I had many proofs of this in the course of my visits to Moussorgsky, when we would talk together unreservedly, free from the constraining presence of Balakirev and Cui. With much that he played me I was quite delighted —the divine enthusiasm of the creative artist burnt steadily within him. He confided to me all his schemes for the future —and he had more than I; one of them was in connexion with *Sadko*; this, however, he dropped and passed on to me; Balakirev approved of the idea, and so I set to work on it."

In spite of the bitter professorial tone of much of this —Rimsky-Korsakov wrote *My Musical Life* just before his death, after he had been professor for forty years in the Petersburg Conservatoire—the passage quoted gives us a lively picture of the intellectual relations of the Balakirev circle at a time when their different views on matters of taste began to show themselves with ever-increasing clearness. It was over the question of opera that these differences, later on, were most strikingly manifested. At the time of which we are speaking, most of the members of the circle—with the exception of Balakirev himself—were making their first experiments in this field, in which they were soon to take such totally different directions; for the present, however, all were inspired by the same ideals, the same principles. The

161

outward expression, the perfect musical embodiment of this ideal, they found in Dargomizhky's opera *The Stone Guest*, that astonishing masterpiece with which the dying composer ended his career. The enthusiasm of the "Powerful Coterie" for this work knew no bounds; we have already described at length in Volume I of these monographs the performances of portions of this opera, in which Dargomizhky sang the part of Don Juan, Moussorgsky those of Leporello and Don Carlos, with Veliaminov as the Monk and the Commander, and Alexandra Purgold as Laura and Donna Anna, while her sister, Nadeshda, as usual, supplied the place of an orchestra. Their enthusiasm for the work increased, if possible, with each performance. One may safely assume that between Dargomizhky and his youthful followers there had been a mutual impregnation of ideas, although the composer's friends —V. T. Sokolov, for instance, in his *Memoirs*—emphatically reject this idea that *The Stone Guest* was in any way influenced by the "Powerful Coterie." At any rate the *Guest* was in the eyes of the faithful adherents the one work that was to mark the beginning of a new epoch in the history of Russian opera. In the free yet melodious recitative to which Dargomizhky set Pushkin's text, without alteration, one could see the foundation on which the New Russian School —the expression now appears for the first time—based all their subsequent efforts in the way of operatic reform.

Dargomizhky had one leading principle which he bequeathed to the New Russian School, and which was variously interpreted by his later followers: "I insist that the note shall be the direct expression of the word; *truth* is what I will have." This dictum, short and decided as it sounds, leaves plenty of room nevertheless for explanation and commentary and gives but a vague idea of the opera reforms that Dargomizhky may have had in his mind. One might well ask, with Pontius Pilate: "What is truth?" and, in the sequence, each of the young composers who swarmed around

Dargomizhky answered the question according to his own inclination and ability. A general systematic confession of faith on the part of the representatives of the New Russian School as to their musical and artistic aims was never drawn up, nor have we any clear, unequivocal statement of their efforts at operatic reform. Neither Stassov nor Cui, the two literary authorities of the "Powerful Coterie," ever succeeded in formulating such a statement in their writings on the subject; they hardly ever got beyond polemics, and like all polemics—especially of a revolutionary kind—their tendency was ruthlessly to pull down rather than to build up. The rest of the literary pronouncements on the subject furnish hardly anything of a positive nature; they are almost without exception passionate outbursts, arising from the enthusiasm of the moment. Amidst the uproar of a heated newspaper squabble it is impossible to raise any firm æsthetic structure for bold artistic schemes; all is uncertain, every moment discovers fresh points of view. This war, too, was waged on several fronts—small wonder if ideas became confused.

The first watchword of the New Russian School was "Down with convention!" With this battle-cry they attacked practically everything; first it was the classical school, with the sole exception of Beethoven in his later manner; then the rage for Italian music, just then at its height in Petersburg; next the followers of the despised Mendelssohn, chief among whom they reckoned, rather unfairly, Anton Rubinstein and the whole crowd of German professors in the Conservatoire; and they were soon up in arms against the new theories of Richard Wagner, which A. N. Serov was making strenuous efforts to introduce into Russia.

When it came to opera, it was naturally the Italian "season" that was the chief object of their campaign, which they waged with unrestrained fury and reckless violence. The young revolutionaries met with but scant support from the public, who either held aloof—undecided or antagonistic—

or watched with an amused air of ineffable superiority the fight against the godlike beings who, it was thought, were beyond the reach of injury, Lucca, Patti, Rubini, Tamburini, Masini—who could suppose that these would ever be dethroned?—it was a ludicrous business! And they were right; the worship of the operatic "stars" was carried to such lengths in Petersburg, and elsewhere, at that time that the public was not in the least interested in *what* was performed, but merely in the performance of individual singers. To the ears of the audience every sound that came from the throats of these leading ladies and gentlemen was pure gold —whether the coinage bore the stamp of Bellini, Donizetti, or Rossini was quite a secondary consideration. Against this state of things the New Russian School discharged the sharpest arrows of its embittered polemic in vain—all were of no avail against the top note of a Tamburini.

Though, as we have said, these brave and tireless warriors never drew up a systematic program for the reformed opera of which they dreamed, certain principles were laid down for their guidance, and these, as in Dargomizhky's demand for "truth," each of them interpreted in his own way. They started with these three fundamentals:

1. The New Russian School demands of opera, equally with the symphony, that it shall be thoroughly "musical." One of the characteristics of the school is its dread of everything vulgar and superficial.

2. What is sung on the stage must correspond exactly to the meaning of the text.

3. The forms for operatic music shall have absolutely no connexion with the forms which convention has dictated; they must spring naturally from the dramatic situation and the demands of the text.

All three propositions contain much that is both vital and judicious; it is difficult to believe that, in their time, they were regarded as the highly dangerous expression of revolutionary, even anarchical opinions. Their apparent dependence upon Richard Wagner's theories of music-drama (which were being advocated at this time, in both word and deed) makes it necessary to insist once more with special emphasis on the fact that the New Russian School's projects for operatic reform—in the late sixties of the nineteenth century—were in no way influenced by Wagner's ideas and had not the slightest connexion with them. By that time Wagner had written *Die Meistersinger*, and the *Ring* was half finished, but no musician in Petersburg, with the exception of Serov, can possibly have known of the these works. Moreover, Wagner's prose writings were equally unknown to them; only after a considerable time did his influence make itself felt in Russia, when it appears most markedly in the later operas of Rimsky-Korsakov. It is true that, thanks to the energetic advocacy of Serov, Wagner's earlier operas had not been long in reaching Russia, but with the members of the "Powerful Coterie" they had found no favour—a remarkable fact, which one is almost inclined to attribute to their violent opposition to Serov's views on music; it is difficult to explain the attitude of the Balakirev circle to Wagner's music on any other grounds.

The first performance of *Lohengrin* in Petersburg took place in the Imperial Opera-house, under K. N. Liadov, in October 1868; Dargomizhky, Balakirev, Moussorgsky, and Rimsky-Korsakov were together in a box. The last-named composer, in *My Musical Life*, refers to the occasion thus: "For our part we expressed an absolute contempt for *Lohengrin*, while Dargomizhky almost exhausted his stock of venomous humour upon it." A strange reception, truly, for the Knight of the Grail on the part of the leading champions of musical reform in Petersburg; Rimsky-Korsakov, however, has the grace to insert a mark of exclamation after this reminiscence and hastens to inform us of his own later attitude towards the question; they had failed to understand,

165

he says, that "Wagner in his wisdom was pointing the way to an artistic goal far beyond the reach of us Russian progressives." But this late recognition cannot alter the fact that *Lohengrin* on its first performance in Petersburg was rejected by just those musicians from whom one would have expected the most enthusiastic recognition. Cui even went out of his way to be offensive in his notorious article "Lohengrin, or Curiosity Punished," one of the coarsest and most brutal pamphlets to be found in the whole of Wagnerian literature.

This is all the more astonishing when we consider the "three fundamentals" quoted above. The theoretical importance as well as the practical application of these was at first greatly exaggerated. It seems to be a biological law in the world of art that the vital germ of any new artistic movement is destined to attain to its later normal healthy development only through an initial phase of boundless exaggeration; so was it here. At the very beginning, final conclusions were reached, from which, as the first blind impulse was diverted into the quieter paths of reasonable reflection, it became necessary to withdraw. The one especially destined to experience this was Moussorgsky, who alone of all the members of the "neo-Russian school" had the blood of the true revolutionary in his veins. It is characteristic of such a temperament that it shrinks from nothing and is not restrained by any enormity apparent or real; irresolution in matters of art was unknown to Moussorgsky—he would always rather take a step too many than one too few. So in this instance. His first attempt in the field of music-drama, after the unsatisfactory experiments of his youthful years, made such extravagant demands upon the resources of the dramatic art, as well as on the possibilities of music as a means of expression, that a step further would have landed him in the realm of sheer caprice, which is outside art. As soon as he realized the futility of this attempt, it must be owned, he at

166

once set to work with no uncertain hand to lay down the
limits within which his theory of music-drama, based on the
three fundamentals, was henceforth to work itself out.

The example of Dargomizhky, who, though he was no
longer very young, and suffered from severe heart-attacks,
was working with almost unnatural eagerness at his opera
The Stone Guest, had a stimulating influence on the members
of the Balakirev circle. In the year 1868 nearly all of them
were busy making sketches for operas, or actually having
them performed. Borodin had begun on *The Tsar's Bride* (a
subject suggested by Stassov and afterwards handed over
to Rimsky-Korsakov), besides being already occupied with
the idea of *Prince Igor.* Cui finished his *Ratcliff*; even Balakirev, for the first and last time in his life, was contem-
plating an opera—*Shar Ptiza* (*The Fire-bird*)—which, however, was never finished. Moussorgsky could not hold aloof.
Since the days when he was working at *Salambo,* his musical mentality, as we have seen, had taken an entirely new
direction. The songs that he had composed in the interval,
many of which had developed into short dramatic episodes,
had confirmed him and his friends in the belief that he was
really destined for a dramatic composer. The success of his
inimitable humorous songs suggested to him the propriety of
attempting something in the way of a comic opera. Glinka
had once advised Dargomizhky to write one, on a subject
taken from the life of the Russian people, a field hitherto
untouched and full of promise. Dargomizhky, unfortunately,
did not fall in with the advice, which he passed on to Moussorgsky, who caught at the idea in a manner that one would
hardly have expected. He chose as his subject Gogol's comedy *The Marriage,* and aimed apparently at producing a
companion piece to Dargomizhky's *Stone Guest.* In that
opera the composer had taken Pushkin's dramatic poem of
the same name, and set it to music without altering a single
word of the original text; in like manner Moussorgsky dealt

167

with the prose of Gogol's comedy, peculiarly unsuitable though it seemed for any such treatment; only those who know the play can estimate Moussorgsky's undertaking at its proper value.

The Marriage is one of Gogol's brilliant studies of Russian lower middle-class life, of which the immortal *Inspector* is the finest example. Gogol's chief concern was certainly with "the truth," as was Moussorgsky's, though in a different sense; while the composer aimed always at giving a faithful picture of the inner life, Gogol's chief concern was to describe incidents and outward appearance with the greatest possible accuracy. "Don't blame the looking-glass if your mouth is crooked!" was the motto he chose for his *Inspector*. "The spirit of drollery," he said once to a friend, "lurks all around us, only we do not perceive it just because we stand in the middle; but when the artist shows it to us on the stage, we all rock with laughter and are amazed that we never noticed it ourselves." It is this all-pervading spirit of drollery that he extracts from the everyday happenings in the two-act comedy *The Marriage*. Podkoléssin is a clerk in a government office who has worked his way up to the position of head of a department, with the title of Government Councillor—a perfect specimen of the official mind, petty, narrow, and stupid, such as only the endless monotony of a government office can produce. This is how his friend Kotchkarev speaks of him: "Heavens, do you call that a man? He's an old stick, a caricature, a bad joke in human shape!" Podkoléssin decides to give up the single life and marry. The only persons to whom he confides his intentions are his servant Stepan—a rude, uncouth boor, quite incapable of understanding his master's ideas on the subject of gallantry, and seeing nothing funny in the whole affair—and a female matrimonial agent who, as is common with those of her calling, has a tongue that is never still. Podkoléssin puts the patience of both to a severe test by always drawing back at the decisive moment, when the matchmaker—in other respects a quite respectable specimen of the lower-class Russian bourgeoisie of the period—thinks she is sure of him. Suddenly the situation takes an unexpected turn; Kotchkarev, his giddy friend, who owes his own rather dubious married happiness to the same go-between, surprises Podkoléssin in a conversation with the worthy dame. He takes in the situation at a glance and resolves to avenge himself for his own unlucky match by filching the business out of the agent's hands. Without saying a word he matures his plan of action. After he has cleverly extracted the name and address of the rich heiress who is proposed as a partner for his friend—the elegant Anna Tikhonovna Kuperdiagina, daughter of a former merchant "of the Third Guild"—he bows the old woman out of the room. As soon as she is safely disposed of—no easy task —he takes his friend in hand and pictures to him the joys of marriage and family life in such glowing and attractive colours, and insists so artfully that there is no time to be lost, that Podkoléssin, moved partly by flattery, partly by fear of losing the prize, calls for his best clothes, which with Stepan's help he manages to get into, after a long tussel with a tight collar, and lets himself be dragged out of the room to wait on the excellent young woman, whose father was a merchant "of the Third Guild." . . .

This is as far as Moussorgsky got with his composition. The humour of the four scenes lies not so much in the situation as in the behaviour of the four characters, who are drawn by Gogol in masterly fashion. It is true, one is inclined to ask oneself at first with some misgivings what this has to do with music. Patience! We shall soon see! In this "attempt at a music-drama in prose," Moussorgsky aimed at nothing less than the creation of a new style of musical comedy—not "comic opera" or operetta (the sort of thing in which almost everything is comic but the music), but a perfect blending of all the comic elements present in action,

169

words, gesture, way of speaking, etc., with the music itself, which, as a contributor to the general effect, was to be considered exactly on a par with all the other factors. The result was not to be obtained by the employment of mere comic devices, such as eccentricity of melody or harmony, absurd orchestral effects, and so forth—such things are not to be found in *The Marriage*, with rare exceptions; Moussorgsky was far too fine a musician to try to work out a new stylistic system by any such primitive means; he was only too well aware how dangerous they are, and he used them only with the greatest caution. He knew that, in this case as in others, where the intention is perpetually in evidence, it has an irritating effect that ends by disgusting the hearer.

As to the stylistic principles by which he was guided in the composition of *The Marriage*, he explains himself in unmistakable terms in a letter to César Cui, with whom he was still at that time on terms of friendship. He writes from Shilovo, the little country-house, which was still (1868) in his brother's possession, and where Moussorgsky was passing the summer (the letter is dated July 3):

"Good-morning, my dear Cesare! Here I am, out at grass. I eat nothing but green stuff, *en forme et matière*; I live in a peasant's hut, drink milk, and am out of doors all day long—only at nightfall they drive me back to my stall.

"On the day I came away—I was vexed at not having seen you again—I finished the first scene of *The Marriage*. There are three scenes in Act I, the first with Stepan, the second with the marriage-broker, the third with Kotchkarev. I have noted down your remarks, as well as Dargomizhky's, and have profited by them. I have considerably simplified the part I showed you. I have had a very happy idea for Podkoléssin's orchestral motif, which I shall be able to use again to the best advantage in the scene of the wooing. Dargomizhky seems to like it very well. The motif makes its first appearance while he is talking with Stepan, at the words:

'Well, and did he not ask?'—in short, while they are dis-
cussing the wedding. One sees at once that it is a fragment
of a theme, which will be heard for the first time in its en-
tirety in the scene of the wooing, when Podkoléssin has really
made up his mind to marry. It goes very well with Podkoléssin's stupid show of embarrassment. In the first scene I have
invented quite an ingenious dodge for throwing light on
Stepan's character; after his master has called him for the
third time, he comes on in an angry mood, though naturally
he tries not to show it, but when Podkoléssin begins again:
'I just wanted to ask you, my good fellow . . . ' he calls
out: 'The old girl is here!' at the top of his voice, in order to put an end to his master's tedious questions. I have
just finished my sketch for the second scene, for the old go-
between—some of it is not bad. The whole scene, I think, will
be amusing; one of the successes is just at the end, where
Podokoléssin gets so absurdly upset about his 'grey hair.'
Now I am turning my attention to Kotchkarev. I mean Act
I to be looked upon as an attempt at '*opéra dialogué*.' I
should like to get it finished by the beginning of the winter;
then we shall be able to lick it into shape. *Kotchkarev sera
fait spécialement pour vous, mon cher.* Tell your wife that
the scene with Thekla has come out all right—she will be
glad of that; I am so grateful for the interest she takes in
my extraordinarily cheeky experiment.

"Contrary to my custom, I have to content myself with
leaving a good deal of it in the rough, as I have no piano
here; as soon as I get to Petersburg, I shall work up my
sketches. In my '*opéra dialogué*' I endeavour, as far as possible, to show up very clearly the slight changes in intonation that occur in the course of conversation apparently for
the most trivial reasons and in the least important words.
It is here, it seems to me, that a good deal of Gogol's humour lurks; e.g., in the scene for Stepan, where his amiable
tone changes into something different, after his master has

worked him up to a white heat over the affair of the boot-pol-
ish. In the scene for Thekla, there are plenty of instances—
with her it is only a step from chatter about her own self-
importance to actual rudeness, or unbridled abuse. However,
when you have my music in front of you, all this will be made
clearer.

"July 10. I was prevented from sending this letter off,
and I am glad of it. I have now finished Act I! It rained for
three days without a break—I worked all the time without
stopping, so you may say the weather and I got busy together. For my part, *The Marriage* would not leave me in
peace. I had to go on writing, and I did so! Now the weather
is fine again and I can take a rest. Instead of three scenes,
there are now four—it had to be so. My love to you, and to
Dargomizhky when you see him!"

As to the artistic views expressed in this letter, no comment is needed; its meaning is unmistakable. We learn from
it that the stylistic principle, on which he laid the greatest
stress, was the faithful reproduction in music of the natural
modulations of the human voice in ordinary conversation.
Under these conditions considerations of musical æsthetics
must naturally be subordinate; and, as matter of fact, in this
particular work Moussorgsky disregards them almost completely. In so doing he acted in conscious opposition to the
opinion of Balakirev, and it is sigificant that in any questions connected with his "extraordinarily cheeky" undertaking he turns exclusively to Dargomizhky and César Cui.
He dared not approach Balakirev on the subject—the composer looked askance on what he considered Moussorgsky's
mad idea; into this new and tangled region in the realms of
art he could not follow him. That Moussorgsky, however,
as every true artist should be, was for a time completely obsessed by his subject is plainly shown in the P. S. to the
letter given above. As Flaubert somewhere remarks: *"Ce n'est*

172

pas nous qui choisissons les sujets, ce sont les sujets qui s'imposent à nous."

Another letter to Cui, dated August 15, 1868, is no less interesting. Take, for instance, the following:

"I am now engaged in arranging what I have written, and keep drumming it into my head, so that I may be able to play it over to you, though to fix a thing in the memory without the aid of an instrument is for me more difficult than composing it. . . . I am still resting after Act I, though I am thinking over Act II and making a mental plan of it; I have so far written nothing down. I feel it must wait a little until I have succeeded in making the character of the merchant at the beginning of the act, and also Shevakin and Yaitchnitza [two other candidates for matrimony, who make their appearance in the house of the tradesman's daughter], just as comic, musically, as Thekla and Kotchkarev. Many plans are shaping in my brain—but how true is the saying: 'The farther into the forest, the more wood there is!' But what a fine and whimsical fancy Gogol has!

"Since I have been here, I have been studying the peasants and their womenfolk once more. There is a lad here with the eyes of an eagle, who looks like Antony in Shakspere's *Julius Cæsar*, when he makes his oration in the Forum over the body of Cæsar—a clever fellow, and artful as they make them! All these good people will be of the greatest assistance to me, particularly the female types—a real treasure trove!

"It is my invariable practice to take note of the right people for my purpose, and then to draw them out, as opportunity offers—that is how I get my artistic impressions —and it amuses me. So that, my dear César, is how I am spending my time just now."

This letter is important as showing that even after finishing the first act of *The Marriage* Moussorgsky fully intended to complete the work and had actually sketched out a part of Act II, though only in his head. It is certainly not true, as some spiteful critics have maintained, that he voluntarily dropped the work because he was disappointed with the results of his *"opéra dialogué"* methods. His reasons for dropping it, as we shall soon see, were very different—so true is it that "The farther into the forest, the more wood there is!"

Act II of Gogol's comedy (i.e., the second half of Moussorgsky's Act I, after the change of scene) and Moussorgsky's second act (for he set only the first half of Act I) are played in the house of the beauty who is bent on marrying. Anna Tikhonovna and her worthy aunt are receiving a whole crowd of suitors, among whom are the two mentioned by Moussorgsky in his letter—Shevakin (the Muncher) and Vaitchnitza (Scrambled Eggs) ; the scenes that follow give full scope for the play of Gogol's wit and humour. Kotchkarev, with his unceasing patter, manages to raise Podkoléssin (who sits dumb and paralysed with nervousness) to the position of first favourite in the lady's eyes; he then by his powers of persuasion works his friend up to such a pitch that he is ready to consent to get married as soon as a priest can be found and the wedding-breakfast prepared. While the bride and her aunt are dressing, and the old go-between sits sentry at the door, Podkoléssin, who suddenly realizes the abyss that yawns beneath him, calls a passing droshky, jumps, in an agony of terror, out of the window, and flies back home to the safe keeping of Stepan, leaving hat, overcoat, and galoshes behind him.

Podkoléssin's attitude towards matrimony may possibly have struck an answering chord in Moussorgsky's own soul—this may have been a reason for his chosing this particular theme. For the marriage tie he had an incomprehensible, almost morbid, dislike. Mme L. I. Shestakova tells us in her recollections of Moussorgsky: "Many people tried to persuade him to marry, but his horror at the idea was almost a disease. He would often say to me: 'When you read in

174

the papers that I have put a bullet through my head or hanged myself, you may be certain that I was married the day before.'"

One must always regret that Moussorgsky did not bring his work to a conclusion; had *The Marriage* been completed, there is no question that it would have a very different place in the history of opera from what the unfinished and little-known production now occupies. So long as his interest in the subject, and consequently the holy joy of the creative artist, were alive in him, he worked at *The Marriage* with unusual rapidity, and had not his enthusiasm flagged, it would not have taken him long to finish it. It took him a month, all but three days (June 11 to July 8, 1868), to compose the first act—the dates are given in the manuscript with that scrupulous accuracy which was characteristic of the composer. The piano arrangement occupies sixty-four pages. Although this work was never completed, he undoubtedly derived great benefit from it; the perfectly natural and expressive recitative that we find in *Boris* and *Khovanstchina* could hardly have been possible without the previous training he had had in *The Marriage*. A more perfect fusion of word and tone than that achieved by Moussorgsky in his "musical prose," which contains long passages of ordinary conversation, cannot be imagined—there is no turn of meaning, no shade of feeling, no fleeting mood, no mimic gesture, no emotional or psychical incident that Moussorgsky does not translate into music. It is true it needs a fine ear to appreciate the connexion everywhere; otherwise the work might seem to be mere trifling, devoid of any real musical substance.

His work on *The Marriage* served to enrich Moussorgsky's musical equipment by some of the most delicate means of expression; it taught him, further, to listen with the greatest care to the intonations of human speech, and to reproduce them under the simple form of recitative. Almost always the speech of each one of the characters is marked by

175

individual touches, finely observed; only very occasionally in *The Marriage* do we find a recitative that has a certain impersonal ring, a thing for which you will look in vain in *Boris* or *Khovanstchina*.

The translation of human speech into a definite sequence of musical sounds became for a time almost an obsession with Moussorgsky. In a letter to Rimsky-Korsakov we have his own confession: "Whenever I hear people speaking, no matter who it is or what they say, my brain immediately sets to work to translate what I have heard into music." The results of the faculty thus acquired of transmuting ordinary speech into musical forms are seen in the wonderful recitatives of *Boris* and *Khovanstchina*, though in these two music-dramas the effect obtained is of course far more profound than in *The Marriage*, on account of the tragic pathos of their emotional incidents. For Gogol's play, despite many clever touches in the characterization, is just a humorous piece of an almost farcical quality; in the shallow course of its narrative the depths of human feeling are naturally never disturbed. The incidents as seen on the stage are amusing, but in themselves are without interest, since they merely float on the surface of psychological experience. But even common things, in the hands of a true artist, may be transmuted into something uncommon.

When Moussorgsky returned to Petersburg in the autumn of 1868, his new work naturally created no little excitement. Rimsky-Korsakov in *My Musical Life* tells us: "*The Marriage* excited enormous interest; all were amazed at the task Moussorgsky had undertaken, admired his talent for characterization, and were struck by some of his chords and harmonic progressions. The composer himself sang the part of Podkoléssin in his own inimitable way, Alexandra Purgold sang Thekla, Veliaminov was Stepan, Nadeshda Purgold accompanied at the piano, and Dargomizhky, who was keenly interested, copied out the part of Kotchkarev practically single-handed and sang it with enthusiasm. Everybody was especially amused by the dialogue between Thekla and Kotchkarev, with its extremely characteristic accompaniment."

Of course no public performance of the unfinished musical comedy was given in the composer's lifetime. The original manuscript, the existence of which was known to very few, lay in the Petersburg Public Library for more than a quarter of a century after his death; its subsequent fate will be related in the last chapter of this book. This manuscript, together with many others of Moussorgsky's, was presented to the library by V. Stassov, in whose possession it had been since 1875. So long as Stassov and Rimsky-Korsakov were alive, it was not accessible to the public, in accordance with a rather obscure condition attached by Stassov to his bequest. Moussorgsky had sent him the manuscript of *The Marriage* on Stassov's birthday (January 2, 1873) with the following letter: "To Volodimer [Vladimir] Vassilievitch Stassov, greetings and homage from Moussorianin. No one has felt more deeply for all my troubles and afflictions than you; no one has explored my inner nature with a truer understanding, none has shown me more clearly the way I ought to go. You know how dear you are to me—I, too, feel that I am dear to you. If we succeed in our common efforts to make live music for living people which they can understand, even though the others, who merely vegetate, pelt us with big lumps of mud, and the musical Pharisees would have us crucified—we will still work on, and with all the greater energy as the lumps of mud get bigger and the cries of our persecutors grow even louder. And indeed the trial will soon arrive! [The reference is to the first performance of *Boris Godounov*, which was just coming on.] It is a comfort to reflect that while we are standing in the pillory, waiting for the verdict on *Boris*, our thoughts are already busy with *Khovanstchina*. Serenely, boldly even, may we look into the distant

177

musical future; it calls us, lures us on—no human judgment can affright us. They will tell us: 'You have trampled all laws, human and divine, under foot!' We shall answer: 'We have!' and think to ourselves: 'Ah, if you only knew what is coming!' I can hear their croaking voices: 'You will be forgotten—and for all time!' Our answer shall be: *'Non, non, et non, Madame!'* In fact, our stock of audacity will suffice for any number of judges!

"This is your birthday, Generalissimo, and I am thinking of you all the time—this is only natural; naturally, too, the thought arises: 'What can I do to please so dear a friend?' Without the least hesitation I answer, like any presumptuous youth: 'By giving him myself!' Take, then, this offspring of my early years, Gogol's *Marriage*—examine this attempt at a new kind of speech in music, compare it with *Boris,* contrast the year 1868 with 1871, and you will see that I give you a piece of myself that can never be given again. I have included the copy made by Dargomizhky [Dargomizhky died on January 5, 1869] of the part of Kotchkarev—a precious witness to all that Dargomizhky was to us in those last days; though he was very ill at the time, and busy working on his *Stone Guest,* he copied out this part.

"I hate to fish in muddy waters, and I am convinced that anyone who thinks it worth while to look into *The Marriage* will have his eyes opened as to the question of my musical audacity. You know how great the value I myself put on this work of mine, so I must now tell you the truth—both Dargomizhky and Cui suggested the idea to me, the one in jest, the other in earnest. I have noted the date of composition, the place, and how long it took me—in short, everything is in order, and nothing kept back. Take me then, my dear friend, and do with me what you will.

"With reference to the *'Non, non, et nón, Madame!'*—Once during a terminal examination at the Smolna Institute for young ladies of noble birth, the Empress Marie

Feodorovna was talking with the head girl, a Princess Volkonsky, and happened to make some blunder in history, whereupon the girl interrupted: '*Non, Madame!*' The Empress rebuked her: 'You must not say no to me, my child!' The Princess at once replied: '*Non, non, et non, Madame!*'—Moussorianin."

This letter, written five years after Act I of *The Marriage* was finished, at the time when the composer was working on *Khovanstchina*, is another proof of the high value he set on this "attempt at speech in music," while the dedication to his dearest friend is further confirmation.

We see, then, that it was not staleness nor disillusion nor dissatisfaction with his work that kept him from bringing it to a conclusion. He put *The Marriage* aside merely because he had become so obsessed by another subject for an opera that for a time nothing else had the slightest interest for him.

This new thing was Pushkin's *Boris Godounov*, the unlucky offspring of the great Russian poet. V. V. Nikolsky, professor of Russian history in the Alexander Lyceum at Petersburg, whom we already know as the recipient of one of the ten complimentary copies of "The Seminarist," had drawn Moussorgsky's attention to this extraordinarily promising subject, so full of historical and psychological interest, at a musical evening at Mme Shestakova's. From that moment, as Stassov tells us, the idea of making an opera out of Pushkin's dramatic material took such complete possession of him that he could think of nothing else. He set to work with feverish haste; it took him less than two months to write the first act, and in one short year the entire opera was ready in pianoforte score; this is the more remarkable when we consider that he had to lay out the scenario and write the greater part of the text himself. To Cui, who also had written the libretto to his own opera *Ratcliff*, he writes as follows: "Well, my dear Cesare, *comment cela va-t-il avec la versification?* Bravo! Bravo! We are indeed a heaven-inspired 'coterie,' to my thinking! If we can't find a text to suit us, we just patch one together for ourselves, plain and honest—and it doesn't turn out so badly, either!"

Happy the creative artist who finds a theme on which he can lavish all that is greatest and most profound in his nature, and so soar to the farthest heights of inspiration! To Moussorgsky this happiness was granted in the two operatic subjects on which he was now to embark, *Boris* and *Khovanstchina.*

VII

B O R I S   G O D O U N O V

1868 − 73

THE YEARS Moussorgsky spent on *Boris Godounov*—as we may rightly call the time from the autumn of 1868 to the spring of 1874—were undoubtedly the happiest of his life. His letters of that period express a firm belief in his artistic mission and the magnitude of his own creative powers, together with an unshakable confidence in his methods of procedure, such as he had not previously known. We have seen something of this at the end of the last chapter. Such absolute certainty brings with it perhaps the intensest happiness of which the creative artist is capable, and is a sure protection against all the petty vexations and misunderstandings of this life. Moreover, the first half of this *Boris* period brought an advantageous change in Moussorgsky's worldly circumstances.

In the autumn of 1868 his brother Filaret, with whom he had been living, was obliged to give up his Petersburg residence and retire into the country. Not only was his financial position getting worse from year to year, but there are signs that the relations between the two brothers were becoming strained. The reasons for this were most probably material; Filaret seems to have been both unskilful and unfortunate in his management of what was left of the Moussorgsky property; in fact he soon afterwards lost all he had. His two small estates of Minkino and Shilovo, where his brother Modest had been visited by so many of his finest inspirations, had to be sold by auction without reserve, and

Filaret turned his attention to theatrical management, though with little success.

However, "Nothing so bad but has its better side," as the Russian proverb says. His brother's departure made it necessary for Moussorgsky to look for another lodging, and this problem found the happiest possible solution. The Opotchinins, who, with Mme Shestakova, were probably Moussorgsky's closest friends, after Stassov, proposed that he should live with them. Moussorgsky, who was bound to Vladimir Opotchinin by ties of sincere friendship, and to his sister Nadeshda by some probably deeper feeling, naturally did not hesitate to accept; he took up his quarters in the so-called Engineers' Palace in Petersburg, where Opotchinin had a roomy official residence. By the irony of fate, just at this time, owing to some official alteration, his work in the Engineering Department came to an end and he had to look out for new employment, since he could not afford the withdrawal of sixty to eighty roubles from his slender monthly salary. His new post was in the Department of Woods and Forests for the Crown-lands. He seems to have suffered severely under this drudgery for some time; in his letters we find frequent complaints of the "dreadful fatigue" he experienced. In the archives of the department there was found a heap of about twenty bundles of documents drawn up by Moussorgsky in his fine, regular handwriting; these are all written in the correct, leisurely, official style and betray no sign of the feverish ferment of creative activity that was working in him at the time. Although they are quite devoid of biographical interest, they serve merely to show that Moussorgsky's official duties were by no means a sinecure and that his complaints of a senseless occupation that wasted so much of his time and strength were fully justified. It is difficult, of course, to estimate the precise value of Moussorgsky's clerical work; his chief, apparently, to judge from the marginal remarks on the occasion of Moussorgsky's resignation, already quoted, had no great opinion of his ability; but there can be no doubt that the composer of *Boris* might have been better employed than in such soul-destroying routine work, in which, as he expresses it, he was "continually engaged in making it hot for dishonest keepers or lazy foresters."

The efforts of Moussorgsky's friends have preserved for us these documents in his handwriting, which ordinarily would have been destroyed, and they are on show in the archives of the Ministry for Agriculture, a tardy act of homage on the part of the authorities to the inspired Civil Servant.

Every minute of his spare time Moussorgsky devoted to his *Boris*. "Diligent," says Stassov, "is not the word—he was simply indefatigable." He worked day and night. Yet in spite of this extraordinary activity *Boris Godounov* was not the result of a single effort; its form underwent many changes at its creator's hands, to say nothing of the subsequent revisions in which the composer had no share.

The foundation for the incidents of the opera was taken, as we know, from Pushkin's drama of the same name, although the original title chosen by the poet was: *The Dramatic Story of the Misfortunes of the Realm of Muscovy, the Tsar Boris, and Grishka Otrepiev.* Pushkin's "dramatic story" was taken from Karamzin's *History of the Russian Empire*, in the tenth volume of which the poet found all the materials for his tragedy.

Godounov, as portrayed by Karamzin's powerful pen, becomes a sort of Russian Macbeth; thanks to the protection of Ivan the Terrible, in whose court he grew up, he attained to high honours and actually became connected with the ruling family, through his sister Irene, who became the bride of the Tsarevitch Feodor. Cunning, clever, and treacherous, Boris Godounov now rose rapidly to power; when the weak-minded, priest-ridden Feodor came to the throne, it was Boris who actually ruled—only the crown was wanting. In order to obtain this he contrived the murder of Feodor's young step-brother, Dmitri, the last legitimate offspring of the reigning house. Boris played his cards well, but when the crown, the "Cap of Monomakh," [1] was actually offered him by the leading statesmen, he sorely tried their patience by his pretended refusals before he finally decided to become the successor of Feodor. As Pushkin makes Prince Shouisky remark:

> He shrinks and hesitates with lowering brow,
> Like some sly toper at the proffered cup.

At last he yielded. His reign lasted for seven years, from 1598 to 1605. He was a wise ruler, as became a pupil of Ivan; but, like him, he was the victim of misfortune. Plague, famine, fire, disasters, broke out in all parts of the country; the people grumbled, though Boris did all that was possible to win their favour. Then came a rumour—none knew how it arose—that Dmitri was still alive, in another country, and would soon appear in Moscow, to wrest the crown from the usurping Boris.

In 1604 the south-western frontiers of Russia were invaded by a host of Polish mercenaries, Cossacks, and Russian deserters, led by Grishka Otrepiev, a runaway novice from the Tchudov Monastery, who claimed to be the young Dmitri. At first the Russian generals repulsed him, but Boris succumbed to the tortures of a guilty conscience, and his death put an end to the struggle. The Russian army acknowledged the claims of Grishka Otrepiev, proclaimed him as Dmitri, and returned with him to Moscow. Boris's son Feodor was murdered and his daughter Xenia dishonoured by the victorious Grishka, who then ascended the throne, only to be slain himself the following year by the mutinous populace. "Thus," says Karamzin, "did the crime of Godou-

---

[1] Vladimir Monomachus (the fighter in single combat) was Grand Duke of Kiev and head of the Russian princes, 1113–25.

nov bring down vengeance on himself, his children, and his
country," for with his death began for Russia those seven
apocalyptic years known as "the time of trouble," during
which the realm was laid waste, plundered, torn in pieces, by
civil rebellion no less than by foreign invaders, until in the
winter of 1613 a new ruler, Michael Romanov, was elected by
general agreement.

It is a big subject and an attractive one—though it
must be confessed that Karamzin's account is not historically
accurate in detail—that Pushkin chose for dramatic treatment. He has handled it in the Shaksperian manner, and in
places with something of Shakspere's vigour, but without
that mighty plastic force which characterizes the great Eng-
lishman. Pushkin's *Boris* is merely a kaleidoscopic series of
historical pictures, but each scene convinces by its combined
simplicity and truth, and the whole is lit up by the poet's
evident sympathy with his subject. No wonder that Moussorgsky was carried away by it—Pushkin's characters are
exactly to his liking; no mere conventional types of villainy,
ambition, treachery, such as the subject might easily have
suggested, but clearly cut portraits of individuals, people of
flesh and blood, as various as we find in life itself. Just as to
Moussorgsky, on his first visit to Moscow, was vouchsafed a
true vision of antiquity, so Pushkin has brought an extraordinarily keen historic sense to bear on the events of several
hundred years ago. Take, for instance, the admirable scene
in the monk's cell, where Pimen, while compiling his annals,
soliloquizes on the world, on men and women, and on the task
in which he is engaged; or the scene in the tavern on the
Lithuanian frontier, or with the crowd in the streets of Moscow; these have no predecessor in literature—they are altogether original. It is precisely this ability to grasp and reproduce the spirit of a former age, rather than the actual
construction of the piece, that constitutes the greatness of
Pushkin's *Godounov*.

Moussorgsky was quick to see that Pushkin's dramatic story, with all its incomparable merits, would not be sufficient in itself for a libretto; he turned, in consequence, to the original sources and plunged eagerly into historical research, with the assistance of Stassov, who was at that time librarian in the Petersburg Public Library. Stassov, indeed, became his most devoted helper, ready to lend him every kind of assistance; he found him the words of the folk-songs, and dug out suggestions for scenery and properties, down to the minutest details, from the notes to Karamzin's *History of the Russian Empire*. Here, for instance, they got the information that parrots were first introduced into Russia in the reign of Boris, and found a reference to the big chiming clock, with its procession of mechanical figures. Here too they met with the Jesuits Tchernikovsky and Lavitzky, for whom Stassov, at Moussorgsky's request, had to find cries of terror in Latin, containing as many *i*'s and *u*'s as possible —a proof of the composer's critical ear for the value of spoken sounds. All these details were introduced, for the most part with remarkable success, in Moussorgsky's arrangement of the Godounov story. For the Jesuits Stassov suggested the Latin ejaculation: "*Salve, sanctissima virgo, juva servos tuos*," which was well suited to the situation. The text of the famous song "Hear, now, what happened in the town of Kazan" Stassov took from a "collection of ancient Russian songs"; he tells how he brought his lucky find with him to a concert of the Musical Free School, and how Moussorgsky pounced upon them and broke out into expressions of admiration even while the music was going on. The text of the great chorus of the people's rising in Act IV: "Loosed and freed from all their fetters, see the people march along," is an old Russian "robber-song," which Stassov discovered in a collection belonging to a friend. Three of the most charming numbers in the score of *Boris*, which appeared first in the second version, were written to words taken from another of Stassov's finds—a collection, by Schein, of Russian songs for children. They are the Hostess's song: "I have caught a drake," and the two singing-games for the Tsarevitch and the nurse—the rhyme of "The Gnat and the Bug," and the hand-clapping game.

As regards the music of *Boris*, the largest and by far the most important part of it is the work of the composer's own unfettered imagination; genuine folk-tunes are very seldom employed, and then only *en passant*—e.g., in the great chorus in praise of Boris, in the scene in the Kremlin, or in Varlaam's second song: "There was a man." The theme of the seditious sermon from the two begging "friars," Varlaam and Missail, in the last act: "Sun and moon will lose their light," is an example of that kind of folk-song, which is the work not of many hands, but of one individual; Moussorgsky had it from a strolling minstrel named Riabinin, a peasant from the Government of Olonetz, whom he had heard in Petersburg in the autumn of 1868, at a meeting of the Russian Geographical Society. There is a whole class of melodies, or melodic turns and phrases, which are so redolent of the genuine folk-song that on a first hearing one might easily take them for originals, did one not know that they are not so—witness the chorales during the scene in the cell, and also in Boris's death scene. Here again we see what good use Moussorgsky made of the musical knowledge he had acquired from Father Krupsky. The songs, on the other hand, are not very convincing—they lack the genuine ring. The fact that the musical sources of some of the episodes in *Boris* are to be found in earlier compositions of Moussorgsky, especially the unfinished opera *Salambo*, has been mentioned in our account of the last-named.

Of his work on *Boris* Moussorgsky tells how it "went on boiling and bubbling" under his hands. The way in which he approached the task showed plainly that he was marked out for a dramatic composer—he united in himself the objectivity and the subjectivity of the creative artist in the highest degree, a rare combination, and a sure sign of a born dramatist. "While I was writing *Boris*," he says in a letter to Stassov (July 15, 1872), "I *was* Boris." Yet this strangely marked subjectivity (which he shared in common with Goethe and Shakspere), this extraordinarily keen sympathy that enabled him to enter into the very soul of his various creations and to identify himself with each in turn, in no way prevented Moussorgsky from employing his unusually quick powers of observation as a sort of brake in the process of composition. Just because he regarded the world of actuality as a stage, he was able to turn the stage into an actual living world. In a letter to Stassov (September 6, 1871) we have the following characteristic passage: "Never have I felt more strongly than I do now that for creative work the one great necessity is peace; concentration is possible only when one shuts oneself up in one's cell and contemplates the world and the people in it as they really are." The world thus seen "through the temperament of an artist" like Moussorgsky is of itself transformed to a work of art of the highest order.

Moussorgsky's letters to Stassov at this time give a most lively picture of the way in which *Boris* was written; unfortunately, only a few have survived, and these lose much of their lively colouring in the process of translation. As a correspondent Moussorgsky always seems to be wearing a mask; one has the feeling that a certain bashfulness prevents him from exposing his thoughts and feelings to the eyes of others; but with his mask on, he speaks with greater assurance, realizing that much may be said from behind a mask which without one would be impossible. One of his favourite disguises when writing letters—especially those dealing with one of his great historical works, *Boris* or *Khovanstchina*— is that of a learned deacon of the seventeenth or eighteenth century. His zealous researches into the monastic chronicles enabled him to reproduce their quaint, often difficult, but

188

always pithy style without the slightest effort. Translated into the smooth language of today, these letters naturally lose the roughness so characteristic of the originals; nevertheless we give a few specimens that by their contents no less than their form may throw some light on the writer's individuality.

In a letter dated September 11, 1871 he writes: "We have the honour to inform your Grace that we have decided to amputate on Pimen, and have also to set Grishka's legs [he means, of course, he has recast the music]. The Corsican Admiral [Rimsky-Korsakov] is of opinion that the music has now quite a noble ring and is a worthy offspring of our genius. We are also considering some new touches of impudent rascality that are highly diverting." This refers, of course, to the musical elaboration introduced into the scene in the tavern, with the object of rendering the figures of the two vagabond friars as convincing as possible.

The following occurs in a letter of a slightly earlier date (August 10, 1871): "I have much to impart to your Grace concerning the business in hand, and am burning with impatience to see you with my own eyes and torture your ears with my horrid croaking voice. The villainous Tsar Boris has now an *arioso*; in the opinion of several musicians —including the Knight of the Stormy Ocean, whom your Grace laudably raised to the rank of Admiral—the said villainous *arioso* is not amiss, and tickles the ear agreeably. The words have been stitched together by my own exalted self. And since to watch and listen to the remorseful outburst of a villain for any length of time is both disgusting and depressing, a crowd of nursery-maids suddenly break into the room shrieking out some unintelligible gabble; the Tsar drives them out and sends his son to inquire what makes the women howl. In the boy's absence Prince Shouisky enters and whispers some secret information in Boris's ear. After he has been got rid of, the Tsarevitch returns, and the Tsar questions him. . . . " Then follows the charming narration

189

of the parrot incident, the words of which are Moussorgsky's own. In the letter just referred to he remarks that this is the seventh occasion on which he has celebrated some "beast" or other in song, at Stassov's instigation; the others being (1) a magpie, (2) a billy-goat, (3) a beetle, (4) a drake, (5) a gnat and a bug, (6) an owl and a sparrow. The letter goes on: "The Tsarevitch's prattle stands out so nicely against the accompaniment that the said musicians pricked their ears up all the time, in order to lose nothing of the pretty music."

The first version, the foundation of the opera—the "original *Boris*," as it is called—was completed and fully scored in the summer of 1870. It differs widely from the work in its present form, consisting of the following seven scenes:

1. The scene in the Tchudov Monastery, ending, however, not with the chorus of blind pilgrims, but with an order from the Boyars to the people (through the mouth of the Pristav) to present themselves the next day at the Kremlin, to which they reply that if the order is to howl, they can howl in the Kremlin as well as anywhere else.

2. The coronation scene, which has remained unaltered so far as Moussorgsky is concerned.

3. The scene in the monk's cell; in its original form it contains the narrative of the murder of Dmitri, in Pushkin's text.

4. The scene in the tavern, just as we have it, except for the later addition of the song about the drake.

5. The scene in the Tsar's apartments (the Terem), considerably altered in later versions.

6. The scene in the Red Square in front of the Cathedral in Moscow. This is one of the few scenes in which the composer keeps closely to Pushkin's text. Later, probably feeling that it bore too great a resemblance to the coronation scene in the prologue, he made several cuts, thereby

sacrificing much good music; at the same time he transferred the incident of the idiot (with slight alterations) to the forest scene near Kromy.

7. The Boyars' Duma and the death of Boris, which remain practically unaltered.

This, then, was the form in which Moussorgsky submitted his work to the advisory committee of the Marie Theatre, and now his troubles began. Gedeonov, the director of the Imperial theatres, seems originally to have been not ill-disposed towards the work; in Moussorgsky's letters of that time to Rimsky-Korsakov and the Purgold sisters he says in one place that Gedeonov had shown himself "severe, but just," and in another that it was proposed that he should be invited to play over his work to the advisory committee. The subsequent fate of the score is graphically described in Rimsky-Korsakov's *My Musical Life*.

"During the season (1869–70) Moussorgsky had finished his *Boris Godounov* and submitted it to the management of the Imperial theatres. The advisory committee, consisting of Napravnik, conductor of the opera, Manjean and Bötz, directors of French and German plays, together with the bass-viol player, Ferrero (notice the international combination: a Russian, a Frenchman, a German, and an Italian), rejected the work—the novelty and strangeness of the music was too much for them. Among other objections put forward was the absence of any leading female role. . . . Some of the committee's objections were ludicrous—for instance, the double-bass waxed furious over the *contrabassi divisi* that accompany Varlaam's second song, with a sequence of chromatic thirds; in fact he could never forgive the composer for such an unheard-of piece of audacity."

Hurt and indignant, Moussorgsky withdrew his score; he might possibly have found some consolation in the thought that Pushkin had hesitated for more than six years before publishing his *Godounov* and that, after all, it was a complete failure; it was many years before it found its way on to the stage. It is not unreasonable to maintain that Moussorgsky's rearrangement, together with his music, were necessary to make Pushkin's drama a stage success. The public for a long time took offence at the apparent dryness—the objectivity, one might say—of the poet's historical conception, while the critics, as might be expected, complained of the want of clearness in the arrangement, and its disregard for the usual rules and formulas. Forty years later Moussorgsky had to encounter precisely the same charges. In Pushkin's case, too, professional criticism, already prejudiced against the poet, failed to observe that this work contained the first perfect description of the life of old Russia; a similar claim may be made for Moussorgsky's music, but it was many decades before this fact obtained triumphant recognition for both works.

Moussorgsky did not remain long in dejection; he soon quieted down, especially when he found that Stassov and his other friends shared the views of the committee on many points. He at once resolved to make a thorough revision of his score; fortunately the creative fever still possessed him, and he set to work without delay. On the 18th of April 1871 we find him writing to Stassov: "I am just finishing the Polish scene—the Jesuit gave me no rest for two nights running. That is as it should be; I mean, that is the way I like to compose." The "Jesuit" refers to Rangoni, an episodical character of Moussorgsky's own invention, woven with considerable poetic and dramatic skill into the action.

The further progress of the work can be traced step by step by the dates that Moussorgsky, as was his custom, has inserted in the original score. The second version of *Boris* was finished on July 23, 1872. It differs from the first in the following details:

1. In the scene in the cell the effective choruses of monks in the distance have been added.

2. In the tavern scene (on the Lithuanian frontier) the Hostess's song about the drake is new—it brings the character into higher relief and raises it almost to the dignity of a role.

3. The scene in the Terem has been substantially altered—we may say that not one stone has been left upon another—i.e., no two bars have been left in their original relation. Entirely new are the story of the gnat and the bug, the hand-clapping game, Boris's second *arioso*, the episode of the parrot, Shouisky's greeting ("O orator of high renown"), and the introduction of the chiming clock.

4. Both scenes of the "Polish act" are new, although the composer had a good deal of material to draw upon, from sketches he had previously made, but had not used in the original version. The addition of these scenes was of great assistance in supplying the lack of feminine interest in the opera; not only were the prima donnas of the opera-house gratified, but the interest of the work itself was greatly enhanced by the introduction of the love-scene between the False Demetrius and the haughty Polish aristocrat, Marina Mnischek, especially as the incident is inseparably bound up with the political and historical happenings.

5. The scene in the Red Square (taken from Pushkin) is cut out, and in its place we have the revolutionary scene near Kromy; with the exception of the incident of the half-wit (the *yurodivy*), which has been transferred from the scene in the Red Square, the whole affair is Moussorgsky's own invention.

Finally, Moussorgsky reversed the order of the last two scenes, and ends with the death of Boris, thus following the advice of the history-professor Nikolsky, who had been foremost in urging the composer to choose this particular subject. This transposition of the two scenes appealed so strongly to Stassov that, as he expresses it, he was "in de-

193

spair" to think that "so brilliant an idea" had never occurred to him!

From the year 1868 onward private performances of portions, and occasionally the whole, of *Boris* took place at the musical evenings given by L. Y. Shestakova, V. P. Purgold, and others. Dargomizhky too, in the last months of his life, was enabled to hear certain numbers of the work, which had aroused his enthusiasm; according to Stassov his verdict on Moussorgsky was: "He will go much farther than I," an opinion in which he was certainly not mistaken. On these occasions, as the composer expressed it, "Boris was dragged around by the hair"; Moussorgsky was generally the sole performer, though he was occasionally supported in the female roles by Alexandra Purgold, while Nadeshda ("our beloved orchestra") presided at the piano. In Moussorgsky's letters of this period, as in those of his friends, we find numerous accounts of these domestic performances; e.g., Moussorgsky writes to Rimsky-Korsakov (July 23, 1870): "I have been twice to Pargolovo [a bungalow village near Petersburg] and given performances of my *indiscretions* before a numerous audience. As for the introduction of the moujiks in *Boris*, some people thought it was mere clowning (!), though some few were successful in detecting the tragic undertone. The song of 'The Peep-show' produced rounds of laughter, but when it came to the tavern scene in *Boris*, quite a lot of people did not know what to make of it, or what they ought to say." His companions of the "Powerful Coterie" certainly could not be included in this category —more especially Cui, as we shall see shortly. Borodin in a letter to his wife (November 12, 1871) writes: "Yesterday at the Purgolds they played the whole of *Boris* except the last act. It was fine! What a wealth of ideas! What admirable contrasts! How finished it all seems now, and on what a firm basis it rests! I was immensely pleased with the work. . . . " The following utterance of Rimsky-Korsakov is

194

vouched for by V. V. Yastrebtzev in his *Recollections*: "I adore this work, and at the same time I hate it. I adore it for its originality, boldness, distinction, and beauty. I hate it for its want of polish, the harshness of its harmonies, and the musical absurdities that are to be found here and there." He adds: "Of course his faithful devotees will not understand this—they confuse style with the want of it, and it is just in the ignorance displayed in *Boris* that they find the highest expression of the composer's individuality." Stassov, the most whole-hearted of the "devotees," and to a certain extent a collaborator in the work, had naturally nothing but the most enthusiastic praise for it.

Gradually the fame of *Boris* found its way into official theatrical circles. Kondratiev, the manager of the Marie Theatre, acted with unprecedented boldness; he decided to give a single performance of three scenes from the opera—the whole of the Polish act, and the tavern scene—on the occasion of his benefit in the spring of 1873, an arrangement that did not necessitate the official acceptance of the opera by the advisory committee. The cast was excellent; the famous Petrov sang Varlaam, Kondratiev himself was the Rangoni. Napravnik conducted and secured a masterly performance, although he had only two rehearsals. Moussorgsky was enthusiastic over the result and wrote him a letter overflowing with gratitude. The composer's exalted mood at the time, his happiness at the realization of his hopes, are clearly seen in the exuberance of this letter. Moussorgsky speaks of *Boris* as a "schoolboy's effort" and considers any remark or criticisms the conductor sees fit to make "as an honour and a help. Only a great artist like yourself," he goes on, "is capable of interpreting a composer's intentions with so fine an artistry. Far be it from me—in spite of the applause of the public—to take any credit to myself for the success; all the honour, all the glory associated with the performance of these scenes from *Boris* belong to you, to Eduard Franzevitch, and to our good friends on the stage and in the orchestra. I frankly confess that I bless your name for giving me the opportunity for such a valuable lesson."

Moussorgsky's state of mind at this time may be inferred from the short note to Stassov (May 3): "Dear, glorious, most glorious Generalissimo! Victory! 'Fomka! Epichan! Now for the Boyars!' [A quotation from the scene near Kromy, in *Boris*.] Victory! I am infinitely happy! I feel I could say, write, commit any sort of folly! And it's all your doing! The treasure we both hold so dear is safe!"

The performance, as we read in this letter, was a really great popular success. After it was over, there was a supper at the Rimsky-Korsakovs' (lately married), at which they drank, in champagne, to the success of the complete opera. A year later this desire was fulfilled, thanks largely to the good offices of a certain lady, who proved a true friend to Moussorgsky. The credit of introducing the complete opera *Boris Godounov* to the stage belongs to the original representative of Marina, Mme L. F. Platonova, an admirable artist, and apparently a woman of great energy, who at that time had all the musical dilettanti of Petersburg at her feet. She was aware of the influence she possessed over Gedeonov, the all-powerful director of the Imperial theatres, and proceeded to exercise it for the benefit of Moussorgsky, for whom she had the highest possible admiration. When the time came to renew her contract with the director of the Marie Theatre, she stipulated as an indispensable condition that *Boris* should be played on the occasion of her benefit. Gedeonov had no choice but to approach the advisory committee once more with the altered version—and once more the stern arbiters of art refused to yield. Gedeonov, who was unwilling to part with Platonova, was now forced to exercise his dictatorial powers over the heads of all boards and committees and produce the fateful opera against their wishes, and also, he declared, against his own better judgment.

Seldom in the history of the theatre has woman's wit and woman's influence been used in a better cause. In a letter to Stassov, dated 1886, Mme Platonova gives a lively account of how she got round Gedeonov:

"On receiving the committee's refusal Gedeonov sent for Ferrero, the former bass-viol player, now the chairman of the committee. When he arrived, Gedeonov, pale with anger, met him in the antechamber.

" 'Why have you turned this opera down?'

" 'By your leave, Excellency—the opera is no good!'

" 'Why not? I have heard excellent accounts of it!'

" 'By your leave, Excellency—another reason: the composer's friend Cui is always abusing us in the Petersburg *News*; only the day before yesterday . . . ' and he drew a crumpled copy from his pocket.

" 'Well, your committee can go to blazes, do you hear? I shall produce this opera without their permission!' shrieked Gedeonov, beside himself with rage.

"The next day his Omnipotence sends for me again. 'Now, my good madam, just see what you've brought me to! I'm likely to lose my place all on account of this *Boris* of yours! I can't for the life of me see what you find in it—and let me tell you I have no sympathy whatever with these new-fangled fellows, for whom I shall probably have to suffer!'

" 'All the more honour to your Excellency,' I replied, 'for interesting yourself so energetically on behalf of these young Russian composers, with whom you are quite unable to sympathize!' "

At last, after the usual difficulties and obstacles had been overcome, the opera was produced on January 24, 1874. The artists who sang at Kondratiev's benefit repeated their success; chorus and orchestra, under Napravnik, were excellent, as the critics all agreed; Boris was sung by Melnikov, one of the most talented opera-singers in Petersburg. It was lavishly and tastefully staged, the scenery and properties

197

being those made for the production of Pushkin's drama; these were as good as new, since that work had met with the same fate as that reserved for the opera—after a few performances it had silently vanished from the repertoire.

From the first, Moussorgsky was forced to agree to extensive cuts in his work—the whole of the scene in Pimen's cell, the Tsarevitch's account of the parrot incident, and many other less important episodes fell victim to the blue pencil. The success of the work with the public was once more very great, not to say sensational—on the first four performances composer and artists were called again and again after each act. There were some high-brows, it is true, who regarded the work as "an artistic disgrace" to Russia —the words are Gedeonov's—and thought that its success boded ill for the artistic future of the country. Its popularity was naturally greatest among the younger generation, who caught up its melodies in a flash. Stassov relates how, while *Boris* was running, one would often meet whole troops of students at midnight in the deserted streets or on the Neva Bridge singing the choruses from that opera—generally the revolutionary choruses from the Kromy scene, so that it is difficult to say whether Moussorgsky's success with the young Russia of the time was a matter of politics or of music.

As on so many former occasions—and not only in Russia—the ring of professional critics displayed a hopeless and impenetrable lack of comprehension. It is strange that really intelligent men, with a good knowledge of art, so soon as they become professional critics, generally go completely astray in their judgment on the works of their contemporaries. As far as *Boris* is concerned, the opinions of the lesser men naturally do not matter; but it is instructive to notice the attitude adopted by the leaders in the world of music. By far the most prominent, indeed the only important critics of the day were Stassov and Cui in Petersburg, and Laroche and Tchaikovsky in Moscow. Stassov's views we know already—he had no hesitation in classing Moussorgsky with Shakspere and Beethoven.

Laroche, who, by virtue of his brilliant articles on Glinka (his *Russlan* especially), had won a great reputation in Russian musical circles, showed in his clever and malicious criticisms of *Boris* a complete inability to understand the work. Its clumsy workmanship, he declared, smacked of the amateur, and although there were "unmistakable signs of considerable power," Moussorgsky belonged, in his opinion, "to that group of contemporary Russian composers who were distinguished rather by their liberal tendencies than by any knowledge, skill, or intellectual culture." He attributes Moussorgsky's choice of a "patchwork version" of Pushkin's drama to the composer's leanings towards "realism" (in inverted commas). He further charges him with musical *gaucherie*, coarseness, and cacophony, "*à la* Serov," and compares the orchestral accompaniment to "a perpetual strumming on the piano, with the loud pedal down most of the time." In similar vein he blames him for the frequent use of keys with many sharps or flats—"These," he remarks, "as we all know, sound well enough on the piano, but are heavy and ungrateful when employed in the orchestra." Laroche concludes this exhibition of "professional criticism" with something like a groan: "It is deplorable," he says, "to find such great talents entrusted to one who is a musical realist." Unfortunately, this one-sided, pig-headed criticism had grave results for the composer's future; for many years Laroche's verdict on Moussorgsky's music, and especially on *Boris*, was accepted as final by the musical conservatives in Russia, with the most mischievous results; the impression thus created became so deeply fixed in Russian "society" that it took years and years of laborious pioneer-work to uproot it. Among those who were influenced by Laroche's opinion was his intimate friend Tchaikovsky, who, although he recognized Moussorgsky's talents, was never able to appreciate his work. About *Boris* he was never called upon to express a professional opinion, since his articles appeared in a Moscow paper, and it was not till the beginning of the twentieth century that *Boris* was produced in that city. In his correspondence, however, we find many bitter utterances; in reference to *Boris* he writes to his brother Modest as follows (October 29, 1874) : "As for Moussorgsky's music, it can go to the devil for all I care—it is a low, vile parody of the real thing." He expresses himself in rather milder terms in a letter to Frau von Meck (December 24, 1877) : "You are right in thinking that Moussorgsky is done for. He is perhaps the most talented of all of them, but he is a man who has no desire to make good his own deficiences and is altogether too deeply impregnated with the absurd theories of his little circle, as well as by a belief in his own natural genius. He belongs, moreover, to a rather low type, which loves what is coarse, unpolished, and ugly. . . . He is in love with his own lack of culture and seems to be proud of his ignorance; he writes just whatever comes into his head, with a blind belief in the infallibility of his genius. It is true that he often has very original ideas. Although the idiom he speaks is not beautiful, it is new, in spite of its vulgarities."

Moussorgsky would hardly have been surprised if anyone had repeated these opinions to him—he knew his man; in a letter to Stassov (September 29, 1872) he writes: "You always hit the mark—you remember your casual comments yesterday on Petia's [Peter Tchaikovsky's] outburst! *Boris* is quite beyond him—and he only asked for the *Nursery* cycle because Balakirev had praised it so highly." He uses still more pungent language to describe Tchaikovsky's attitude in another letter to Stassov (December 26, 1872). "My dear Generalissimo," he writes, "for some days past I have been in the company of the worshipper of *absolute beauty* in music, and our conversation has left me with a strange sense of an internal void! This feeling was succeeded by another, still stranger and more insistent, for which I can find no name; it was just what one feels when one has lost a very near and dear friend. While he lived, life seemed indescribably fair and precious; now he is taken, one finds oneself suddenly groping, by night, in a gloomy forest, full of mysterious sounds, which frighten one with a sense of something uncanny. That was the experience I went through last Sunday. . . . The *Opritschniky* was not performed on Sunday—the composer had not brought the score with him.[1] In its place we did several other things, in the following order:

" 'Thisbe'—a fiasco!

"*Mlada* was a success, with the exception of 'Morena,' which fell flat.

"*The Nursery* made no impression as a work of art; they declared that the composer's rendering of it made one forget the deficiences of the composition—otherwise there was nothing in it.

" 'The Tramps'—a fiasco!

"The parrot story—a furore![2]

"Sadyk-Pasha seemed to be half asleep and half awake —probably he was dreaming of sherbet; perhaps, too, of Moscow kvass [a sort of light beer made in Russia]—at any rate, he looked quite as sour while the extracts from *Boris* were being played. I was watching my audience—always an instructive pastime!—and saw Sadyk-Pasha grow sourer and sourer, till I quite expected him to begin to ferment!

[1] The *Opritschniky*, an opera by P. I. Tchaikovsky, whom Moussorgsky refers to several times as "Sadyk-Pasha." This name had been taken by a certain Michael Tchaikovsky, a Polish author (1808–86), who had got himself much talked about owing to his having turned Mohammedan and taken service in the Turkish army.

[2] "Thisbe," the heroine of Cui's opera *Angelo.—Mlada*, a ballet opera by Gedeonov, director of the Imperial theatres, which had been entrusted to the "Powerful Coterie" to compose—we shall refer to it later.—By "The Tramps" are meant the wandering friars, Varlaam and Missail.

This actually happened after the parrot scene—he began really to boil, and the bubbles he threw up burst with a dull, hollow sound that was very unpleasant. All I could gather from these sounds (they were not many), was the following: 'He has power' (you can guess whom he meant), 'but his powers are wrongly employed . . . it would be useful . . . to work at a symphony' (in strict form, of course). The powerful one thanked the Pasha profusely and the incident closed. Next day I met the Pasha at Bessel's [the Petersburg music-publisher] ; 'twas the same old story: 'Our aim in music must be beauty—nothing else but beauty!'" In these plain, unvarnished statements by the two great Russian composers of what each thought of the other, we see how radically they differed, both as men and as artists.

Almost more decisive than Laroche's criticism in forming public opinion was César Cui's estimate of *Boris,* which appeared after the first performance in the Petersburg *News,* the official organ of this "Powerful Coterie." It was known that Cui was the literary spokesman for the Balakirev circle, and expectation was on tiptoe to hear what he had to say about the work of one of its members. The result was a big surprise for everyone, and a cruel blow to Moussorgsky. Of course Cui praises *Boris,* but his praise is so interwoven with spiteful and venomous attacks on not merely the details, but the essential quality of the work, as utterly to nullify his expressions of approval. His strictures are directed against "the slender musical interest of many of the scenes" (e.g., the scene in the cell and the garden scene), "a preference for coarse splashes of colour in the tone-painting" (one wonders where he can have found them!), "musical portrayal of unimportant details," "the short, choppy recitative," "the vagueness of the musical ideas," "the awkward mixture of comedy and tragedy," "the composer's inability to work up the symphonic accompaniment or to develop his musical ideas," and the "immaturity" that is conspicuous throughout! Finally Cui complains of the "absence of any effectual self-criticism" and of Moussorgsky's "self-complacent, slapdash way of composing."

Cui's outburst is all the more surprising when we remember that at that time the "Powerful Coterie" still hung together, and that its members, apparently, were still in perfect agreement. One would have supposed that *Boris Godounov*—the first serious and connected attempt to justify the operatic theories they held in common—would have called forth a storm of enthusiasm from that quarter. Cui may perhaps have been moved by a quite natural, though unbrotherly, feeling of jealousy, for his own opera of *Ratcliff*, which had been in existence longer than *Boris*, still lay in the composer's desk. Possibly, too, he may have felt it his duty, after the great public success of *Boris*, to put a damper on Moussorgsky's hopes, lest they should soar too high. In any case, Moussorgsky was most bitterly hurt by Cui's behaviour; he thought he had a right to very different treatment at the hands of his "friend"; after such an experience we cannot wonder that he hastened to describe the members of the "coterie" as "soulless traitors." He relieved his feelings by writing to Stassov, whom he knew to be true as steel; the excited tone of this letter, to the one friend who never failed to understand and sympathize with him in all his activities, whether as man or as artist, is, under the circumstances, quite understandable. It seems that on the day of the production of *Boris* there had been a serious disagreement, for some unknown reason, between the two friends; four days after the performance—i.e., on January 28, 1874—Moussorgsky wrote to Stassov: "My dear and well-beloved Generalissimo—yes! in spite of all!—I was mad—furious and raging like any jealous woman. . . ! Now I am only a little sad and angry. What is one to say about Cui's article? I will begin at the end; no decent well-bred man would behave as Cui has done, in his efforts to be witty—it was disgraceful to make fun of women, whose courageous conduct (as I have heard) deserved nothing but sympathy. (As to how it affects me personally, that is my own affair—I shall say nothing—but I shall never forget a kind action like theirs.) I was so angry with you, dear friend, for refusing my request that I lost control of myself—politeness might go to the devil! I was cross and sulky with you in the theatre— when I get angry I am capable of anything. Still, neither at dinner at Dmitri's, nor even in the theatre was I really false to you. I will say it once again: whatever happens, *I cannot part from you.* I love you passionately, and your pale face showed me that you love me in no less degree. I am glad we quarrelled—it is a good and wholesome thing sometimes for people to fall out like this. Now I have told you all, and I am myself again. It seems as if the production of *Boris* was necessary for the revelation of certain people's characters. What a spiteful article that was of Cui's! What childish nonsense about the women, and then to charge me with 'self-complacency'! Doesn't he know that I have always failed through excess of modesty? . . . 'Self-complacency'! 'Slap-dash way of composing'! 'Immaturity'! Who is immature, I should like to know! You have often said to me: 'I don't trust Cui in the matter of *Boris*'; your foreboding was a true one and was doubtless inspired by your loving care for me; never fear, then, that my love for you can alter. . . . Moussorianin."

The expression "childish nonsense about the women" requires an explanation. Some lady admirers of Moussorgsky wished to present him with a laurel wreath on the first performance of *Boris*, a design that was prevented by the intrigues of the management. In a letter to one of the most widely read Petersburg newspapers the ladies in question appealed to public opinion, and openly charged the conductor, Napravnik, with having prevented the handing of the wreath over the footlights. "Is it necessary, then," wrote the injured ladies, "to send in a formal petition, stamped and sealed, before one can get a wreath handed up to the stage?" Moussorgsky, who was unwilling to make trouble with the management, and still less with Napravnik, was very awkwardly placed; in a letter to the Petersburg *News* (Cui's paper) he protested against the insinuations against the ladies and took all the blame on himself. The terms in which his protest was made were rather unhappy, owing, no doubt, to the excitement of the circumstances. "While the first performance of *Boris Godounov* was in progress," he wrote, "the composer was informed by some members of the public that they intended to offer him a laurel wreath in the presence of the audience. The composer shrank from any such public demonstration and tried to leave the theatre; he was prevented, however, and it needed his earnest entreaties to prevent the wreath's being exhibited before the public had gone home. After the performance was over, the presentation was made in one of the dressing-rooms of the theatre."

This incident afforded both Cui and Laroche an opportunity to indulge in the usual journalistic witticisms at Moussorgsky's expense. "When the three ladies," writes Laroche, "had delivered the wreath at the box-office in the regular way, their waited, full of expectation, to see what would happen. Nothing happened! The wreath was not handed up! The ladies were furious, and the pages of the Petersburg *News* were agreeably adorned with a number of anonymous letters. Someone had told the ladies that Napravnik was to blame for everything, whereupon they set to work to inform the public of the fact. . . . Three days later the composer himself enters the arena, hastily, excited, still glowing from his recent triumph, courteously inclined to the ladies, full of respect for Napravnik, and—most important of all—highly delighted with the wreath, and also with the fact that it had not been handed up to him—for by this means he was enabled to talk about himself in an important

newspaper and thus to add the laurels of a publicist to those
of a poet and composer. . . . When Moussorgsky heard
of the honour that was proposed for him, he decided to decline it; his nerves gave way, and he implored them not to
show him the wreath. So frightened was he at the thought
of the laurels, ribbons, inscriptions, to say nothing of the
three unknown beauties, that like the bride in Gogol's story
he resolved on flight; someone brought him back, however,
and blushing, yet happy, the composer wrote an article to
tell us all about the honour that had been proposed for him
on the occasion of the first performance of his first opera—
quod erat demonstrandum!"

Cui, in his paper, dealt with the incident in the same
kind and gentlemanly manner.

Such was the discordant note that followed the first
performance of *Boris*—an exhibition of petty, spiteful en-
mity on the part of a man whom Moussorgsky had always
believed in as artist and as friend; it is not surprising that
it awakened a discordant echo in the breast of the composer.
Rimsky-Korsakov maintains that after the first performance of *Boris* a sinister change came over Moussorgsky, especially in his relations to "those who had formerly been his
intimates." Can we wonder if this was so? But the musicians
were not the only ones who raged against the "audacity,"
the "shameless impudence" of *Boris*; from the ranks of the
literati too there came a cry—a few individual voices at
first, but later a whole angry chorus thirsting for vengeance,
who made no secret of their desire to have Moussorgsky's
blood in return from his sacrilegious treatment of Pushkin.
The literary historian N. V. Strakhov wrote three furious
letters to the editor of the *Grashdanin* (the *Citizen*)—at that
time no less a personage than F. M. Dostoievsky—protest-
ing against the "literary outrage" committed by Moussorgsky and charging him, as the author of *Boris*, with "an im-

pudent striving for originality, absolute sterility of invention, the absence of any artistic idea," and so forth.

The truth is that in the case of *Boris Godounov* the general public, and by no means for the first time, showed a better understanding of an "advanced" work of art than the recognized intellectual authorities. This experience made an indelible impression on Moussorgsky, which had a marked influence on the whole of his later career.

*　　*　　*

Let us now see what truth there is in the charges brought against Moussorgsky by the literary and musical critics. Of the four and twenty scenes contained in Pushkin's "dramatic story" only fourteen are used in the opera, and only a small part of the poet's very numerous characters appear on the stage; on the other hand, Moussorgsky has introduced quite a number of persons of his own invention, the most important of which is the strong dramatic figure of the Jesuit priest Rangoni; while the numerous individuals in the chorus—the Mitiukhas and Fomkas—with their short passages of highly coloured dialogue, are also an interpolation. It must be confessed that, taken altogether, Moussorgsky is rather unscrupulous in his handling of the poet's verse, but it is only fair to add that this is not due to levity or carelessness; his procedure is always the result of his profound artistic insight and is in every instance justified by the effect obtained. In some scenes Moussorgsky merely shortens or slightly alters Pushkin's original; in others he runs two or three scenes together, with cuts and transpositions; sometimes he takes single passages, lines, or sentences from Pushkin and works them into his own text; it is seldom that he leaves the original absolutely untouched. It is impossible not to regret the absence of some of the scenes he has left out—e.g., the banquet at Prince Shouisky's house, which ends so effectively with the "grace after meat" from one of the

Prince's pages; or the conversation of the two courtiers about the hallucinations from which Boris suffers:

FIRST COURTIER: . . . With a magician
    Into his room he went, and shut the door.

SECOND COURTIER: . . . That is the way he loves to spend
    his time—
    Prophet, astrologer, or fortune-teller,
    From each and all he seeks to learn his fate,
    Like some fond maiden waiting for her lover.

Strakhov, in a passion, declares that Moussorgsky has given us "bad prose, with neither rhyme nor reason," instead of "Pushkin's divine poesy." The accusation is hardly fair: Strakhov surveys the world of the theatre merely "from his own church-tower," as the Russian proverb says; that is, from the standpoint of the literary historian; he forgets that an operatic composer and a dramatic author look at things from widely different points of view. Moussorgsky had learned this truth from Dargomizhky's treatment of the *Stone Guest,* and his own experience with Gogol's *Marriage.*

It was after full deliberation that he decided against any slavish following of the actual words of the poet; he had come to the conclusion (which so few operatic composers seem to reach) that the conditions proper to spoken dialogue and sung dialogue are entirely different, and therefore different artistic methods must be employed in drama and opera respectively. Pushkin in his *Boris Godounov* had achieved such a miracle of expressive writing as no other Russian poet had yet attained to. Just as Karamzin in his history imitates the style of the old chronicles in masterly fashion, so Pushkin appreciably heightens the effect of illusion by the strong, simple, antique speech he puts into the mouths of his characters. But Moussorgsky too, as we know from his letters, had made the ancient language of his country his especial study and in consequence was able to write both prose and verse of such distinction that with few exceptions they may well stand beside those of Pushkin. It requires an unusually fine literary sense to be able to distinguish Moussorgsky's lines from those of Pushkin in some of the altered passages—e.g., the scene where Boris bids his son farewell. There is never any question of "bad prose without rhyme or reason"; in any case Pushkin's literary drama as adapted by Moussorgsky for the theatre becomes a real stage-play, powerful and effective beyond all expectation.

Of far greater importance than mere external changes, affecting the arrangement of the scenes and the actual wording of the text, are certain esoteric differences in Moussorgsky's conception of the Godounov tragedy, when compared with that of Pushkin. The *Boris* of the latter is essentially a literary product; every line is packed with meaning; it is as suitable for quotation as Shakspere. Though characterized by the loftiest intellectuality, the language fails in that directness and that purely emotional quality which are the first consideration with the composer; just as the plot fails to provide effective dramatic incidents. It is a question whether Pushkin ever intended his *Boris* for the stage; he evidently realized that it was a drama for the study rather than a play in the true sense of the word. The critics of his day had described it, not unfairly, as "a shadow-play in the Chinese manner." The four and twenty kaleidoscopic tableaux, some of which last no longer than a minute and consist of just one short question and answer, would seem an almost intolerable patchwork on the stage, though they make no such impression when read, since the reader's imagination can adjust itself, far more easily than the spectator's, to the constant changes. Moreover, there is no denying that Pushkin erred in shifting the chief interest, in the course of the action, from the Tsar Boris to the second principal character, the False Demetrius. Moussorgsky spared no pains to render the work more effective for stage purposes; with a firm hand he cut away the many side-growths that concealed the direct line of dramatic development, and reduced the psychological details (e.g., in Boris's monologue) to an almost primitive simplicity, to the great advantage of the opera. With his instinct for dramatic effect Moussorgsky realized that in the theatre it would not be sufficient merely for Boris to talk about the tortures of conscience—they must actually be seen; accordingly he introduces the very singular episode of the chiming clock. Moussorgsky knew quite well what an overwhelming effect might be got from the contrast between the harmless whirring and tinkling of this "foreign toy" and the frenzied terror of the conscience-stricken, half-mad Boris. He had reckoned rightly—the effect of this scene is startling. Moussorgsky saw also that it was essential that the death of the unhappy Tsar should take place in sight of the audience. In Pushkin, the part of Boris ends with the stage-direction: "The ceremony of the clothing now begins" (at that time it was customary for the Tsar of Russia, just before dying, to take monastic vows), while Moussorgsky prolongs the scene to the actual moment of death, which is led up to with excellent effect. In both these scenes the "dramatic crescendo" (to use A. N. Rimsky-Korsakov's striking expression) rises to a climax, *fortissimo*, which, in the case of the death scene, is maintained even during the few moments between Boris's death and the fall of the curtain. This short time is occupied by a dumb show in which the spectator is made to realize the hopelessly tragic future that awaits the Tsarevitch Feodor (who was murdered soon afterwards). The boy, overcome with grief, throws himself in despair on his father's body, watched by the cold, unfeeling eyes of the Boyars and Patriarchs, while in the distance are already heard the shouts that acclaim his fortunate rival, the False Demetrius.

Pushkin's work certainly gains in dramatic vigour by

the changes that Moussorgsky has made in the character of
Boris, as well as in the general arrangement; the three great
scenes for Boris become the axis of the piece, on which all the
rest revolves.

While the elaboration of the part of Boris deals chiefly
with externals, in the usurper Moussorgsky makes such radical alterations as to exhibit this character in an entirely new
light. In Pushkin the False Demetrius is simply a daring
impostor, with no illusions as to his past or his real origin,
who makes unscrupulous use of the circumstances for his
own advantage; in his speech—especially in the scenes with
Marina—he often reaches the height of cynical self-revela-
tion; for example:

> Whether I be Demetrius or not,
> What matter, so I furnish good excuse
> For murder and for war?

Moussorgsky's Demetrius is quite different; he is somewhat
of a dreamer—like Gogol's Khlestakov—who believes in the
fables of his own invention, and is able to move those around
him by the force of his conviction—as when he talks of
"winning back his hereditary throne in honourable fight."
In the scene with Marina in the garden he rises to visionary
heights, and his frank and honourable sentiments contrast
almost attractively with the cold-blooded calculations of the
scheming Polish aristocrat. Similarly in the scene near Kromy, where he appears as the chosen representative of the
people, the sympathies of the audience are with him; when
the jubilant trumpets give out the theme connected with the
Tsarevitch Dmitri, we are confused for a moment—we are
not certain who it is that stands before us, the rightful Tsar
or the impudent impostor. With this tremendous note of
interrogation Moussorgsky brings his opera to a close—it
is an extraordinarily clever dramatic effect, of which we find
no hint in Pushkin.

A. N. Rimsky-Korsakov in his exhaustive analysis of Moussorgsky's work observes very finely that in the musical treatment of the False Demetrius we may reasonably discern, if not the lawful son of Ivan the Fourth, an abstract force of equal importance—the personification of the vengeance that lies in wait for the frightful crime of the Tsar Boris. Step by step the music brings the inner tragedy in the mind of Boris plainly before our eyes and provides a striking parallel at the moment of his mental collapse. This peculiar psychological conception of the character may perhaps explain why Moussorgsky uses one and the same musical motif for both the murdered Tsarevitch Dmitri and Grishka Otrepiev, the usurper. The question whether it is the real Dmitri or a pretender does not affect the course of the tragedy in Boris's soul—he dreads not so much an actual force as the symbol of that terrible vengeance which fate has in store for him.

In one respect Moussorgsky has substantially enriched the drama of Pushkin—in his scenes for the crowd, whether interpolated or merely extended and consolidated by him. Here again he has endeavoured to bring before our eyes things that in Pushkin are only talked about; we are certainly made to feel that the real tragic protagonist of the play is the Russian people, but they hardly ever come into the action, although their presence in the background is everywhere felt to be the psychological motive-power. Moussorgsky brings the people on the stage, lets them talk and act, and makes us spectators of their outbreaks of feeling and passion, and scenes that Pushkin has given merely in outline are enriched with endless characteristic details. The revolutionary scene near Kromy—Moussorgsky's own invention—in which the proletarian crowd give full rein to their passions, makes a startling impression today on us, who have so lately witnessed similar events throughout the length and breadth of Russia. One is inclined to think that the composer's visionary gaze was privileged to peer not only into the recesses of bygone centuries, but also into the future, even down to our own day. Similiar reflections are aroused by the remarkably prophetic words that the composer puts into the mouth of the half-wit (the "blessed innocent"), a figure that in Pushkin is merely episodic, but in Moussorgsky is raised to a much higher plane of importance by his ominous warning: "Flow, flow, ye bitter tears! Wail, ye faithful Christian folk! For the foe is at hand, and thick darkness shall fall upon your country. . . . Woe, woe to you, poor starving folk!"

In the original version Moussorgsky calls his work simply an "opera," and nothing is said on the title-page as to the origin of the libretto; later on he names it a "musical folk-drama, after Pushkin and Karamzin," thus clearly indicating the principal source of his inspiration—the people. We know how great an interest the lower strata of his countrymen had always had for him; but hitherto he had confined himself to the investigation of individual characters, whose picturesque emotions he used for his artistic purposes with such striking effect; but in *Boris* he deals for the first time with the people as a collective entity. He knew quite well that his peculiar artistic endowment drew him especially to the study of mass-psychology and he realized at the same time how entirely aloof he was, in this respect, from the musicians of his time. He touches on the subject in a letter to Stassov (October 18, 1872): "To seek out the essential, intimate peculiarities, not only of the individual, but also of the crowd, to explore this region and to bring all its beauties to the light of day—that is the mission of the artist!" And again: "In the great masses of people, just as in the individual, there are hidden treasures which no one yet has touched; to discover their presence, to seek till one has found them, then to offer them to humanity as a new and wholesome diet—that is the problem, nor is there any greater happiness."

If we examine the massed scenes in the prologue, in the courtyard of the Tchudov Monastery, or in the forest near Kromy, from this standpoint, we shall see that these have nothing in common with the usual choruses of conventional opera. Here every member of the crowd appears to have an individual existence; there are no "members of the chorus," no "supers," but all these Fomkas and Mitiukhas, so finely distinguished, are thoroughly characteristic types of the Russian peasantry. Moreover, the crowd behaves throughout exactly as it would do in each of the given situations—no action, no gesture, is emphasized merely for effect. When the people, in dread of the Pristav's knout, rashly beseech the Boyar Godounov to accept the Imperial crown, or with equally blind confidence acclaim him as Emperor, or when at last, broken by famine, plague, and oppression, they rebel and join the usurper's party, hurling abuse and ridicule at Boris's Boyars—in every place we find the same delicate psychological motivation; every tone, every word, is true to nature. Moussorgsky saw from the beginning that the effect he wanted was not to be obtained by musical finish or stylization of any kind, and in seeking a solution of his difficulties he discovered, quite independently, that method of artistic representation that has come to be known as naturalism or realism in music and to which he owes his unique power of giving direct impressions.

Moussorgsky has been reproached with painting historic Russia in too gloomy colours, with neglecting many sides of the national character and giving a false impression of the people as a brutal, drunken crew, given to bestial excesses. This reproach is undeserved; we must not forget that many of the acting characters—e.g., the Hostess, the "Nanny," the two begging friars—are just as representative of "the people" as are the stupid, howling mobs in the mass scenes. It is precisely this insistence on the multifarious aspects of the people's psychology—their capacity for enjoyment, their sense of fun, their unfailing good humour, etc.—that makes Moussorgsky's work so matchless as a monument of Russian art. If *Boris* is an indictment of "the people," it is equally an act of homage to their worth.

Another charge continually brought forward even to this day is that the dramatic conception is wanting in unity. It was Cui who wrote: "The work is merely a succession of scenes, which may be said to have a certain common relation to one definite object, but otherwise are strung together loosely, with no real organic connexion. You may rearrange them as you please, cutting out some scenes and introducing new ones, without altering the look of the opera." That, of course, is transparent nonsense; the events in *Boris Godounov*, far from being loosely thrown together, are inseparably connected, and it is impossible to detach any one scene from the position assigned to it without injuring the logical development of the whole. On the other hand the highest praise is due to the fine dramatic instinct that Moussorgsky has shown in preserving the main line of construction, while excluding all that is superfluous. Naturally, neither Pushkin's nor Moussorgsky's play preserves "the unities," in the classic or pseudo-classic sense of the term; we have to deal not with one hero only, but with two or even three, if both "the Russian people" and "the Muscovite Empire" may count as such.

It was just this apparently conflicting variety of material that enabled Moussorgsky to conjure up so comprehensive a picture of bygone Russia, in which the widest contrasts are included. We must in any case admit that in this one work alone the composer has given proof of the universality of his talents—here every emotion of the human heart finds its fitting expression; whether he deals with the tragic utterance of the conscience-stricken Boris, or the haughty dignity of his demeanour in the presence of the Boyars, whether with the burlesque humour of the drunken Varlaam or the toadying bully Rangoni, his success is equally extraordinary. He is no less convincing in depicting the cold-blooded coquetry of the haughty Marina Mnischek than in finding the right music for the simple, kindly humour of the scenes between the imperial children and their old nurse; the childish tricks with which the village children torment the village idiot are expressed in tones as true to life as the tragic strain in which the poor boy gives vent to his grief, while Prince Shouisky, the cunning coward, aware of his advantage, is as unforgettable a figure as the wise and saintly monk Pimen.

In his employment of musical means to characterize the various persons and situations of the drama, Moussorgsky displays the same freedom and unconventionality in *Boris* that we are accustomed to in his earlier work; the intuition of the artist, even a certain touch of the improvisatore, are certainly more in evidence than any signs of painstaking revision or the careful elaboration of details; yet on the whole the details in *Boris* are wonderfully consistent and appropriate; one has the feeling that here is a peculiar kind of creative art, which works, like nature, through certain deep instincts, unwitting of the ends they serve. The result is that the choice, employment, and development of the descriptive methods are far from seeming casual or without a plan —all follow in logical order and are never without an inner artistic justification. Especially in the matter of leading themes did Moussorgsky show his independence, thereby throwing new light on the right employment of this device. Musical symbolism, indeed, he very seldom used; his mind was too concrete to admit of his attaching any great importance to so abstract a system; consequently he used the leit-motiv rather for the purpose of distinguishing the different characters than as the musical embodiment of an idea. Generally speaking, we find in his treatment of it the instinctive delicacy of touch that goes with an unfettered artistic imagination, not calculating and working out its effect according to a preconceived scheme, but following the inspiration of the moment. A. N. Rimsky-Korsakov in his analysis of *Boris* aptly remarks that with Wagner, who deals mostly with such emotions and conceptions as can be docketed and reduced to a formula, the leitmotiv is the very leaven of the musical structure; with Moussorgsky, on the other hand, who is interested in the actual man as he is, and not as he ought to be, who seizes upon the particular example, and shows it to us in all its complicated psychological ramifications, it is only exceptionally that the leitmotiv is used to describe emotional experiences.

Accordingly we find the leading character, the Tsar Boris, without a leitmotiv of any kind—Moussorgsky saw at once that here no leitmotiv would serve his turn. The range of emotional experiences to which Boris gives explicit or implicit expression is so extensive that to illustrate them by a system of leitmotivs would have been too complicated a task for anyone to contemplate. The variety of these emotions seems truly inexhaustible; the range from the solemn composure of fervent prayer, through the majestic consciousness of sovereign power, to a mood of profound parental tenderness for his daughter and of frank affection for his growing son—from dark and gloomy brooding, mingled with superstitious fears at the thought of a coming Nemesis, and a wild desire for vengeance on the traitorous nobles, to the cold politeness and exaggerated irony of his interview with Shouisky, and so on up to his frenzied outburst of rage, typical of the oriental tyrant, followed by the maddening pangs of remorse for the murder committed—then from the smooth urbanity, the assumed indifference of the practised politician, to a state of terror, and, last of all, the sudden defiant, frantic challenge in the face of inexorable death: "I still am Tsar!"—what endless revelations of an unfathomable nature! To find a leitmotiv for so complex a psychology was manifestly impossible and Moussorgsky, with his unerring instinct, made no attempt to do so.

The other characters in the drama offer no such complex task; their part in the development of the plot demands only a more or less limited emotional endowment. Each of them fixes his or her emotional impulse on a certain definite object and in consequence is a fitting subject for the leitmotiv treatment; but though Moussorgsky was of course aware of this, he is very sparing in his use of this particular method—his artistic instinct invariably avoided exaggeration of any kind.

The usurper, who is hardly so much a human personality as the incarnation of an idea—i.e., of the approaching Nemesis in the form of the murdered Tsarevitch—has, as we have said, the same leitmotiv as the real Demetrius, a theme that at one time suggests, in its touching simplicity, the innocence of childhood, and at another sounds the note of triumph, in the ringing tones of trumpets and horns.

For Marina Mnischek, the noble Polish lady, there is no leitmotiv, but she is associated always with a characteristic rhythm—either mazurka or Cracovienne (the national dances of Poland)—which serves to characterize this episodical figure in apt and striking fashion.

Pimen, again, the old monkish chronicler, in whom all human passions have long been extinguished, has a tranquil theme that is wonderfully effective—its two bars seem to sum up all the wisdom of a soul that after many struggles has attained to perfect interior peace.

Highly successful too is the cringing theme that suggests so well the fawning character of Prince Shouisky—a theme that, as Rimsky-Korsakov remarks, "insinuates itself into the score just as the Prince himself might do into the apartment of his rival Godounov." No less masterly is the short theme, of only four notes, assigned to Varlaam, the

218

mendicant friar, which in its many different forms illustrates with inimitable humour the various drunken moods of that magnificent toper. The motif dominates the orchestra, just as Varlaam dominates the stage, yet never become tiresome.

The music of *Boris* is naturally and by intention national; the Russian people, with whom we are here chiefly concerned, must needs be represented as Russian and using the Russian idiom; but whenever the specifically national quality is outweighed by the purely human element (e.g., in the two big scenes for Boris, or the scene in the cell between Pimen and Grishka Otrepiev), the music loses all its national characteristics. The voice parts float above the orchestra in a free but always melodious recitative, which follows the delicate inflexion of the text as closely as possible. This method, it may be remarked, renders the task of the translator wellnigh impossible, since each note is written for a particular syllable of a particular word, and will fit no other. The varied intonation in the translation would be quite different and would need to be expressed by different notes.

Separate numbers, in the traditional forms, occur only in places where they spring naturally from the dramatic situation.

The opera can also show some very remarkable instrumental episodes—e.g., the introduction to the second scene of the Prologue, when we have an imitation of a festal peal from all the belfries of the Kremlin in honour of the Tsar's coronation. This short piece, built as it is on only two chords, is an experiment in sound-painting, of an audacity unprecedented at that date, and still surprisingly effective. Even Cui remarked that the clashing bells in Moussorgsky's orchestra sounded almost "more natural" than those in the steeples.

The big Polonaise in the garden scene has the right

ring of festal splendour. It was Moussorgsky's original intention to orchestrate this for strings only, in imitation of the "*quatre-vingt violons du roi*"; he came to the conclusion, however, that it was impossible to create a musical setting of sufficient brilliance without the aid of both wood-wind and brass. The somewhat archaic flavour of the piece, in keeping with its period, is due to the fact that the composer employs the Lydian mode throughout—whether consciously or not we cannot tell. The old Polish folk-tunes, like the Russian, always show a preference for the ecclesiastical modes, and of these (as we see in many of Chopin's dances) they seem to prefer the Lydian and mixolydian. It is doubtful if Moussorgsky was aware of this—with him the intuition of genius often hit upon the right way.

In the history of Russian opera *Boris Godounov* represents a height of achievement that has never yet been surpassed—Moussorgsky alone succeeded in reaching it once again with his *Khovanstchina*. If one proceeds to compare *Boris* with Glinka's *A Life for the Tsar* and *Russlan and Ludmilla*, or Dargomizhky's *Stone Guest*, it is rather with the object of showing the musical development of Russian music than of drawing attention to points of resemblance that might raise any doubt as to the absolute independence of Moussorgsky's work.

The national spirit, which we see stirring in the operas of Glinka, celebrates its first real triumph, freed from all conventions, in *Boris Godounov*, and it is here too that Dargomizhky's tentative gropings after musical truth result for the first time in the discovery of a stylistic principle that is equal to all demands. Neither Glinka nor Dargomizhky had any idea of the possibilities that Moussorgsky was to bring to fulfilment, although the germs of them were contained in their own operas. No doubt Moussorgsky's artistic nature drew nourishment from the soil prepared by his two great predecessors; nevertheless its development was perfectly free and independent, nor did he ever entertain even a thought of conscious imitation.

It is clear enough from what has been said that it was *Boris* which first gave Moussorgsky his unique position among European composers; he was fully aware of this, and in the concluding paragraphs of his *Autobiography* he has the following very apposite remarks: "Neither by the nature of his compositions nor by virtue of his views on art does Moussorgsky belong to any of the musical movements of the day. His confession of faith may be summed up in these words: art is a way of communicating with one's fellow-creatures, though that is not the object of art; all creative work is conditioned by this guiding principle. Starting from the assumption that human speech is subjected to strict musical laws (see Virchow and Gervinus), he [Moussorgsky] perceives that the musician's task is to reproduce not only the voice of emotion, but, more especially, the varying modulations of human speech. He considers that it is only the great reformers, such as Palestrina, Bach, Gluck, Beethoven, Berlioz, and Liszt, that have given laws to music; not that these laws are unalterable—on the contrary, he is convinced that they, in common with the whole world of intellect, are subject to change and progress."

This recognition of the fact that all rules which in their day are recognized as absolute are subject to alteration preserved Moussorgsky from ever standing still in his artistic development or being hampered by too great a fidelity to his æsthetic principles; as a convinced believer in the axiom of Heraclitus: "All things are in a state of flux," in music as in everything else, he gave only a conditional assent to authority, with the implied reservation that it is always permissible to change one's opinion. On the other hand, his belief in his own vocation as a reformer led him to respect the established rules of art until he believed himself able to replace them by others that had come to him either by inspiration or after due reflection.

In the field of music-drama Moussorgsky never made any essential departure from the principles embodied in *Boris*; while engaged on that work all the problems connected with dramatic composition had become perfectly clear to him, and hereafter there was to be no more groping in the dark. Indeed, that masterpiece contained many fresh lights that illuminated the whole of his future career.

VIII

KHOVANSTCHINA

WHILE THE family estate was owned by his mother, Moussorgsky always spent the summer months there; later on he stayed with his brother on one of his small country properties. When these, too, had been sold, Moussorgsky lost his regular summer holiday resort, and consequently he did not leave Petersburg for any length of time during the summer of 1871; he had to be content with visits to the *datchas* (bungalows) of friends, in those summer colonies that mostly dot the course of the Finnish Railway, on the shores of the Gulf of Finland. Most of his friends, like the great majority of Petersburgers, had escaped from the heat and dust of town —it was the proper thing in Russia to own, or at least rent, a *datcha*; and from June to August Petersburg was deserted. This year only one of his friends shared Moussorgsky's fate —Rimsky-Korsakov, chained to Petersburg by his official duties, was spending the summer months at the town house of his brother, a high official in the Russian Admiralty. This fact had important results, for the two young composers, thrown on their own resources, saw a great deal of each other and became close friends; they had been acquainted for years, having met at Balakirev's musical gatherings, but had never been on intimate terms. This summer, however, their relations developed into a real friendship, which was to last for some years before it was broken off.

Rimsky-Korsakov tells us that Moussorgsky was often at his brother's house that summer and played them much of the music of *Boris*. The two composers went on bungalow trips together, especially to Pargolovo, where the Purgolds lived; Rimsky-Korsakov had already formed a tender attachment in that quarter, which was later on to develop into something stronger.

The growing pleasure that the two young composers took in each other's society, as men and as artists, suggested a plan, which they carried out at the beginning of autumn and which was not without influence on their artistic development—in August 1871 they took a lodging together. Stassov remarks, with truth, that such an event had never happened before in the history of music; for this lodging, as we know from the avowal of one of the two occupants, consisted of a single room, in which the two lived and composed. Rimsky-Korsakov declares that the plan worked out quite successfully. "How could we possibly help disturbing each other? Very simply; Moussorgsky used the piano till noon, while I copied music or orchestrated some passage that I had already thought out; about noon he went to his work at the Ministry and I sat down to the piano. Then, too, twice a week I had to be at the Conservatoire at nine in the morning, and Moussorgsky often lunched at Opotchinin's. So all went on smoothly." Happy are the young, who are quite content if only they can follow their own inclinations! In this case it was the fire of creative art that inspired the two friends. Moussorgsky worked feverishly at those scenes of *Boris* that had still to be finished—i.e., the "Polish act" (so-called) and the forest scene near Kromy—and Rimsky-Korsakov laboured at his opera *The Maid of Pskov*.

The stimulus and help that the two composers found in living and working together would have made up for greater discomforts than they had to endure. It can hardly have been a very comfortable way of living; their one furnished room was of the most ordinary kind. Moussorgsky states his exact address in a letter to Stassov, and this gives

us a fair idea of the quarters occupied for a time by two
of the greatest of Russian composers. The address is "Zaremba's house in Panteleimon Street, Apartment No. 9. along
the corridor to the right from the stairs, first door on the
left." It does not sound inviting, but neither of the two young
composers could afford much. Moussorgsky had to live on
his meagre official pay; and Rimsky-Korsakov, who had resigned his post at the Admiralty and had no settled income
but his stipend as Professor of Composition at the Petersburg Conservatoire, was probably not much better off.

Borodin gives a substantially true account of the *ménage* of the two composers, in a letter to his wife (October
26, 1871). We cannot doubt for a moment which of the two
appealed most to the composer of *Prince Igor*. He himself
was characterized by elegance of manner rather than by
natural impetuosity, and Korsakov's muse, all combed and
curled, attracted him more than Moussorgsky's inspired but
rather dishevelled Egeria. Borodin says in his letter:

"The other members of our circle are more united than
ever. In particular Moussinka and Korsinka, since they
have shared the same diggings, have come on greatly. Musically they are diametrically opposed; each is the complement
of the other, and their influence on each other has been of
the greatest advantage to both. Modest [Moussorgsky] has
developed Korsinka on the recitative-declamatory side; and
the latter has got Modest out of his craze for rugged originality; he has toned down the roughness of his harmonies,
his orchestral mannerisms, his illogical way of developing his
subjects—in short, he has made Modest's work far more
musical."

No doubt Borodin was right in his remark that the association of the two composers was good for both. Rimsky-
Korsakov, in his opera *The Maid of Pskov* (*Pskovitianka*),
the scene of which is laid in the time of Ivan the Terrible,
was treating a subject with which he was certainly not so

familiar as was Moussorgsky, whose studies for *Boris* had made him an authority on that particular period of Russian history. The subject that Korsakov had chosen was attractive to Moussorgsky, since it glorified the free life of the old Russian Hanse town, Pskov, with its Town Parliament (*vetsche*), as opposed to the despotism of Moscow. Moussorgsky expresses himself so enthusiastically about Rimsky-Korsakov's music, especially the great chorus scene of the Town Council, a counterpart of the chorus scenes in *Boris*, that he seems almost as proud of it as if it had been his own work. In a letter to Stassov he writes: "I have just heard something really distinguished—a specimen of Korsinka's genius; he has grasped the true essence of music-drama. He has worked out the chorus scene of the Council in *The Maid of Pskov* wonderfully, exactly as it ought to be. I could have laughed aloud for sheer enthusiasm."

On the other hand, Moussorgsky certainly profited not only by his friend's somewhat pedantic professional accuracy, but also by the niceness of his critical faculty, which rarely erred. Already Rimsky-Korsakov was "editing" his friend's music. How he did it he explained very clearly in after years to his Boswell, V. V. Yastrebtzev, who has published two volumes of *Recollections of N. A. Rimsky-Korsakov*. He was almost abnormally sensitive on the question of musical keys; every key, to his ear, had its own strongly marked individuality, and any falsification of this (or what he regarded as such) made him furious. For instance, E flat major, for him, was the proper key for "cities and fortresses." In the "geography lesson" in *Boris Godounov*—that is, the Tsar's conversation with his son over a map of Russia—Boris sings the phrase: "With one glance, as if from heaven, thou canst survey the whole Empire, its frontiers, rivers, cities." The three last words are accompanied (tremolo) by the chords of F major, G minor, and E flat major, respectively. As Rimsky-Korsakov tells his Boswell: "Moussorgsky originally put the word 'cities' before 'rivers' (the melody and harmonies being the same) ; this irritated me greatly, because the chord of E flat did not come in the proper place. I begged Moussorgsky to alter the order of the words, so that 'cities' came on the last chord; and, do you know, I feel absolutely satisfied now whenever I hear that E flat." For similar purely subjective reasons he would have liked to transpose the scene by the fountain from E flat major into E major, "the proper love-making key," but reconciled himself to E flat, which "was also suitable." F major, however (he adds), would have been quite impossible in such a passage. "Besides, Moussorgsky was too great a master of tonecolour ever to make so gross a blunder."

The house where the two composers lodged belonged to Nikolai Ivanovitch Zaremba, who had been brought to Petersburg by Anton Rubinstein as director of the Musical School of the Russian Musical Society, afterwards turned into the Imperial Conservatoire. Besides the relations between landlord and tenants, this brought the two into contact with the official musical world of Petersburg, especially with the "German musical Pope" of Russia, Anton Rubinstein. Rimsky-Korsakov, as we have mentioned, had, after long hesitation, accepted the post of Professor of Composition at the Conservatoire, and even Moussorgsky was sometimes kindly disposed to the musical academicians, though he often ridiculed them unmercifully. This is shown in his letter to Stassov of September 11, 1871 :

" . . .1. Yesterday I saw dear old Rubin face to face; he was as keen as we were on having a meeting.

"2. He fixed Wednesday that purpose.

"3. He will come on Wednesday with his new opera, to show it to us—*us* includes General Bach [one of Moussorgsky's nicknames for Stassov], Dmitri Vassilievitch [Stassov's brother], the Admiralty [Rimsky-Korsakov], Kvehe [Cui], and poor me.

"4. He wants Borodin and Balakirev to hear him too, but we are not likely to get them.

"5. He will sing his opera himself and begs us not to let anybody else be present. So I should like to know where Rubinstein is to bring his opera, to you or to Dmitri Vassilievitch. Make up your mind and let us know (in person if possible). Rubinstein was delightfully keen—as an artist he is full of life and charm."

The meeting, at which Rubinstein played his opera *The Demon*, which was to have an immense success in Russia, took place at Dmitri Stassov's house. Besides those mentioned in the letter, there were present Laroche, W. Bessel, the music-publisher, and Nikolai Rubinstein, just back from Moscow, who played the music with Anton as a piano duet. For Moussorgsky such musical "peace conferences" had no practical result; he was always absolutely incapable of any sort of diplomacy in questions of art, and any chance of establishing better relations with other musicians was sure to be destroyed by his uncompromising frankness—such was probably the case on this evening. In Bessel's *Recollections* there is a short but significant notice of this important first hearing of *The Demon*. He says: "Notwithstanding the composer's marvellous playing, the new opera made no very favourable impression on the audience. The dances, the march, and the procession of the caravan (introduction to Act II, Scene ii) pleased them best. Only after supper, when the great artist sat down to the piano, their mood changed and they became enthusiastic; when he left, they all escorted him to the door, expressing their admiration."

At that time Moussorgsky might have made peace with honour, not only with the Conservatoire—the "musical synagogue," as he called it—but with the other stronghold of official music at Petersburg, the Imperial Marie Theatre, whose stage was the goal aimed at by all Russian operatic composers. He reached that goal later with his *Boris*, but only after overcoming many obstacles. In 1871 a most promising opportunity was offered to Moussorgsky, and not only to him but to all four members of the "Powerful Coterie"—all except Balakirev. In the winter of 1870–1, according to Rimsky-Korsakov—in the winter of 1871–2, according to Stassov (the latter date is the right one, as is shown by a letter of Moussorgsky's)—an important proposal was made to the composers of the "Powerful Coterie." S. A. Gedeonov, the manager of the Imperial Theatre at Petersburg, who had literary and dramatic ambitions of his own, formed a plan of giving a great spectacular performance at the Marie Theatre, a blending of opera, ballet, and fairy pantomime. The attractive subject of the piece, one full of fantastic scenes and fine stage pictures, he took from the Slav legends of the Balkans.

Princess Mlada, beset by all the good and evil spirits of a chaotic mythology, formed the centre of a plot that had hardly any dramatic connexion, but found room for almost anything, from the sacred horses of heathen idolatry to processions of ghosts and a final apotheosis. To the general astonishment, Gedeonov ordered the music for this grand spectacle from Cui, Moussorgsky, Rimsky-Korsakov, and Borodin. He employed Stassov to negotiate with them; and it is highly probable that Stassov, who was at that time more than ever under the spell of the pan-Slavonic vision, was responsible for the whole plan of the piece. It was only natural, under these conditions, that the music for such a play should be entrusted, not to German professors at the Conservatoire, but to these musical cranks, who, if they had no other merit, were beyond dispute (except Cui) thoroughly Slavonic and national in feeling. Stassov believed, firmly and rightly, in the genius of his friends and hoped that out of heathen Slav mythology and ancient Slav customs they would make a musical and dramatic masterpiece. The four composers went to see Gedeonov and were allotted their parts.

César Cui, who, on the strength of his *Ratcliff*, considered himself the greatest dramatic composer of the time—an opinion in which his friends supported him—undertook the first act, in which the few traces of dramatic construction occurred. Borodin chose the fourth act, in which his passion for the Slav heroes of hoary antiquity hoped to find rich material; it included scenes of strange heathen rites, and the apparition of the ghosts of dead Slav princes, a temple engulfed by the sea, and a general catastrophe. Moussorgsky and Rimsky-Korsakov were to divide the second and third acts between them; Moussorgsky chose some peasant scenes, a grand procession of Slav princes, and a big fantastic scene of sorcery, the orgies in honour of the "Black God" (Tchernobog) on the hill of Triglaff.

All four composers started their work energetically. The working-out of the scheme offered enticing opportunities; the outlay on the staging and orchestra was to be unexampled, and the composers could give rein to their fancy, unhindered by any question of money. Most of them, including Moussorgsky, acted as people generally do in such cases, when they get a definite order for music; they turned up all the old works that were gathering dust in their desks, and looked to see what could be used, with alterations, for *Mlada*. This was necessary, from the fact that the composers had only a very short time allowed them to finish their work. Moussorgsky had the choruses from *Œdipus* and *Salambo* lying by, waiting for a resurrection; he now adapted them, by hook or crook, to the new piece. The orchestral fantasia, *The Witches*, which he had begun in 1866, but had not completed, seemed made for the pan-Slavistic Brocken scene. He dug it up, to serve for the witches' sabbath on Mount Triglaff, instead of on the Blocksberg. Only the "March of the Slav Princes," and some scenes in the second act, were new.

But the composers soon lost interest in their combined

work. There were many reasons for this; Borodin was in the first flush of ardour over his opera *Prince Igor*; Rimsky-Korsakov confesses that the work did not appeal to him, "owing to the vagueness of the subject and the inadequate working-out of the scenario." Moussorgsky felt much the same, as he said frankly in a letter to Stassov (March 31, 1872): "But Mlada! Mlada!

> Even in the gloomy grave
> I have no peace
> From the wan dead. [1]

"I feel ashamed to take up my pen to compose music to 'Sagala, hush!' and similar rubbish—the author must have been fuddled when he wrote it; how can one get inspiration from the fumes of delirium tremens? Disgusting! I have long been struggling against the irritation that certain people arouse in me; but when the causes of this irritation persist, or when it is not in my power to remove them, the struggle changes from an acute attack to a chronic complaint (the simile is quite accurate; bad temper, which casts a gloom over a man's life, is just a disease, and continual relapses make it chronic). The way they have of treating the composers of *Mlada de haut en bas*, the lack all decency on the part of our worthy entrepreneur, and the consequent (and impending) moral fiasco of our society—that is too much for me. My dear friend, you know that I can't stifle my anger; still less can I go on cherishing a grievance. I must take the offensive; it is simpler, better, and more straightforward. I have told Korsinka and Borodin, as moderately and tactfully as I could, that in order to preserve the maiden innocence of our association and save it from being prostituted, from henceforth *I* mean to give the orders

---

[1] "Who is lying 'in the gloomy grave'—whether the author of the piece or Mlada or both I leave you to decide" (note by Moussorgsky). The verses are taken from the libretto of *Mlada*.

instead of obeying them, in all that concerns our common undertaking; *I* shall ask questions instead of answering them—of course in agreement with Korsinka and Borodin for them and for myself—let our entrepreneur say what he likes."

What the "entrepreneur" said to this is not known and was of no further importance, for shortly afterwards he was dismissed and the whole *Mlada* business fell through. Later on, Rimsky-Korsakov took the subject in hand alone and made one of his finest fantastic operas out of it.

In connexion with this abortive undertaking Rimsky-Korsakov suggested that Moussorgsky should write a musical satire—a sort of companion to his "Peep-show"—in which Gedeonov should appear as the beneficent Euterpe, and the members of the "Powerful Coterie" as his satellites.

"It is a capital idea," wrote Moussorgsky, "for Korsinka insists that I shall give us all a good trouncing—myself included. If I succeed, our reputation is saved. It is not the Philistines who will be our judges, but we ourselves, and we know what chastisement our own folly deserves."

Unfortunately Moussorgsky never carried out this "capital idea," and nothing more was heard of it.

*   *   *

His life with Rimsky-Korsakov lasted only till the summer of 1872. The frequent trips to Pargolovo had their result; Rimsky-Korsakov left his friend in order to get married. His wedding with Nadeshda Ivanovna Purgold took place on June 30th, and Moussorgsky acted as best man.

This separation from his chum had serious results for him, as might be expected; in Rimsky-Korsakov he lost not only a pleasant companion, but a moral support, for lack of which he fell more and more into the ways of an irregular, irresponsible, but highly uncomfortable Bohemianism.

In the year 1872 an event occurred that, though unimportant in itself, marked for Moussorgsky the culmination of a long process of mental development. Most of the members of the "Powerful Coterie," under similar influences, had gradually been shaking off the artistic control of Balakirev, when that composer most unexpectedly put an end to it himself. He withdrew, not only from his own circle, but from all the public musical activities of Petersburg.

In the previous year Balakirev had shown a waning interest in musical matters. Moussorgsky, who now met him less often than before, was deeply affected by the report, which he had from Stassov. He wrote in answer to his friend (April 18, 1871) : "Your letter about Mili [Balakirev] has quite upset me, although I have not myself remarked his growing coolness. My imagination drew a terrible picture of it. Your words were like a funeral oration on Mili's artistic career—it is frightful if it is true, and not partly affectation on his side. It is too soon, far too soon, *for a man to be wearied out*! Or is it the result of disillusion? Perhaps; but where is his courage, and the consciousness of his duty and of the artistic aims that cannot be reached without a struggle? Or was art only a means and not an end for him? *Diavolo! diavolo!*"

Clearly it was not only the growing independence of the former disciples of his circle that caused Balakirev to take this surprising step. He had so far met with nothing but disappointment in his musical career; the Petersburg public was unmoved by the nationalistic ideals of art which he and Stassov followed with a zealous and narrow fanaticism, but which had not spread beyond the pan-Slavistic group. He had broken with the Russian Musical Society owing to his obstinacy on this point; the war that he waged with the society, as director of the symphony concerts of the Free School of Music and as the champion of progress against hidebound reaction, ended, as might have been expected, in complete defeat. The public preferred the great European names of the Musical Society, and the "Internationalism" of its programs to the national Russian propaganda of the Free School. Balakirev's concerts were given to empty halls and very soon swallowed up all his reserve funds. The last concert was in March 1872. An array of empty seats greeted Balakirev when he appeared to lead the orchestra. He called the concert his "musical Sedan" and retired, in a huff, from public life; indeed it seemed as if his disgust at the stupidity of the public gave him for a time a distaste for music itself —for some years he gave it up completely. Besides, Balakirev, who in his youth had been a convinced atheist, now fell under the influence of the obscure religious and political powers then so influential in Russia and became an Orthodox bigot, with a strong leaning to the dogmatic teaching of the Old Believers. Not till the end of the seventies did Balakirev put an end to his voluntary exile (he had spent the time as a minor official at one of the railway stations in the outskirts of Petersburg) and return to his musical work, but no longer in the circle of the "Powerful Coterie," which had now completely broken up.

The last work that Balakirev conducted at his last concert was the Polonaise from the just completed "Polish act" of Moussorgsky's *Boris Godounov.* The composer had sent Balakirev the score on March 22, 1872, with the following letter: "If you think the Polonaise worth putting on the program of your concert, I shall be glad. I shan't mind in the least if you put it right at the end; those who are interested in the piece will stay on. It will be a great help to me to have the Polonaise performed; it is essential that I should hear my music played by the orchestra alone, without the chorus, and I have not had a chance to do so till now."

This last symphony concert of the Free School of Music, and Balakirev's consequent withdrawal from the musical world, mark the close of an epoch in Moussorgsky's life —they are the outward signs of that inner development

234

which ended in freeing him from a control that had at first given him a wholesome stimulus and a fellowship with kindred spirits, but had gradually grown into an intolerable despotism on questions of art and life. The composer of *Boris Godounov* saw the way of his art clear before him and had no more need of leading-strings.

*   *   *

In the interval between the completion of the score of *Boris* in its original form, 1871, and the first performance of the work in its final shape, on January 24, 1874, Moussorgsky composed but little. The continual revision of the score, the composition of the Polish scenes, and other additions, the many difficulties connected with getting the opera accepted and rehearsed, especially the dress rehearsal and performance for the benefit of Kondratiev, the manager, gave the composer, who had only half his day free, no time for other important work. During that time, besides his "Peep-show," *The Nursery* was the only thing he completed. This composition is of special importance as being the only work that made Moussorgsky's name known abroad in his lifetime. Not only this, but it brought him into closer relations with the Petersburg music-publisher Bessel, whose sure and happy instinct led him to secure the rights in nearly all Moussorgsky's later compositions.

Vassili Vassilievitch Bessel was one of the most popular men in Petersburg musical society during the second half of the nineteenth century. Everybody knew him, not only as the founder and head of the well-known publishing house, but also as publisher of two widely read musical journals, the *Musical News*, (*Musikalny Listok*) and the *Musical Review* (*Musikalnoie Obosrenie*). He issued instructive treatises on many subjects allied to music, and organized various literary and musical societies, exhibitions, the Rubinstein Museum, etc. As a music-publisher Bessel, who was himself a skilled

musician and had studied under Vieuxtemps at the Petersburg Conservatoire, was the first to recognize the importance
of the "New Russian School." But he did not undervalue the
importance of the Conservatoire and its head, Anton Rubinstein, many of whose works he published and to whose *Demon*
he owed the great expansion of his firm. This made it possible for him to publish many works whose future was more
than doubtful, but whose merits Bessel's artistic instinct di-
vined, if it did not quite grasp. In his journals Bessel did
not venture to declare himself definitely on the side of the
"New Russian School"; he used their columns for a far-
reaching and successful propaganda in favour of the leaders
of the other side. That was obviously his only course, since
Serov and Laroche were two of the chief contributors to his
journals; moreover, it was not mere commercialism, but sincere conviction, that made Bessel hail Rubinstein and Serov,
and, later on, Tchaikovsky, as the greatest leaders of Russian music.

V. V. Bessel founded his firm, with his brother Ivan, in
1869. In 1871 he published the first short pieces by Mous-
sorgsky—the songs "The Magpie," "The Ragamuffin,"
"The Orphan." He seems to have hesitated at accepting *The
Nursery*, as is shown in a letter of Moussorgsky's to Stassov,
May 1, 1872:

"My dear Generalissimo, I beg you will come tonight to
Cui's—the business of *The Children* can still be arranged;
I have seen Bessel, and he will be at Cui's, too. I wish we
could talk over how to manage the business. Bessel insists on
having a picture for *The Children*. I beseech you to come to
the help of your Moussorianin."

And Stassov, ever ready, came to the rescue. He got
the (at that time) celebrated painter Ilia Riepin, whom
Moussorgsky came to know personally, to draw a cover for
The Nursery. Bessel had his picture—a festoon of toys round

236

the title of the work, which contributed not a little to make it popular—and so "the business was managed."

In the summer of 1873 Bessel went to Germany. One of his reasons for the trip was to form a connexion with the German musical world and to spread some elementary knowledge of Russian music in Germany, where no one had any idea how individual and highly developed a school of music had arisen on the banks of the Neva. Some years later (1878) Bessel began, in regular annual reports in the *Neue Musik-Zeitung*, to inform the German musical world of the progress of music in Russia. In 1873 his first visit was to Franz Liszt at Weimar. He gave him presentation copies of the operas that had just been published by his firm—Dargomizhky's *Stone Guest* and Cui's *Ratcliff*. In his *Recollections* Bessel gives the following account: To help Liszt to understand Dargomizhky's work, it was necessary to put a German or French text to the opera (*Ratcliff* had a German translation). Consequently Bessel asked Moussorgsky, who knew German perfectly, to fit Bodenstedt's translation of Pushkin's dramatic poem to the piano score of Dargomizhky. Moussorgsky, who was very anxious to bring this original Russian opera, and Russan opera generally, to the knowledge of Liszt—and in the circle of the "Powerful Coterie" Liszt was rightly accounted as the most progressive musician of his time—did what Bessel asked him and wrote Bodenstedt's translation, with a few necessary alterations, into the piano score of *The Stone Guest*. But Liszt never got this copy. Bessel, who did not want to give away Moussorgsky's autograph, made another copy the night before he called on Liszt. The story is significant, since it shows Bessel's opinion of the composer of *The Nursery*.

Besides these two piano scores Bessel apparently brought the old master at Weimar other publications of his firm, including Moussorgsky's *Nursery*; perhaps it was Stassov, who was in Germany at the same time as Bessel and also called on Liszt, who gave him or sent him a copy of this example of the "New Russian School." Between Moussorgsky and Stassov there was naturally a lively correspondence while the latter was abroad. Stassov's letters, unfortunately, were not kept, so that Moussorgsky's letters are all the more instructive. From these we find that Stassov had the idea of getting Moussorgsky to take a trip abroad, in order to make Liszt's acquaintance. It is a pity that this plan was never carried out; such an acquaintance would undoubtedly have had the most important results for Moussorgsky's life and artistic career; the great-hearted Liszt would never have left the gifted composer to wear himself out at the daily grind of a junior clerkship.

Moussorgsky's letters to Stassov gave eloquent proof of his high opinion of Liszt and his understanding of the great man. His first mention of him is in a letter of July 23, 1873, addressed to Vienna. The letter also contains some most interesting remarks on Russian music.

Moussorgsky writes: "Bessel's brother (Bessel has seen Liszt several times at Weimar) stopped his droshky and came up to me to tell me that Liszt is quite enthusiastic over the latest Russian music and that he had told V. Bessel that my *Nursery* so delighted him that he was in love with the composer and wanted to dedicate '*une bluette*' to him. If that is true, and no exaggeration, it is surprising, *almost incredible* from Liszt. I may or may not have a gift for music, but I have done pretty well in *The Nursery*, for I understand children and regard them, not as mere dolls to be played with, but as little men and women in their own little world. That is all right; but still I should never have thought that Liszt, who generally treats only colossal subjects in music, could *really* understand *The Nursery*, praise it, and even become enthusiastic over it. The children in the work are little Russian children, who reek of the soil. What will Liszt say, or rather think, when he sees *Boris*, if only in a piano score? In short, if this *great event* really has happened, Russian music is happy in finding recognition from a giant like Liszt. I am thinking not of myself alone, but of the fact that he (as Bessel's brother told me) is always talking of Russian musicians and is never weary of reading their works. God send him long life, and perhaps I may yet manage to travel to Europe to see him, and give him a pleasant hour with all sorts of novelities—but only with you, Generalissimo, of course—instead of which I must stay here and rot, wasting time and work on things that could be done better without me. It is my fate, though I can see the entire uselessness and superfluousness of it all, that I must go on wearing myself out on the Woods and Forests. It is uncanny! What new worlds would open before me could I but meet Liszt! What hidden corners would we three explore together! Liszt, who is bold and fearless, would not fear to journey into unknown lands with us.

"Shall you be seeing Liszt, Generalissimo? If even in Petersburg, among our half-decayed human corpses, something seems to stir, if a good idea springs up here and there and the creative spirit of Russia is waking from its agelong sleep, what must it be like in Europe? The old Russian genius is like a frightened sparrow, afraid to open its mouth; when it flies 'up to the clouds' it sits on a cloud and goes to sleep, and when it comes 'down into the vale,' it gets into a shop and is mixed up with all sorts of petty affairs that are of no importance, and can never free itself from the old habit of saying: 'As Monsieur pleases!' That mystical music picture, the '*Danse Macabre*,' in the form of variations on the theme of the '*Dies Iræ*,' could only have come from the brain of a daring European like Liszt—in it he has shown the true artistic relations between the piano and the orchestra. The conception is so simple; it is a set of variations and (apparently) nothing more; but I would

239

compare it to Riepin's picture 'Bourlaky'—that too is a group of portraits and, at first sight—nothing more.

"The colossal 'Te Deum,' which stands in relation to Beethoven's Titanic Second Mass as St. Peter's at Rome does to our Isaac's Cathedral, could only have been reared in the brain of that other daring European, Berlioz. I can only compare it, as far as its form goes, with the introduction to *Russlan*—the work of the Europeanized (heavens, what a word!) Glinka. *Et nous autres?* . . . We need Europe, not to drive round there on a pleasure trip, but to learn to know it; we do not want to admire the eternal Swiss waterfalls or the view from the Brühl Terrace at Dresden or to find where you can get the best dinner, in Paris or in Vienna—no, that is not what we want. We leave that to our landed proprietors—all that are not yet ruined—and to fat-pursed financiers. Unfortunately even our musical travellers have little more than that to tell us about Europe. That's the way of the Empire of All the Russias—always half asleep! In the world of science and letters, where brains *have* to work quicker, the heads of all branches of learning are in constant communication, and so are the great men of all countries. I don't know how it is with the other arts, but in the musical world such an idea has never entered the heads of our musical commercial travellers. 'She sleeps, she sleeps, and no one knows when she will wake' [a quotation from Borodin's song, 'The Sleeping Princess']. . . . But if our mere parleyings in the antechamber of Europe have proved so profitable, full relations with the Continent would naturally do much more for our progress."

The immediate effect of this letter was that Stassov urged Moussorgsky to come to Germany at once, if possible, to become personally acquainted with Liszt, and evidently offered to remove any money difficulties in the way of this plan. Nevertheless Moussorgsky felt compelled to de-

cline his friend's invitation; how it went to his heart to do so
is shown in the answer he sent to Germany on August 6th:

"This is the answer a Russian musician has to give you,
my dear Generalissimo! He must give up realizing his dearest wish, must deny himself a real life and go on sweating
away at his dirty work. It is frightful, but it is true. Your
ardent appeal almost made me resolve to chuck my job for
good; but there is always a catch somewhere—I cannot bring
myself to desert my friend and chief, whose sight is failing
—it would be cruel and wrong. He has helped me before, so
I must help him now—it would be caddish not to do so.

"What might a meeting with Liszt have led to! But
no! I must look to some other possibility *of earning my daily
bread*; if only I could succeed in finding a way to satisfy the
wolves and save the sheep! As you are going to see Liszt, I
should like to ask you to hand him a note from me, but I
won't risk it; firstly—what am I to write? Secondly and
lastly—dare I do it? So I will observe perpetual silence, like
a Trappist. Besides, I believe in my star; it cannot be that
I shall not at some time see the musicians of Europe face to
face. Still, if it is my fate not to, I shall have to bear it, as I
bear all the rest.

"I really should not tell you everything, dear friend,
yet this is just what I am doing—there is safety in distance.
Your proposal that I should come to you to see Liszt, and
your guarantee of expenses—well, it is just like you—but
I must throw it all away, there's no way out of it. Your plan
has left on me a vivid impression, nevertheless—so vivid
that I can see Liszt, hear him, chat with him and you. That
is not empty talk; you have managed, thank God, to bring
the mighty form of the great European artist to my mind
in living reality, to set the cells of my brain working on all
he has done, to bring me near him in spirit, to let me speak
to him and hear him answer. Without your help I could not
have projected myself into Liszt's presence in this way and

have seen him so vividly. Such a vision is vastly important —*how important I know now,* especially since he, as Bessel's brother tells me, has come to know me musically, though of course only in part. That was what I wanted to tell you, my friend! You may call it *pure Platonism* if you like; but the important thing is that it has stirred up my brains—which is always good for Russian brains, since every Russian (whoever he be) is like the Petersburg droshky-drivers, who fall into their sweetest slumbers as soon as they have got a fare."

Stassov was not satisfied with this answer. He sent his friend a second, still more pressing invitation, in which he tried (and rightly) to shake Moussorgsky's exaggerated view of his duty to his official superior. But he was unsuccessful. After a month, on September 6th, the zealous clerk in the Woods and Forests sent him another refusal, in which he repeated the word *"impossible,"* underlined numberless times. Stassov had to take the answer as best he could and go to see Liszt alone. Moussorgsky himself may have bitterly regretted his obstinacy later; the chance of going abroad never came again. The only long journey he took after this was the one from which no traveller returns.

In his second letter to Stassov he mentions not only his official duties as preventing him from leaving, but quite different considerations, which probably had had weight with him a month before, but of which he did not tell Stassov, as they might not seem to his friend, as they did to him, important enough to justify his refusal.

He had been seized by the fever of creation. He wrote to Stassov, apparently quite cool and collected: " . . . I am convinced that I *must* start seriously on *Khovanstchina*—it is full time . . . " but his own mind was not so calm—it was "bubbling and seething" again as when he first began his *Boris.* He was all on fire for his new subject, and the flame of his enthusiasm burnt up all other interests—Stassov and Liszt and all Europe together.

Khovanstchina is a formidable name, especially when written as *"Chowánschtschina,"* in the German transliteration. The word (the accent is on the first *a*) looks as if it were invented to display the tongue-twisting properties of the Russian language. The last syllables hiss like a brood of snakes. What is the meaning of this monstrous word? Nothing much—its sense is more innocent than one would fancy. The last syllables are only a contemptuous suffix in Russian, like "-ery" in English. When the young Tsar Peter (not yet "the Great") was told of a plot that the two Princes Khovansky had formed against him, with the design of seizing on the crown of the Russian Tsardom, he dismissed the whole affair with a contemptuous shrug, and the word *"Khovánstchina!"* and gave orders to let the matter drop. The "dropping" meant that the two Princes Khovansky, father and son, were publicly hanged; but otherwise the conspiracy had no further result, so far as the Russian Empire was concerned. Moussorgsky, however, did not keep to historical facts in the denouement of his opera.

The idea of taking the subject of an opera from the times of the regency of the Tsarevna Sophia and the revolt of the Streltzy at Moscow came to Moussorgsky from his trusty literary adviser V. Stassov, in the year 1872, when *Boris,* only just finished in its second form, was still awaiting representation at the Marie Theatre.

"It seemed to me," writes Stassov in his biography of his friend, "that the fight between old and new Russia would give a fine field for a drama or an opera, and Moussorgsky agreed with me. In the centre of the plot I wanted to put the majestic figure of old Dosifei, the leader of the Raskolniki, a strong, energetic man of keen intellect and vast experience, who, as a controlling force, guided the acts of two Princes —Khovansky, the representative of the old, fanatical, gloomy Russia, and Golitzin, the representative of the culture of western Europe, which was beginning to find favour among the courtiers of the Tsarevna Sophia. Various characters and scenes in the German quarter of Moscow and in the barracks of the Streltzy, the German pastor and his old sister, their young niece, two members of the sect of the Old Believers, one, Marfa, aflame with youth and passion, the other, the withered, soured, fanatical Susanne, both always at strife, young Peter, with his youthful bodyguard, clever, energetic Sophia, with her savage guards, the monastic settlement of the Raskolniki, the sectarians burning themselves at the close of the opera, when Dosifei realizes that 'old Russia' is passing away and a new age beginning—all that seemed to us a most promising plot for an opera."

Stassov was right; but the subject was almost too rich in material and in the possibilities of effective situations that it offered the dramatist to admit of a straightforward dramatic handling. Moussorgsky took up the subject with enthusiasm. With all the ardour of his impulsive nature he plunged into the study of this obscure period of Russian history, devoured all he could get hold of in the way of historical material on the beginning of Peter's reign, on the rites and customs of the Old Believers, the so-called "Raskolniki" ("*raskol*" means "schism"), who seceded from the Greek Church when the Patriarch Nikon ordered the revision and correction of the old Church books, and clung to the old traditions with obstinate fanaticism, rejecting all religious innovations. The subject must have interested him on the musical side, for the liturgical melodies of the Old Believers provided unique material that had never before been put to artistic use, and that traced its origins to a past beyond the reach of historical research.

All this appealed to Moussorgsky, who had a keen artistic interest in the spirit of the Russian nation, and its expression. Mass-psychology, the spontaneous outbursts of popular passions, the "herd instinct" in its stark primeval forms, are best revealed in times of revolutionary violence,

when the power that once kept the people together in sub-
jection is shattered—as it was before the accession of Peter,
and also in the "Time of Troubles" that brought Boris
Godounov to the throne. The nation as a collective organ-
ization was as interesting to Moussorgsky as its individual
leaders. In *Khovanstchina* he found more than one opportunity of expressing in music the emotional reactions of the
masses in the face of events by which each one of them was
individually affected. In spite of the varied dramatic action
and the intricate episodes that serve to bring the different
characters into relation with each other, the protagonist in
this play is the soul of the Russian people. *Khovanstchina,*
like *Boris,* was called "a musical folk-drama," and even more
strongly than in his earlier work Moussorgsky felt the connexion of the distant past with his own age. "The past in the
present—that is my theme," he said. What he meant by this
is explained in the following passage of a letter to Stassov
(June 16 and 22, 1872):

"'We have made progress!' That is a lie! We are
still at the same point. On paper, in books, we have progressed, but really we are still just where we were. So long
as the people itself cannot make out what is being done with
it, so long as it does not *itself* will what is to happen to it—
it is still *just where it was.* Public benefactors play their
part magnificently, win glory, and record it, but the people
still groans, and drinks to stifle its groans, and groans all
the louder—and is *exactly where it was before.*"

Apparently this idea had come to Moussorgsky when,
at Stassov's suggestion, he began to study the epoch of the
end of the sixteenth century, since this letter is the first in
which he mentions the Streltzy, the ancient bodyguard of
the Muscovite tsars, whose revolt is the centre of his new
drama. And on July 15th, he writes:

"To Vladimir Vassilievitch Stassov, with the dedication
of *Khovanstchina.*

"There are no previous instances of dedications of works that are not yet written, but that does not bother me, nor will I let it. I find nothing in my heart that will frighten me into keeping back my dedication till the work is finished. I look forwards, not back. I dedicate to you the whole period of my life during which *Khovanstchina* will come into existence; it is not nonsense when I say: 'I dedicate to you myself and my life for that time,' for I remember clearly that in *Boris* I *lived* as Boris, and that experience has left a precious eternal memory behind it. Now begins something new, *your* work; I am just beginning to live in it—how many precious experiences, what undiscovered countries, lie before me! So I beg you, with the dedication of *Khovanstchina*, *which you yourself set going*, to accept my whole 'incongruous being.' Moussorianin."

Moussorgsky's letters to Stassov, and, from 1877 onwards, those written to his motherly friend Ludmilla Shestakova, give a clear and almost continuous picture of the growth of *Khovanstchina*. It is interesting to follow its course in these papers, for they throw many characteristic sidelights on the mind and methods of the composer.

From the dates of these letters we can see that Moussorgsky worked especially hard at *Khovanstchina* in the summer and autumn of 1873, again in the autumn of 1875 and the summer of 1876. In the summer of 1873, as we know, he gave up his journey abroad to see Liszt, for the sake of this work.

At first we find him studying chiefly the history of his period. He was delighted with the *Pilgrimage to Palestine* of Lukianov, a priest of the Old Believers, at the end of the sixteenth century, in which he discovered a great deal of characteristic detail of the period in which he was interested.

He always speaks in his letters to Stassov of "our opera," "our *Khovanstchina*." He dwells on the smallest details and submits them to his friend's judgment. The historical

246

accuracy that he thus secures is more striking than even in *Boris*; at the same time there is no denying that this elaborate archæological research, which was often lost in a desert of unimportant details, was quite unnecessary in face of the intense interest he felt in the tragical motive of the story.

On July 13, 1872, Moussorgsky writes:

" . . . When you return, dear Generalissimo, all the materials for our future opera will probably be collected. I have bound up a whole big bundle of papers, and called it 'Materials for the musical folk-drama, *Khovanstchina*.' On the title-page are my authorities—all nine of them—not bad, that! I am over head and ears in books, my head is like a soup-kettle. If you have anything good on hand, throw it in!"

Then he names his authorities—heavy historical works —and says finally: "Then comes Avakum [one of the Fathers of the Russian Church]—as the dessert." The further he plunges into the study of his authorities, the more the style of his letters resembles that of his period, so that in some places he is hardly intelligible on account of the antiquated phrases and obsolete expressions that he uses.

The first considerable interruption in *Khovanstchina* was caused by the production of *Boris Godounov* in January 1874. Although during this time Moussorgsky "had his head full" of ideas for his new opera, the troubles connected with the first performance of *Boris* did not allow of any profitable work. Not till March 9th can he report to Stassov: " . . . At last, work on *Khovanstchina* is going full steam ahead," but it is not till August 7, 1875 that he tells his friend: "The first act of *Khovanstchina* is finished in spite of the hindrance of my duties; I am starting on the second act."

It was not only the demands of his official duties, of which Moussorgsky is always complaining more frequently and freely, that delayed his work on *Khovanstchina*. Moussorgsky's imagination was already busy on the plan of a second piece, the comic opera *The Fair at Sorótchintzy*, which we shall speak about in the next chapter. Besides this, a whole series of compositions, smaller in bulk, but in artistic value ranking with his greatest works, came to birth during this period. Thus he did not devote his energies so exclusively to *Khovanstchina* as he had done to *Boris Godounov*. The work itself, too, was harder, for here, having no settled framework ready, he had to work out the whole dramatic scheme himself and write every line of the libretto with his own hand. Stassov only performed the "hodman's work" of furnishing material—most valuable, but not helpful to the essential construction of the opera. He supplied numerous details for the historical background and the language, but took no part in artistic creation.

The further the work developed, the more clearly Moussorgsky became conscious, not only of the greatness, but also of the difficulty of the task. In the letter last quoted he goes on to say: "What a hard job you have given me! Yes, indeed. 'If once you say A, you must also say B.' It's got to be done! I have said it: 'On to new shores!' and there is no turning back; he who ventures on the high seas must not give up! How gladly would I share it all with you, all that has to be done, all those things in which my faith does not fail! How many unknown, unheard-of worlds, what new forms of life, are opening to our view! How enticing they all are, asking to be known and understood! And how hard it is to attain to their possession! It makes one anxious and fearful; but when one has once made a start—and knows that *only daring can succeed*—how happy one feels!"

The completion of the second act took Moussorgsky only four months; he announces the glad news to his friend on December 29, 1875, thus: "The second act of our *Khovanstchina* is ready—I have written right through the holidays, and all night. I think it is a success." Later on he completely altered the act—the difficult scene of the dispute between the Princes Khovansky and Golitzin, and Dosifei, had given him a great deal of trouble from the start—and nearly a year later (on August 31, 1876) he informed Madame Shestakova: "Your Moussinka, lazy dog though he is, has finished Act II of *Khovanstchina*."

But this statement was not strictly true—the second act was not finished; it was to contain a quintet which Moussorgsky wanted to write at Petersburg "under Rimsky-Korsakov's superintendence," since "the combination is an odd one—an alto, a tenor, and three basses"—and the entrance of the Boyar, who brings the news of Peter's having been informed of Khovansky's treason, and of his answer, which gave the name to the piece. The act was to end with a "threatening chord *pp*" to express the stunned and palsied terror of the crowd on the stage. Of all this the manuscript contains only the entrance of the Boyar.

The further the work progressed, the slower was the pace. Moussorgsky had once more to realize the truth of the Russian proverb: "The farther into the forest, the more wood there is!" We get the impression that Moussorgsky finally lost his way in the labyrinth of the material that he was working up into his historical music-drama. Scenes of popular life, types, dramatic situations, picturesque, religious, and political details, accumulated in boundless profusion. The drama grew into an epic poem with endless ramifications, into the chronicle of a whole epoch of Russian history. Moussorgsky wanted if possible to take the whole mass of those "unexplored, unheard-of worlds" that rose before his artist's eye, and pack them into his musical drama. Every detail that he could not bring in was a grief to him and he struggled hard to keep it. Gradually he lost confidence —he felt, more and more clearly, that a collection of interesting, picturesque, individually striking, even thrilling scenes, would not make a drama, without a central interest and a construction that leads straight to the denouement of

249

the tragedy. His work seemed to be splitting at the seams and threatened to fall to pieces in his hands. So he began to reconstruct, to abridge, to cut, to omit whole scenes, but unfortunately his power of distinguishing between the essential and the unessential sometimes failed him; he cut out indispensable parts and refused to sacrifice superfluous details.

A critical day of great importance for the fate of *Khovanstchina* was the composer's name-day (June 15th) in 1876. He mentions this to both his correspondents. In a letter to Madame Shestakova, we read: "I have been in retreat again lately—it was necessary, my nature needed it. In my solitude I have thought a great deal about *Khovanstchina* and I find a great deal of it not what it ought to be. I am almost dissatisfied with myself, but now I am more inclined than ever to believe that I need to be more often alone to collect my thoughts for the sake of my art."

The alterations proposed by Moussorgsky in Stassov's dramatic plan seem to have led to a mild dispute between the friends, but that did not prevent the composer from doing as he thought right. In questions of art Moussorgsky was almost obstinately positive and would not make the slightest concession, even to his dearest friend, if he was not fully persuaded that it was right. You could not force him to change his opinion against his will. The letter to Stassov is as follows:

"My dear Generalissimo! You have for the first time been pleased to frighten your Moussorianin, by apparently getting angry with him. It was not his design to arouse your wrath; but it has happened—well, believe me, my dear friend, that Moussorianin will take your wrath all in good part and try to bear it. For some time—quite a long time— he has been tormented by evil doubts, misgivings, scruples of all sorts—that's the sort of country holiday he has had! He is working—but he wants quiet for his work. *Khovanstchina* is too big, too extraordinary an undertaking. You,

Generalissimo, I am sure, will not suppose that I have taken your remarks and suggestions otherwise than I generally do. *But I have stopped my work—and am thinking over things.* The substance of my thoughts—today, yesterday, weeks ago, tomorrow—is still the same—the wish to emerge a conqueror from the strife and to say to mankind a new word of friendship and love, right out, till it echoes over the whole breadth of the Russian plains—the true word of an obscure musician who is a champion of the true ideals of real art."

In both of these letters one hears the longing that becomes more insistent in all creative minds, the older they grow—the longing for quiet, for solitude, for conditions fairly favourable in which to live and work. But Moussorgsky was never allowed to enjoy this good fortune for any length of time; the Bohemian life that he had had to live since he parted from Rimsky-Korsakov, sometimes alone, sometimes with some room-mate or other, now took a downward course; he was never more to enjoy the happiness of undisturbed creation in congenial surroundings. We must always keep this fact in mind if we wish to understand Moussorgsky's last years. It was chiefly this that continually slackened the pace of his work on *Khovanstchina*.

When he succeeded in retiring for a short time into the quiet of country life, he would soon begin to revel once more in the joys of composition. In the summer of 1876 he had escaped for a little while from the city and was living at a *datcha* with an acquaintance (Naumov). The following letter to L. I. Shestakova shows us his state of mind:

"Dear, kind Ludmilla Ivanovna, I have moved here. The *datcha* is charming; the trees climb right up into the windows, and whisper to me—I don't know what, but I fancy it is something beautiful. God grant that in the company of these kindly and peaceful, if sometimes rather noisy friends, I may succeed in accomplishing my desire, to finish my work—I dream of nothing else. If I keep my health and—may

251

Heaven grant it!—find the needful peace of spirit, you may
be sure that *Khovanstchina* will not let me down. Last night,
being in a strange place, I hardly slept at all. In the evening I took a long walk with N.; we went for five or six
versts at least [about four miles], all along the loveliest
roads; we were both very happy, and afterwards—neither
of us closed an eye. Silence all around us; in the distance
one heard the horn of the signalman on the railway embank-
ment, or a trusty watch-dog barking; now and then, like a
glissando on the harp, a sleepy breeze rustled the leaves—
who could get to sleep? To add to it all, the 'invisible moon'
stole through the leaves on to the head of my bed—softly
and tenderly she stole in. After the 'regulation' noise of
Petersburg, after the restless rumble of the capital, it is impossible to enjoy the quiet all at once—at first one is merely
irritated, one misses the noise and is always asking oneself
what has happened to it. Yesterday, as I sat in the arbour
on the balcony, I was comforted by the merry song of a
band of passing idlers. They were singing a song with accompaniment on the harmonica; I caught the melody, but
was unfortunately too shy to stop the people and ask what
the song was about—I am sorry for it now. I sat on the
balcony and thought about *Khovanstchina* and with good
results. If only I could have leave of absence—my pen would
simply gallop over the music paper. It is high time! Nearly
everything is composed—I have only to peg away at the
writing out. But my duties don't allow of it.

"Dear, good Ludmilla Ivanovna, I wanted to chat with
you about what is nearest to my heart—and I have done so.
I'll write again soon. Keep well, my good, kind friend!
August 2, 1876. Your Moussinka."

Moussorgsky began the third act of *Khovanstchina* on
"New Year's Eve of the year 1876" and finished it on May
29th (at Oranienbaum). The first scene of the fourth act
bears the date of August 5, 1880; the second scene of the

same act was probably composed in 1879. The sketches for
the music of the fifth act go back to the year 1873, but Moussorgsky worked them out and put them together only a few
months before his death.

At last, on August 22, 1879, he was able to tell Stassov:
"Our *Khovanstchina* is finished; there is only now a little cut
to make in the final scene of the burning; we must discuss
this together, for the rascal [he uses the German word
'*Schelm*'] is completely dependent on the technical possibilities of the theatre." Moussorgsky never mastered this "rascal" of a scene. That was left for his musical executor, Rimsky-Korsakov.

Although Moussorgsky had eagerly caught at the subject that Stassov suggested for his opera, he was, as we have
seen, by no means inclined to follow out his friend's plan
slavishly—he had his own ideas, he was an artist first of all,
while Stassov was a historian and archæologist. That explains
their very different conceptions of the same subject. In Stassov's original sketch there is a complete lack of the dramatic development required for any theatrical work. Moussorgsky saw this clearly; he understood, what Stassov failed
to notice, that a political intrigue, a fight between two parties, is not a dramatic conflict. His first dramatic work had
had several "heroes," but among them was the outstanding
personality of the Tsar Boris, who, even when not on the
stage, remained the centre of dramatic interest. Among the
numerous characters of *Khovanstchina*, all equally important for the story as Stassov had thought it out, such a
primus inter pares was wanting. We have Prince Ivan Khovansky, the rough, ruthless leader of the Streltzy, the Tsar's
bodyguards, who were often more dangerous to the ruler
whom they were supposed to defend than his worst enemies;
there is Prince Golitzin, a clever and in some respects cul-
tured nobleman, a friend of European reforms, but at the
same time an irresolute waverer, whose western European

varnish is so thin that every moment the real nature of
the benighted reactionary shows through. Then there is the
third Prince, the *staretz* (venerable old man) Dosifei—in his
worldly life, now long past, known as Prince Mischetsky—
the intellectual and spiritual head of the sect of the Old
Believers. He is bound to Prince Ivan Khovansky by their
common espousal of the old tradition and its petrified formulas; but the latter is more interested in the political side
of the question, while the fanatical Dosifei clings to the
heritage of the olden time with the firm faith that is the inner light of his soul. All three are really heroes of tragedy,
who succumb, in either active or passive conflict with Destiny, which here is the New Age, personified in the character
of the young Tsar Peter. All three characters undoubtedly
hold the attention in a high degree, especially through the
extraordinarily impressive musical setting that Moussorgsky's art has given them; and yet with none of the three does
a listener feel that he has the real central figure of the plot
before him. This soon struck Moussorgsky, in spite of Stassov's intention of making old Dosifei the chief hero of the
drama. Moussorgsky rightly doubted whether a fanatical
old man, whose religious mysticism is out of harmony with
the spirit of his times, however interesting and attractive in
himself, would have the personality to hold the interest of an
audience through five acts as the hero of the tragedy. He
understood just what was necessary to give Dosifei an inner dramatic life and at the same time to make him effective
for the stage. By a stroke of genius he supplemented the
story by weaving a love-interest into the plot and thus created a closer sympathy between the audience and the story
told on the stage. He made *Khovanstchina* the tragedy of a
woman's soul, torn asunder between overpowering sensual
desire and religious ecstasy, and seeking to reconcile herself with Heaven by sharing in the fiery death of the lover
she has lost. Instead of three heroes, or, rather, beside them

and above them, he brings in the figure of a woman, whose soul stands out in grand relief from the confused background of historical action, as the centre of his work.

She is the "wicked heretic" Marfa, the leader of the Sisterhood of the Old Believers, who cannot tear from her heart her sinful love for her former lover, young Prince Andrei Khovansky, on whose behalf his father aspires to the Imperial crown. The girl's uncontrollable passion provides a strange but truly Russian contrast to the ardent ecstasy of a religious fanaticism bordering on madness. You cannot tell whether these two feelings are struggling in violent opposition, or spring from a common source and express a single craving for the absolute surrender of body and soul. The pathos of dramatic and musical emphasis, which Moussorgsky, the apostle of truth in art, generally avoids with exaggerated care, for fear of making it "insincere," finds full scope in the character of Marfa—greatly to the advantage of the music.

It seems as if Moussorgsky wished to make up for the restraint with which his art had hitherto treated love, by this outburst of passion on the part of one woman. Nearly all his efforts in the field of love-lyrics, as we have seen, were failures. In *The Marriage* he had given a malicious caricature of the awaking of "tender feelings" in a half-dead sexuality. In *Boris*, that grand picture of the soul, there was no question of love, unless we count the maidenly lament of Xenia, "the child-widow," as such. But now, in *Khovanstchina*, he puts into Marfa's mouth a song burning and glowing with sensual desire. Here, however, the outburst of passionate imagination does not lead to a free exaltation of soul and spirit, but only drags the woman down to the dust. Carnal desire seems to her the greatest of sins; only by fire can she be cleansed, only by a voluntary death can she expiate her guilt.

One has the feeling—vague and unsupported by any

evidence—that this conception has its source in the composer's own feelings. Towards the close of his life two profound ideas exercised an ever-growing influence on Moussorgsky's art and life: the poetry of death, and the poetry of the love that savours of mysticism, all bound together by secret and invisible threads. One of the finest passages in the score of *Khovanstchina*, which never fails to startle by its imaginative truth, is Marfa's confession, which she makes to Dosifei, of the "fearful torment" of her sinful sensual love for Andrei Khovansky. These bars of music are surpassed in effectiveness only by the short recitative that follows, the comforting answer of the old man, who understands and pardons all, expressed in the words: "All earthly things pass away." Such music—tones that go straight to the heart—no man can write except from his own experience. Marfa seeks and finds atonement for her sin in death alone.

It is significant that the first scene that Moussorgsky worked out in lyrical and musical detail was not one of the stirring pictures of the historical panorama that he intended to unroll in his piece, but this close of Marfa's love tragedy and its terrible sequel of the fiery death of the heretics. Nevertheless this one scene was the only one that Moussorgsky never finished, though it was the persistent thought of it that furnished the motive for the whole structure of the opera. He was busy with it even in 1873. A letter to Stassov of July 23rd in that year contains a remarkable description of this scene, as it shaped itself in the imagination of the poet-composer. Moussorgsky writes: "Our work goes merrily on—I am getting just the right atmosphere—only I want to be alone, to think it over properly. It is too early as yet to write down what I have thought out—it wants time to ripen; you cannot trifle with a folk-drama. What splendid things I've got for our dear lady heretic—my word! . . . Just in passing I can only tell you that when I showed people the 'Requiem of Love,' their eyes started out of their heads, the whole affair is so novel—the Jesuits are nothing to it! It is the death-sentence, and its execution, of a woman in love deserted by her lover. And in a way it brings out the stupidity of Andrei Khovansky, who has preferred a German girl as stupid as himself to this haughty, passionate woman. Marfa does not reproach Andrei with his love for the German girl, but only pities him and her. Clothed in a shroud, with a lighted candle in either hand, she circles round him, to the sound of Hallelujahs; the theme of the incantation is heard, only in another key and with different harmonies—Dosifei appears, also with shroud and candle, and declares that 'the hour has come when we must be cleansed in the baptism of fire, and so enter into the heavenly mansions of the Lord, where Antichrist hath no power, and our souls shall be saved.' "

A week later, on August 2nd, Moussorgsky completed this sketch. "The women appear from the forest, all in white shrouds, with candles in their hands; one of them utters a piercing cry: 'Death is upon us,' and runs after the Brothers, bidding them also clothe themselves in white and take candles in their hands. Andrei Khovansky is bewildered—the fool cannot imagine what is going on in the settlement. After the love-theme from the incantation, the heretic whispers in his ear: 'Beloved, thy last hour is at hand, embrace me for the last time—I am true to thee till death; to die with thee is but to sink into a pleasant sleep. Hallelujah!' (She bows low before him.) This Funeral Mass of Love pleases *everybody, without exception,* and I even like it myself." This scene is followed by the suicide by fire of the sectarians, who by this voluntary death seek to escape from "Antichrist" (Peter).

Marfa, as the real centre of dramatic interest (in its restricted sense), comes naturally into contact with the other chief characters in the action. She is connected with Dosifei by their common religious faith, and holds the leading

257

position among his female disciples. Prince Golitzin regards her as a "soothsayer"; his leaning to mysticism and occultism is partly the result of European "culture," partly a relic of the gloomy superstition of his Russian surroundings. Beset by well-founded fears of the fate that threatens him amidst the political upheavel of the time, he sends for the "heretic" from whom he hopes to learn the future. Marfa duly foretells his imminent fall and the burning of the others. Moussorgsky, whose rationalistic temper refused to accept any interference of the supernatural with the logical connexion of his plot, accounts for this by the fact that Marfa, the heretic (a historical character, the former Princess Sitzky, who fled from the close, incense-laden air of the palace, that sink of iniquity, to join the seekers after God), during her attendance at the court of the old Tsaritsa Natalie, naturally heard all the gossip of Moscow and was especially well informed as to Golitzin's position, whereas the latter, excluded from the court of the old Empress by his western European views, would not have known the young Princess. This rather roundabout explanation enabled Moussorgsky to enrich his score with one of its finest scenes—that of the "incantation" lately mentioned. Its ending is characteristic of Golitzin—and Moussorgsky; after Marfa has gone, the Prince, concerned about his reputation as a champion of enlightenment and European morality, rings for his servant and orders him to "drown the woman in the swamp, to prevent any scandal." The order is carried out, frustrated at the last moment by the young Tsar Peter's "Horseguards."

These "Horseguards" of Peter are brought into *Khovanstchina* to make the contrast between the dark, mysterious, and therefore alluring mysticism of the old age, and the naked, unadorned "enlightenment" introduced by Peter the Great, plain to eye and ear: their blaring trumpets and the blatant vulgarity of their march tune often break rudely into the very different picture that Moussorgsky has used all the arts of musical suggestion to bring before us.

Marfa's successful rival for the love of young Andrei Khovansky is Emma, the niece of the Protestant clergyman in the "German quarter" of Moscow. Moussorgsky had originally intended to give the "German quarter" an important place in his piece. The picture of this simple, clean, peaceful society, taken in conjunction with Peter's "Horse-guards," would have formed a striking contrast to the rude, primitive nature and sulphurous atmosphere, political and religious, of their Muscovite surroundings.

Rimsky-Korsakov relates in *My Musical Life* that Moussorgsky often played him long passages of the music that he had composed with this view, "in the style of Mozart" (!), and that this music was "very fine." But the composer had to give up all idea of this German idyll, since the dramatic compass of the work was getting beyond all bounds; and the little of it that he kept in his score fell a sacrifice—as we shall see presently—to the revising zeal of the editor of *Khovanstchina*, Rimsky-Korsakov.

The character of Emma, rather vague in itself, was thus made even more colourless. She and her equally unimpressive cavalier, whose stupidity—he is the tenor—even Moussorgsky emphasizes, wander like unreal shadows through the opera, which is otherwise so rich in living and individual characters. We would gladly leave them out altogether if they were not necessary for the plot.

The moving spirit of the political intrigue round which the piece revolves is the Boyar Shaklovity; it is he who writes the anonymous denunciation of the Princes Khovansky, thus causing their fall, and the discovery of the Streltzy conspiracy, for which they were responsible and which Peter put down with an iron hand. Shaklovity is a very remarkable character—he is actually a common scoundrel, but has a certain dignified, even majestic bearing, in spite of his blood-thirsty nature and his passion for intrigue. Moussorgsky, by the way, commits a historical inaccuracy, which, however, does not affect the essence of the opera or the significance of its actual events. The action of the opera takes place—as can be verified by several facts—in the year 1682; Peter was then only ten years old, and his wrath could terrify nobody. The revolt of the Streltzy, in which the Khovanskys were involved, broke out nine years later. Shaklovity dictates his anonymous denunciation of the Princes and the Streltzy—which is addressed to "the Mighty Tsars of White, Great, and Little Russia"—in the Red Square, in front of the Kremlim, to a certain notary, apparently of clerical standing, who is one of the most successful comic figures in the piece, a worthy counterpart of the begging friars, Varlaam and Missail, in *Boris Godounov*. This begins the opera. But it is Shaklovity, also, who brings to the "Princes' Council," at the end of the second act, the news of the discovery of the plot, the anger of the Tsar, and his contemptuous branding of the affair with the name "*Khovanstchina!*"

Prince Ivan Khovansky, threatened by the anger of the young Tsar (or rather of the young Tsars, since at that time both brothers, Peter and Alexei, ranked as rulers of all the Russias, while their sister, Tsarevna Sophia, acted as regent), has withdrawn to his estates in the interior of the Empire. There Moussorgsky shows him to us in one of the most effective pictures of his musical drama. The stage represents a richly furnished hall in the Old Russian style, in the country-seat of the proud magnate, who thinks himself powerful and splendid enough to aspire to the crown of Russia. The Prince is at table. Along the wall are ranged a host of maids of honour, who are there to entertain their great lord with song, but fail in their attempt. In spite of song and dance, there is a feeling of calamity brooding over the scene. This is broken by the entrance of a servant, who

announces a messenger on horseback. The old Prince, whose
uncontrollable temper threatens to break out at any moment,
asks: "Who dares disturb me here?" It is a message from
Prince Golitzin: "Prince Golitzin sends word: 'Danger
threatens thee, it is at hand! Beware, Prince!'" "What! In
my very house? Will thy Prince insult me in my own ancestral manor?" Khovansky, in a towering passion, gives
orders for Golitzin's messenger to be handed over to the
stablemen "to be used as he deserves." We know what that
means—the slave must run the gauntlet of the ostlers in
the stable-yard. After this disturbance the spirit of revelry
needs reviving. The Prince calls for his Persian slave-girls,
and now begins the familiar "Dance of the Persian Girls,"
which has rightly been described as the most precious pearl
of oriental music in the world. Hardly is it over when the
Boyar Shaklovity enters again, unannounced, and excuses
the rudeness of his intrusion by the importance of his message. This time he comes as the envoy of the Princess Regent; disturbed and alarmed by the continual troubles and
the doubtful state of both home and foreign affairs, Sophia
is summoning a great council of her Boyars and dignita-
ries; Prince Khovansky is the first to be invited. The latter,
whose arrogance is flattered by this open preference, sends
for his most splendid clothes, his high beaver cap, and his
prince's staff; while he is robing, the girls must hymn his
praises. They sing *pianissimo*, with voices faint with fear,
making an unexpected and extraordinarily striking effect:
"Glory and honour to the White Swan, *ládu, ladú*!" At last
the Prince rises heavily and moves towards the door, supported by two servants; on the threshold, he falls, the death-
rattle in his throat. An assassin, evidently hired by Shaklovity, has plunged a dagger in his heart from behind; the
singing-girls scatter with shrill screams: Shaklovity steps
up to the body of the Prince, who has fallen like an oak cut

261

down, and with a scornful smile repeats—still *piano*—"Glory and honour to the White Swan, *ládu, ladú!*" Curtain. . . .

In all operatic literature there are few scenes more effective than these, where the tremendous dramatic excitement is raised to the utmost possible height by the magnificent music. Few passages even in Moussorgsky's works are equal to them.

Moussorgsky called *Khovanstchina*, like *Boris Godounov*, a "Musical Folk-drama." What was meant by this ambiguous expression was discussed in an earlier chapter. In any case Moussorgsky did not mean to say that his plays were dramas "for the people," nor did he mean to represent the people as an actor on the stage. He rather represents the people as the passive, suffering part of society—not on account of chance conditions or the especially unfavourable conditions of the periods of which he treats, but from the very nature of things. The lot of the people is eternally tragic; there is no way out of it, nor can there be any. Consequently the people, in Moussorgsky's works, does not act consciously and independently, does not guide its own fate by its own creative ideas into paths that lead to a tragical or happy end, but is always the helpless tool of higher powers or of invisible wire-pullers, all the more when it thinks it is acting consciously and independently.

And it is just this that is the real drama of the people, the drama of every people at all times, but especially of the Russian people, and especially in the times of those "revolutions" that Moussorgsky treats of in his operas. Two striking examples of this are the revolts against Godounov and against the Boyars in *Boris*, and the rising of the Streltzy in *Khovanstchina*; in both the people thinks it is acting freely and yet is only a ready tool in the hands of ambitious intriguers.

In regular "folk-scenes" *Khovanstchina* is not so rich as is *Boris*. There is, in fact, only one scene that deserves the

262

name, the beginning of the first act, where the people welcome and accompany the Dictator of Moscow, Prince Khovansky, as he rides through the streets to the Red Square. The original version of *Khovanstchina* also contains an animated scene before this, in which the people urge the "learned" notary to read out to them the government proclamation on the notice board and when he will not, smash up his booth. This scene was sacrificed by the editorial blue pencil of the reviser. Apart from these scenes in the first act, in which the people takes part as a collective body, Moussorgsky in *Khovanstchina* shows us only separate groups of the population, who are rather a sort of morbid excrescence on the healthy body of the nation. On one side are the Streltzy, the unspeakably brutal soldiery, sunk in dirt and drunkenness, of whom the notary says: "Are these men? No, they are beasts in human shape, wading in blood, causing tears and cries of terror wherever they go." On the other side are the Old Believers, the fanatical heretics, who see nothing before them but the gate of heaven, open wide for them alone, and seem to wander through life in ecstatic apathy, untouched by all external happenings. The strangeness of each of these had a great attraction for Moussorgsky. His love for the unusual explains the interest with which he worked at the artistic and musical development of the material that the Streltzy and the Raskolniki furnished by their mental attitude and the visible and audible expression thereof.

Two scenes of *Khovanstchina* are devoted to the Streltzy. One shows them in their own quarters, the Streltzy-Sloboda. Here Moussorgsky takes the opportunity of sounding every note, so to speak, of the varied passions of these unruly guardsmen, corrupt, but sometimes open to better human feelings. First comes an outbreak of brute instincts, during a wild drunken revel, and the consequent fight with the women, who are enraged at their husbands' behaviour.

Directly afterwards there is a complete change of tone; the cunning, intriguing notary stirs up the Streltzy by stories of the exploits of Peter's "Horseguards"—whom they rightly regard as a threat to their own existence—to sheer madness, mingled with the cowardly fear felt by all violent natures. Their "little father," Ivan Khovansky, tries to calm · their perturbed spirits, but even he lets out the truth: "Beware of Tsar Peter!"—at which the Streltzy remember that there is a God, and in a marvellous, short, unaccompanied chorus, *pianissimo*, implore the Lord's mercy on their guilty and imperilled heads. On this, with a soft roll of the drums, the curtain falls.

The last scene but one of the opera shows us the Streltzy condemned to death after their unsuccessful mutiny— in the Red Square near the Kremlin, as in the first scene. By the Tsar's command each of them carries the block and the ax with which he is to be beheaded. This mournful procession is accompanied by the wailing of the women, in reproducing which Moussorgsky goes to the utmost limit of realism that is æsthetically possible. A Boyar is to read their sentence again to the Streltzy. Instead of this he brings them pardon from "the young Tsars, Peter and Alexei." In all the literature of music there is hardly another such effective employment of the chord of six-four as in the short recitative of the Boyar, at the word "pardon"—it sounds like a note of deliverance, at which not only the unhappy criminals on the stage, but the entire audience breathes a sigh of relief.

The Raskolniki, the sect of the Old Believers, do not take an active part in the story at first. But their presence broods like a nightmare over almost all the scenes of the musical drama, as they cross the stage singing, or their hymns are heard behind the scenes. It is hard to breathe in this close atmosphere of gloomy superstition; their self-immolation impresses one not as a shining act of martyrdom, but as a cruel, brutal crime, a senseless flinging away of life with all its healthy instincts. The crushing effect of the final scene is increased by the quick march of Peter's "Horse-guards"—it sounds like the mockery of fiends as the guards come on to the stage, but stand powerless before the raging flames of the terrible *auto-da-fé*. With this, Moussorgsky's drama closes. The author has no mercy on us—not a ray of light brightens the future. The lament of the *yurodivi* would be as appropriate here as in *Boris*; the folk-drama is ended, but the drama of the Russian folk is not ended—cannot and never will be ended. . . .

The music of *Khovanstchina* shows considerable differences in style from that of *Boris Godounov*, but these must not be regarded as the result of a conscious and consistent development; the style of *Khovanstchina* is not an advance on that of *Boris*—the latter, in its own way, could hardly be improved on. Nevertheless, Moussorgsky does not repeat in his second opera the methods he employed in the first; in none of his varied experiments does he follow a set pattern, and whatever may be his guiding principle, he never allows it to stiffen into a formula. He had no need to fear lest this mental and creative versatility might lead him astray, for in the whole course of his work as a composer he found, times without number, that his infallible instinct invariably discovered the right form in which to clothe each poetic or dramatic idea as it arose; his artistic creations are always "made to measure," so to speak—he fits every line with the musical garb that suits it and goes with it and with no other—the sureness that he displays in this respect almost suggests the clairvoyant.

Thus, though there is no one absolute guiding principle in respect of style in *Khovanstchina*, any more than in *Boris Godounov*, nevertheless we feel that in both works the stage action, the words, and the music form an ideal stylistic

265

combination such as is only possible with elements inseparably connected and inevitably fitting together.

The essence of the vocal style of *Boris* was recitative;
even in moments of the greatest dramatic stress it was still
his ideal means of musical expression. In *Khovanstchina* it
is replaced by broad, flowing melody of intense significance.
Of course it is a melody of a special kind, which Moussorgsky believed he had discovered—and who would care to con-
tradict him? In a letter to Stassov, of December 25, 1876, he
writes: "I am now deep in the study of human speech; I have
come to recognize the melodic element in ordinary speech
and have succeeded in turning recitative into melody. I might
call it 'melody justified by the meaning'; diametrically opposed as it is to the much beloved classical forms, it will one
day perhaps be understood by each and all. I should consider that a new conquest for the field of art if I could only attain it—and attained it must be. . . . I have already made a
start in *Khovanstchina*."

The melodies in the part of Marfa, richly expressive
both as speech and as song, and to a certain extent in that
of Dosifei, help us to understand what Moussorgsky meant
by "melody justified by the meaning." On the other hand,
in the parts of Golitzin and Prince Ivan Khovansky he does
not develop the recitative, incomparably fine as it is as a
setting of the words, into the same full-blown melodic form.
Obviously this is intentional and not the result of mere
chance or incapacity; a certain emphasis that is suitable and
characteristic for the lofty and exalted imagination of the
"seeker after God" and her "prophet" would have been in-
appropriate to the rather commonplace phrases of the bland
Golitzin, or the sheer rudeness of the rough General of the
Streltzy. In *Boris* the actual songs are mostly—with the
exception of certain lyrical episodes—interpolations—e.g.,
the songs in the nursery scene, Varlaam's song about the Tar-
tars in Kazan, the entrance song of the hostess—they do

not belong to the structure of the piece. This is not so in *Khovanstchina*; in this opera there are some numbers that have the character of "set pieces," but nevertheless fit perfectly into the framework of the drama. This is partly a consequence of the "justified melody" that is here employed —e.g., in the confession of her love that Marfa makes to Dosifei, or in the wonderful *aria* in which he makes his peace with God and the world before he leads his community to a fiery death. It is true that there is also a whole series of songs in *Khovanstchina* that have not the slightest connexion with the story and are sung by the chorus, or by single characters, either by themselves or to others. Among these are the wonderful song of Marfa "By all the ways the maiden went," the song (cut out by the editor of the opera) of the Strelitz Kuska on "Gossip," a pendant to Don Basilio's "Calumny" *aria* in *Il Barbiere*, the song and dance of Prince Ivan Khovansky's maids of honour, the songs of praise with which the people or his servants are required to hail their vain master over and over again—almost too often—the first chorus of the Streltzy in their barrack yard, which is a regular drinking-song, etc. Among all these songs and choruses, which seem like the fairest flowers of Russian folk-song, really only three are actual folk-songs: Marfa's first-mentioned song, whose melody (and words?) Moussorgsky found in the old collection of Villebois, the song of praise for Ivan Khovansky (really a wedding song), and the melody of young Andrei Khovansky's last song before his death. Yet even Rimsky-Korsakov, who included Marfa's song and the "Song of Praise" in his collection of folk-songs, expressed well-founded doubts as to the "genuineness" of the last-mentioned melody, where the perfect fifths are a departure from the usual style of Russian folk-songs. All the other songs in folk-song style in *Khovanstchina* are Moussorgsky's own melodies. It is astonishing how completely Moussorgsky made the musical speech of his nation his own. There is no doubt that the opposite process would be as easy; if Moussorgsky's melodies had an opportunity of penetrating among the people, they would unquestionably soon rank as folk-songs; the choruses of the scene of the peasant revolt in *Boris Godounov* were on the way to become such. Moussorgsky has a wonderfully infallible instinct for a free, unsymmetrical, and yet perfectly natural rhythm in his "popular" music. The "prime-number rhythms,"[1] to which musicians outside Russia have only gradually become reconciled, are very numerous in his work. The "Song of Praise," with which old Khovansky is hailed by his maids of honour, is the only example of continuous 17-4 time (6-4+5-4+6-4) in all music. We have seen 11-4 time in Moussorgsky's earlier works (it was also used very happily by Rimsky-Korsakov in his opera *Sadko*) and 7-4 and 5-4 times are quite common in *Khovanstchina.*

Especially remarkable, and unique in all musical literature—even in Russia—are the original hymns of the Old Believers used by Moussorgsky in *Khovanstchina.* Chief among these are the "Æolian" chorus in the first scene of the opera, and the "Phrygian" in the last. The melody of the latter was sent to Moussorgsky by the singer Madame L. Karmalina, Dargomizhky's intimate friend, who had found it somewhere in the innermost recesses of Russia. The Old Believers even now use for their worship, almost exclusively, old manuscripts where the music is written in neumes, or *kriuki* (hooks), as they are called, whose history goes back without a break into the grey mists of the early Middle Ages; hence the authenticity of their songs is beyond doubt. Moussorgsky has been reproached with having harmonized these songs and arranged them for several parts, although in the worship of the Old Believers only unison singing was customary, as it still is, and his arrangement was called

[1] i.e., bars or phrases of 5, 7, 11, etc.

"unhistorical." The reproach is unfounded, since just at the period of which he treats, the rudiments of part-singing had made some way among the Old Believers (as is clearly proved by some *kriuki* manuscripts), although it was only occasionally used.

But even without this excuse Moussorgsky is not to blame. Historical truth in a work of art is not attained by pedantic accuracy, but only by artistic intuition, which is able to reproduce the spirit of an age by what methods it chooses. It is not the photographic correctness of the representation, but the æsthetic conception of the life and feeling of an epoch, that gives the impression of historical truth, and this Moussorgsky fully succeeded in doing with the choruses of the Raskolniki. These austere arrangements, usually for two parts, breathe the spirit of an exaggerated asceticism and gloomy religious bigotry. Rimsky-Korsakov relates in *My Musical Life* that Moussorgsky had originally written the "Phrygian" chorus in the last scene in consecutive fourths, but was inclined later on to soften down this "barbaric" music. In the present version, which has gone through the cleansing process of Rimsky-Korsakov's revision, hardly a trace of the consecutive fourths is left.

Moussorgsky is even more sparing of his use of leading themes in *Khovanstchina* than in *Boris Godounov*; hence they have all the more striking effect when he uses them. Only one of the chief characters in the drama has a leitmotiv—old Prince Khovansky; strictly speaking, that is the only leitmotiv in the whole opera. Still, it is used in all sorts of ways, even for purposes of musical symbolism, which Moussorgsky entirely avoided in *Boris Godounov*. The composer uses it to indicate the vague idea of *Khovanstchina* as such—that is to say, the whole vast body of events that mark the time of the young Tsar Peter's accession—the measureless arrogance of the Boyars, attempts at a *coup d'état* to bring back the old customs, and leanings towards religious mysticism and political

269

reaction among those classes of the nation that saw salvation only in the old traditions. The same theme, pregnant alike in melody and harmony, appears also in the picture of the Streltzy (whose commander Khovansky was), each time in a greatly changed form, in keeping with the tone of the scene. Besides Khovansky, only one minor character in the drama has a leitmotiv—Varsonofiev, Golitzin's servant, whose appearance on the stage is each time announced by a short throbbing phrase, as if someone were knocking at the door.

A novelty in style, as compared with that of *Boris Godounov*, is the employment of particular musical forms to indicate the events that are happening. In a sense, these musical reminiscences come under the head of leitmotivs, not relating to characters, but to conceptions; there is nothing of this in *Boris*. An example may make the meaning plainer. At the beginning of the last scene but one, as the coach taking Prince Golitzin into exile rolls across the back of the stage, the orchestra plays the melody (now but a melancholy echo) of which the wonderful sinuous phrases were first heard in the incantation scene, when Marfa prophesied to the Prince his impending fall; and the same melody accompanies the weird mysterious consecration to death that she utters to her lover, young Prince Andrei, before she leads him to his fiery death.

Descriptions of nature are not often found in Moussorgsky; when they appear, they are without exception tone-pictures of striking effect. Two of the loveliest musical landscapes that Moussorgsky has painted are contained in *Khovanstchina*—one is the prelude to the first act; Moussorgsky calls it "Dawn on the Moskva River." It consists of five "melodic variations"—varied no less in their harmony, rhythm, and figures—on a lovely, clear-cut theme of truly national character.

The form of melodic variations is a method of musical

expression long familiar to the Russian people, through their popular songs. When a song is sung in a Russian village—especially by several singers in succession—no two stanzas are usually sung alike. Each singer tries to introduce individual variations in the melody to suit his or her own voice and mood, and in accordance with the meaning of the particular verse. Thus the song loses all rigidity and seems to be a living, breathing organism, capable of varying with every moment. This pecularity of Russian folk-song becomes in Moussorgsky's hands a most effective means of musical expression, which he employs in many of his works, and nowhere more successfully than in this prelude; it is always the same landscape, somewhat melancholy and monotonous, that we see before us, and yet it seems constantly to change its appearance, in accordance with the changing light. It is not (as is often erroneously supposed) the sunrise that Moussorgsky means to depict in this prelude; the music entirely lacks the pomp and circumstance usually employed for such effects. Nature-painting in Russian art has always a specially intimate character, owing partly to the landscape itself (in which there is really "nothing to see"), partly to its effect on the thoughts of the beholder, who when he tries to give them artistic expression, usually avoids any striking effects. So, perhaps, ears used to musical colour thickly laid on would find "nothing to hear" in the prelude to *Khovanstchina*; but if you abandon yourself to its beauty, you will learn to understand the charm of a Russian landscape and you will not hesitate to hail this fine piece as one of the greatest achievements in musical landscape-painting.

Hardly less successful in its suggestive charm is the other musical landscape that Moussorgsky gives us in *Khovanstchina*. The restful unison passage in the prelude to the last scene, with its quavers ascending and descending apparently without beginning or end, paint for us in masterly fashion the audible and visible impression the composer had in mind: "The rustling of the pine woods by moonlight, growing stronger, then dying away, like the breaking of waves upon the beach" (letter to Stassov, August 2, 1873). Against this background Dosifei makes his confession to God and to his own conscience; then follows the whole strange business of the "funeral mass of love," leading up to the terrible act of fiery martyrdom, until the quick march of Peter's "Horseguards" breaks in as a shrill discord, upon the storm-laden air, now rent by the lightning of terror.

Moussorgsky knew the secret of dramatic contrast; with great artistic delicacy he sets the sharpest opposites against each other—old Khovansky's rough clumsiness is set against the inspired dignity of Dosifei, or the amiable, polished, half-education of Golitzin; the burning, self-sacrificing passion of Marfa against the bourgeois respectability of Emma; the drunken brutality of the Streltzy against the religious ecstasy of the Raskolniki, or the commonplace punctilio of the "Horseguards." This method is employed not only in the drama, but in the music, where Moussorgsky lets us see, or rather hear, the vast extent of the scale of feeling that he commands by means of musical expression.

It is wonderful what economy of means he observes. One of his chief æsthetic axioms is: "Too much is as bad as too little." Moussorgsky had a natural horror of musical loquacity—hence the parsimony with which he keeps back his musical reserves seems almost miserly, and his scoring thin and poor, when compared with the din and crash of the modern orchestra. The fact that in spite of this he succeeded in attaining such incomparably striking effects is only one more proof that quantity of sound takes quite a subordinate place in the list of musical factors—never has so much been said with so few notes as in *Khovanstchina*.

It was not given to Moussorgsky to finish his second opera himself, although he completed it in the piano score, up to the last scene of all; hence a performance of the work was naturally impossible during his life—a few fragments of *Khovanstchina* were all that he ever heard.

In the winter of 1879–80 Rimsky-Korsakov undertook to revive the orchestral concerts of the Free School of Music, after a long interval, and conducted them himself, in place of Balakirev. In the second concert he inserted in the program some fragments of *Khovanstchina,* the chorus of the Streltzy, Marfa's song, and the "Dance of the Persian Slave-Girls," Moussorgsky himself providing an orchestral accompaniment for the first two numbers—they are almost the only pages of his opera that he ever scored. He could not finish the dance soon enough, and Rimsky-Korsakov offered to orchestrate it for him. Moussorgsky, as Rimsky-Korsakov reports in *My Musical Life,* accepted "gladly," and was "delighted" with the orchestration, although Rimsky-Korsakov made many changes in the harmonies and counterpoint. But as the score of the "Persian Dance" in Rimsky-Korsakov's version is really a little masterpiece of orchestration, it is not hard to believe that Moussorgsky's remark was sincere.

Khovanstchina is not printed in the form in which Moussorgsky wrote it; soon after his death Rimsky-Korsakov undertook the revision of the work. This revision and the subsequent fate of the opera will be discussed in our last chapter.

The only piano edition of *Khovanstchina* ever printed was that arranged from Rimsky-Korsakov's version; Moussorgsky's original piano score has remained till now in safe keeping in the Public Library at Petersburg, awaiting its resurrection, which we hope will not be too long delayed.

IX

ISOLATION

1875 — 8

THERE is unfortunately hardly any material in existence for a psychological biography of Moussorgsky—nothing on which we can found beliefs or assertions that go beyond more or less probable, but always doubtful, hypotheses. The only trustworthy materials for such a biography are his own letters, but even these must be used with some caution, since letters are always the birth of a moment, especially with so impulsive and vivacious a character as Moussorgsky's; and while they faithfully reflect the feelings of the writer at a particular moment, they afford but little ground on which to base any definite conclusions as to his more deeply rooted and permanent psychological principles and tendencies. And in Moussorgsky these were of so individual and complicated a character that they revealed themselves fully to none of his contemporaries, at least of those who have left accounts in writing of their friend.

One of the literary narrators of the last and saddest years of the composer, V. V. Stassov, seems to have appreciated this fact. He, who is generally so eloquent, is coldly laconic in describing the last years of Moussorgsky's life. Except for some chance remarks on the apparent decline of his talents, he has nothing to say—or nothing he cares to say. This singular silence probably arises in part from an unnecessary tactfulness and a desire to spare his friend's reputation, in part from a certain feeling of self-defence, which would not allow him to disclose his own part in the tragedy of Moussorgsky's last years—and lastly, assuredly, from his inability to understand his friend's psychological development, and his conviction that it would be best to say nothing about it.

The second of the authors who have written about the last period of Moussorgsky's life, Rimsky-Korsakov, was not so wise. In *My Musical Life* he speaks at length of his dead friend, but displays such an impenetrable lack of comprehension of the man himself, as well as of the artistic labours and sorrows of his latter years, that we wish he too had kept silence. Korsakov's words only help us to understand why Moussorgsky turned from friends who could think so of him. For Rimsky-Korsakov could hardly have concealed in their daily intercourse the opinion of his friend that he expresses so frankly in his recollections. We wonder no longer at the "fatal change" that took place, according to Rimsky-Korsakov, in Moussorgsky's nature and his attitude to his friends after the performance of *Boris*; only we are inclined to give other reasons for it. Rimsky-Korsakov maintains that Borodin, Cui, and he himself were as fond as ever of the talented composer of *Boris*; but one can easily understand that the latter in a friendly but decided manner declined an affection such as was expressed in Cui's criticism of *Boris*. The natural consequence of this was that the "Powerful Coterie" broke up completely.

The visible cause of the dispersal of the Balakirev circle was the retirement of its leader. This marked the beginning of the end of their friendships, and the commencement of cooler, though still amicable relations between the individual members. Naturally this cooling of friendship did not happen so suddenly as did the change of their former intellectual leader into a railway official; but when it had once begun, it went on without a break. Sometimes fresh groupings took place between the friends. Rimsky-Korsakov and Borodin drew together after the former's association with Moussorgsky was broken. Cui usually kept apart from the rest. Only Moussorgsky was really isolated by this break-up of the Balakirev community. He clung longest to Stassov, the only one who tried to stay at his old friend's side as long as possible, at least in matters of art, although he did not manage to endure till the end.

The same occurrence may take on a very different appearance according to the point of view from which it is regarded and the temperament that throws light on it. The different conceptions formed of one and the same event give glimpses of the temper and nature of those who formed them, which are often instructive. Both Borodin and Moussorgsky have spoken of the breaking-up of the "Powerful Coterie" in their letters. If we compare these two views, it is at once clear that a union between such different temperaments and views of art and life could not last long. Borodin, in April 1875, writes to Madame L. I. Karmalina—well known from Dargomizhky's biography:

"No doubt you have heard a great deal about dissensions in our circle—in fact, its dissolution. I regard the case differently from Ludmilla Ivanovna and many others. In the first place I see in it nothing but a very natural state of things. As long as we were still under that broody hen (I mean Balakirev), we were as like as one egg to another. But when we were hatched and fully fledged, it was evident that naturally no two of us had the same feathers; and as our wings grew, each flew away in the direction that he fancied. Difference of aim, work, taste, and character in our artistic creations is a good thing and by no means to be deplored— it must be so when artistic individuality matures and grows strong (Balakirev could never understand this and does not understand it even now). Many are troubled by the fact that Korsinka has turned back and devoted himself to the study of old music. I am not sorry—it is perfectly intelligible. Korsinka has developed in the opposite direction to myself, for instance—he began with Glinka, Liszt, and Berlioz and is naturally tired of them and is now trying to explore unknown fields that have still the charm of novelty for him. I began with the old masters and have now come to the new."

In these few lines we see the whole of Borodin—a quiet, clear-sighted character, assuming the rational attitude of a man of the world with regard to a fact that seems to him natural and inevitable. When people see that they no longer agree, when former ideals have vanished to give place to more "reasonable" views, then they shake hands, bid a friendly good-bye, and each goes his own way. From the standpoint of social ethics and the judgment of the average man, there is no possible objection to this. So, in another field of life, many myriads of aspiring revolutionary enthusiasts have turned into law-abiding citizens and honest fathers of families. That the ardent heart of an artist might regard such a proceeding as treason to the common cause, take it as a grievous breach of friendship, and feel deeply wounded—this probably never entered Borodin's mind as possible.

But that is how Moussorgsky's morbidly sensitive nature was affected by the changed attitude (so quietly accepted by Borodin) of the members of the "Powerful Coterie" with regard to the common cause, the fight against routine, authority, and tradition. Whether Moussorgsky was right or wrong is another matter; but it is obvious that a nature like his was bound to kick over the traces when there was a chance. Any objective judgment on the facts naturally had not the slightest influence on his own convictions; he felt betrayed, and if he could have pardoned treason against himself, he could not forgive it against art, the highest and holiest, the only sacred thing in his life, which he was ready to defend at any moment with all the passionate abandonment of his being.

This inner severance from his former friends, which

dates practically from the autumn of 1875, was the crowning sorrow of Moussorgsky's later years; if it is not the only key to the course of his later life, yet it undoubtedly was largely the cause of his falling into harmful ways. The passages in Moussorgsky's letters dealing with the matter are characteristic of the state of his feelings, growing from sarcastic jesting to fiery wrath or open contempt.

In a letter of August 7, 1875 he writes to Stassov: "I met the Roman [*Rimsky* in Russian means 'the Roman']. We both jumped down from our droshkies and embraced with a will. Then he informs me that he has written fifteen fugues, each one a greater tangle than the other—just this, and nothing else!

> "Oh that his ink had dried up quite,
> Before it helped the quill to write!

"César (I can't keep away from Rome today), they say, has finished the third act of *Angelo*. I have not been to see him. I am afraid—not of him, but of his third act. I did not even ask the Roman about César.

"When will these people, instead of writing fugues and conventional third acts, read sensible books and mix with reasonable men—or is it now too late?

"That is not what we expect from art today. That is not the mission of the artist. *Life*, wherever it is shown; *truth*, however bitter; speaking out boldly, frankly, point-blank, to men, that is my only aim, that is what I want, and that is where I am afraid of making a blunder. There's a certain somebody who spurs me on to this adventure, and I mean to stick to it."

His faith in this "somebody"—namely, Stassov—lasted longer, almost to the end of his life. It is doubtful whether he ever realized that even Stassov at last had renounced his friend's artistic faith. Though Stassov lets slip the confession of this fact in his biography of Moussorgsky, he seems to have succeeded in concealing it from his friend in their personal intercourse. Moussorgsky, to the last day of his life, calls him "My only Generalissimo, you, the *only* man who understands me." And Stassov, apart from Ludmilla Ivanovna Shestakova, was the only confidant to whom he poured out his heart about the breach with his other friends. He believed—and at first rightly—that he was as sure of Stassov's sympathy as of the moral support of Glinka's sister, whose attitude with regard to the breaking-up of Balakirev's circle is evident from the paragraph quoted from Borodin's letter. On October 19, 1875 Moussorgsky vents all his griefs in a letter to Stassov, in which at the same time he takes the opportunity of expressing his confidence in him and his admiration for his previous pioneer work in art. Stassov had sent him a photograph of his own portrait, painted by Riepin (it is now in the Tretyakov Gallery in Moscow). Moussorgsky answered:

"I often look at you. You are gazing with strained attention into the distance, as if you scented something there. Power and knowledge of the truth speak in every feature— bravo, Ilia Riepin! . . . It is this honest, living gaze *into the distance—forward*—that inspires me. When I think of certain artists who are now stuck fast 'behind the barricade,' I am overcome not only with impotent wrath, but with nausea. The whole aim of these gentlemen is to express themselves, as it were, *by drops*, one drop after another, all nicely measured. They enjoy it, but a real man is wearied and enraged at it. Oh, do manage to get out of yourselves, my dear sirs, something that will show that you are alive! Show whether you have claws or web feet, whether you are beasts of prey or amphibians!—Well, what do *you* think about it? What about the barricade? Without understanding, without any will of their own, these 'artists' have voluntarily allowed themselves to be bound in the fetters of tradition, they are nothing but walking examples of the law of inertia, and yet they fancy they are doing great things. All this would be merely uninteresting and slightly annoying but for the fact that they—these artists—had once hoisted another banner and tried *to bear it proudly aloft before men.* Caught up in Balakirev's eagle talons, they breathed the upper air for a time with him, though not so deeply as he, and aimed at heights that would have baffled greater men than they. Now the iron grip of Balakirev has slackened—and they feel suddenly that they are tired and want a rest. Where can they find rest? Naturally, in traditions handed down from old times; 'as our fathers have held, so will we hold.' They stuck their gallant standard in a corner, carefully *hid* it behind old lumber, locked it up with seven locks behind seven doors. So they found peace, and now they are at rest. *Without a banner,* without an aim, without looking into the future, they sit brooding over what has been done long ago and does not want their assistance. And the croaking critical frogs, hopping about in their native swamp, now and then puff themselves out and give them—these same artists—a croak of praise. How could they do otherwise? The 'Powerful Coterie' has broken up into a horde of soulless traitors, its scourge has proved a child's toy whip. I say that in the whole world there is nothing more deadly, nothing more useless to the art of today than such a set of—artists!"

This letter sounds as if it had been written in the excitement of some especially painful moment, under the impression of some especially bitter experience. But it was more than this—Moussorgsky is dealing with something against which his whole soul rose in rebellion; this is plain from a letter that he wrote more than four months later, on the night of the 28–9th of February 1876, to Ludmilla Ivanovna Shestakova. In this, after an allusion to her brother Glinka, we read:

"You have comforted me greatly with your kind, splendid letters. You are right, it is so; there *must* still be true men in the world, even though we have to suffer horribly from those who play us false—and almost everybody plays false in our glorious age, in which everything progresses—except *humanity*. Openly and boldly, without concealment, treason has attacked the noblest, mightiest, and truest principles of art; and this in the very house where once a new young life flourished, where new powers of thought awakened, new artistic plans were formed and carried out. But let us leave C. Cui and N. Rimsky-Korsakov in peace, for 'the dead fear not the knout' [a quotation from *Khovanstchina*]. All that I am writing now came to my knowledge in your house, I felt it in your house. 'Truth loves not the company of liars.' There was no lying then at your house, neither on our side nor on theirs—and even the walls told no lies on that memorable evening; all was *truth*, and what truth! The gentlemen in question (Cui and Korsakov) have finally abandoned the most sacred aim of art—to speak to humanity in the language of truth. . . . I am almost sure Borodin would not have taken their side; but it is now too late to settle that and it would do no good. *Oh, if Borodin could only get in a rage!*"

But Borodin could not, at least on account of the matter at issue, as is evident from the passage just quoted. He too joined in the "point-blank betrayal" of the common cause, though in a more diplomatic way than Korsakov and Cui. The decisive breach between these two and Moussorgsky had taken place, according to this letter, at Madame Shestakova's house.

Ludmilla Ivanovna Shestakova, who practically never appeared in the public musical life of Petersburg, seemed to all those who had the nurture and growth of Russian national art at heart to wear the aureole of her great brother's deathless crown of glory. Especially after Glinka's death she seemed to the members of the "New Russian School" a living token of the new spirit that the creator of *A Life for the*

Tsar and *Russlan* had breathed into Russian music. Her house was a sort of stronghold of Russian art and Russian traditions, where the hostess, one of the last representatives of the declining Russian aristocracy as it was in the days of serfdom, played her part with true Russian hospitality. It was a distinction coveted by the greatest minds of her time to be admitted to the musical society that Ludmilla Ivanovna gathered round her, although this society abstained from all outside advertisement and was confined to a very intimate circle. In the middle seventies Ludmilla Ivanovna undertook a work that won for her name a place of special honour in the annals of Russian music. She had the score of her brother's second great work, the opera *Russlan and Ludmilla*, printed at her own expense, in order to protect the work from all arbitrary alteration by officious conductors, and from any other dangers. In the year 1859 one of the two manuscript copies of the score in existence was destroyed in the fire at the Great Theatre at Moscow. Ludmilla Ivanovna took note of this warning of fate. The publishing of the work, which was engraved by Röder at Leipzig, she entrusted to Balakirev and Rimsky-Korsakov, who performed their task with admirable care.

Between Moussorgsky and Ludmilla Ivanovna there sprang up in the course of years a close friendship, which almost took on the character of a family relationship. Especially after the death of Nadeshda Petrovna Opotchinina, Moussorgsky attached himself with all the unsatisfied longing of his craving heart to his motherly friend. The poet of *The Nursery*, like so many other men of genius, remained a grown-up child all his life long; he had a craving, unconscious, but none the less real, for a woman's hand to soothe his violent nature with its tender care. After his mother's death Nadeshda Petrovna Opotchinina took up the task; when she died, in 1875, to the unspeakable grief of her friend, Ludmilla Ivanovna took her place. There is no doubt that the kind sympathy of this noble woman did much to brighten the gloom of Moussorgsky's latter years, while at the same time she was a moral support to him in battling against the fatal craving that arose from a morbid predisposition and grew stronger with his misfortunes, till at last it ruined him body and soul. But when their friendship began, he needed no support in this respect.

In his letters to Ludmilla Ivanovna, Moussorgsky never mentions or refers to himself except as "Moussinka," a pet name that only this friend was allowed to use. This was a sort of token of the exceptional position that Moussorgsky accorded her among his nearest friends. He writes with reference to this: "I thank you, dearest Ludmilla Ivanovna, for now and then calling me 'Moussinka.' A warm breath of love comes from the word and I would never allow anybody but you to call me so." He himself used the tenderest and most moving phrases, only to be found in the inexhaustible Russian language, and sounding in another language forced, sickly, and clumsy: "My dear little dove," "my little mother," "I cover your little hands with burning kisses," "yours with a warm heart and whole soul," etc.

Moussorgsky's friendship with Ludmilla Ivanovna was some compensation for all that he had lost in love, true friendship, and sympathy during the latter years of his life —no one knew that better and appreciated it more fully than he himself. "I will confess to you," he writes in a letter of August 31, 1875, "that every letter of yours expresses so much love, such a sunny, life-giving feeling, that your moral support can even reconcile me to the inhuman monstrosities of modern society. How unalterably *good* you are, my little dove!"

It is clear that Moussorgsky sought the friendly sympathy and "moral help" of Ludmilla Ivanovna, not only in artistic matters, but in the intimate questions of his personal life. Besides the growing coolness between him and his former musical comrades, Moussorgsky seems to have finally broken with his own brother. In all the letters of this period he only once mentions his brother, who "kept him from work" a whole day; and Ludmilla Ivanovna writes to Stassov after the death of their friend that she feels justified in speaking of their friendly relations with Moussorgsky, since he made no secret to her "of his attitude towards his brother and other people." If we read Moussorgsky's letters to Ludmilla Ivanovna, one after the other, we realize that the writer gradually brought more and more of his own life and experience into his relations with his friend, because he found less and less sympathy in the rest of the world. Though he possibly became doubtful even of Stassov in matters of art, he was always sure of Ludmilla Ivanovna.

At the close of the year 1876 Moussorgsky audited the accounts of his artistic work of that year and was content with the result. It was less pleasant when he considered for whom he had done his artistic work, and what thanks he had earned for it. He wrote to L. I. Shestakova on the first day of the Christmas holidays, apparently without any special reason, as follows:

"Dear, darling Ludmilla Ivanovna, you alone with your wonderfully kind heart have recognized what your Moussinka has done for art in the past year. Whether I have done art any real service, I don't know; I cannot make up my mind, and my ideas are all upside-down. But I feel that I have done some good work and that for me there is no looking back. *You alone, and you only,* my dearest Ludmilla Ivanovna, have given me the comforting consciousness that I am fully understood. I have only just realized how stupidly tired I am."

Moussorgsky's love for Ludmilla Ivanovna, in the course of the few years that it lasted, grew into adoration. He saw in her the incarnation of all the powers of good that watched over his life and art; he was troubled about her health; he sought with anxious tenderness for anything that might make her life fairer and pleasanter, and he readily accepted from her many a serious warning and kindly reproof. By her recognition, her sympathy, he felt guarded against the temptations to which his former comrades had fallen victims. "Yes, dear, dearest Ludmilla Ivanovna," he writes in one of his last letters to his friend, "how could I dare to play the traitor, to surrender like a coward, to despise art and myself, so long as I bear in mind the words you have said to me, and with which you have—*hallowed* me! Those words are sacred, for they come from you. . . . You have given Glinka to the world in his work of genius *Russlan and Ludmilla*. And in spite of that engrossing labour you have found in your wonderful heart the kindest of words for me. I repeat again, you have hallowed me, dearest Ludmilla Ivanovna, *hallowed* me as artist and man."

After these proofs of the purest and noblest emotions it is particularly painful to turn to Rimsky-Korsakov's assertion that in Moussorgsky's conduct during his last years he noticed signs of "moral degeneracy" and "mental decline." Moussorgsky, to whom this harsh criticism was, as we can safely infer, not unknown, replied by a "reserved and dignified demeanour" in the circle of his former friends, where he appeared less and less often. Nevertheless, for some little time after the performance of *Boris*, he still sought the society of Rimsky-Korsakov and Borodin, whom he often met at Ludmilla Ivanovna's house. Madame Shestakova describes one of these meetings in her *Recollections of Moussorgsky*, which she published soon after his death. From her narrative, which describes many attractive traits of her friend and is a fitting memorial of her friendship, a short extract may be inserted here. Ludmilla Ivanovna writes:

"From my first meeting with Moussorgsky (it was in 1866, when he was twenty-seven) I was struck by his delicacy of feeling and his unusual air of good breeding and courtesy.

He was an uncommonly well-bred young man, very tactful, always keeping himself under complete control. I have known him for fifteen years, and during all these years I have never known him give a sign of irritation or forget himself in any way, never seen him impatient or violent, nor ever heard him say a single unkind word to anybody. When I once told him how I wondered at his complete self-control, he answered: 'I get that from my mother; she was a saint.'

"Moussorgsky and Rimsky-Korsakov, who were then still great friends, though they lived rather far apart, found it convenient to meet at my house. They generally both came early, so as to have time, before the other guests arrived, to talk over their latest works. In the course of such conversations amusing episodes often occurred. Rimsky-Korsakov used to sit down at the piano and play what he had written since their last meeting. Moussorgsky, who listened most intently, gave his opinion. The moment Korsakov had heard it, he jumped up and began to stride up and down the room, while Moussorgsky quietly sat down at the piano and began to play. After he had quieted down, Rimsky-Korsakov came back and asked Moussorgsky to explain his opinion, which he generally did.

"It was my custom to go to bed early. About ten o'clock I generally gathered up my work. Moussorgsky never failed to notice it and said loudly: 'The first bell.' After a while, if I looked at the clock or got up, he said: 'The second bell! I think we won't wait for the third, or it will be like the bit in Gogol's *Marriage*—"Out you go, you idiots!"'"

These stray sketches of the friendship between Glinka's sister and his greatest successor are enough to show what a treasure the impulsive composer of *Boris* possessed in the kind, understanding friendship of Ludmilla Ivanovna. This friendship must have helped him over many hard places in a life that had little else to brighten it.

*　　　*　　　*

Moussorgsky's circle of friends and acquaintances was naturally composed chiefly, but not exclusively, of members of the musical world, down to this latter period of his life. He never went into the "great world" now, since his interests were completely those of art, and his financial position had grown so bad that he was compelled to earn his livelihood as a subordinate government clerk. He kept up friendly relations with representatives of other arts, however, especially those whose artistic views did not clash with his own progressive temper and his impulse to shatter the traditional rules of art. With some eminent poets and authors who were in sympathy with the original aims of Balakirev's circle he had been personally acquainted since the days of the "Commune"; some artists, also, to whom he was drawn by similar artistic views and interests were reckoned among his nearer friends. Among these, besides the sculptor Antokolsky and the painter Riepin, was the architect Victor Hartmann, a friend of the Stassov family. Stassov's function at that time was to act—and he did so with conspicuous success—as a connecting medium between the different branches of Russian art; his far-reaching activity as a writer, endlessly industrious and wonderfully prolific, was by no means confined to the field of music. In his writings, which fill three quartos, nearly six thousand pages, music occupies a relatively small place, about a quarter of the whole.

Victor Hartmann, to whom Petersburg owes some fine buildings, was on intimate terms with the whole Balakirev circle, but especially, as we have said, with Stassov and Moussorgsky. It was he whose sudden death, in the year 1874, brought the composer his first great sorrow. This premature loss—Hartmann was only thirty-nine—made a deep impression on Moussorgsky; he seems almost to have felt that he himself would be the next to follow into the land from which there is no return.

Stassov was abroad when Hartmann died. Moussorgsky speaks in a letter of the death of their common friend. The letter possesses great psychological interest in its expressions of self-reproach and the bitter attacks made on contemporary society. It reads as if the writer had looked into the future and seen his own death and heard the same comments as Hartmann's death drew from him. The letter, of August 2, 1874, runs thus:

"My very dear friend, what a terrible blow!'Why should a dog, a horse, a rat, live on?'—and creatures like Hartmann must die! When Vitiuschka [a pet name for Victor] was last in Petersburg, I was walking home with him from Mollas's (where we had waited in vain for your Grace) when at a street-corner, just opposite St. Anne's Church, dear old Vitiuschka turned white and leaned against the wall of a house. As I know that feeling by experience, I asked him (*carelessly*): 'What's the matter?' 'I can't breathe,' answered Vitiuschka. And in spite of that, as I know how prone artists are to get nervous heart-attacks (palpitations), I said, *still carelessly*: 'When you've got your wind again, old boy, we'll go on.' That was all I could say, when I knew that his death-warrant had been signed! What clumsy fools we are! . . . When I recall that talk, I feel wretched, because it was fear that made me a coward—I did not want to frighten Hartmann, and so behaved like a schoolboy. Believe me, Generalissimo, I acted to our friend Hartmann like a silly fool. Cowardly, helpless, mean! A man—and such a man—feels ill, and one comes to him with a silly 'Old boy,' and unmeaning, commonplace words, and feigned indifference, and all the rubbishy social conventions! And the root of all this is just vanity, the base coin of society. I shall not soon forget what happened, it will haunt me—perhaps I may grow wiser in time.

"That is the mischief of it—that we never see the danger until a man is drowning or at the point of death. Man is a blockhead! And if he had a forehead seven feet high, he would still be a hopeless blockhead! All we little, little men are fools; so are the doctors, who strut about with the importance of gobbling turkeys, settling questions of life and death.

"This is how the wise usually console us blockheads, in such cases; 'He is no more, but what he has done lives and will live.' True . . . but how many men have the luck to be remembered? That is just another way of serving up our self-complacency (with a dash of onion, to bring out the tears). Away with such wisdom! When 'he' has not lived in vain, but has *created*—one must be a rascal to revel in the comforting thought that 'he' can create no more. No, one cannot and must not be comforted, there can be and must be no consolation—it is a rotten morality! If Nature is only coquetting with men, I shall have the honour of treating her like a coquette—that is, of trusting her as little as possible, keeping all my senses about me, when she tries to cheat me into taking the sky for a fiddlestick—or ought one rather, like a brave soldier, to charge into the thick of life, have one's fling, and go under? What does it all mean? In any case the dull old earth is no coquette, but takes every 'King of Nature' straight into her loathsome embrace, whoever he is—like an old worn-out hag, for whom anyone is good enough, since she has no choice.

"There again—what a fool I am! Why be angry when you cannot change anything? Enough, then—the rest is silence. . . . "

Not only did Hartmann's death move Moussorgsky to the misanthropic outburst of this letter, which he sent to Stassov at Wiesbaden; his grief soon found artistic expression, which will probably keep the name of the Petersburg architect in remembrance longer than his buildings.

V. Stassov, after he returned from abroad, sought to honour the memory of Hartmann in every possible way; with this purpose he held, in the summer of 1874, an exhibition of water-colours and drawings by his dead friend. This exhibition was the occasion of one of the most charming instrumental compositions that Moussorgsky has left behind him, the *Pictures at an Exhibition,* a series of ten piano pieces, connected by an interlude, which is repeated four times in varied forms. Schumann's cycles of pieces (*Papillons, Carnival*) undoubtedly served Moussorgsky as models for this attractive piano suite, so far as the form went, but the connexion between the two writers does not go beyond mere external similarity.

We have already noticed that Moussorgsky's musical fancy had full play only when it had some objective reality to work on. It is as if his creative genius always needed some slight impulse from outside, to guide it into the right way. This was so here. Hartmann's pictures and drawings, of very varied subjects, gave every possible opportunity for musical interpretation. Moussorgsky, like most creative minds who draw their inspiration solely from some chance "idea," was entirely dependent on the caprice of his own feeling; he could not compel this source to flow more freely than it chose. Consequently with him periods in which work progressed with wearisome slowness alternated with others in which the flow of creative energy was so strong that he could not escape from it. The result was that his compositions in their first conception usually had the appearance of genius, while the technical working-out was difficult, and sometimes unsuccessful. His work on the *Pictures at an Exhibition* evidently coincided with a period of great creative fertility. He writes to Stassov, to whom he afterwards dedicated the series, "some day in June 1874": "Hartmann is bubbling over, just as *Boris* did. Ideas, melodies, come to me of their own accord, like the roast pigeons in the story —I gorge and gorge and overeat myself. I can hardly manage to put it all down on paper fast enough." This combination of the highest pitch of his creative faculties with

290

a happy impulse helped to make the "Exhibition Pictures" little masterpieces, in which the technical detail, too, seems inspired. Even Moussorgsky himself, who was seldom satisfied with his own work, thought the pieces a success. He was especially delighted with the "Promenades," the intermezzos, in which he depicts himself straying from picture to picture through the exhibition. These musical portraits of himself are not without a certain delicate and genial humour. Moussorgsky was right when he said that his "own physiognomy peeps out all through the intermezzos"—they reveal a clever and intelligent face "*nel modo russico*," which reflects the objects seen, but in a form transfigured by art— take, for instance, the "*Vecchio Castello*," from which the beholder apparently cannot tear himself away. The truly Russian theme, in 11-4 time, that is the foundation of these "Promenades" is particularly fine.

The ten pictures of which Moussorgsky gives his impressions in music, are as follows: "The Gnome"—the drawing of a dwarf who waddles with awkward steps on his short, bandy legs; the grotesque jumps of the music, and the clumsy, crawling movements with which these are interspersed, are forcibly suggestive. This number, like some others of the cycle, in which the composer respects mere "musical beauty" as little as ever, naturally struck his contemporaries as an incredible piece of audacity. "The Old Castle," an old tower of the Middle Ages, before which a minstrel sings his song, a long-drawn, unspeakably melancholy melody. "The Tuileries, children quarrelling at play" —Hartmann's picture shows a walk in the Tuileries gardens in Paris, crowded with playing children and their nurses. The musical picture, as always when Moussorgsky was dealing with those "of whom is the kingdom of heaven," is full of magical tenderness; highly diverting, too, are the quarrelsome cries that rise from the crowd of romping children. "Bydlo" is a big Polish dray, drawn by a team of oxen on its high, rumbling wheels; the reproduction of this would not be very musical had not Moussorgsky introduced a swinging folk-song in the Æolian mode, evidently sung by the driver. The "Ballet of Unhatched Chickens" is a costume design of Hartmann's for a performance of the ballet of *Trilby* —in Moussorgsky's musical rendering, a "Scherzino" of the greatest charm. The next piece is called "Samuel Goldenberg and Schmuyle." "I mean to try to get Hartmann's Jews," Moussorgsky writes to Stassov, and he has certainly succeeded. The piece, as regards its subjects, is perhaps the boldest venture in program music that was ever attempted in miniature form. We owe to it one of the most amusing caricatures in all music—the two Jews, one rich and comfortable and correspondingly close-fisted, laconic in talk, and slow in movement, the other poor and hungry, restlessly and fussily fidgeting and chatting, but without making the slightest impression on his partner, are musically depicted with a keen eye for characteristic and comic effect. These two types of the Warsaw Ghetto stand plainly before you—you seem to hear the caftan of one of them blown out by the wind, and the flap of the other's ragged fur coat. Moussorgsky's musical power of observation scores a triumph with this unique musical joke; he proves that he can reproduce the "intonations of human speech" not only for the voice, but also on the piano. The next piece, "The Market at Limoges," is also a "study in intonation," where the scolding of the wrangling market women is reproduced in masterly fashion. "The Catacombs"—in this picture Hartmann shows himself exploring the depths of the catacombs of Paris with a lantern. In Moussorgsky's original manuscript after the remarkable introduction he has written, above the *andante* that follows, these words: "*Cum mortuis in lingua mortua* (With the dead in a dead language)" and then, in Russian, "Hartmann's creative spirit leads me to the place of skulls, and calls to them—the skulls begin to glow faintly from within." The next picture shows "The Hut of Baba-Yaga," the witch of Russian folk-lore, whom Pushkin has handed down in immortal verse in his introduction to *Russlan and Ludmilla*, with her hovel perched in bird's claws. Moussorgsky has written for this a wild scherzo—a sort of witches' ride—and carries out his pictorial design only in the trio, where the strange harmonies and halting melodies produce a weird effect of unreality. The final number is a somewhat conventionally designed apotheosis—"The Great Gate of Kiev," from one of Hartmann's architectural sketches.

During Moussorgsky's life this original cycle of piano pieces, rich in thought and music, was completely ignored. It was first printed six years after his death; it was hardly ever heard in the concert hall, and it was impossible for amateurs to play at home, owing to its great technical and musical difficulty. Only since 1920 has the cycle been added to the European concert repertoire.

* * *

The performance of *Boris Godounov* in January 1874 not only brought Moussorgsky recognition as an artist—though the tide of reputation soon ebbed, leaving only a stronger self-confidence in the composer's spirit—but won him a friendship with one of the greatest artists of the Russian operatic stage.

Osip Afanasievitch Petrov was sixty-seven years old when he created the part of the drunken friar Varlaam in *Boris*. He had had a brilliant stage-career; on the day memorable in the history of Russian opera, the great first performance of Glinka's *A Life for the Tsar*, November 27, 1836, he appeared on the stage of the Marie Theatre as the creator of the part of Sussanin. The equally distinguished singer Anna Yakovlevna Vorobieva, who afterwards became his wife, soon rivalled him in this opera as an unsurpassed and unequalled Vania. In Glinka's second opera, *Russlan and*

293

Ludmilla, which was almost more important for the development of Russian operatic art than his first work, the chief parts (Russlan and Ratmir) were entrusted to the two Petrovs. Petrov's "mighty bass," which Glinka cannot praise enough in his *Recollections* and his wife's "wonder voice," a magnificent contralto, whose rich, soft tone, in the opinion of contemporaries, had not its equal in all Europe—these vied successfully with the most remarkable voices of the Italian opera in Petersburg. But the other artistic qualities of this exceptional pair of singers far surpassed even the wonderful tone of their voices. The great dramatic talent possessed by both artists, which was far beyond the average operatic standard, now rising to thrilling heights of tragic pathos, now expressing itself in brilliant, irresistible humour, enabled them to make such memorable and impressive figures of all the parts they played that Petersburg theatrical gossip lived on them for many years. "The Petrovs" passed into legend in the history of Russian opera.

Geniuses can generally understand one another perfectly well; and often they experience a strong mutual attraction, even outside the field of their art; in the regions above the level of average humanity a finer atmosphere prevails, and none can endure to breathe it for long except those whose spirits were born to live on the heights. But if there is to be a true companionship between them, it is necessary that such exceptional intellectual and artistic natures should be alike in their powers, but unlike in their activities. The ideal conditions for a friendship between them are, first, a mutual understanding, based on their individual natures and talents, and, secondly, an avoidance of any interference in the particular sphere of action that each has made his own. These conditions were satisfied in the relation between Moussorgsky and Petrov. Moussorgsky, as we know, possessed a remarkable talent for acting, without any ambition to display it in public; Petrov had remarkable musical talent, which enabled him to keep pace with the impetuous musical development of his great contemporary, without ever encroaching on the province of the creative artist. A close friendship grew up between him and Moussorgsky, founded on heartfelt personal sympathy. In the Petrovs' house Moussorgsky found, from time to time, that "family life" which he sorely missed in his bachelor life in Petersburg.

He often speaks of the Petrovs in his correspondence with Ludmilla Ivanovna Shestakova. On April 21, 1876, the fifty-year stage-jubilee of O. A. Petrov was celebrated with a splendour unusual even for the Petersburg Imperial Theatre, and Moussorgsky eagerly took part in it. Petrov was presented with a golden laurel crown, on the hundred leaves of which were engraved all the parts that he had sung at the Marie Theatre in the course of fifty years. In his letters to Ludmilla Ivanovna, in which this jubilee is often mentioned, Moussorgsky always calls Petrov "our dear grandfather," since Ludmilla Ivanovna, too, had long been a friend of the pair who had done so much for her brother's works.

Moussorgsky's friendship with O. A. Petrov had important results, inasmuch as it inspired him to begin a work which unfortunately was not completed, but which contains some of the finest gems of his musical humour, and several of the best of his dramatic lyrics. We refer to his opera *The Fair at Sorótchintzy* (the accent is on the second syllable), the libretto of which is founded on one of the burlesque episodes of Gogol's immortal *Evenings on the Dikanka Farm*. Moussorgsky began work on this piece when *Khovanstchina* was only half done. He had, as he said of himself, "the greedy eyes of a priest" in matters of music; thus his creative fancy, for several years, vacillated between the gloomy religious mysticism of *Khovanstchina*, and the rather broad and drunken comicality of Gogol's humour—which formed the opposite poles of his own mental experience.

The plot of *The Fair at Sorótchintzy* was born of the

desire to write a Little Russian part for O. A. Petrov. This
wish coincided with his long-cherished design of again entering the field of comic opera (which he had not touched
since he had laid his *Marriage* aside and given the piano
score to Stassov), as well as his scheme of raising a worthy
monument to Gogol, whom he loved and honoured. Petrov
himself was a "Khokhol"—that is, a Little Russian—and
in confident anticipation that the association of Gogol and
Moussorgsky would give excellent results seems to have zeal-
ously forwarded his friend's work. The scenario of the opera, in Moussorgsky's handwriting, which was found among
V. Stassov's papers, and is now in the Public Library at
Petersburg, with most of Moussorgsky's autographs, bears
the note: "On May 19, 1877, at the house of A. Y. and O. A.
Petrov at Petrograd." (Moussorgsky sometimes used this
name—which, though not generally employed in his day,
came into use for a short time during the Great War—for
Petersburg, to express his love for old Russia.) This seems
to point to a close co-operation of the pair in planning the
work. The question of the libretto may well have caused
Moussorgsky some difficulty. Little Russians speak a very
distinctive dialect, full of idiomatic expressions, which is regarded by over-zealous patriots as a separate "language."
Moussorgsky, like all Great Russians, had a very incomplete
command of "Ukrainish"; and though the libretto of the *Fair*
is not written throughout in this dialect, it is sprinkled with
Little Russian phrases and expressions, which give it a special stamp and exhibit the characters on their comic side in a
most entertaining way. Probably Petrov rendered invaluable
assistance to Moussorgsky, who was his own librettist again
in this work. In the musical setting of the plot, which is full
of local humour, Petrov must have given the composer much
good advice, founded on his wide knowledge. Moussorgsky,
as his work in *Boris Godounov* and *Khovanstchina* had already shown, was painfully exact in reproducing details of

place, period, and nationality in his compositions—he dreaded nothing so much as faults in style, in any of these respects, such as might throw doubt on the "truthfulness" of his music. On these principles he worked out *The Fair at Sorótchintzy* with great thoroughness. He studied Ukrainian folk-song, which, through the Polish influence to which it had always been exposed, was really far more "Western" in character than the music of Greater Russia. He collected Little Russian tunes whenever he could get hold of them— Petrov probably helped him—and amassed a treasure of "materials" for his opera, of which he made very little use.

The story of Gogol's tale is as follows:

It is the annual fair in the village of Sorótchintzy. The peasants from all the country round are there, among them Tcherevik, the marvellous type of a Ukrainian blockhead, whose western European counterpart could only be found in Lower Bavaria. Tcherevik brings an old mare and a few bushels of wheat to sell at the fair. He has also his talkative and far from attractive wife, Khivria, and his charming young daughter, Parássia, on his cart. At the entrance of the village, on the bridge, an altercation occurs between a group of lads and the occupants of the cart, and ends by one of the young fellows stopping the mouth of the too eloquent Khivria with a well-aimed lump of mud. This is the tying of the dramatic knot; the sequel is obvious—love at first sight between Gritzko, the "Párobok," as such lads are called in the Ukraine, and the fair Parássia. Tcherevik welcomes Gritzko as a son-in-law, especially after he has given proof of an astonishing capacity for drinking in the tavern. They shake hands on the betrothal; but they have reckoned without the temporarily gagged Khivria—nothing in the world shall make her accept the culprit as her son-in-law. Khivria shows such extraordinary energy, compared with her husband, that it is clear who will get the best of it—the affair of the lovers seems hopeless. Then as the *deus ex machina,* as Moussorgsky remarks in his manuscript, appears a gipsy. These cunning, inventive fellows, who ply their trade in great numbers in the Ukraine, love to use the opportunity a fair gives for fishing in troubled waters. Among the peasants the tziganes, although somewhat dreaded, are much liked for their cheerful, light-hearted temperament, always ready for some merry prank or subtle practical joke. Gogol's tzigane has contrived to fleece the stupid peasants by playing upon the dark superstition and proverbial dread of the Devil, so prevalent among these people, absolutely uneducated and still belonging to the Middle Ages. He spreads abroad the report that there is something uncanny about the Sorótchintzy Fair—the Evil One in person has taken up his quarters there in an out-of-the-way barn and now and then appears in the form of a pig's snout, or a ragged red waistcoat. Woe to the man that meets him face to face! The result is a most uncomfortable and apprehensive feeling among the people at the fair, who crowd together at every noise, imagining that they see the dreaded swine's snout, everywhere, and, in fact, every now and then, finding among their stalls a rag of a red waistcoat, planted there, obviously, by the gipsy. When the gipsy hears of the sorrows of the Párobok Gritzko, he good-naturedly resolves to help him. This does not make him forget business, however; he undertakes to bring about Gritzko's betrothal to the fair Parássia if he will sell him a yoke of oxen for twenty roubles. Gritzko gladly agrees to the bargain. Meanwhile evening is coming on. In their gossip's hut, where Tcherevik and his family have put up, Khivria is awaiting what she regards as her own particular fairing. In spite of her advanced age, she is not averse from love, and has found a customer for her over-ripe charms, and still more for her cookery, in the person of the priest's son, the divinity student Afanasi Ivanovitch. When she has succeeded in getting rid of her sulky husband, who has been sleeping off his debauch on the settle by the stove,

298

she sets to work to prepare a royal banquet for her lover. At last he appears, climbing over the hedge and making his entrance by falling into a bed of nettles. But the excellent Khivria's wonderful cookery soon comforts him for his mishap; his ardour grows as the food diminishes. At last he ventures to drop his shyness and proceed to actual caresses. Immediately—oh horror!—comes a knock at the door— Tcherevik, his gossip, and some of their boon companions are back from the fair! The priest's son, half paralysed with fright, mumbles some pious ejaculations, while Khivria's strong arms push him up a ladder into the loft. The excited company now enters with strange stories of the fair, among which the gipsy's tale of the Devil, the pig's snout, and the red waistcoat naturally plays a leading part. They do their best to cheer one another up, but the general feeling becomes more apprehensive, in spite of the bag of *sivukha* that Khivria has thoughtfully placed on the table. Meanwhile the creaking of the rafters under the weight of the priest's son sets their teeth to chattering with fear—Khivria alone manages to put a bold face upon it. Then, when the suspense is at its height, the window of the hut suddenly flies open, and with a terrible grunt a pig thrusts his snout into the room. A scene of indescribable confusion follows—the Ukrainian divinity student tumbles down from his hiding-place with a crash and a clatter, Tcherevik and his mate take to flight in wild terror, while the tzigane and his accomplices, who of course are answerable for the practical joke, manage to get away with the booty in the form of various oxen and horses. Tcherevik and his mate in the course of their flight along the high-road are taken by the enraged villagers for horse-stealers and well cudgelled. The Párobok, Gritzko, prompted by the gipsy, comes to their aid, explains the mistake, and rescues the prisoners from the hands of their tormentors. This friendly service must not go unrewarded. Gritzko is assured of the hand of the fair Parássia, for Khivria is too ashamed to make any objection. The tzigane gets his oxen, and all ends happily.

From this material Moussorgsky drew up the following notes for a scenario:

Orchestral introduction: A hot summer day in Little Russia.

1. The Fair (Chorus).
2. Entrance of the Párobok with his friends (reference to Parássia and Khivria).
3. Tcherevik and Parássia (their characters—wheat, beads).
4. Chorus of the dealers at the fair, concerning the red waistcoat—leading to a scene for four persons.—The gossip and Tcherevik.
5. After a little while Tcherevik intervenes in the Parássia-Párobok affair. Scene in recitative: the Párobok declares his intentions to Tcherevik (Tavern).

   N. B. The gipsy is witness of all this from the other side of the stage.
6. Entrance of Khivria—scene with Tcherevik (the Párobok is present). Khivria drags her husband away.
7. The Párobok alone. Appearance of the gipsy (deal in oxen, with reference to Parássia).
8. Short Gopak [dance].

   N. B. Intermezzo?

Act II (the gossip's hut)

1. Tcherevik asleep. Khivria wakes him (domestic conversation, chiefly aimed at getting rid of the husband).
2. Khivria's recitative—Cooking—entry of Afanasi Ivanovitch. Short duet.

3. Return of the rest from the fair. Story of the red waistcoat. Big comic scene.

Act III

1. Night. Great excitement and confusion (with a prelude—the gipsy). After their escape from the red waistcoat Tcherevik and his gossip sink down, wearied out. A cry raised that horses and oxen have been stolen. Both are seized. Comic conversation between the prisoners. The Párobok sets them free.
2. Soliloquy (*dumka*) for the Párobok.
3. Dawn. Parássia comes out into the garden. Soliloquy. Thinking of Khivria—independence—Triumph and dance.
4. Tcherevik and Parássia—dance.
5. The gossip and the Párobok come in laughing. Big betrothal scene (talk about Khivria's selfishness).
6. Finale.

   May 19, 1877. At A. Y. and O. A. Petrov's in Petrograd.

The music for *The Fair at Sorótchintzy* left by Moussorgsky in piano score consists of the following numbers: the orchestral introduction, "A hot summer day in Little Russia," leading directly to the fair scene. This fair scene includes the following sections: an entrance chorus, Parássia's *aria*, with interpolated remarks by Tcherevik ("wheat, beads" in the scenario), the gipsy's tale of the red waistcoat, a trio (Parássia, Gritzko, and the gipsy), Gritzko's proposal to Tcherevik, Chorus (all the bustle of the fair). This is followed by the Párobok's *dumka* (the Little Russian name for a lyrical outburst of feeling, always solemn in character), and a Gopak for the merry young villagers. The *dumka* has a wonderful swinging melody in the "Phrygian mode," which often occurs in Little Russian folk-songs; the melody, however, is not folk-song, but an original creation of Moussorgsky's. There is besides a scene between Tcherevik and his gossip, which is not mentioned in the scenario, but obviously belongs to the first act; the two friends come out of the tavern, drunk, and sing in blissful forgetfulness the song of "The Cossack who goes over the Steppe to Poltava" and then a fine Ukrainian roundelay, "Oi, ru-du, ru-du-dú." All that is lacking in the first act is the entrance of Khivria, planned in the scenario, and the "deal in oxen."

Nearly all the music of the second act is in existence, down to the first words of the gossip's story of the red waistcoat, just before the "*grande scène comique*." These delightful scenes of the second act, with their inimitable humour, bringing out the characters of the three figures (Tcherevik, Khivria, and the priest's son, Afanasi Ivanovitch), have only one counterpart in Russian music-drama, the scene in the "tavern on the Lithuanian frontier," in *Boris Godounov*. In his musical portraiture of the priest's son Moussorgsky has evidently had in mind a former and equally amusing creation of his, "The Seminarist." Like the latter, Afanasi Ivanovitch in his dalliance with Khivria cannot escape from the influence of Church psalmody, and regularly closes the phrases of his sinful love-making with flourishes in the sixth or some other ecclesiastical tone, which, in this connexion, gives an irresistibly comical effect.

There is little to say of the music of the third act—we have only one out of the six scenes contemplated in the scenario—namely, the third, Parássia's *dumka*; but if quality can make up for the lack of quantity, it does so here. This *dumka* is one of Moussorgsky's finest musical conceptions.

As an "Intermezzo" between the first and second acts, which Moussorgsky himself marked with a question in his scenario, he proposed to insert a piece of music that had gone through manifold metamorphoses already, without finding any settled place—his orchestral fantasia *A Night on the Bare Mountain.* Here it was to represent the "dream of the Párobok," inspired by the gipsy's ghost-stories. Moussorgsky had conceived the "Intermezzo" originally as an orchestral interlude; later on he thought of using this music as the accompaniment of scenic action, a sort of ballet-pantomime. It was his way to think out all his plans at once in the minutest details and to set his brains to work—though the idea had only just occurred to him—over costumes and scenery. "For heaven's sake," he writes to Stassov, "what am I to do with my devils in *The Fair?* What ought they to look like? . . . What would a drunken Ukrainian village lout see in his dream? Do please help me." So the "Tchernobog" of the Triglaff Hill was to be transplanted from the pan-Slavonic regions of *Mlada* to the "Bare Mountain" in the Ukraine; and no objection could be made to this, for the subject was the same, sorcery and devilry. Moussorgsky got no further with this idea—*The Fair at Sorótchintzy* and the "Intermezzo," too, were left unfinished. His work on this opera, so eagerly pursued at first, was suddenly interrupted by Petrov's death in 1878. Clearly this event was not the only cause that induced Moussorgsky to drop working on his Little Russian opera; but the loss of a direct incentive to complete the piece must have considerably lessened his creative impulse. That he never completely gave up the idea of going on with *The Fair* is shown by the letter about the "Intermezzo" just quoted, which is dated August 22, 1880, half a year before the composer's death. This fact contradicts the view expressed by some Russian writers that Moussorgsky was convinced that he could not succeed in finding the musical phrases, steeped in the local colour of the "black-earth" country, which were necessary for the description of Little Russian conditions. This statement is belied by the completed scenes of *The Fair at Sorótchintzy,* which contain pictures of Little Russian life that a born "Khokhol" could not have done more convincingly.

Some numbers of *The Fair* appeared in print as piano pieces during the life of the composer; sheer lack of money compelled him to sell them singly for small sums to the music publisher Bernard; otherwise he would hardly have consented to the premature publication of an unfinished work intended for the stage.

We cannot too deeply lament that Moussorgsky was not allowed to complete his work on *The Fair at Sorótchintzy*. Apart from its other qualities, the work would have been unique in Russian music as a purely comic opera and, as the existing scenes clearly prove, would have been a model of its kind. As it is, the Russian stage is still without any masterpiece of comic opera; Glinka wanted to write one, Dargomizhky ought to have written one, Moussorgsky, as we have seen, failed to do so.

The fragments of *The Fair at Sorótchintzy* contain much charming music, displaying riotous spirits, kindly humour, and irresistible comicality, as well as deep feeling; it is all the more to be regretted that the work remains merely a torso, which has yet to be adapted for the stage. Several attempts have been made in this direction; when Moussorgsky, forty years after his death, suddenly and unexpectedly became the fashion, many hands took up *The Fair at Sorótchintzy* and it was put on the stage in various versions. We shall consider these attempts in another chapter—the last—in which we give a survey of the fate of Moussorgsky's works after the composer's death.

* * *

The Fair at Sorótchintzy was not Moussorgsky's last operatic scheme, nor is it the only one that he left unfinished.

Stassov relates—not in his biography of his friend, but in a comparison between the painter Perov and Moussorgsky—that the latter had planned to make an opera on Russian country life in the time of serfdom. We know that it was

Moussorgsky's way to steep himself in impressions, as it were, and if occasion served, to embody them in a work of art; in this opera he meant to utilize firstly the impressions that he had received at the breaking up of his own landed estate, when the Moussorgsky family, like all the lesser Russian nobility, was compelled by the abolition of serfdom to dispose of its lands; and secondly the experience he gathered in his past as senior clerk in the Ministry of Woods and Forests, where, as he says, he was always battling with dishonest and refractory gamekeepers and foresters. The opera was to be called *The Bobil*, which means "the loafer," the landless and homeless peasant, who is generally considered a troublesome member of a Russian village and is treated accordingly. This work, too, would apparently have been a "folk-drama" in a special sense—perhaps more so than Moussorgsky's two historical operas. Stassov speaks of a scenario of the opera, which was found among the composer's papers, but unfortunately he does not say where it is to be found today. He gathered from his conversations with Moussorgsky that the composer intended in this work to bring on the stage the type of a tyrannical landowner, such as existed among the "planters" in the age of serfdom, and such as he depicted in *Khovanstchina* in the form of old Ivan Khovansky, though only in historical perspective. Such a landowner is sometimes kindly and dignified, sometimes harsh and cruel, inflated with ancestral pride and the vanity of power, enforcing his likes and dislikes with reckless caprice, organizing joyous banquets in his domestic harem, ready to fly into a madness of rage, but able to show a princely magnanimity, full of superstition and prejudice, and treating all around him as a horde of hereditary slaves. There were many such figures among the greater Russian landed nobility, about the middle of the nineteenth century. We can realize that so wide a scale of emotions offered rich material for Moussorgsky's plan of musical characterization. Part of the music of *Bobil* was completed and, after Moussorgsky had abandoned the scheme, found a place in his other works— for instance, a fortune-telling scene, which was put straight into Marfa's "prophecy" scene with Golitzin in *Khovan-stchina*. Stassov tells us that Moussorgsky had high hopes of a scene representing the manorial court, sitting in judgment on some poor devil of a loafer who was caught poaching. The material for this scene was probably used later on in *Khovanstchina*, in the scene where a spiritual court of the elders of the Old Believers sits to try "the heretic and sinner" Marfa—a scene with which Moussorgsky was long busy, but which he did not work out. The fragments we have mentioned are all that exists of the music of *Bobil*.

When *Khovanstchina* was finished, Moussorgsky took up the plan of a third historical piece, the subject for which he again took from the disturbed periods of Russian history, in which the excited, surging passions of the masses offered him such a field for his power of reproducing mass feeling. The central figure of the opera was to be the Ural Cossack, Emelian Pougatschòv, who pretended to be the murdered Tsar Peter Alexeievitch, and gave Catherine the Great so much trouble when he drove the Empress's troops back to the Volga with his horde of adventurers and threatened to set all Russia aflame. Here again the real hero would have been not merely Pougatschòv, but his age, with all its confusion and terror. With *Boris Godounov* and *Khovanstchina* this work would have formed a trilogy of all the Russian revolutions that had happened down to Moussorgsky's time.

It was only in the very last months of his life that this operatic scheme began to take a settled shape in Moussorgsky's mind. He had already begun to collect some musical material for it; for his libretto he probably used Pushkin's novel *The Captain's Daughter*, the historical background of which is the revolt of Pougatschòv. César Cui afterwards made a rather weak piece out of the story. But besides the episodes depicted by Pushkin, Moussorgsky intended to weave many new and original elements into his work. The painter Perov, whom we have mentioned, painted a picture of Pougatschòv, representing the false Tsar on the terrace of a manor-house, surrounded by his companions and his Russian irregulars. Near them is a priest in threadbare cassock, with a crucifix in his hand, barefooted, shivering with cold and fright. On the other side, near a group of cowering landowners, are some figures of those merciless butchers of men, those "beasts in human form," that every revolution brings to the surface. This picture Moussorgsky wanted to put on the stage; no doubt he would have painted it in startling colours.

In the Public Library at Petersburg there are a few pages on which Moussorgsky has noted down some folk-songs of the Russian borderlands, among them a remarkably characteristic Kirghiz melody with words, headed: "For my last opera, *Pougatschòvstchina.*" This tune, a tender lullaby ("I sought thee and found thee in the garden, where the apples ripen; sleep, sleep, Fariduschka, my sweet love"), is the only trace that remains of Moussorgsky's "last opera."

X

DECLINE AND DEATH
1878 – 81

WHEN Moussorgsky found himself once more alone, owing to Rimsky-Korsakov's marriage, he looked out for another room-mate. Solitude for any length of time was not to his taste; a *ménage*, or at least a lodging, shared with another, gave him the semblance of a home of his own, a thing that he had always longed for, but could never compass.

At first he was fortunate; his partner in the new diggings—that is to say, in the furnished room that was all he could afford, since a badly paid government clerk could not rise to a flat—was a young man distantly related to him on his mother's side, Count Arseni Arkadievitch Golenishtchev-Kutúsov, aged twenty-four, another impoverished aristocrat, who had to put up with a Bohemian life in Petersburg. Their new lodging was near the centre of the city—at the top of a letter to Stassov we find the address: Espalier Street (Spaliernaia), No. 6.

His association with young Count Golenishtchev-Kutúsov was not only personally a great boon to Moussorgsky, who soon became sincerely fond of his fellow lodger, but unexpectedly proved of great advantage to his art. It turned out that the young Count was a poet, not one of the numerous dilettante verse-writers who were found everywhere in Petersburg society, but a poet by God's grace, an artist in the best sense of the word, one who had the gift of turning facts of experience, without effort, into artistically beautiful pictures of faultless poetical form. This spontaneity of artistic creation, which in the young Count seemed as easy and inevitable as a natural function, strengthened Moussorgsky in his former conviction of the superfluousness, even harmfulness, of any technical training in art. Hans von Bülow, when asked how a man became a conductor, said: "One fine day you sit down at the conductor's desk, and then you find either you can do it, or else you can't, in which case you'll never learn to." This axiom, which is undoubtedly true of the art of conducting, but is otherwise open to grave objections, was, in Moussorgsky's opinion, true of all departments of art. He was glad to support his opinion by the example of Count Golenishtchev-Kutúsov, especially as he wanted an argument against the opposite doctrine, more and more strenuously maintained by Rimsky-Korsakov, of the necessity of severe technical training.

Stassov was naturally one of the first whom he told of his happy discovery. He wanted to make his young protégé acquainted with his old friend, and introduced him in a letter (June 19, 1873), as follows:

"Since Pushkin and Lermontov, I have never met with what I find in Kutúsov; he is not a manufactured poet like Nekrassov, and you do not notice the birth-pangs in his inspiration, as in Mey (I prefer Mey to Nekrassov). In Kutúsov there is unadulterated truth of sentiment; in almost all that he writes you feel the fresh breath of a lovely warm spring morning; besides this he has an incomparable technique, which was born with him. It is remarkable that he is at the University, at a time of life when people usually—well, you know—but our young poet (*he is very young*) is not inspired by bourgeois motives, never follows the fashion, and does not ape Nekrassov's grimaces. He hammers out into verse his own thoughts and the impulses that belong to his own artistic nature. This independent *lordship over his own brain* greatly delighted me when I looked into Kutúsov's rough copies (they are written sometimes in pencil, some-

309

times in ink, with blank pages between—a true photograph of the artist's brain-work)—it delighted me immensely! Kutúsov is *himself* a good judge (an 'esoteric critic,' as Balakirev used to say), as every real artist must be. I will pledge my word that Kutúsov toils like a blacksmith—yes indeed, in the sweat of his brow, like poor me—and how attracted he is to the people and to history! One word more: an artist cannot treat a subject honestly unless it is near to his heart, and Kutúsov has always realized this."

This cursory analysis of Kutúsov as a poet is on the whole very just. One remarkable point about Kutúsov's poems (only a few of which he has published), a feature rarely found among contemporary Russian poets, is their complete absence of "period"—if we did not know this poet's date, we could hardly say when his poems were written. Kutúsov, though his works include some dramatic sketches, is primarily the poet of inner currents of feeling, of the quiet beauties of nature, of the effort that strives to get at the heart of things, to attain the peace of the sages and their painless renunciation. Nothing could be better for his purpose than his even and plastic verse, often breathing the almost passionless tone of an epic, despite the lyrical intensity of the subject. But he often has great success in picturing the strongest dramatic situations, thanks to the bright and lively colouring of the language at his command.

Kutúsov's literary art was exactly in harmony with Moussorgsky's music, which can boast of precisely similar merits. It almost seems as if the young poet, in spite of their difference in age, sometimes exercised a decisive influence on Moussorgsky's views of the world, and hence, indirectly, on his art; though of course it is possible that there was no such connexion of cause and effect and that his acquaintance with Kutúsov coincided, by chance only, with the period at which a remarkable change in Moussorgsky's attitude towards life and art took place.

310

Moussorgsky built his views of the world and his environment on the sandy soil of his own personal experiences, which certainly reacted on him with extraordinary intensity. His capacity for entering into all events that excited his interest was, as we have seen, boundless, and he forgot that outside impressions are not the experience of the world within. He sympathized so much with the griefs and sorrows of others that he made them his own and intensified them in his art, by his love and sympathy. Moussorgsky very seldom used his own feelings as a subject for musical expression, as is especially plain from his songs; when he did, as in his few love-songs, the necessity for self-expression fettered him, and his artistic modesty caused him to lose himself in mere commonplace. But a change came over him in this respect, during the seventies, just at the time when Golenishtchev-Kutúsov crossed his path. He turns away from depicting the outer world, to the inner depths of his own experience; instead of letting his own feelings flow out through the channels of other men's thoughts, he draws his impersonal pictures from his own innermost feeling, and presents them as musical works full of personal colour. So we get the surprising spectacle of Moussorgsky at last becoming a lyrical artist, without really knowing it himself. It was probably this change in Moussorgsky's artistic attitude, joined with his growing tendency towards brooding pessimism and torturing self-analysis, that came as an unpleasant surprise to Stassov, who was steadily growing calmer and clearer in mind, and caused him to talk of the decline of his friend's talents and to write that absurd passage in his life of Moussorgsky, which would stultify all his earlier criticisms if the psychological explanation were no obvious: "His compositions became nebulous, unnatural, sometimes disconnected and tasteless." This hostile criticism is entirely explained by Stassov's disapproval of the increasingly introspective tendency of Moussorgsky's art; it had completely lost the national tone, which seemed to the zealous Russophile, Stassov, indispensable to any creative work by a Russian artist. When Moussorgsky became a lyrist and wove his own personality into his music, national characteristics fell into the background. In the glowing furnace of his own emotions all the dross was purged away, and only the shining crystal of pure humanity remained.

At the beginning of the preceding chapter it was pointed out that unfortunately there is practically no trustworthy material in existence for a psychological biography of Moussorgsky. We should be even worse off if we had not his music; this does give us a glimpse now and then into the secret depths of his emotional life, which he carefully guarded not only from the eyes of intruding strangers, but even from his friends. In the course of his remarks on the "change for the worse" in his friend's character, Rimsky-Korsakov relates that Moussorgsky in his latest years talked in a forced, unnatural way, and affected a whimsical manner. As an example of this he relates in a tone of tolerant disapproval an occasion that clearly shocked his sense of propriety. At the dress rehearsal for a performance of *Boris Godounov*, when the tolling of the monastery bell had been finely rendered *pianissimo* in the orchestra, Moussorgsky rose and, crossing his hands on his breast in Eastern style, made a low salaam to the musician who played the bell. We have already spoken of the "masks" that Moussorgsky assumed in his letters, as soon as he began to fear that he might blunder into revealing his inmost feelings. All these were defensive tactics—a sort of psychological mimicry—with which Moussorgsky shielded the secret cells of his soul from curious eyes. But he did not employ them in his music; had he done so, music, in which he demanded above all truth, truth, and again truth—not in the sense of photographic truth to nature, but in the sense of unadulterated truth of feeling—would have lost all its worth and meaning to him and suffered sheer desecration.

Moussorgsky never confessed that he expressed his own

nature in the setting of *Without Sunlight*, a song-cycle by
Golenishtchev-Kutúsov, and during his life no one would
have thought that he had done so. Today the outlines of the
real man are more clearly visible, no longer obscured by the
influence of his personal demeanour, and it is hardly to be
doubted that these songs are a true reflection of his state of
mind at the time. Golenishtchev-Kutúsov, only twenty-four
years old, could scarcely have drawn the autumnal melancholy of these songs from his own heart. We can scarcely be
wrong in thinking that in these songs we have the poetical
echo of the emotions of the composer, as he confessed them to
his new friend, the poet, in an hour of confidence; that Golenishtchev-Kutúsov was susceptible to such poetic suggestions is shown by other lyrics he wrote for Moussorgsky.

The six songs of the *Without Sunlight* cycle are all confined to the same mood of autumn melancholy, from which
there is no escape but the way of death.

This consciousness of "no escape" calls forth feelings
that range from sorrowful resignation to dull despair. Whether in the narrow enclosure of "Interior," or the vastness of the
moonlit plain in "On the River"—always there is the same
tormenting thought of the uselessness of all that happens
and the irremediable loss of vanished happiness. Twice is the
vision of happiness that has long since passed away darkened
by the figure of a woman, who presents herself to the artist's
mind as an ominous incarnation of the aimlessness and hopelessness of all strong and true feeling—in the second and
fourth songs, "Thine eyes in the crowd," and "Ennui." The
third song, "At last 'tis over, the heat of day," and the fifth
("Elegy"), "The night dreams in a mist," show the composer yet once again the unforgotten vision of his early love, to
whom he is prepared to surrender his whole soul, while he
must keep back the tears that tell of a grief that no one
knows. The last song, "On the River," has an almost weird
power of suggestion; in bright moonshine the waters of the

river lie dark under the shadow of the banks; a whisper seems to sound from its depths, the whisper of a mysterious voice:

Should she bid me listen, I could not stir;
Should she drive me forth, I would flee and never look round;
Should her call invite me—I would leap into the abyss.

No one can escape from the deep impression this song is sure to make. Moussorgsky here is so sparing in his use of musical expression that the setting would seem thin were it not justified by its effect. On a ground-bass, slowly rocking to and fro on the two notes of a minor second, we have a few vague, strangely related harmonies and an equally strange short, melodic phrase, which catches the ear at once and leaves behind it an aching sense of unsatisfied longing. From time to time the monotonous movement is interrupted by a close, as if the shadow of a passing cloud held back the flow of the water—that is all; ghostly as they came, the notes vanish in the darkness of a dying chord.

In the other songs of the cycle Moussorgsky is true to his principle that too much "expression" is just as inadmissible as too little. He could allow himself to follow this dangerous rule, since no one knew so well as he how to bring the verses out in relief by slight, hardly noticeable touches of musical shading. The first two songs of the *Without Sunlight* cycle are models of this wise moderation; even in the song "The night dreams in a mist," which gives the widest scope for natural description, he successfully escapes from the danger of the usual "tone-painting." The desired effect is conjured up with just two bars of wavering triplets, so harmonized that they seem to blend like shadows. The fact that the songs of this cycle sometimes close with a soaring chord of the sixth, sometimes with *morzando* harmonies of the seventh, instead of a straightforward common chord of the tonic, was, at that time, a breach of the rules that gave rise to great excitement and high disapproval among musical

314

Philistines. Long after, these delicate touches of musical colouring and characterization were properly esteemed, and recognized for what they were, the individuality of a natural musical expression and an addition to the language of music. Moussorgsky was right when he maintained that such progress is possible only when the creative intuition of genius, breaking through traditions and formulas, disregarding all rules except those it makes for itself, reaches boldly out for new means of expression; time alone will decide what is well and what is ill done.

To about the same period as the cycle *Without Sunlight* belongs a short song that Moussorgsky composed to his own prose words. In musical style it differs greatly from the *cantabile* manner in which he set Kutúsov's poems, and resembles his former attempts at "recited prose." The song is called "The Sphinx," and bears the dedication: "To Marie Ismailovna Kostiurina" (later Madame Feodorova), with the note: "To the little lady under the Christmas-tree." The words show that this is an occasional composition, referring to some event in the "little lady's" life. They run thus: "She is so quiet, so discreet. That silent mouth frightens you, you herd of prying chatterers! Perhaps sometimes she can look mockingly—if so, what matters it to you? Proud, is she? Can that be possible? You cunning impostors, do you dare attack her with your spiteful accusations? . . . " Moussorgsky contrived to raise this musical tirade far above the level of a mere personal affair, as it really is.

*   *   *

Can we detect any settled philosophy of life in Moussorgsky? Had he any? Clearly we cannot suppose that the composer of *Boris Godounov*, who was solely an artist to the innermost fibres of his nature, could have had any cut and dried philosophical views, or have subscribed to any definite doctrine or system. But as a man of intelligence, of wide cul-

315

ture and reading, Moussorgsky had his own settled views on the world and mankind, which we might with some justification call philosophical. One question which is closely connected with this, and which keenly interested him from his youth up, comes more and more to the front and fills a wider space in his art as time goes on—the question of death and dying.

This is the point at which Moussorgsky's art touches that of his great fellow-countryman, Dostoievsky. In his autobiography Moussorgsky had mentioned the name of Dostoievsky as one of his friends and acquaintances among Russian authors, but he afterwards struck his name out. There is no doubt, however, that he was familiar with the works of the author of *The Brothers Karamazov*, though he never refers to him in his letters; we may even point to a certain influence that Dostoievsky had on Moussorgsky's art (perhaps partly through Golenishtchev-Kutúsov's agency), which found expression at last in a disillusioned, dourly fatalistic conception of life.

Still, the course of Moussorgsky's mental development, as regards these questions, ran in exactly the opposite direction to Dostoievsky's—it led from an almost *exalté* religious feeling to cold scepticism. Dostoievsky, on the other hand, found on his death-bed the consolations of that religion which Moussorgsky laughed at, while all his life his soul was the battle-ground of the ceaseless conflict between God and the Devil. In his early youth Moussorgsky was deeply religious, even in the orthodox sense; he believed in the immortality of the soul and was enthusiastic for Lavater's doctrine of its survival after death. To this side of him, too, we may trace the mysticism that he "caught," and the ecstatic fits that occasionally took him. At that time telepathy, clairvoyance, occultism, etc., were as much in vogue as they are today and always have been, except that they had other names—and Moussorgsky, too, was influenced by them. Through Hol-

316

bach's *Système de la nature* and the study of Darwin, which he took up enthusiastically, he gradually changed to a cold, rationalistic atheism, which did not prevent him from preserving an artistic interest in the darkest corners of the spirit-world, and all the grotesque aberrations of belief and superstition. This profound understanding of the religious ideas of the masses and their fantastic delusions is shown by his treatment of the character of Pimen in *Boris Godounov,* and the picture of the Old Believers in *Khovanstchina.* He appreciated the force and beauty that lies in every popular belief and superstition and contrived to use these motives with remarkable skill for his artistic ends.

His own view of life, of mankind, of the destiny of man, and of death took on, in course of time, largely through the nature of his own personal experience, a tone of deep pessimism. Like Ivan Karamazov, he is ready at any moment to hand back to God with many thanks his "ticket of life." Death occupies an ever greater space in his thoughts as in his art, but it is not fear of death for himself that frightens him, but the repellent thought of the inevitable destruction of human personality. Yet for him, as for Dostoievsky, the fact of annihilation attracts him as a subject for literature. Death and everything connected with it were always a leading motive in his artistic work; the monologue of Mathô before his death, the death of Boris, the destruction of Sennacherib, the song "Cruel Death," the "Catacombs" in his *Pictures at an Exhibition,* are the artistic tribute that he paid to Death, the almighty master of all living. Even in *The Nursery* he touches on the problem of death in the song "The Beetle"— we have almost the feeling that the artist himself is as frightened and bewildered in the face of death as the child is when confronted by the dead insect. Death never appears to him as a peaceful, natural ending, but always as wanton cruelty, a senseless *cul-de-sac,* a hateful outrage. In referring to the passing of his friend Hartmann he could find no other symbol for death than that of the damp earth, which like an old prostitute takes every "lord of the earth" into her repulsive embrace.

One of Moussorgsky's favourite melodies was the *"Dies Iræ,"* which he knew from the works of Liszt and Berlioz. Here, too, he to some extent agreed with Dostoievsky, who had a special love for the scene of the apparitions in *Robert le Diable,* "because it smells of the churchyard."

Moussorgsky expressed his final "philosophy of death," if we can call it so, more plainly than ever in a work that he wrote at the same time as the cycle *Without Sunlight*; this was the set of songs, to words by Golenishtchev-Kutúsov, collected under the title *Songs and Dances of Death*: "Trepak," "Cradle-song," "Serenade," and "Field-Marshal Death."

For the initial idea of this work, with which Moussorgsky crowned his achievement in the field of vocal music, Stassov again claims the credit—as he expressed it himself, it was he who "set the task" to Moussorgsky. The pupil did his teacher honour, though, it must be confessed, he could hardly have carried out the scheme so completely without the congenial collaboration of his young poet-friend. Kutúsov sketched out four pictures of thrilling tragedy for this strange musical Dance of Death; Moussorgsky made them into weirdly impressive musical scenes. They are written for voice and piano; but it is possible that he himself thought of arranging them for orchestra, as was afterwards done by Glazounov and Rimsky-Korsakov. The piano part is elaborately worked out and, as in many of Moussorgsky's former songs, is as effective as the vocal part.

The first piece, "Trepak," depicts a drunken peasant who has lost his way in a snow-storm and staggers along over the lonely waste. There the Man with the Scythe finds him and dances a breathless Dance of Death with him in the whirling snow-flakes, till the peasant, exhausted, sinks down in the soft snow to his last sleep. Death bends over him with a mocking smile, and whispers in his ear: "Sleep, friend, sleep sweetly. . . . See, the summer is here! The sun is shining on the meadows, far away a song is heard. . . . The sickles are swinging up and down . . . and a pair of doves are flying overhead." The words are not meant as consolation, but are spoken in contemptuous scorn, and their mocking grin is made more uncanny by the magical music to which Moussorgsky has set them. The entrancing dance-tune leaps up for the last time and dies away, and three chords of bare fifths, like an endless covering of frozen snow, seem to spread over the whole scene.

The second scene, "Cradle-song," shows us a death-chamber, where a mother watches by the cot of her dying child. There too stands the Skeleton at the foot of the bed and sings in a soft, monotonous voice, to a strangely haunting motif, his lullaby: "*Eia popeia*, slumber sound!" The heart-rending appeals of the mother break in vain against the stark serenity of Death, who goes on undisturbed, singing his song to the end, till the fevered child draws its last, long breath. "See how my song has brought the boy to rest! *Eia popeia*, soundly he sleeps!"

In the third song, under the window of a sick-room, Death, the knight, sings a "Serenade" to a maiden dying of consumption. His wooing sounds ever more entrancing, more seductive, till, with the triumphant cry: "Thou art mine!" the song breaks off. This is an example of music "beautiful in itself," rare among Moussorgsky's songs, and has a regular scheme, which is justified by the strophe form of the "Serenade."

The imposing effect of a great fresco is produced by the fourth and last song, of "Field-Marshal Death," who appears on his charger on a battlefield strewn with corpses, and, as a conqueror, holds a review of the dead. The march motif, in which Death ironically and arrogantly proclaims his victory to the combatants, is imitated from a Polish revolutionary song. In the form that Moussorgsky has given it, it is wonderfully picturesque.

The first three numbers of the *Songs and Dances of Death* were composed between February and May 1875 and were dedicated to the singer Osip Afanasievitch Petrov, his wife, and Ludmilla Ivanovna Shestakova; "Field-Marshal Death" was composed in the summer of 1877 and dedicated to the poet. The *Songs and Dances of Death* were not printed during the life of the composer. Mussorgsky had planned to extend the cycle of songs, still on themes suggested by Stassov; the sketch of a monkish fanatic, who dies in his cell to the heavy tolling of the convent bell; a political exile, who comes back, is wrecked in sight of home, and perishes in the waves; a dying woman whose fevered fancy calls up memories of love and visions of youth; and several others. "Moussorgsky liked these ideas," writes Stassov, "but he never succeeded in carrying them out, although he played fragments of them to me and others." In fact the poet I. P. Polonsky, who knew Moussorgsky well, relates that he had heard him play a piano piece (?) picturing the feelings of a political prisoner in the Fortress of Peter and Paul, with, as a musical background, a chiming clock, which played Bortniansky's hymn "I pray to the power of love" out of tune. According to this account, Moussorgsky had altered one of Stassov's themes or combined two—the monk and the political prisoner.

Akin to these figures of the Dance of Death is another poem by Golenishtchev-Kutúsov, called "A Ballad" ("Forgotten"), to which Moussorgsky set one of his finest and most effective songs. A mother and child are laughing and playing, expecting the return of the father, who has fallen in battle and is lying alone and forgotten, a prey to greedy vultures, on the deserted field. The sharp contrasts in mood —always a speciality of Moussorgsky's, are here worked out with great artistic power. The two tenths with which the song ends seem to span the whole wide horizon of the desolate plain and of human sorrow. The immediate inspiration of this song was a picture, "Forgotten," by the celebrated Russian battle-painter, Verestchagin, who was famous in his time for his startling realism and had found his subject on the battlefields of the Turkish war. It was said that this picture aroused the high displeasure of the Tsar Alexander II, who suspected antimilitarist and pacifist views in this terrifying portrait of the realities of war. Although this report, as was made clear later, was unfounded, the picture, which is now in the Tretiakov Gallery at Moscow, vanished for a time from public sight, and the printing of Moussorgsky's "Ballad," dedicated to Verestchagin, was suspended, although the licence of the censorship had been obtained. The "Ballad" was first published six years after the composer's death.

Moussorgsky's peaceful life with young Count Golenishtchev-Kutúsov, so profitable to his art, did not last long. Their connexion was broken off by the same fate as had brought his companionship with Rimsky-Korsakov to a sudden end—Count Golenishtchev-Kutúsov married. This separation affected Moussorgsky much more than his parting from Rimsky-Korsakov, since he had been really drawn to the young poet as a man, whereas only their common artistic interests bound him to Korsakov. He expresses his grief to his trusty friend Stassov in the bitterest terms. Perhaps he felt instinctively that this change would have a fatal effect on him, by leading him into other paths that he wished to avoid. His life with Kutúsov had lasted little more than two years. On the night of December 29–30, 1875 Moussorgsky writes to Stassov:

" . . . One more bit of news, my dear friend! A lad has gone astray, drawn by various wishes and desires—no other than Arsenius Golenishtchev-Kutúsov, the Count; and the temptation to which he has succumbed is merely that he thinks he would like to get married! Not as a joke, but *really and properly*. So yet another is setting off for those 'home countries' from which none return. O God! Here am I sitting bemused in a government office, running after any little idea that appears in the distance (and how happy one is when one catches it), and gentlemen who don't know the misery of an office go and get married right away, without even having been led astray! I scolded Arseni well and said no end of rude things to him. Come what may, *I can't tell lies*. He wanted me to go with him to call on his fiancée (I know her), *but I am not going*; I should have to tell lies if I did. I don't like what he is doing and *I won't go in*—I won't! Such things make me want to work harder than ever. And if I am left all alone—well, alone I shall be! In any case I shall have to die alone. . . . I'm sorry about Arseni, Generalissimo."

"In any case I shall have to die alone"—Moussorgsky did not know then how soon and how sadly these prophetic words would come true.

*　　*　　*

After the break-up of the *ménage* with Kutúsov, Moussorgsky sometimes went to stay with an acquaintance, the painter Naumov, who played a not very creditable part in the composer's subsequent life. Naumov himself seems to have had a taste for drink and probably gave an impetus to this unhappy weakness in his fellow lodger, which soon led to his final ruin. That Moussorgsky's old friends had no very high opinion of his new acquaintance can be seen from some remarks in Rimsky-Korsakov's *My Musical Life* and in the letters of Ludmilla Ivanovna Shestakova. His anxious friend writes (on August 9, 1878) to Stassov: "If it were only possible to get him [Moussorgsky] away from Naumov, we could save him yet."

But Moussorgsky himself was of quite a different opinion; after all, one prefers those friends who do not quarrel with one's weaknesses, but rather indulge them, careless of the consequences; and in any case Naumov must have possessed some good qualities to attract so exacting a spirit as Moussorgsky's; otherwise the latter would not have had such a strong liking for him. Probably Naumov appealed to the human side of the composer by a certain hearty familiarity that made him feel that he was one of the family; in a letter to Stassov he calls the Naumovs "the family that pets and spoils me." It is evident that he makes a special effort to set Naumov in as favourable a light as possible in his letters to his friend and to Ludmilla Ivanovna. From this effort we can infer, if we choose, something like an uneasy conscience. Now he assures Ludmilla Ivanovna of the true devotion his new friend feels for her—so we can infer that Naumov and Madame Shestakova were acquainted—now he begs Stassov to be so good as to show Naumov and his son the Public Library, of which Stassov was director; or he writes: " . . . My host Naumov sends you his kindest regards. He is delighted with your letter; I could not help reading it to him; he is enthusiastic over your consideration and kindness for poor creatures like us."

Naumov is mentioned for the first time in a letter to Stassov, of August 7, 1875. Moussorgsky was then still living with Golenishtchev-Kutúsov, and the poet's absence of mind was the reason alleged for Moussorgsky's having to stay for a time at Naumov's. He seems to have been so comfortable there that after his parting from Kutúsov he at once moved over again to Naumov's rooms in the Vassili Ostrov, a quarter of Petersburg on the other side of the Neva. In a letter to Stassov he gives Naumov's address and goes on to say: "How I am faring—I, your *shy* Moussorianin [a play on his Christian name, Modest]—you can see by the address. It is easily explained; Arseni took our latch-key with him to the country, and consequently I am, so to speak, boarding with my estimable friend Naumov, in whose rooms, in spite of my official duties, I have finished the first act of *Khovanstchina*."

Naumov was not the only friend that Moussorgsky cultivated outside his usual circle of musicians and people of intellectual distinction. His reasons for this are sufficiently plain from what has already been said. Among his new acquaintances he found more human—and perhaps also artistic—sympathy than among his comrades "in the profession." Rimsky-Korsakov, from the height of his moral superiority, mentions this fact with reproach, without understanding the true reason for it, which his short-sighted primness could not appreciate. He writes in *My Musical Life*:

"About that time we found that he [Moussorgsky] used to sit in the Maly Yaroslavetz Restaurant and other taverns till the small hours, over a bottle of brandy, alone, or in the company of new-found friends and boon companions, whom none of us knew. When he dined with us, or elsewhere, Moussorgsky generally refused wine at table, but later in the evening he was irresistibly drawn to the Maly Yaroslavetz Restaurant."

Moussorgsky had long struggled against the injustices of life—Fate spared him nothing. He had to bear one trial after another: the death of his early love, which left an unhealed wound in his heart; the death of his mother, at a time when he was still unable to do without her tender care and loving guidance—by which his "hearth and home" were for ever destroyed; the complete financial collapse, which precluded all possibility of an easy life, and dashed all his hopes for the future. Then followed the years of oppressive, soul-destroying labour for beggarly pay; sore disappointments in art, not only as regards insufficient recognition of his works—that his combative nature would easily have overcome—but "betrayal" in a quarter where he least expected it; the premature death of the only woman whom he loved, but had never possessed; the quarrel with his brother, which severed those last ties of kinship that had given him some feeling of belonging to a family. In addition to all this his *Boris Godounov*, which first brought him honour and recognition and had a lasting success with the public, which all the cavilling of foolish critics could not damage, was suddenly, and without any reason, taken out of the repertoire of the Marie Theatre and never again performed during the life of the composer. There were rumours that the opera had displeased "the All-Highest," and this naturally impaired the composer's position with the official musical world, which was none too strong already. Is it a marvel that all this broke down a nature so incapable of resistance as Moussorgsky's? We must remember his "terrible illness," which caused him and his family great anxiety in his youth, just after he joined the Preobrazhensky regiment. Even then he showed signs of a "morbid" craving, in the full sense of the word, for the narcotic effects of alcohol; the fact that these signs vanished again as suddenly as they had come was an irrefutable proof, from a medical standpoint, that he was the victim of a hereditary tendency, which weakened his free will in this respect.

The biography of an artist is not the place for a medical history of pathological symptoms; but we must at least draw attention to the medical explanation of a fact that might otherwise arouse other feelings than an understanding sympathy. Moussorgsky during his last years of life was cruelly misjudged even by his nearest friends; we might at least spare his memory. The usual method of hushing up and smoothing over such cases, by refusing to call things by their right names, never answers, since it often gives rise to unfounded suspicions of something worse and confuses the logical sequence of psychological causes and outward behaviour, instead of explaining it. The frank confession of the truth is the right weapon to oppose to malignant slander or the unfounded exaggeration of a narrow bourgeois morality.

Yes, Moussorgsky in his latest years took to drink—the fact cannot be denied—but this is no reason for refusing our sympathy to the creator of so much noble music, as some of his former friends did. The composer of *Boris* is not the only genius who has had to buy his "faculty divine" at the price of a so-called "moral failing"—a reflection that should lead us to abandon the habit of judging genius from the standpoint of average morality. It is hard to keep one's temper when one reads in Rimsky-Korsakov that Balakirev "already suspected that Moussorgsky had a love for alcohol" and had "dropped him on this account." The writer of these words himself—as we plainly see—also deserted his friend "on this account" and he was followed by all the other less intimate friends of the "fallen genius." It is a lamentable spectacle, from which one would prefer to turn away. It is easy, and hardly heroic, to condemn the sinner; but want of sympathy and the desertion of friends may sometimes be in themselves a crime.

Except for Ludmilla Ivanovna, there was no heart that responded freely and unreservedly to the emotional needs of one who had given so many artistic proofs of his true and real humanity; still less was any purse opened for his relief. And how easy it would have been to help him! There is no doubt that Ludmilla Shestakova was right when she said in a letter to Stassov: "If there was any possibility of getting him away from Naumov, we might still save him." "Naumov" is obviously here only one of a class, a symbol. It was not a matter of "getting Moussorgsky away" from anybody, so much as of taking steps to give him a more worthy existence and make it possible for him to devote himself freely and without "official hindrances" to art and creation. But it is always the shyness of the rich that lets the "poor and proud" perish. Nobody, of course, thought of such a very simple method as giving material help, in his case, any more than

in that of numberless poverty-stricken artists, whose wretched fate ought always to be remembered as a warning example.

Ludmilla Ivanovna's appeal was not answered, or at
least did not result in any practical help. She herself, a mere
weak woman, who, like all Russian "great ladies," was unac-
quainted with the realities of life, could do nothing; probably, too, the idea of coming to his rescue never entered her
mind, since, like most people for whom the material side of
life has never been a "problem," she could hardly understand what a decisive influence freedom from financial worry
might have on a man's spiritual life, as well as on his artistic
work—a thing that no one realizes until he has lost his own
independence. It is pathetic to see Ludmilla Ivanovna's helplessness, her wish to remedy what was wrong, and her complete inability to find a way out of the difficulty. At last she
made up her mind to use her moral influence to the full; her
efforts met with some success, though naturally it did not
last; the counter-currents were too strong. The letter to
Stassov just quoted (of August 9, 1878) reflects her state
of mind. The old lady writes: "And now I want to speak
about one of your closest friends; I mean Moussorgsky. I
have been silent about him all this time, so as not to grieve
you. Last week he came to see me several days in succession,
and every time he was in a terrible state, and sat with me a
long time; when I saw he was getting worse and worse, I felt
I had to do something to save him and protect myself. I
wrote him a letter begging him not to come to my house
again in a state of nervous excitement (as he calls it) ; I told
him in my letter all that was in my heart, of course as dis-
creetly as possible. Well—only think of it!—yesterday my
Moussinka appeared, *absolutely* sober, and promised that he
would never vex me again. We shall see what happens, but I
am convinced he will abstain, at least for a time. . . . It is
such a pity about Moussorgsky, he is such a fine man!" But
well-meant advice and pathetic appeals, even from so kind a

327

heart, did not help matters much. If Moussorgsky could have had an independent income as the foundation of a peaceful mental state, he would have been far more amenable to sympathy, friendly advice, or even medical treatment. But, as we said, nobody thought of this until it was too late; till then they only gave vent to moral indignation and shook their heads at the failings and weaknesses of a man whom they no longer understood or cared to understand, though they still pretended to be his friends. Many a great mind has been ruined by the conflict between social prejudice and the natural moral instinct.

Moussorgsky sank ever lower in the scale of society. How high the others had risen! Stassov, Cui, Borodin, were now Excellencies, Rimsky-Korsakov a professor. The gulf that had opened between them and him grew ever wider and deeper. From the heights of their official position they looked down with astonishment and disapproval at the drowning struggles of the irreclaimable Bohemian and thanked their Creator that they were not as he was; they were quite wrong, for in spite of the outward unseemliness of his way of living Moussorgsky had kept his soul and his artistic conscience pure as crystal, which was more than could be said of any one of them. We cannot for a moment admit the "moral ruin" of the author of *Boris*—he had a right to hold his head up and look any man in the face. It was not he who would have to blush when Art asked her sons to give an account of their stewardship—no one had served her more faithfully. In life as in art he never made the slightest concession that his conscience would not have approved. The only reproach that could be brought against him was that he—to use the hackneyed expression—tried to drown his sorrows in the bowl. And he was less to blame for this than were those around him, who withheld from him the practical help, the human and artistic sympathy, for want of which he was driven to seek comfort elsewhere.

328

His inner estrangement from his former friends and comrades naturally resulted in their meeting less frequently. Instead of the "Powerful Coterie," there was formed in Petersburg another musical circle, including all the members of the "Powerful Coterie" except Balakirev and Moussorgsky. This group later found a centre in the wealthy timbermerchant and patron of art M. P. Belaiev, who was an enthusiastic lover of music and won an honourable place in the history of Russian music by founding his publishing house in Leipzig, by establishing symphony concerts in Petersburg, which were specially devoted to Russian music, by giving yearly prizes for compositions, and by liberally assisting young and rising talent. All this was of no use to Moussorgsky, since Belaiev only began his patronship of music in the eighties. The lost members of the old community, Balakirev and Moussorgsky, were replaced by fresh and younger spirits—Alexander Glazounov, still a schoolboy, whose astonishingly precocious talents were the wonder of all, and Anatol Liadov, whose first efforts as a composer had been welcomed by Moussorgsky in 1873, in the following words, from a letter to Stassov: "A new and unmistakable genius has appeared; original and purely *Russian*, the son of Constantine Liadov, and a pupil at the Conservatoire, who, I remember, when we were there together, never talked drivel about such things as chords of the 6-4. . . . He is a real genius. Easy, natural, without any humbug, daring, fresh, and *strong*. Yes, he is all that." Moussorgsky was not mistaken in his judgment, but he himself did not have the pleasure of observing the greatest period of Liadov's musical activity. That no closer personal relations were formed between them was not because of the difference in age, but because Liadov naturally attached himself to his teacher, Rimsky-Korsakov, and his circle, rather than to Moussorgsky, who was steadily acquiring the reputation of an eccentric wastrel.

Few separate works were composed by Moussorgsky in the years 1877 and 1878. The time he could give to music was mostly taken up, as we know, with his work on *Khovanstchina* and *The Fair at Sorótchintzy*. Besides these his only output was a series of songs to poems by A. Tolstoy, Golenishtchev-Kutúsov, and Pleshtcheiev, and a biblical chorus, *Joshua,* for which he employed some of the unused material from his opera *Salambo.*

The five songs with words by A. Tolstoy are the only compositions of this period that in a measure justify Stassov's opinion that Moussorgsky's artistic power had not maintained its former level. But if we consider the other works of this period, it is absolutely unjust to draw any conclusions from them as to a general decline in the composer's talent. Two of Tolstoy's poems, "Not like the lightning," and "At last retires," like "The Wanderer," by Pleshtcheiev, and the cycle *Without Sunlight*, come under the head of autobiographical songs. We cannot doubt that Moussorgsky chose these words because they expressed his state of mind at the time. Tolstoy's first song is a passionate protest against the pin-pricks of destiny, which are sometimes harder to bear than a crushing blow: "Not like the lightning did misfortune strike, not like a rock that shatters once for all. No, it gathered like the rising mist that shrouds the heavens in heavy clouds—like the fine rain that drizzles through the endless autumn nights! And still it beats down, ceaselessly, pitilessly, without rest or pause. Misfortune, why despoil the oak-tree twig by twig, and leaf by leaf? To others Fate has been kinder, bursting on them like the thunder-storm and tearing the tree up by the roots." Autumn sadness speaks in the second poem of Tolstoy, which ends with the words: "The old sorrow comes back again, bends again over thy soul; thy head droops as of old—joyless, hopeless." And the Wanderer sighs:

330

"All those I loved are, ah! so far away;
Would I could clasp them to my heart today."

All these words found a sorrowful echo in the heart of the composer.

The third of Tolstoy's songs ("The Spirit in Heaven") expresses a milder pessimism: "Softly glideth a soul through the fields of the blest," and he longs, amid the joys of heaven, to return to earth, "so that I may pity and comfort a mortal." The somewhat sickly conventionality of the words left Moussorgsky's fancy no scope for raising them to the eternal heights of musical beauty. His conception in this song, like that of the poet, keeps to the path of traditional drawing-room sentiment, and even the accompaniment sometimes drops into the mere conventional formulas, a thing which hardly occurs elsewhere in his work. The two last songs of the series strike quite another note; the "Minstrel's Song" is like an improvised folk-song, a style in which Moussorgsky always excelled; the song "Master Haughty (Arrogance)," is nothing but a musical caricature, a *genre* in which Moussorgsky is a master, especially when, as in this instance, national character comes into the theme. Russian folk-songs often personify and satirize some undesirable trait of character; and this ironical style is imitated in the incisive humour of Tolstoy's words and Moussorgsky's music. In the dedications of the Tolstoy lyrics we notice a difference from Moussorgsky's previous works, in which he seldom went beyond the circle of his closest musical friends. On "Not like the lightning" and "Master Haughty" stand the names of F. A. Vanliarsky and A. E. Paltchikov, probably members of the club at the Maly Yaroslavetz Restaurant, of which Rimsky-Korsakov speaks so contemptuously in *My Musical Life*. Two of the Tolstoy series, contrary to Moussorgsky's custom, bear no dedication; the song "At last retires" is dedicated to Countess O. A. Golenishtchev, wife of the poet, with whom Moussorgsky had apparently been reconciled during the two years that had passed since Kutúsov's marriage. Only once did Moussorgsky set another lyric by his former comrade. The poem is called "The Vision," and once more the theme is the apparition of the lost love before the eyes of the poet—or is it the composer? This was always the favourite motive that Moussorgsky chose for lyrical expression on the rare occasions when he was under the spell of passionate longing. The song, dedicated to Elizabeth Gulevitch, the mother-in-law of the poet, does not rise above the usual level of Moussorgsky's love-lyrics.

Very fine is the chorus of *Joshua*, which shows us the young Moussorgsky of the *Salambo* period in his most impetuous vein. The composer adapted the scriptural text himself; the original Hebrew themes, which are developed in the chorus with a fine sense of style, were picked up by Moussorgsky from an old Jew who chanted his prayers in the courtyard over which the composer lodged. The new version of the chorus, according to Stassov, was written in the years 1874 and 1875, although the copy was made, according to the manuscript, on July 2, 1877. The chorus is interrupted in two places by solos: a short recitative for baritone: "Behold, O Israel, the sun stands still," and a long-drawn lament for mezzo-soprano in the style of the old Jewish temple chants: "Weeping wander the women of Gibeon." This work was first published and performed after the composer's death, in Rimsky-Korsakov's orchestral arrangement.

*　　　*　　　*

So Moussorgsky's uneventful life went on from month to month in almost unbroken monotony. It was no great alteration when, in 1879, he exchanged his post in the department of Woods and Forests for another in the Ministry of Imperial Control. One of his non-musical friends, T. I. Filippov, director of the Board of Control, who greatly admired Mous-

sorgsky's art, obtained this new post for him; as on a former
occasion, his old official superiors were, if anything, glad to
get rid of him, while his new chiefs took him on as a matter of
course. Again his morning hours were given up to the soul-
destroying routine of subordinate office-work. His absolute
lack of zeal or ambition or of any interest in his work prevented Moussorgsky from ever rising above the lowest position in the government service. He devoted his afternoons to
work at his two operas, *Khovanstchina* and *The Fair at
Sorótchintzy*; his evenings were usually given up to social
life—which takes up more time in Russia than elsewhere.
Less and less often did he appear in the circle of his old
friends, even of Ludmilla Ivanovna and Stassov, more and
more often at the table at the Maly Yaroslavetz Restaurant.

In the summer of 1879 something happened to break
the monotony of his existence, something that counts among
the great events of his life. He went on a tour through the
whole of southern Russia, the Crimean towns and the Black
Sea provinces.

Madame Daria Michailovna Leonova was one of the
favourite singers of the day at Petersburg, and, owing to
her engagement at the Imperial Marie Theatre, her name
was famous all over Russia. Legends had grown up around
her—for had she not studied, "herself," with Dargomizhky
and Glinka? At the first performance of *Boris Godounov*,
in 1874, she took the part of the Hostess in the scene on the
Lithuanian border. César Cui writes about her in his *Memoirs*: "By far the most prominent figures among the artistes
of the Marie Theatre were the *basso* Petrov, and the alto
Leonova, two wonderfully gifted singers, who must undoubtedly be classed among the greatest in their profession." Rimsky-Korsakov, who is extremely sparing of praise, mentions
Madame Leonova's "beautiful" contralto voice, but adds
that it had not been properly trained and that the artiste's
singing in consequence had sometimes a touch of the gipsy

about it. However, he allows that Madame Leonova, who had now passed the zenith of her powers, was "often inimitable" in parts with a strong dramatic or comic appeal. This rather equivocal appreciation shows at least that Madame Leonova, like Moussorgsky, had great natural talent and was fitted to render his songs, in which both sides of her talent found scope for display. Moussorgsky himself often gratefully recognizes this in his letters.

Madame Leonova, who had lately returned from a tour, which took her to Japan, San Francisco, New York, and also to London and Vienna, undertook a concert tour for the summer of 1879 through all the large towns of southern Russia. She asked Moussorgsky to accompany her, in both senses of the word. He gladly accepted the offer, and did not regret it. The tour not only brought him honour and success, to which he had long been a stranger, but was rich in impressions that Moussorgsky's receptive mind did not allow to remain unused. Although his success was mainly due to his piano-playing, which, as we know from the verdict of expert contemporaries, was in many respects "inimitable," his own works, too, found a readier acceptance in the provinces than might have been expected. The impression made by his compositions was not sufficient to prevent them from falling into oblivion for more than thirty years; but this Moussorgsky, enjoying his momentary success, fortunately did not know, and no gloomy forebodings darkened the generally pleasant impressions of the tour, which greatly raised his artistic self-confidence.

The idea of using his talent as a pianist for a source of income had occurred to Moussorgsky before. In a letter to Stassov, June 15, 1876, there is the following postscript: "By the way, Fate has kept me going so far, but who knows what may happen to one in the present general state of affairs? I have been really working at my piano of late and am gradually coming to think that if Fate wills, I can manage to earn my daily bread by strumming." This almost careless attitude towards one of the most important matters of life is characteristic of the writer. In Moussorgsky's day there were still traces of that aristocratic musical dilettantism which demanded anything from art rather than material gain. Art was the high goddess whom men served without hope of pay—rather would they sacrifice all they had to her, like many of the great Russian nobles who ruined themselves with their orchestras and theatres. The idea of making a milch cow of art was almost blasphemous; consequently it occurred to Moussorgsky only towards the end, when he had borne the yoke of office work for nearly twenty years, not without grumbling, but without seriously rebelling against his fate. For his compositions he, like Glinka, never got anything worth mentioning. When at last he made up his mind to use his musical talent and knowledge to earn his livelihood, he came to utter ruin.

Apart from his two trips to Moscow, Moussorgsky had never gone beyond the limits of Petersburg and the Government of Pskov, where his family estates were. We can guess with what eagerness his impressionable temperament and his vivid mind took in and worked up all the new things that he saw and heard, nature, mankind, manners, and customs. The tour took him to Poltava, Elizavetgrad, Nikolaiev, Kherson, Sebastopol, Yalta. In a letter to Stassov (September 10, 1879) he gives extracts from his "Travel Diary," as he calls it, briefly setting forth the impressions made on him by the towns of southern Russia from an artistic point of view. It is interesting to follow him on his journey with the help of these remarks. Moussorgsky was surprised to find that those Russian cities that were usually frequented by artistes and singers from the two capitals— Odessa, Nikolaiev, Sebastopol—seemed to have little understanding for music and art, while in places lying off the main

335

routes, such as Elizavetgrad, Kherson, Poltava, he found true
enthusiasm for music and a profound understanding of it.

"They know all our musicians there, through and
through, and conversation flowed as easily as in Petersburg,"
he says of Kherson and Elizavetgrad, where, as he writes,
"after the '*Erlkönig*' they loudly applauded even poor me."
In private houses at Kherson he was "enchanted by their intelligent appreciation of the artistic aims of the new movement in music."

He reports of Poltava, the "capital" of the Ukraine,
that *Khovanstchina,* especially Marfa's last scene with Andrei Khovansky, "capitally rendered by Leonova," produced
a startling effect. Of great importance to him, naturally,
was the reception given there to some numbers out of the
Ukrainian opera on which he was working. To his joy he
found that his fears lest he had blundered in catching the
local colour in music and words were quite unfounded. "*The
Fair at Sorótchintzy,*" he writes to Stassov, "aroused the
greatest sympathy there [at Poltava] and in the whole of the
Ukraine. Ukrainian men and women assured me unanimous-
ly that the character of the music was thoroughly national,
as I too have realized since I have been here." This remark
absolutely contradicts the view that after O. A. Petrov's
death Moussorgsky completely lost interest in his Little Russian opera and gave up working at it. In Elizavetgrad, the
native town of Petrov, the great singer, he thought of him.
"I have been in Petrov's native town," he writes to Ludmilla Ivanovna, "and looked over the limitless steppe, wide
and free as his mighty soul."

"But Odessa! O *bella donna* of the South!" he goes on.
"She cares nothing for art, dead or alive; she is interested in
nothing but the price of wheat and the exchange." No better was the impression made on him by Sebastopol, "where
one hardly dares utter the word 'art.'" He was struck by the

336

devastation wrought in the town by the enemy artillery during the Crimean War, so long ago.

He writes humorously from Yalta, the "Pearl of the Black Sea," a spot far superior in natural beauty to Nice, the pearl of the Mediterranean: "A team of four quadrupeds with absurdly long manes and tails brought us here; the road led through the plain of Baidarki up a steep approach, through the famous gate, and along the slopes, from which precipitous rocks, bathed in sunshine, seem to dive into the depths of the sea. Here they put us up in a hovel that was more like a cave, inhabited by centipedes that bite and a kind of snapping beetle, which also bites, and other insects that bite hard—their only *raison d'être* is to embitter human life; but the magic hand of Sofia Vladimirovna [Madame Fortunato, Stassov's daughter, the owner of the celebrated Grand Hôtel de Russie at Yalta] rescued us from the aforesaid nest of bugs (recommended by Verestchagin), and transplanted us into Europe . . . into a hotel astonishingly clean, comfortable, and luxurious." At Yalta the two artistes were the objects of the most delicate attention, not only from their friend, the owner of the hotel, but from all the visitors, who are numerous at that time of the year.

The programs of the concerts, which do honour to Leonova's taste, included songs by the chief Russian composers, and some European; Moussorgsky gives them conscientiously in a letter to Ludmilla Ivanovna—Glinka, Dargomizhky, Serov, Balakirev, Cui, Borodin, Rimsky-Korsakov, Schubert, Chopin, Liszt, Schumann—he forgets to mention his own name. "On such stilts as these," he adds, "one can stride over the wide world." Moussorgsky not only acted as accompanist in these concerts, but had also to play solos, for people were not yet accustomed then to concerts of songs only—they wanted variety. The doyen of the staff of the Board of Control possessed no grand "repertoire," for he had never taken the trouble of getting one together. So he had to get out of

337

the difficulty as best he could. That is the ironical comment in Rimsky-Korsakov's *My Musical Life.* "Truly an odd sort of repertoire," says this stern judge of musical morals; "the overture to *Russlan and Ludmilla,* by Glinka, in an improvised rendering, or the coronation chimes of the Kremlin bells out of *Boris*!" Rimsky-Korsakov need not have been so indignant—even greater, or at least better-known pianists, have, on occasion, filled out their programs by improvisations.

We can scarcely be mistaken in supposing that two "Capriccios" for the piano which were composed during this tour, and called by the composer "Gursouf" (a place in the Crimea) and "On the South Coast of the Crimea," were specially written to fill out the programs. Both pieces are unimportant in subject and careless in structure—one can see that they are only occasional compositions, and only a few harmonic and rhythmical subtleties betray whose work they are—such as the slow introduction to the capriccio "Gursouf," reminiscent of the "rustling of the pine wood" before the fifth act of *Khovanstchina.* Whether the composer would have published these two pieces in the form in which they were written is questionable—in any case he never troubled himself to do so.

Among these half-improvised occasional concert pieces we may safely include a longer piano fantasia, "A Storm on the Black Sea," mentioned by Stassov and also by Rimsky-Korsakov. Although Moussorgsky often played this piece at Petersburg to his friends, he did not think it worth the trouble of writing down, and not a trace of it is to be found among his manuscripts.

The musical raw material that Moussorgsky brought back from his tour was certainly more valuable than these compositions. As his habit was, he wrote down, helped by his wonderful memory, everything that he heard and that he hoped to make use of later on. From the Ukraine he brought

back a whole string of Little Russian folk-melodies and motifs for *The Fair at Sorótchintzy*, only a very few of which,
unfortunately, he was able to utilize. Even in situations
where people do not usually think of composition, his pen
was never weary of catching snatches of real popular music;
he tells Stassov: "On the steamer between Odessa and Sebastopol, not far from the Tarankhunkut lighthouse, when most
of the passengers were getting seasick, I wrote down a Greek
and a Hebrew melody, sung by two women. In the latter I
accompanied them, and they praised me and called me *'Meister'* [he uses the German word]. By the way, in Odessa I went
to the service at two synagogues and enjoyed it greatly. I
have got two Israelite themes, one delivered by the cantor,
the other by the choir in the gallery, in unison; I shall never
forget these two melodies as long as I live."

That Moussorgsky, a pure-blooded Aryan, loved Hebrew music so is remarkable and a proof of his complete absence of prejudice as a man and as an artist. In his "Hebrew
Song," in his youthful works, in his choruses *The Destruction of Sennacherib* and *Joshua*, in *The Fair at Sorótchintzy*
(in the gossip's story of the red waistcoat), he has given
striking proofs of his deep insight into the true significance
of Hebrew music. He is always captured afresh by these
slow, mournful melodies, with their slightly oriental elaboration of outline. He had always loved to be the musical champion of all the "disinherited by fate," and among these he
certainly reckoned the Jews, who were still persecuted in
Russia at that time.

Moussorgsky announced in a letter to Stassov, of August 5, 1880, a very singular work that he wanted to con-
struct, mostly from the musical material he had collected
during his Crimean tour. He writes: "I have begun a suite
for orchestra, with harp and piano, on themes that I have
collected from various honest pilgrims of this world: the program takes you from the shores of Bulgaria over the Black

Sea, into the Caucasus, on to the Caspian and Ferghana, as far as Burma." Unfortunately this geographical suite, which would have been unique, was never finished; indeed, not even the sketches for it were found among the composer's papers.

Quite outside the musical studies that Moussorgsky made on the Crimean trip, is a work which brings out all the composer's sunny humour, so long obscured, and which may well rank with his best songs in this kind. It is "Mephisto's Song of the Flea," in Auerbach's Cellar, from *Faust*. The song is composed rather "in the style of Schumann," perhaps a tribute to the German Goethe; it is full of sparkling wit and ironical humour. Moussorgsky wrote it to Strugovstchikov's Russian translation of Goethe's words. It is a proof of the closeness of the translation that the original German words can be fitted to the tune without alteration. The song is dedicated to Madame Leonova, who—as a female Mephistopheles—first performed it on the tour and was enthusiastically applauded everywhere.

From the Crimea their tour went through the towns of the Don country and the Volga, back to Petersburg. Unfortunately no descriptions by Moussorgsky of the second half of the journey have come down to us.

What a very beneficent effect this long journey, with its manifold impressions, had on the composer's state of mind can best be seen in a letter written to Ludmilla Ivanovna Shestakova from Yalta. From the words of this letter we can see that he brought back from his journey new courage to defy fate, and fresh vigour to begin once more the brave fight against the stupidity of his contemporaries. It was the last flicker of his energy before the final collapse. Moussorgsky writes: "How much that is new, reviving, enchanting, Nature has to offer us! How many new, sometimes important meetings with new people, who can discuss real art a trifle better than certain advance agents of Russian publicity! This journey, which has refreshed and renewed my strength, has also been of great profit to me educationally. I feel as if many years had fallen from my shoulders! Life calls me now to new work for music, to a wider musical activity; farther and ever farther must I wander; my task is clear; with ever greater eagerness I press forward *to new shores* in the shoreless seat of art! To seek for new countries, never resting, never stopping, without fear or wavering, *to set foot firmly* on the ground of the Promised Land—that is a great and beautiful aim!"

*   *   *

During the concert tour, which kept him away from Petersburg for several months, Moussorgsky came to a decisive resolution—to give up his degrading office work and devote himself entirely to music. The success that he had gained everywhere as composer and pianist may have strengthened his confidence that he was really capable of "earning his daily bread by strumming." Still it was some time longer—over half a year—before he carried out this resolution. The new courage that he had gained from his journey did not abandon him after his return; an eloquent proof of this is a letter that he wrote to Stassov on January 16, 1880: "In spite of some unimportant drawbacks, I do not, and will not, give way to depression. My battle-cry, which you know so well, remains the same: 'Go boldly on! Forward to new shores!' If fate allows me to widen and extend the path on which I have entered—the path that leads to the living goal of art—how I shall rejoice! The demands art makes of her servants are so immense today that they call for the *whole of a man*. The times are past when one could compose *in one's spare time*. Give yourself wholly to mankind—that is what art requires of you now!"

Give yourself wholly to mankind! When he did so at last, without hesitation, without restraint, without looking

341

back, his reward was bitter enough—a lonely death-bed in a soldiers' hospital.

Moussorgsky used his freedom at first to throw all his energy into completing *Khovanstchina.* Apart from this, only a few pieces were composed in 1880, and it is doubtful whether they belong to this year or are earlier works, which he looked up and arranged for his own use as a pianist. They are mostly piano pieces. The manuscripts, on which he always put the exact date, were unfortunately not preserved, or at least have not yet been brought to light. These piano pieces are not among the composer's important works. The best of them is a scherzino, "*La Couturière* (The Dressmaker)," a conversational modern counterpart to Mendelssohn's "Spinner." The very exacting technique of this composition shows that Moussorgsky did not spare himself—for at that time he was the only interpreter of his own piano pieces. There are some pretty bits in the little *genre* picture, "*Au village,*" in which Moussorgsky has treated folk-song themes, or imitations of them, with his usual skill and taste. He has nothing arresting to say in two "lyrical" pieces for piano. Even the names, "*Une Larme* (A Tear)" and "*Méditation* (Dreaming)," are unpromising. In these Moussorgsky, as was usual when he had no immediate motive for musical expression, takes refuge in watery, meaningless musical commonplaces. The better of the two pieces is "Dreaming," which, though very primitive in form, gives us two interesting themes. When Moussorgsky ventured into the field of "absolute" music, his lack of professional technical training showed itself painfully. Inspiration is the mark of genius, but the logical development of abstract musical themes, without the definite lines of a program—"continuous musical inspiration"—is always the result of acquired skill. The fact that Moussorgsky was not at his best in works that required what he lacked does not derogate in any way from his great achievements in other departments of musical art, which were all his own. Among the four piano pieces, the little fantasia "In the Village" is dedicated to the famous Russian actor and humorist, Ivan Feodorovitch Gorbunov, while the others have no dedication.

To the year 1880 belong, apparently, three Russian folk-songs, arranged for four- or five-part male chorus, which Moussorgsky worked out with his own unerring feeling for style. It was an especially hard task, for such a thing as a part-song for men's voices does not exist in a Russian village, and there was a danger of falling into the stereotyped glee-club style, which the composer most skilfully avoided.

In 1880 Moussorgsky, for the last time, was asked to join in a common musical enterprise with all the other members of the old "Powerful Coterie." In this year fell the twenty-fifth anniversary and jubilee of the Emancipator Tsar, Alexander II, and a gala performance was to take place in the Marie Theatre. The words were written by two authors of no particular note, Tatistchev and Korvin-Krukovsky; the approval of the sovereign, however, was obtained for the performance. The poem these two had written consisted of a dialogue between the Genius of Russia and History, illustrated by living pictures. The music for these tableaux was to be entrusted to the Russian composers living at Petersburg. Rimsky-Korsakov wrote a chorus, *"Slava* (Glory)"; Borodin his "Sketches from the Steppes of Central Asia," afterwards so popular; the composer Sike, a musical picture, "The Black Sea." Napravnik, too, was among the musicians taking part in this common work. To Moussorgsky fell the task of illustrating the "Capture of Kars" in music. He managed it in a very simple way, by taking the "March of the Slav Princes" that he had composed for the projected legendary opera of *Mlada.* In order to connect the piece with Turkey, he composed a trio in oriental style, for which he used a Kurdish theme, which he had probably written down during his Black Sea tour. The projected performance fell through, however, like the opera *Mlada*; the poets disappeared silently from Petersburg, and the music was not used.

It was natural that Moussorgsky's association with Madame Leonova, after the joint experiences of their successful tour, should develop into a cordial friendship. It almost seems as if Madame Leonova, who was clearly a very energetic lady, reserved the composer of *Khovanstchina* exclusively for herself during the last year of his life. Their relations, of course, had no tinge of romance, for Madame Leonova, who was married to the dramatist Gridnin and living with him, was then fifty-five. This new friendship was as distasteful to Moussorgsky's old friends, especially to Ludmilla Ivanovna, as had been his acquaintance with Naumov, who was now quite forgotten. According to the reports of contemporaries, there is reason to suspect that Madame Leonova so far followed in Naumov's footsteps that in the goodness of her heart and her desire to please her friend she, too, encouraged his fatal craving for drink. Rimsky-Korsakov is of the opinion that Madame Leonova used Moussorgsky merely for purposes of advertisement, to give new lustre to her fading artistic reputation. However that may be, we cannot deny that Madame Leonova was a real friend to Moussorgsky, as far as lay in her power. It is at least doubtful whether this was merely for her own advantage, for long before she had had the chance of using Moussorgsky's name as an advertisement for her own artistic enterprises, she had expressed high admiration for him. She herself, in her *Recollections*, finds eloquent words to express the impression that Moussorgsky had made on her from the beginning. She writes:

"Long before the performance of *Boris* I made Moussorgsky's acquaintance. Although he was peculiar in some respects, I noticed qualities in him, as a man and as an artist, that were in every way so attractive that I was seized with a desire to know him better. . . . Moussorgsky was a man who, I think, had not his like in the whole world. He was always ready to satisfy anybody's wishes and he never even thought of suspecting anything wrong in anyone. He judged others by himself. When one came to know him better, one was forced to think that he had an exceptional nature. He was so innocent in the things of life that it seemed to him quite impossible that any educated and well-bred man could ever cause pain to his neighbour, or even play a dirty trick on him. In one word, his was an entirely ideal personality."

He spent the summer of 1880 at Madame Leonova's bungalow (*datcha*) at Oranienbaum, one of the most frequented summer resorts near Petersburg. The artistic result of his stay there was, as we know, the completion of *Khovanstchina*. Whether it was otherwise good for him is doubtful, if we may judge by Professor I. I. Lapschin's account of the personal recollections of his colleague, S. V. Rozhdestvensky, professor at the University of Petersburg, who was only a boy at the time:

"In the year 1880 I was living with my parents at Oranienbaum, in the bungalow belonging to the singer D. M. Leonova. I saw M. P. Moussorgsky every day in the garden and the courtyard. He looked remarkably like his celebrated portrait by Riepin. He was always very shabbily dressed, and a friend of his told me later that he had often had to buy left-off clothing for the unlucky composer. Once a week D. M. Leonova gave a musical soirée, preceded by a supper, which was usually served by 'Moussinka.' From the dining-room you could hear the clatter of plates and uncorking of bottles; every time he came out of the room, Moussorgsky's manner was more and more excited. After supper the concert began. Moussorgsky, who by that time was generally 'full,' acted as accompanist and solo pianist. He played his own

345

pieces perfectly, and with thrilling effect upon his audience."

We may add to this account another and a kinder one, also from a contemporary. In the summer of 1923 an old Russian general, A. von Leontiev, living at Zurich as a refugee from the Russian Revolution, published a "Souvenir" of Moussorgsky in the *Neue Züricher Zeitung*, apropos of the first Swiss performance of *Boris Godounov*. The old General's words give such a graphic picture of Moussorgsky that they deserve to be rescued from oblivion.

He writes: "Was it a dream? Or did it really happen? Anyhow, an unforgettable experience. At Petersburg in the year 1879—perhaps 1880—it doesn't matter. Late in the evening, in a private house, after a sumptuous dinner, an intimate gathering, not more than six or seven guests. Among them Leonova, the *diva* of Russian opera, Gorbunov, the famous actor, story-teller, and delineator of national character, and—Moussorgsky; not quite forty years of age, and yet with an old, haggard face. Unhappy Moussorgsky, seeking comfort, strength, forgetfulness, and inspiration more and more in alcohol and going rapidly to ruin!

"The piano is open, the candles lighted. Gorbunov has been telling stories, when suddenly the laughter stops—Moussorgsky sits down to the piano. He strikes the opening chords of a melody strange to us . . . and at once Leonova takes her stand close to the player. Now comes the tender, heart-thrilling song:

> He glides, he glides, the white swan,
> Ládu, ladù, the white swan.

> He glides, he glides with the young swans,
> Ládu, ladù, with the young swans.

> Sing to the praise of the white swan,
> Ládu, ladù, the white swan!

"This song was followed by some other pieces from the latest and greatest work of Moussorgsky, on which he was then engaged—*Khovanstchina*. Leonova stopped singing. She could not follow Moussorgsky's playing—he was playing and composing at the same time.

"We listened breathless to these achievements of his rapt genius, gradually rising into ecstasy, wrestling victoriously with a theme that was new to us, but that seemed to expand and soar ever higher as we listened. It appeared as if the composer in Moussorgsky was striving with the performer—and he was a great pianist, as we know.

"What was the meaning of this torrent of ideas expressed in sound? Whither would it lead? It was as if an uncontrollable will—a mighty force, shattering all that came in its way—had struck upon something equally stubborn, invincible, firm-rooted in the earth—and in truth it was nothing less than the birth of the new Russia. We get the first impression of the mighty form of Peter the Great in the blaring trumpet-blasts of his new-raised regiments, coming to storm the fortress of the old Russia and the old faith. Closer and closer they beset the remnant, the handful of Old Believers. But these do not fly—the flames from their ruined settlement, now become their funeral pyre, rise to heaven from the dense clouds of smoke, while the broad, sublime hymns of the men of Old Russia sound grandly as they go to their death. 'Father, deliver us from the words of the Evil One, from the power of the tempter and the Antichrist!' Two worlds, two civilizations, Asia and Europe, tradition and progress, faith and science, are wrestling together.

"Finally the last mighty chords die away. While he was playing, Moussorgsky seemed to us indescribably changed, with eyes half shut, then suddenly looking up for a moment, staring upwards as if at something he sought to fathom. . . . When he had finished, he closed his eyes, and his arms fell powerless at his side. We all shuddered from head to foot. Why? From suspense? From fear? Fear for whom? For Moussorgsky? For Russia? For ourselves? Or rather because we had been face to face with a revelation of the divine in the person of this weak and suffering man? Nobody ventured to break the silence. Leonova, who had been standing motionless at the piano, turned quickly round and retired with noiseless steps to the end of the room. Tears were streaming down her face. Gorbunov sat still, crouching forward, with his massive head bowed to his knees. We were all as if rooted to our seats.

"At last, as Moussorgsky still sat completely exhausted, his host ventured to ask: 'Modest Petrovitch, perhaps you would like to stay the night here?' Moussorgsky turned on him, his eyes still flashing with the fire of inspiration, and a kindly, grateful smile lit up his face for a moment. But he stretched out his hand so firmly in farewell to his host that the latter did not dare to repeat his invitation.

"And Moussorgsky was the first to leave the house. After he had gone, no one could bring himself to say a word of condemnation."

This scene gives a startling picture of a genius driven inevitably to his end by the dark powers of fate, while those around him stand impotent—paralysed, as it were—and can do nothing to avert or even delay the impending doom.

Towards the end of 1880 Moussorgsky's fight for existence, in the full meaning of the words, began—he was faced by the threatening spectre of poverty and even starvation. He had wished to give himself wholly to the service of mankind, but mankind did not want such a sacrifice and turned coldly away. He had tried to smooth the road "to the living goal of art," but the path led him to the grave instead.

In the endeavour to find some settled means of livelihood to replace the clerkship that he had resigned, Moussorgsky had consented to take the position of assistant teacher in the school of singing opened by D. M. Leonova at

Petersburg; but as the undertaking did not pay and took up so much of Moussorgsky's time, it was sheer waste of energy. Rimsky-Korsakov remarks that Moussorgsky did not realize the degradation of such a position, and dwells with irony on the spectacle of the composer of *Boris* teaching the elementary theory of music, and writing "various trios and duets, shockingly incorrect," for Madame Leonova's pupils. But the lash of his scorn falls not so much on Moussorgsky as on Petersburg society and its musicians, who could allow so degrading a spectacle.

Moussorgsky had resolved to "devote his whole personality to art"; but all he found to do was to accompany the singers at numberless concerts, by which usually he won a storm of applause, but nothing else, except a few wreaths, which were, soon after, laid on his grave. The great majority of these concerts were given for the benefit of needy students in colleges and academies of every description—a form of charity epidemic in Russia—and Moussorgsky never dreamed of asking to be paid for his help, although he himself was quite as much in need of assistance as the host of students, male and female, among whom the proceeds of the concerts were divided. Moussorgsky's last public appearance but one was at a commemoration of Dostoievsky's death, which took place on January 25, 1881. When the portrait of the author, veiled in crape, was placed on the platform, the audience rose and listened, standing, while Moussorgsky improvised a funeral march. It was the last "farewell" that he addressed, not only to the dead poet, but to all living men. Only once more—on February 9th—he appeared on the concert platform, to accompany a singer.

Even in the face of the poverty resulting from giving up his clerkship and becoming a "professional" musician Moussorgsky never lost courage. His astonishing energy never failed, he held his head high, however hardly fate might treat him. In his last letter to Stassov (August 20,

1880) we find the same unconquerable bravery: "Mousso-rianin is true to the principle that he has always proclaimed —with a new and unexplored path before me, am I the man to falter? Never! Forward! Full speed ahead!"

At last the end came, sooner than was expected, per-haps, by all those who stood and looked on at his hopeless struggle and would not stir a finger or spare a penny to help him. His mind kept up the fight, but his body gave way. The only account of his final collapse is contained in the *Recol-lections* of Madame D. M. Leonova. She writes:

"It is probable that two causes undermined his health; his moral sufferings (especially in connexion with the boy-cotting of *Boris Godounov* by the directors of the Imperial Theatre) and his material privations. He was living in ter-rible poverty. One day he called on me in a state of great nervous excitement; he confessed to me that he did not know what to do, that he had no means of support, and that noth-ing was left him but to beg in the streets—in short, that he saw no way out of his position. . . . On the same evening we were going to a party at the house of General Sokhansky, whose daughter, my pupil, was to sing for the first time to a large audience. . . . It seemed to me that her really fine singing made an impression on Moussorgsky, for I noticed that he was obviously nervous while he accompanied her. After the musical recital was ended, the young people began to dance, and I was just going to sit down at the card-table when young Sokhansky entered the room in some agitation and took me aside. He asked me if Moussorgsky suffered from epileptic fits. I assured him that I had never seen or heard of anything of the sort. I was then told that he had just fainted away. A doctor who was among the company at-tended to him; when the time came to go, Moussorgsky was quite restored. We took a droshky together. When we were near my flat, he pressed me to allow him to stay there, on ac-count of the state of his nerves, which was alarming him. I readily consented, for I knew that he could get no help in his lonely lodging. I got a room ready for him and told my maid to sit up and to call me if there was the slightest need. Moussorgsky slept through the night in a sitting position. When I came into the dining-room in the morning to have my tea, he was apparently quite well. I asked him how he was. He thanked me and said that he was all right. Hardly had he uttered the words when he turned half round and fell full length on the floor. We hurried to his help and got him up, and I sent for a doctor. Two more fits followed during the day; in the evening I sent for some of his friends who had shown their sympathy before, including Vladimir Stassov and Tertius Ivanovitch Filippov. We held a consultation. As we anticipated a long course of medical treatment, requiring constant attention, we decided to persuade him to go to a hospital. We explained the importance, the necessity even, of this step, and promised that he should have a private room. He resisted for a long time and declared he wanted to stay in my rooms; at last he consented. Next day we took him in a carriage to the hospital."

The hospital in which Moussorgsky was received was the Nikolai Military Hospital in the Smolna suburb of Petersburg. To allow of his admission, he was put down on the list of patients as an officer's servant. But he had a private room, as was promised. What his illness really was is naturally hard to determine after the event, nor it is of any consequence. Rimsky-Korsakov briefly and bluntly says "the white fever"—the Russian for delirium tremens. The official report by the physician attending him, Dr. Berthenson, does not call it that, but speaks of heart trouble and lesion of the spinal marrow. A French writer on music, Robert Godet, has taken the trouble to have Moussorgsky's illness diagnosed on the evidence of dates. The doctor he consulted, Dr. Rist, head of the Laënnec Hospital at Paris, came to the conclusion that the disease of which Moussorgsky died was

351

the last stage of chronic nephritis (Bright's disease, chronic inflammation of the kidneys)—but, as we said, the name is of no consequence.

At first he made good progress towards recovery. Dr. Berthenson, by the unanimous testimony of his friends, did all that could be done for his patient. His friends too, now rather alarmed, paid him frequent visits, as in duty bound. If they did not come in person, they showed the patient "little attentions"—Cui, for instance, who sent Moussorgsky his dressing-gown, as the composer of *Boris* naturally had nothing so fine in his second-hand wardrobe. In this dressing-gown he sat for the painter Riepin from the 2nd to the 5th of March, for the famous portrait, the original of which is in the Tretiakov Gallery at Moscow. Riepin painted the picture without an easel, on a little table. "It was fine spring weather then," writes Stassov in his Necrology, "and Moussorgsky's room was flooded with sunshine." All seemed to be going on well. His strength returned, and the sick man's looks improved. He often declared to his visitors that he had never felt so comfortable in all his life. Suddenly an unexpected change for the worse took place—a paralytic stroke deprived him of the use of his arms and legs. But his reason and his consciousness never left him till the last moment, nor did his hope of recovery. On the day he died, he had some lively talk with Stassov and Rimsky-Korsakov, who came to see him.

A description of Moussorgsky's last moments and the environment in which he died is found in an article by the Russian composer and writer on music M. M. Ivanov, the well-known critic of the *Novoye Vremya*, a paper that always set its face against all progress, whether in politics or in art. The notice appeared in the journal called *Molva* (*Rumour*). It was this:

"I went into the private room at the Nikolai Hospital. My heart failed me. The environment in which Moussorgsky was doomed to die, the setting in which this genius was extinguished, made one shudder . . . you could see at once that a true Bohemian had died here. . . . Close to the door stood a cupboard, a desk, two chairs, and two small tables with newspapers and five or six books, among them Berlioz's *Traité de l'instrumentation.* He had died like a soldier, sword in hand (just as A. N. Serov had done). A feeling of bitterness rose up in me—strange is the fate of our countrymen! That a genius like Moussorgsky (all recognized his genius, even when they did not share his artistic views), possessed of all the qualities that fitted him to scale the highest heights of life, should die in a hospital, among strangers, without one friendly hand to close his eyes! . . . What a fate has pursued our great artists! . . . About five in the morning he drew his last breath. No one was present except two hospital attendants. They told us that he gave just two loud cries, and in a quarter of an hour all was over. Soon after, some friends of the dead man arrived—V. V. Stassov, D. V. Stassov, N. A. Rimsky-Korsakov, Keltchevsky, the officer of Uhlans who had lived with Moussorgsky, and a few others, including two ladies (one of them, I think, was Rimsky-Korsakov's wife). The rules of the hospital do not allow a corpse to remain in the sick-room, and no coffin must be brought in there. Hence we had to provide for the speedy removal of the body. We could not think of taking Moussorgsky's mortal remains to any private house; they were therefore removed to the hospital mortuary. When the corpse had been dressed, Dr. Berthenson sent for a stretcher. The body of the dead composer was laid on the wide linen covering of the stretcher and hidden with a sheet. All those who were present, nine or ten persons, carried the bier through the quiet corridors of the hospital, down the staircase to the ground-floor, then across the wide courtyard to the little chapel. A melancholy procession in melancholy surroundings! Moussorgsky's body had to wait in the chapel till eve-

ning, with two other patients just dead, for the arrival of the
coffin. About seven o'clock it was carried over to the hospital
church, where the first mass for the dead was said."

Moussorgsky died on the morning of his forty-second
birthday, March 16, 1881.

So ended the short but momentous life of one of the
greatest musicians of Russia, nay, of all mankind. He went
through life a lonely man, in spite of many more or less lasting friendships, his artistic aims misunderstood, in spite of
some superficial successes, which were not concerned with the
real substance of his art. Is there any comfort in the fact
that he shares this fate with so many other great spirits and
that his works survive him? For posterity, perhaps; but the
burden of his life was not lightened by any consciousness of
having created immortal works, and could he have foreseen his own end, he would have included it in his *Songs and
Dances of Death*, where the tragic and the grotesque are so
finely mingled.

*   *   *

What usually happens happened in this case also—
Moussorgsky's death opened the eyes of his friends and enemies alike to the irreparable loss that Russian art had sustained by his early, far too early, departure. Like the old
shepherds in Pimen's story, they saw clearly only by the
side of the new-made grave. People now tried to make up
to the dead what they had put off doing for the living; the
funeral of the composer, which took place on March 18th,
was a celebration the cost of which would probably have been
enough to keep him comfortably for a long time while he was
alive. Moussorgsky's mortal remains were laid in the ceme-
tery of the Alexander-Nevsky Monastery, close to the grave
of his great predecessor Michael Glinka. Among the many
costly wreaths that were borne before the hearse were some
from the Conservatoire, the Imperial Theatre, and various

354

musical unions and societies, which had not troubled about him in his lifetime, as well as from those various schools and colleges for which he had always lent his art to numberless charity concerts. There was no lack of more or less sincere speeches, and a poet of the fourth order (Lishin) had written a poem, which he recited by the open grave. The friends of the "Powerful Coterie" had all assembled, with numerous official and unofficial representatives of the musical world, and an endless train of spectators.

Only one friend was not present—Ludmilla Ivanovna Shestakova, who was kept at home by illness. Ten days after the funeral she sent Stassov Moussorgsky's letters, with the following note:

"I am sending you, Vladimir Vassilievitch, our dear Moussinka's letters. You cannot imagine how painful it is for me to think that I did not see him during his illness. A note from him, which I got by post, prevented me; he told me he was going on so well that he hoped to get out some day soon and would come to see me. The only thing that comforts me is that in the whole course of our long friendship I never gave him the slightest hint that I disapproved of his behaviour; I may well say 'our friendship,' for he concealed nothing from me, not even his feelings towards his brother and other people. He is an irremediable loss to art, as well as to his friends; but there was no hope of a happier future if he had lived. You will admit that with his pride, his education and breeding, it was hard to endure the protection of D. M. L. [Leonova] and the man she was living with (I forget his name). I can only say that for me Moussorgsky will always live, not only as the author of *Boris*, but as a remarkable personality, kindly, upright, and noble. I am ill and confined to the house; as soon as I can get out, my first visit of course will be to Moussorgsky's grave."

*　　*　　*

Not to all Moussorgsky's friends was it given to atone for the wrong they had done him so amply and remarkably as did Rimsky-Korsakov, who unselfishly devoted nearly all his labours for several years to the task of making the artistic achievements of his friend accessible to posterity. His action gives one a vague impression that it was a sort of penance for some—perhaps unintentional—fault. It may be questioned whether in carrying out his gigantic task Rimsky-Korsakov always acted with proper tact; but the purity of his motives is beyond all doubt.

Stassov, too, did what lay in his power to ensure that the memory of the author of *Boris* and *Khovanstchina* should be duly honoured. In the year of Moussorgsky's death he published his biography of his friend, written with almost fanatical enthusiasm, which, however, goes no further than that period of Moussorgsky's life when Stassov was really in sympathy with his work—i.e., down to 1875. This brief biography is still the most trustworthy source for the first half of the composer's life.

Apart from the literary and musical monuments that Rimsky-Korsakov and Stassov raised to Moussorgsky's genius, all the friends of the dead man soon united for the purpose of immortalizing his memory in stone and metal. The idea came from the painter Riepin. Though for obvious reasons no monument to Moussorgsky could be erected in any of the public squares, at least there should be a memorial on the grave, worthy of the composer's creative genius. Riepin himself, Rimsky-Korsakov, Liadov, Glazounov, contributed considerable sums, and the rest of what was needed was obtained by subscription in less time than it would have taken to raise an old suit of clothes for the composer when he was alive. The Petersburg architect Bogomolov, one of the best men in his profession, furnished the design for the monument; Ginzburg, then a young and unknown sculptor, with the assistance of his teacher, Antokolsky, and of Riepin, carved the life-size portrait in high relief that occupies the front of the imposing monument.

The unveiling took place with great solemnity, on November 25, 1885, the anniversary of the first performance of Glinka's *A Life for the Tsar*. The four corners of the sheet under which the monument was hidden were drawn off by Borodin, Balakirev, Rimsky-Korsakov, and Cui. Borodin, Pauline Stassov, and Madame Rimsky-Korsakov delivered addresses. Stassov distributed among the spectators his pamphlet *In Memory of Moussorgsky*. So all rites were duly paid; yet among those present there can have been but few who were not oppressed with a sense of guilt, while many may well have recalled the words of the dying Tsar Boris:

My God!
Cannot a sin be purged away by prayer?

*   *   *

The story of Moussorgsky's life is ended. Pure as crystal against the dark background of his tragic destiny stands out the soul of this incomparable artist. Whether we consider him as artist or as man, we can discover no flaw, either of thought or of feeling; and few men have proved so convincingly the truth of the dictum of the sculptor Antokolsky, his friend in earlier days: "He only is an artist who loves humanity as passionately as he loves his art—who dedicates his whole life to art for the sake of humanity. Only in such favoured beings is the divine spark to be found, bright and unquenchable; and that, in art, is the one thing needful, for when the soul ceases to lend its sympathy, the death of art begins."

XI

SUBSEQUENT HISTORY OF THE WORKS OF MOUSSORGSKY

It is certainly an exceptional case, when the life of a composer's works really begins with his death—not merely the history of their varying fortunes, but the growth and development that give them their final form, or at least the only one in which for the present they are accessible to the public; this, however, has been the singular experience of nearly all Moussorgsky's music as we have it today. Some further additions were necessary if the children of the composer's mind were to make their way in the world after his eyes were closed in death; for Moussorgsky had left some of his greatest works in so incomplete a state that they had no chance of surviving. The reconstruction of his music went further than this, partly owing to the questionable but well-meant attempt of his musical executors to win wider acceptance for the artistic legacy of a great genius by adapting it to the prevailing taste, partly from the desire to give his musical ideas a worthier setting than he had chosen, as, for instance, by orchestrating his piano pieces and the accompaniments of his songs.

First among the editors of Moussorgsky's musical works comes N. A. Rimsky-Korsakov; the others follow far behind—the chief are César Cui, V. Karatigin, A. Tcherepnin, A. Glazounov.

How Rimsky-Korsakov came at the start to have the single and undisputed charge of the dead composer's ar-

tistic legacy he relates himself in *My Musical Life*; the harsh
and almost hostile terms in which he describes Moussorgsky's method of writing music may be explained by his wish
to explain and excuse his own rather drastic way of dealing with his friend's intellectual property:

"After Moussorgsky's death all his manuscripts and
sketches came into my hands. They had to be looked through,
arranged, completed, and prepared for the press. During
Moussorgsky's last illness T. J. Filippov, at V. V. Stassov's
suggestion and with the composer's consent, was appointed
as his official executor, so that, in case of his death, no difficulties might be raised by his relations with regard to the
publication of his works. Moussorgsky's brother, Filaret
Petrovitch, was still living; we knew little about him and had
no idea of his attitude towards the fate of Modest Petrovitch's works, so it was thought best to choose an executor
among the disinterested admirers of the composer—such as
T. J. Filippov. He at once made an agreement with the firm
of Bessel, giving them the right of publishing all Moussorgsky's works, and binding himself to hand them over,
without exception, as soon as possible; the firm did not pay
any advance on the contract. I, for my part, undertook to
revise and complete all Moussorgsky's compositions that I
thought suitable, and hand them over to Bessel without pay-
ment. I worked at my late friend's compositions for a year
and a half or two years after this. Among his papers were the
following works: not quite completed and not orchestrated
(except for a few single numbers), the opera *Khovanstchina*,
and sketches for a part of *The Fair at Sorótchintzy*; then
quite a number of songs, of earlier and later date—all completed; the choruses *The Destruction of Sennacherib* and
Joshua, a chorus from *Œdipus*, a female chorus from *Salambo*; *A Night on the Bare Mountain* in various versions;
other orchestral works—a Scherzo in B flat major, an Intermezzo in B minor, and a March (Trio *alla turca*) in A

flat major, various tunes of folk-songs, sketches written in youth, and an *Allegro* in C major, in sonata form, also an early work. All was left in very incomplete shape; here and there were meaningless, disconnected harmonies, and loose part-writing—incorrect modulations or none at all—badly orchestrated passages—the bumptiousness of the amateur over it all—occasional signs of technical skill, and more often a complete lack of technique of any sort. In spite of all this, the great majority of these compositions were so full of genius, so individual, had so much originality and life about them, that it was absolutely necessary to publish them; but they had to be put into shape by an expert hand, or their publication would have had only a bibliographical interest. If Moussorgsky's works are destined to live and flourish fifty years after the death of the author—after which period they will become common property—an archæologically correct edition can still be undertaken, for all his manuscripts passed from my hands to the Public Library. For the time being, however, we needed an edition for practical artistic purposes, so as to be able to have his works performed and to display his great genius, but not to study the psychology of the composer and his technical faults."

Rimsky-Korsakov here speaks so clearly and plainly of the considerations and aims by which he was actuated in revising Moussorgsky's works that we can hardly understand the false view of them that a part of the musical press has persistently taken. We are almost inclined to suspect that this misrepresentation was due to motives that have nothing to do with art. The artistic indignation often takes on a moralizing tone, even questioning the purity of Rimsky-Korsakov's motives—a view that is quite unfounded and cannot be too strongly reprobated. It is significant that in Russia itself, which is most nearly interested in the question, not a voice has been raised against Moussorgsky's musical executor during more than forty years that have elapsed since Rimsky-

Korsakov's revision. Naturally there is a growing desire to consult the original forms of his works, especially *Khovan-stchina,* but nobody has thought of questioning the great practical artistic value of Rimsky-Korsakov's versions, still less of doubting the moral motives of his actions.

If, from our present standpoint, many of the alterations that Rimsky-Korsakov has made in Moussorgsky's works seem superfluous, sometimes quite incomprehensible, we must not forget when his versions were made. Forty years ago men's musical conscience was not so elastic as it is now —this explains many changes that now perhaps strike us as merely the result of narrow professorial pedantry. According to modern ideas, Rimsky-Korsakov undoubtedly went much too far in his revision, especially in *Khovanstchina,* but it would be unfair to exact from an artist whose conception of music was founded on the works of the older masters that he should share in views that now seem obvious. That Rimsky-Korsakov did not always hold to his first opinions is proved, not only by the remarkable widening of his own musical ideas, but by the fact that he revised some of Moussorgsky's compositions (including *Boris Godounov*) several times, always with more indulgence to the originals, even restoring much that he had cut out at first. What marked out Moussorgsky as an exceptional genius is the fact that he was far in advance of his time, even from a purely musical standpoint. Rimsky-Korsakov was not the only one who could not keep pace with him.

The case was especially complicated by the circumstance that in Moussorgsky—owing to what Rimsky-Korsakov calls his "obstinate, bumptious amateurishness"—great musical originality was united to grave technical defects. It was no easy task to make the distinction between quality and defect with a sure eye and a steady hand; even Rimsky-Korsakov's artistic intelligence, though far above the average of musicians, occasionally failed to do so. It would be unjust to

361

reproach him with this, for the history of music shows hundreds of examples proving that the greatest minds were unable to separate the wheat of artistic intuition from the tares of "bumptious" incapacity. Rimsky-Korsakov could never quite make up his mind as to Moussorgsky's works, as he confessed when he said: "I hated *Boris*, and yet I worshipped it." This expression in the mouth of the reviser can be made to cover his feeling as to all Moussorgsky's works, and even towards the composer himself. He sometimes felt himself repelled by them, and yet he always yielded anew to their irresistible attraction.

We have indicated before that Rimsky-Korsakov probably felt a certain remorse as regards his dead friend—what he had neglected to do for him as a man during his life, he wanted to make good as an artist after his death. With all the honesty of his rather hard but strictly just mind, and the almost unexampled conscientiousness of his nature, he set to work. Laroche once said of Rimsky-Korsakov that "he suffered from the mania for perfection." This mania, which could always find in the smoothest, most polished surface a place where one last touch of the file was needed, showed itself in his revision of Moussorgsky's works, often, but not always, to their advantage. He felt himself justified in such action, not only by his artistic conscience, but as a man—he expressed his views to his trusty Boswell, V. V. Yastrebtzev, very plainly: "The more I consider Moussorgsky and his style, the more firmly I am persuaded that Moussorgsky was not really cut out for the uncompromising naturalism on which he so prided himself. If you look at his earlier works, you will find in them a striving after beauty, and unmistakable feeling for form, and even a tendency towards correct part-writing. . . . Then a crisis occurred in his musical style. Backed up by his friends (Stassov, Mollas, etc.), he ended by persuading himself that it was his vocation to revolutionize the whole art of music. He became fanatically possessed with this opinion and laid on the colour thickly with a liberal hand, where it was not wanted, fully convinced that every musical utterance of his was sacred, every chance combination of sound artistic and lawful." From this point of view Rimsky-Korsakov was persuaded that he was doing right in smoothing down the rough outlines of Moussorgsky's works, for he believed that he was thus restoring their true artistic form, of which, as he held, the composer, in his inconceivable blindness, had deprived them.

Rimsky-Korsakov's *bona fides* in his revision of Moussorgsky's works can no more be doubted than his conscientious diligence. If Moussorgsky, while composing his first great drama, said of himself: "I live as Boris, in *Boris*," Rimsky-Korsakov, who sometimes lost himself in working at *Khovanstchina*, could say of himself: "I often could not tell who I really was, Rimsky-Korsakov or Moussorgsky."

His methods were justified by the artistic result. He himself felt almost the joy of an author in his new version. Even before he heard "his" *Boris*, he said to Yastrebtzev: "Do you know, to speak the truth, I should rather not hear *Boris* again in the earlier edition; I have worked at the improvement of it again, and the new form is so clear to me that I do not care for the old." And after the performance of the work in the form he had given it, he writes as follows in *My Musical Life*: "My revision and orchestration of *Boris Godounov*, which I heard for the first time by the full orchestra, caused me a feeling of unspeakable satisfaction. The sworn Moussorgsky-worshippers turned up their noses and seemed to disapprove. . . . But I have not destroyed the original form of the work by my revision—the old frescoes, so to speak, have not been permanently painted over. If the people are ever persuaded that the original is better and finer than my version, they will put this aside and perform *Boris* from the original score." This has not happened yet, in the thirty years that have passed since the appearance of the new version, although the original score has remained accessible to everybody, in the library of the Marie Theatre—a strong testimony in Rimsky-Korsakov's favour.

Rimsky-Korsakov's versions undoubtedly have their faults, as we have remarked more than once—and we shall have to notice some of these defects again—but still they have the enormous advantage of being the work of a master hand. This is especially true of the orchestration, which is like the finest work of a skilled jeweller, giving the uncut gems of Moussorgsky's inspiration their proper lustre and imperishable value.

The revision and orchestration of Moussorgsky's works was absolutely necessary if they were to be generally accessible to the public. Who could have been better qualified and more clearly fitted for the work than his old friend, who was familiar with all the peculiarities of the composer's nature, even if he did not understand them all—who had sometimes worked with him side by side and shared all his artistic cares and struggles?

Rimsky-Korsakov in his self-sacrificing labour on Moussorgsky's works performed a task of the greatest importance in the history of art, for he made it possible for the two masterpieces of the unfortunate composer, *Khovanstchina* and *Boris Godounov,* to make a triumphant progress over the whole world. For this he deserves the thanks of every intelligent critic, even if we recognize that his work, like all human work, has its faults.

*   *   *

Khovanstchina

The first work that Rimsky-Korsakov took up immediately after the composer's death was *Khovanstchina.* In the years 1881 and 1882 he devoted all his powers to it and completely suspended his own original work during this time. It was no easy task. First he had to compress the enormous mass of musical material into something like the limits of an evening's performance. How Moussorgsky had exceeded these limits is evident when we learn that the cuts that Rimsky-Korsakov had to make comprised more than a thousand bars —nearly enough for another opera. Of course there will always be critics who think that the bars that were cut out are the best and who would rather have sacrificed those that were retained; but these are matters of purely personal taste, which, as we know, can never be settled so as to satisfy everybody. It is beyond dispute that considerable cuts had to be made to fit the work for the stage. The editor was confident in his own artistic judgment—Rimsky-Korsakov, a dramatic composer *par excellence*, was far better qualified for the work than many of his critics. Not only had whole scenes to be struck out, but those that were kept had to be compressed as much as possible. It is unfortunate that the editor in preparing the piano score omitted all the passages he had cut out of his orchestral score—possibly in order to avoid, at least for a time, irksome and tedious explanations and disputes, which could lead to nothing. The skill he showed in making the cuts deserves the greatest admiration, apart from the question of principle. One great difficulty was the danger of making the intricate plot of the drama still more obscure by omitting necessary links; Rimsky-Korsakov succeeded rather in making it clearer. The composer himself had not aimed especially at securing unity and consistency, and in these respects the work has lost nothing by the revision— you do not notice the joins.

The chief cuts were as follows: in the first act, the scene in which "strangers" read the placard, with the help of the Notary, and finally wreck his booth (more than two hundred bars). Here, no doubt, the editor has blue-pencilled a scene, interesting in music and words, such as only Moussorgsky, the master of Russian "mass-scenes," could have written; but the episode has nothing to do with the plot, and in fact hangs up the real action of the scene—Shaklovity's dictation of his anonymous letter to the Notary. In the second act two scenes are cut; the first is the reading of a long letter from Golitzin's mother to the pretender, a passage of a hundred bars (as the editor justly remarks, to read two letters, one after the other, would be tedious, and the letter of the Tsarevna Sophia has still to be heard); the second is the entrance of the German pastor, and his conversation with Golitzin, which contains some charming music; but this episode, as Moussorgsky never wrote his intended scene "In the German quarter," has no real significance, and in any case is not indispensable. The dispute between the three Princes, following on the prophecy scene, effective in words and music, but far too long, is shortened by about a hundred and fifty bars. A big cut of about the same size is made in the third act, in the scene between the Notary and the drunken Streltzy. The other cuts, scattered over the whole piece, vary from one to fifty bars. Many of them—e.g., the cut in Shaklovity's *aria*—appear to have little or no reason; but if we once admit the principle of revision—and in this case it was necessary if the work was to be made possible for the stage—it is useless to argue over every single bar.

Rimsky-Korsakov's additions to Moussorgsky's work are only such as are absolutely necessary; they occur chiefly in the fifth act, in which some scenes were only sketched out, and there was no real Finale. Only the theme for the final chorus (an original chant of the Old Believers, communicated to Moussorgsky by L. I. Karmalina) was in existence. Rimsky-Korsakov makes the chorus sing the melody in unison, as it should be sung, but nevertheless has provided it with full orchestral accompaniment—a lambent, serpentine figure for strings symbolizes the flames of the pyre. The idea is not bad, and its execution is masterly, but it is the only passage in the revised version that is not quite in the spirit of Moussorgsky, who had no liking for this sort of mere musical beauty and conventional symbolism. A more inspired idea of Rimsky-Korsakov's is the bringing of Peter's "Horseguards" on the stage again at the Finale, to see the terrible *auto-da-fé* of the sectarians. This sudden contrast, which thrills the spectator, was certainly in the spirit of the original author. The editor has taken the music for a speech of Dosifei in the fifth act note for note from the first act. Besides this, Rimsky-Korsakov—quite unnecessarily— has inserted four bars in the E flat major chorus of the first act ("Hail him, hail him")—a sort of trio that divides the chorus—and extended some of the fanfares, for stage purposes.

Unfortunately the editor has not confined himself to making the necessary improvements in Moussorgsky's original version—removing obvious blunders in the vocal parts, making alterations in chords and their resolutions, etc.—he has gone far beyond this. First and foremost, he has completely altered the tonality of the opera, making Marfa throughout sing a semitone and Andrei Khovansky a whole tone higher than Moussorgsky had done. Besides the general raising of the keys, he introduces various transpositions, which do not always seem justified. In some cases, however, we must agree with him—for instance, when he writes on the relation of keys in the third act: "I have said already that Moussorgsky, who was often excessive in his use of modulations, sometimes, on the other hand, kept to the same key for quite a long time, thereby producing an effect of sameness and monotony; for instance, in the second half of the third act he remains in E flat minor from the entrance of the Notary to the finale. That was intolerable and quite uncalled for, as this part unquestionably falls into two divisions: the scene with the Notary and the Streltzy's appeal to old Khovansky. I kept to E flat minor for the first part

367

and transposed the second into D minor, thus making it more effective and varied."

In his correction of particular harmonies and of the part-writing in *Khovanstchina* Rimsky-Korsakov sometimes goes so far as completely to distort their meaning. Had he revised *Khovanstchina*, not in 1881, but twenty years later—about the time when he undertook to edit *Boris Godounov*—his treatment of the score would probably not have been quite so drastic. It is, as we have said, impossible to justify the editor's methods in every detail; we can agree with him unconditionally only when his corrections are founded on considerations of orchestral technique. In spite of this, the score of *Khovanstchina* has on the whole the effect of being the offspring of one mind, not of two. Was the dramatic and emotional power of Moussorgsky's music so great that the counter-currents of Rimsky-Korsakov's style could make no difference to it? Or had the latter so entered into the composer's ideas that he came to speak his language, though in more measured terms? Probably both these causes contributed to the effect. We shall be able finally to estimate the value of Rimsky-Korsakov's revision only when a second version, closer to the original, has been made—which is hardly to be hoped for under present conditions.

But even if all Rimsky-Korsakov's alterations in *Khovanstchina* had been sins against the spirit of the composer, he would have atoned for them by his feats of orchestration. Rimsky-Korsakov once declared he would far rather orchestrate than compose. This preference is displayed in the score of *Khovanstchina*, in which the orchestration of every single bar is worked out with loving care. Just as in his own works, Rimsky-Korsakov has given us here an ideal example of what we may call the musical graver's art. As instances of this it is enough to mention the wonderful tone-picture of the overture, the "Dance of the Persian Slave-girls," and the subtle orchestral variations in the accompaniment to Marfa's song in the second act. Moussorgsky himself had orchestrated only a few numbers of *Khovanstchina*; among others, these same variations, the Streltzy Chorus in the second act, and the *aria* of Shaklovity, the score of which is lost. Rimsky-Korsakov has re-orchestrated these numbers.

The first performance of *Khovanstchina* in Russia took place in February 1886, by an amateur company in Petersburg. Previously there had been a dispute with the Imperial Marie Theatre, which added nothing to the fame of that institution in the annals of Russian opera. Rimsky-Korsakov had handed in his score in April 1885 to the musical advisory committee of the Imperial Theatre, the same body that won such lamentable notoriety by its action in the case of *Boris Godounov*. Later on he and César Cui became members of this committee, but for reasons easy to understand they took no part in the discussion of this work. This was unlucky for *Khovanstchina*; the committee not only declined the work, but, contrary to its rules, refused even to consider it, on the declaration of the president, the chief conductor, E. F. Napravnik—whom Moussorgsky had thanked so profusely after the performance of *Boris Godounov*—that "one radical opera" was enough for the repertoire of the Marie Theatre. This "one radical opera" was, of course, *Boris Godounov*, which, though it was never played, was officially in the repertoire of the theatre. Rimsky-Korsakov and Cui met this outrageous behaviour of the opera committee in the only proper way; they gave in their resignations from that body and never attended another meeting. Stassov, who rightly considered this action of the almighty conductor—himself no Russian, but a Bohemian—as an insult to Russian art, wrote fiery protests in the columns of all the journals that would print them. But it was no good—*Khovanstchina* was rejected and stayed so. The performance of the work by the Petersburg Musical and Dramatic Society in the Kononov Hall was a protest against the stupid and reactionary atti-

369

tude of the Imperial Theatre. The work, which needed a big stage-setting and made heavy demands on the chorus and the orchestra, could not naturally get from amateurs a worthy performance, capable of bringing out all its beauties. There were altogether eight performances, which passed almost unnoticed. The case was made worse by the narrow-minded interference of the "religious censorship," which forbade any mention of religious dissensions and required the fanatical priest of the Old Believers, Dosifei, to be made into a harmless "Wanderer," named Koreny ("the Root" —of all evil?) and the members of his sect into something like a Purity League. The public was bewildered and probably believed in Moussorgsky's reputed "madness"; only the initiated knew what it was all about.

Not till February 1911 (!) did the directors of the Imperial Theatre realize their duty to one of the greatest musical geniuses of Russia and on November 7th give *Khovanstchina* a performance worthy of the piece. The appearance of the great Chaliapin in the part of Dosifei helped largely to win for the piece such a triumphant success as rescued this mighty example of Russian opera from oblivion and made it immortal.

The first performance of *Khovanstchina* outside Russia took place in 1913 at the Opéra at Paris. S. P. Diaghilev, the herald of Russian art outside his own country, included this performance in the Russian season, which had been one of the standing features of Paris music since 1907. It was Diaghilev who, after seeing Moussorgsky's manuscript, declared that Rimsky-Korsakov had left "not one stone on another" of the original work and in high indignation entrusted the preparation of a new version of *Khovanstchina* to Igor Stravinsky and Maurice Ravel. It was a failure—nothing has ever been heard of the new version since. All that was published was the final chorus, rewritten by Stravinsky, which shows no especial improvement on Rimsky-

Korsakov's version. When, in 1923, *Khovanstchina* was included in the regular French repertoire of the Opéra, Rimsky-Korsakov's version was reinstated.

In Germany, Frankfort am Main has the credit of having first performed Moussorgsky's second masterpiece, on February 19, 1924.

Boris Godounov

The revision of *Khovanstchina* was necessary; that of *Boris Godounov* was not. The author of *Boris* had finished the score down to the last bar, and the work had been successfully presented in this form. It could not, indeed, be denied that the orchestration was often clumsy, for it was the composer's first serious attempt in this department. If the editor had confined himself to making necessary or desirable corrections in the orchestration, posterity would have given him grateful thanks. But, as things stand, it is hard to avoid feeling something like indignation at Rimsky-Korsakov's action; our feeling is softened only by the conviction that he was firmly convinced that he was doing the late composer and his work a real service by his new version.

The first impulse to revise *Boris* came from Rimsky-Korsakov's wish to arrange the fine Polonaise for concert use. He had then, by the end of the eighties, become better acquainted with Wagner's scores and was astonished at the possibilities revealed therein of new orchestral effects of colour and gradation of tone. The first practical application of his new knowledge, especially in the use of the brass, was the brilliant orchestration of the Polonaise from *Boris Godounov*, in the purest Wagnerian style.

The successful re-orchestration of the Polonaise suggested to Rimsky-Korsakov the idea of making a thorough revision of the whole work, which he "hated and worshipped" —not only to remove from the score all that he did not like, but to silence those critics who—rightly, as he thought—reproached the work with "unnecessary difficulty, raggedness in the melodic phrases, uncomfortable intervals in the vocal parts, harshness in harmonies and modulations, weak and thin orchestration—in short, numerous technical defects." He made it his aim to get rid of these technical defects and was persuaded, as he openly declares in the preface to the piano edition arranged from his version, that "the correction and regulation of the technical side would set the worth of the opera in a clearer light, make it accessible to all, and refute the charges brought against it." His attitude towards the task he had undertaken was, as we can see from this quotation, fundamentally different from that towards *Khovanstchina*; while in that work he had so entered into the spirit of the composer that he sometimes did not know whether he was Rimsky-Korsakov or Moussorgsky and had tried to *create* in accordance with the author's mind, here he sat down seriously at his desk to *correct*, without for one moment forgetting that he was Rimsky-Korsakov. Alas, alas! in his regrettable blindness he has sacrificed some of the fairest and tenderest flowers of Moussorgsky's inspiration to his academic pruning-hook. This is especially so when he makes the recitative of the master of musical speech "more singable," or turns the psychological and logical sequence of a dramatic scene into the direct opposite—as in the duet between Marina and the False Demetrius by the fountain, which in Moussorgsky's version dies away in murmuring whispers of love, to the covert mocking laughter of the Jesuit Rangoni, while Rimsky-Korsakov makes it rise to a *fortissimo* of conventional operatic bravura—a sufficiently effective ending in its own cheap way, but artistically far inferior to Moussorgsky's fine dramatic point.

Particularly unhappy are many of the "simplifications" that Rimsky-Korsakov, chiefly to oblige conductors, has made in the score of *Boris*. He has generally done them poor service, however, since the shifting of the melodic stress to a part of the bar where it does not belong gives the sensation of having to beat time against rhythm and melody. The most conspicuous example of this is the first theme of the overture, which, in Moussorgsky's original, begins with the first (and strongest) of the four crotchets, while Rimsky-Korsakov makes it start on the third, so that it seems to be always limping. Another example is the "Drake" song of the Hostess in the "Scene on the Lithuanian border." Rimsky-Korsakov shuts the "Drake" up in the cage of a rigid two-four time, while Moussorgsky lets him fly at his ease in and out of the bars. Many more such examples could be given.

Unjustifiable too are the extensive cuts which Rimsky-Korsakov made in the 1896 edition of his version—he saw this himself afterwards, and restored them, for the most part, in the 1908 edition. These included six long scenes: Pimen's story of the Tsar's life, the scene between Boris and Feodor over the map of the Muscovite Empire, Feodor's story of the parrot, leading to the scene between Boris, Feodor, and Schouisky, the incident of the chiming clock, the scene between Rangoni and the False Demetrius, and the usurper's monologue by the fountain. In the second edition only the first scene of Boris's children in front of the chiming clock is omitted. A worse example of arbitrary alteration was that Rimsky-Korsakov, contrary to the express wish of the author, changed the order of the last two scenes of the opera, thus ending the piece with Boris's death, instead of the revolutionary scene "in the woods near Kromy."

Finally we cannot, unfortunately, say that the excellence of the orchestration in this score of Rimsky-Korsakov's makes amends for any faults in his revision. The orchestration is in itself masterly, as it could not but be with Rimsky-Korsakov; but the brilliant, carefully polished sound-fabric does not always suit the occasionally rough and simple outlines of the music. Here his study of Wagner has been more

373

hurtful than profitable to the score, as regards purity of style. Rimsky-Korsakov began his work on *Boris* eagerly, but completed it against the grain, feeling it a heavy burden. He frankly confesses his "weariness of the irksome task" in *My Musical Life*. Perhaps this distaste for the work, in spite of his conscientiousness, explains the obvious exaggeration of his "corrections." It is psychologically easy to understand.

All things considered, we cannot wholly deny the justice of the unfavourable comments made on this version, although the criticism is often as exaggerated as was the zeal of the editor. So long as the composer's original score rests hidden in the archives of the Marie Theatre, we are thrown back on Rimsky-Korsakov's version. All attempts by musicians to re-orchestrate the work from Moussorgsky's piano edition and put the opera on the stage in this form—as was done in 1924 at the Latvian National Opera at Riga—have been doomed to failure; only a rival editor equal to Korsakov in every respect could compete with the technical mastery displayed in every bar of Korsakov's version, and this will hardly happen for some long time to come.

One great service Rimsky-Korsakov's action unquestionably has done—it has contributed enormously to popularize Moussorgsky's art. In the new smooth shell the rough kernel of the original form pleased everybody. Rimsky-Korsakov's version of *Boris Godounov* had a triumphal progress through the whole world. In Russia the first performance of *Boris* in its new shape took place in the autumn of 1904 in the Marie Theatre at Petersburg, when Chaliapin made the unhappy Tsar Boris a most impressive dramatic figure. Since then the work has held a high place in the repertoire of all the chief opera-theatres in Russia.

From Petersburg it soon found its way to all the capitals of Europe, and then across the ocean to America, where it has become one of the favourite pieces in the repertoire

374

of the Metropolitan Opera House in New York. In Germany too the work has found its way in two years on to the stage of almost all the larger cities. The first performance in German took place at Breslau, October 29, 1923.

The Fair at Sorótchintzy

Of all the works Moussorgsky left behind him, this one has experienced the most varied fortunes. The fact that Rimsky-Korsakov, through whose hands nearly all Moussorgsky's musical papers passed, did not touch *The Fair at Sorótchintzy* not only kept all other would-be editors from having anything to do with it during his lifetime, but also prevented it from attracting general attention.

Rimsky-Korsakov's authority in Russia was so great that for a long time no one would taste the strong meat of Moussorgsky's music without knowing that it had been prepared, or at least approved of, by him. Thus *The Fair*, or what was left of it, remained practically unknown in Russia, till in 1912—Rimsky-Korsakov had died in 1908—part of it was published by Bessel, the Petersburg music-publisher, in an edition arranged by V. Karatigin, the music-critic. Before this time only a few early issues (long reckoned as bibliographical rarities) were in existence, and no one troubled about them. The publication in the year 1912, including the introduction, "A Hot Summer's Day in Little Russia," arranged and orchestrated by A. Liadov, coincided with the revival of interest in Moussorgsky, which was now at last taking place in Russia. Rimsky-Korsakov, though he would not himself touch *The Fair at Sorótchintzy*, had no rooted objection to a revision of the work. In a letter to the publisher Bessel, June 11, 1903, he states his view of the question. He writes:

"A. K. Liadov's idea of orchestrating all that exists of *The Fair at Sorótchintzy* is one with which I fully sympathize. He told me that his plan was to revise and orchestrate the introduction, Parássia's song, the Gopak, and the second act; he played me his version of the introduction. Clearly it is very desirable that these should all be published. My view is that, as regards the second act, it should be printed complete in large opera *format*. In my opinion this act will be most suitable for stage performance (as a one-act fragment), and the rest for concerts."

The event was different, however, from what Rimsky-Korsakov had supposed. While Karatigin was working on *The Fair*, he conceived the idea of performing all the fragments of the opera together, at first privately, without costumes or chorus, in concert form. This was first done as a commemoration of the thirtieth anniversary of the composer's death, on March 16, 1911, at a musical "day" given by Baron Driesen, the editor of the *Imperial Theatre Annual* in Petersburg. Its success with the audience, who were drawn from the musical and social élite of Petersburg, was striking; and now the whole world became interested in Moussorgsky's "new" opera. This led to the idea of attempting a performance on the public stage. It took place in the Comedia Theatre in Petersburg on December 17, 1911, as an extra performance, organized by the musical journal *The Musical Contemporary*.

The success of all these attempts, due to the irresistible charm of Moussorgsky's inspiration, caused the manager of the lately founded Free Theatre in Moscow, Mardshanov, to determine on the inclusion of Moussorgsky's newly-discovered work in his program. The chief difficulty was that there were only disconnected musical fragments in existence. Mardshanov resolved to produce *The Fair* as an opera with spoken dialogue; what music there was was to be sung and played, and the scenes that were lacking were to be filled in, not set to music, but merely spoken. The Moscow music-critic and composer I. Sakhnovsky was employed to look over the musical material. Sakhnovsky used and orchestrated everything published and unpublished, in the way of numbers and scenes of the opera, including Karatigin's version. The scenes that were wanting were supplied by dialogue adapted from Gogol's novel. The scenario drawn up by Moussorgsky was followed fairly closely, up to the third act; this was done, apparently, as a pious duty, but it was going a little too far. It is possible that Moussorgsky himself would have made considerable changes in his scenario—so much, at least, is indicated by the fact that there exists a scene of *The Fair* in his own handwriting that is not provided for in the scenario and is thus hard to incorporate into the plot.

The first performance of *The Fair at Sorótchintzy* in this form, half opera and half comedy, took place on October 8, 1913 in the Moscow Free Theatre. The impression produced by it was a mixed one; the magic charm of Moussorgsky's music and the incomparable humour of some of the scenes could not fail of their effect, but the work in its hybrid form could not achieve a really striking success. The Moscow performance showed that the idea of bringing the work on to the stage in this form was wrong. If *The Fair* was to be made safe for the theatre, it must be completed as an opera pure and simple, not as half opera and half comedy. Consequently, the music that was lacking would have to be supplied. But who would be so daring as to match himself against Moussorgsky? Someone was found, unexpectedly, where one would least have thought of looking—César Cui, now at the beginning of the ninth decade of his life, set to work in 1915 to complete the opera left behind by Moussorgsky, whom he had so slandered.

The first performance of *The Fair at Sorótchintzy* in Cui's version took place on October 13, 1917 in the Musical Drama Theatre in Petersburg. Any impression made by the work was entirely eclipsed by the Bolshevik revolution which broke out a week after and threw the Russian theatre into

377

complete chaos—in any case the success of the piece was only moderate.

After this a Russian composer living in Paris, N. Tcherepnin, a pupil of Rimsky-Korsakov, made a third attempt, quite independent of the previous ones, to preserve Moussorgsky's work for the stage. He approached the task from a point of view entirely different from Cui's. The latter had regarded Moussorgsky's scenario as the unalterable scheme, which must not be tampered with; thus all that was left for Cui to do was to compose new scenes to fill up the gaps left in the music-plot. For Tcherepnin, on the other hand, Moussorgsky's music, the completed scenes and the sketches for others, were the only real elements of the work. In order to restrict himself to these, he had to make important cuts and changes in the scenario; still the music, as we have it, is throughout either composed by Moussorgsky himself, or founded on motifs—folk-tunes or his own inventions—which were found in the composer's sketches for his opera and were handed over to the reviser by the publisher Bessel, who was then living in Paris. Contrary to Cui's method, Tcherepnin, in *The Fair at Sorótchintzy*, acts only as an arranger, not as an original composer; where the existing musical material is not sufficient, he takes other melodies of Moussorgsky's; for instance, in the love duet at the end of the first act he uses a beautiful theme from the song "By the River Don." From a merely musical standpoint Tcherepnin's work deserves the greatest credit; for whole pages you are persuaded that you have before you an original work by Moussorgsky, so excellently is his style imitated; only once—in the duet just mentioned—does the reviser forget his part and come obviously near to the style of his master, Rimsky-Korsakov. Whether *The Fair at Sorótchintzy* in this shape will keep the stage has yet to be seen. The first performance of Tcherepnin's version took place on March 16, 1923 at Monte Carlo and was a great success both with the audience

378

and with the critics. The City Theatre at Breslau came next, with the first German performance of *The Fair at Soró-tchintzy,* on May 6, 1925.

The Marriage

This first "attempt at setting a prose drama to music" of Moussorgsky's slumbered for thirty-eight years after it came into existence, and twenty-four years after the composer's death, carefully guarded from curious eyes by Stassov, in the Manuscript Section of the Public Library at Petersburg, before it was drawn from its hiding-place. Rimsky-Korsakov gives the following account of it in *My Musical Life:*

"With Stassov's consent, *The Marriage* was performed one evening at my house by Sigismund Blumenfeld, my daughter Sonia, the tenor singer Sandulenko, and young Gury Stravinsky [a brother of the composer]. Nadeshda Nikolaievna [Rimsky-Korsakov's wife] accompanied at the piano. The work, thus brought to light, in spite of a certain intentional unmusicality, surprised all who were present by the obvious inspiration of its ideas. After we had discussed and considered the matter, I resolved, to the great satisfaction of V. V. Stassov, to hand it to Bessel for publication, but first I proposed to look it through and make necessary corrections and simplifications, with the intention of perhaps orchestrating it later for the stage."

Rimsky-Korsakov did not succeed in carrying out the plan he stated—he died when the task had merely been begun. Among his papers only the first twelve pages of a score of *The Marriage* were found written out.

The piano edition, revised by him, was soon afterwards brought out by Bessel. This time the "corrections and simplifications" by Rimsky-Korsakov consisted, as a matter of fact, of a few unimportant alterations, every one of which

379

was noted with punctilious accuracy, the original text being given with them.

It was not the fate of this singular torso of a comic opera to have a successful career on the stage, and it is hardly to be expected that it ever will—a dramatic "fragment," however fine, can never count on exciting the interest of the public. This was proved by some attempts that were made in Russia to bring *The Marriage* on to the stage. The first public performance in Russia, still with piano accompaniment, took place in Petersburg on March 19, 1909. On October 13, 1917 it was performed for the first time with orchestral accompaniment, together with Cui's version of *The Fair at Sorótchintzy*, at the Musical Drama Theatre in Petersburg. The orchestration was provided by a student at the Petersburg Conservatoire (!), Hauk. This version foundered, with Cui's version of *The Fair*, in a chaos of the Revolution. Later on, the only act in existence was orchestrated by Maurice Ravel, but has not yet appeared on the stage in this form. In April 1923 some semi-public performances were given in Paris, and there the matter ended. In spite of the almost enthusiastic reception that the work found from the majority of French press critics, no theatre has yet ventured to put it into the repertoire.

Orchestral Works and Choruses, Songs and Piano Pieces

As soon as he had finished *Khovanstchina*, Rimsky-Korsakov set to work revising the other pieces that the composer had left unfinished or not ready for the press. The task went on smoothly. The first compositions that he sent to press, in 1882, were the *Songs and Dances of Death*, with five songs to words by Tolstoy and the song "A Vision." His editing in these was limited to quite unimportant corrections of clerical errors, such as were likely to occur with a com-

380

poser who, as Laroche put it, "could not even get the sharps and flats right." Of the longer works Rimsky-Korsakov edited only one, which gave him much trouble. He writes about it in *My Musical Life*: "At first I could make nothing of *A Night on the Bare Mountain*; Moussorgsky had planned the piece originally in the sixties, under the influence of Liszt's 'Dance of Death,' for piano and orchestra (it was then called *Midsummer Eve*, and came under Balakirev's harsh but just criticism), and then left it lying for a long time. While he was working on Gedeonov's *Mlada*, Moussorgsky used the material of the *Night*, with the addition of vocal passages, for the Tchernobog scene on Mount Triglaff. That was the second form of the piece. A third form was given it while working at *The Fair at Sorótchintzy*, when Moussorgsky had the singular and absurd idea of making the Párobok see the witches' sabbath in a dream. . . . This time the piece ended with the chime of the village bells, at which the demon crew vanish in terror. The quiet passage descriptive of dawn was founded on the theme of the sleeping youth, who had had the frightful nightmare. I used the latest reading for the close of the work. . . . But none of these versions, as a whole, was suitable for publication and performance. Consequently I resolved to make a purely orchestral piece from Moussorgsky's material and did my utmost to keep all the best and most connected parts without change and to put in as little as possible of my own. But first I had to create the form into which Moussorgsky's ideas could naturally fall. It was a hard problem, and for two whole years I did not succeed in solving it satisfactorily. I could manage neither the form, nor the modulations, nor the orchestration. The work on my friend's other pieces went on well."

This proves the truth of the proverb, "Slow and sure." Rimsky-Korsakov finally succeeded in solving his problem in a masterly way; the *Night on the Bare Mountain* is one of the best of his revisions of Moussorgsky. The score appeared in 1886.

The other works, the editing of which gave Rimsky-Korsakov less trouble, were as follows: the Scherzo for orchestra in B flat major, and the *Œdipus* chorus, which he merely prepared for press, the "Intermezzo *in modo classico*" and the "Turkish March," which he orchestrated, and the chorus *Joshua* (*Jesus Navinus*), the "Chorus of Women" out of *Salambo*, and the song "Night," which he orchestrated, the latter after the orchestral sketches left by Moussorgsky. Besides these he prepared for press the unpublished songs "Kallistrat," "By the River Don," "The Naughty Puss," "The Hobby-horse" (these two he included in *The Nursery*), "The Pilgrim," and "Mephistopheles's Song of the Flea." All these compositions appeared in 1883.

This exhausted the unpublished music left by Moussorgsky, so far as Rimsky-Korsakov thought it ripe for publication; he did not know of the songs in the so-called "Paris manuscript," which came to light only in 1909. Later on, he edited and published the following works of his former friend: *Pictures from an Exhibition* in 1866; the chorus *The Destruction of Sennacherib*, which he re-orchestrated; the song "Gathering Mushrooms"; the "Serenade" and "Field-Marshal Death," from the *Songs and Dances of Death*, which he arranged for orchestra (the first two numbers, "Trepak" and "Cradle-song," were orchestrated by A. Glazounov) in 1891. In 1908 followed a new edition of all Moussorgsky's vocal music that had previously appeared. In bringing out nearly all the music left behind by Moussorgsky, Rimsky-Korsakov not only performed a giant task, but did invaluable service to the memory of his dead friend. The balance sheet of his activities as musical executor of his distinguished friend certainly leaves a heavy credit, both moral and artistic, in his favour. In the memory of posterity his name is inseparably associated with that of the creator of *Khovan-stchina.*

Nearly all the compositions of Moussorgsky that Rimsky-Korsakov thought not worth publishing have appeared since Rimsky-Korsakov's death. In 1911 and 1912 V. Karatigin brought out the songs "Mournfully rustle the leaves," "The Tempest," "I fain would pour forth my sorrow," the "Evening Song," "Cruel Death" (in his ending to which he showed a complete lack of understanding of the composer's intention), and "The Sphinx"; also the two piano pieces called *Recollections of Childhood* (in the second of these, which was unfinished, he added a coda of thirteen bars, this time with more justification), "*Souvenir d'enfance,*" "*Impromptu passionné,*" and "*Rêverie.*" The Scherzo in C sharp minor, written for piano, but originally designed for orchestra, and the "Prayer of Salambo" appeared in 1917, arranged for orchestra by Senilov. Finally Bessel in 1923 published in Paris the "Paris manuscript" (seventeen songs of the years 1857–66), under the title *Youthful Years,* given it by the composer, leaving out the Italian duet "*Ogni sabbato avrete il lume acceso,*" which is not an original composition of Moussorgsky's.

Thus at the present day all Moussorgsky's dramatic works, and nearly all his orchestral, piano, and vocal compositions (also in collected editions, all with German, French, and English words) are in print. The unpublished works are merely a few quite unimportant youthful pieces for the piano, *Schamyl's March,* the *Allegro* in C major, for a sonata, for piano duet, besides the original version of *Boris Godounov* and the original piano score of *Khovanstchina.*

Two orchestral arrangements have been made of the *Pictures at an Exhibition*; an incomplete "Russian" version by Toushmalov, which is in print, and a complete "French" version by Maurice Ravel, which is the exclusive property of the Russian conductor S. Koussevitsky and is at present still in manuscript.

*　　　*　　　*

It is a shameful thing for Russia, but none the less a fact, that the composer of *Boris Godounov* and *Khovanstchina* was completely forgotten after his death. *Boris*, the only dramatic work that he had left ready for the stage, was not performed again, and in concerts his works were hardly ever met with. In the concert programs of the Imperial Russian Musical Society at Moscow, for instance, the name of Moussorgsky appears only five times in the course of its fifty years' existence! Apart from the obvious causes of this fact—the general lack of understanding for this new *genre* of art-song in Russia (where even Schubert and Schumann were little known), the overshadowing reputation of Tchaikovsky, the spite and hostility of critics—there was a special reason for this neglect of Moussorgsky, which made the performance of his music impossible for a time; he had no one to interpret him. The artistes of the old guard, the great Petrov, Melnikov (the first Boris), the singers Petrovna-Vorobieva, Platanova, and Leonova, who were such warm admirers of the art of the author of *The Nursery*, the *Songs and Dances of Death*, and all the many other unique songs—all these were either dead or had retired, and there was no second generation to carry on their work. As for Moussorgsky's few piano works, he himself had always been their only interpreter. So Russia remained silent, in spite of the labours of Rimsky-Korsakov, who gave the world the works of his dead friend, one after another; they found no response, either among musicians, who, with few exceptions, were still under the influence of a diametrically opposite artistic tendency, or among the general public, who knew and cared nothing about them. Moussorgsky's name was forgotten, or, at best, used as a warning. It was long before peo-

384

ple in Russia realized what they possessed in Moussorgsky and what was the importance of his art to the intellectual development of his country.

At last there came from abroad the news that interest had suddenly awakened in the art of the bold pioneer of musical expression, who had been ignored or grossly misunderstood in his own home. The movement spread farther and farther over all civilized countries. There is no possible doubt that the first source of Moussorgsky's fame was France, and especially Paris.

Involuntarily we ask the question—how came the French to show such enthusiasm for a Russian composer? The first and principal cause for this remarkable event was entirely outside the field of art. It was to be found in the political combinations and intrigues towards the end of the nineteenth century. If the Franco-Russian Alliance had not come into existence in 1896, people in Paris would hardly have been so enthusiastic for Russian art and music as they were after that date. These tendencies were naturally stimulated on the side of Russia—rather by the Russian Government than by Russian artists—for keen-sighted politicians well understood that nothing was so sure to create a lasting sympathy for Russia as the popularizing of Russian art and especially Russian music in an allied country. So Russia gained great advantages from her art, and rightly so. The success of the propaganda for Russian music in Paris was extraordinary; but it soon took a direction that no one in Russia had expected. At first matters went exactly as was wished; the surprise began when French taste began to take shape. Not César Cui, who was powerfully supported by Countess Mercy d'Argenteau, not Borodin, not Rimsky-Korsakov, both of whom found an enthusiastic patroness in Countess Gréful, not Balakirev, still wearing the halo of a "leader" of the "New Russian School," achieved the greatest success and won real popularity in Paris. No! it was the one outsider in this musical race for the favour of the French public—a man who, even among his colleagues and friends, was thought half cracked, and who moreover had been dead for twenty years —Moussorgsky.

It is not hard to trace the reasons for which the French singled out Moussorgsky from all the Russian composers. These reasons had nothing to do with politics, but were purely artistic. In the first place, it was the healthy musical naturalism that Moussorgsky displays in all his works that attracted the French. A nation that counts as its own Balzac and Zola, Meunier and Rodin, could not remain insensible to an artist who was the first to treat music in a similar spirit. This effect was helped by the unusual musical language that Moussorgsky speaks, a language that sometimes disregards grammatical propriety, but is always interesting, original, and magnificently impressive. That was the right kind of music for the French, who have always had a certain weakness for the overthrow of traditional ways of thought. The seed of revolution could always find congenial soil in France.

But some other obvious causes contributed to this result, as we shall now show. The honour of having discovered Moussorgsky in France is officially due to Pierre d'Alheim, the husband of the singer Marie Olenine, the talented interpreter of Moussorgsky's songs. In 1896 he wrote a fine pamphlet on the composer and delivered a course of lectures in Paris, which appeared soon after in book form. His wife supported his literary propaganda by giving between 1896 and 1900 more than sixty concerts of Moussorgsky's works in France and Belgium, concerts that met with increasing success, rising to absolute enthusiasm. Rightly can Madame Olenine d'Alheim maintain: "France and Belgium, gifted with so clear and subtle an intellect, in no way prone to mysticism, were the first to understand Moussorgsky's intimate realism."

D'Alheim's publications were soon followed by others,

throwing further light on Moussorgsky's works. Camille Bellaigue (1900) wrote a brilliant notice of the author of *Boris* in his *Impressions musicales et littéraires,* and, soon after, a more comprehensive essay in his *Études musicales* ("A Great Realistic Musician: Moussorgsky"). He was followed by Claude Debussy, with a detailed study in the *Revue Blanche* (1901), and Pierre Lalo, with three long articles in the *Temps.* Lastly, in 1908, appeared the well-known book of Calvocoressi, and *Moussorgsky's Legacy* by Marie Olenine d'Alheim.

Moussorgsky was unofficially known to intimate circles in Paris long before Pierre d'Alheim appeared on the scene. As chance would have it, he was introduced to Paris by a musician whom he himself thought unworthy of notice. In a letter of Moussorgsky's to Stassov occurs the following characteristic passage: "We are not to be led by the nose by any pretty little tunes. The lady of the house may offer her dear friend a box of bonbons—that is no business of ours! . . . Oh, this Monsieur Saint-Saëns, who plumes himself on his originality! With every fibre of my brain I loathe him; with every pulse of my heart I renounce him! What have we to do with him, this worker in miniature?" Yet it was no other than Saint-Saëns who in 1874 brought the piano edition of *Boris Godounov* back to Paris from a concert tour to Petersburg. It was this piano edition with which, though some time later, Claude Debussy became acquainted, through Jules de Brayers. Moussorgsky's art touched more than one string in the heart of the young French composer and exerted a decisive influence on his development, especially when he became acquainted with the songs of the author of *Boris.* The "pointillistic" method of many of Moussorgsky's piano accompaniments, the light and shade of his harmonies, his vivid musical declamation, and the free sweep of his rhythm were the models for Debussy's own musical style; though we are far from charging the author of *Pelléas* with any lack of

387

individuality, or deliberate imitation. So it was that Moussorgsky's art, so rich in the seeds of future development, although decried at home, became abroad a living source of an important artistic movement, far removed from his own original views—the new French musical "impressionism."

But these matters were known only to a few of the initiated, till the enthusiastic and genuine propaganda of the d'Alheim couple began to work—then was the right moment to bring Moussorgsky's name into official relations with the new and audacious musical movement in France. We may add that possibly a strong motive for this action was the fact that the Russian master's art was a welcome set-off against the ever-encroaching influence of Wagner.

After succeeding in France far beyond her wildest hopes Madame Olenine d'Alheim carried her noble and ideally unselfish crusade in favour of Moussorgsky's songs into the composer's own country. She sought to revive interest in Moussorgsky by giving concerts in Petersburg, Moscow, and the Russian provinces, from 1900 to 1906, which must have reached a respectable total in three figures. And, by a miracle, she succeeded—succeeded in a measure beyond all expectation. A Moussorgsky renaissance arose in Russia, which spread far and wide and converted more than one of the noteworthy musical critics of the press from a persecuting Saul into an apostolic Paul. No doubt it would have happened, sooner or later, in any case; still, this remarkable woman and remarkable artist deserves the glory of having given the first impulse to the movement.

A fortunate chance brought it about that Moussorgsky, about the same time as this revival of interest in his songs, came before the public again as an operatic composer. *Boris Godounov* in Rimsky-Korsakov's version—which, even in 1896, when it was proposed for one of the gala performances at the Tsar's coronation in Moscow, had been struck off the list by the sovereign's own hand—about the beginning of the new century, made a conquest, not only of the theatres, both State and private, in the two capitals and the provinces, but also of the hearts of the audience. In Moscow and Petersburg Feodor Chaliapin's art in the part of Tsar Boris greatly contributed to this result. Besides this, Chaliapin in the concert hall, next to Madame Olenine d'Alheim, was one of the most zealous champions of the composer of the *Songs and Dances of Death*, the "Ballad," "The Seminarist," the "Song of the Flea," and all the other fine songs that gave his mighty dramatic and comic talent such incomparable opportunities for full expression.

Moussorgsky's victory in Russia was now complete; at last the prophet had come to fitting honour in his own country. From France and Russia Moussorgsky's name and his works soon penetrated into all lands. In Germany, Italy, England, Spain, America, there is hardly an opera-house of any note that does not include *Boris Godounov* in its standing repertoire.

His songs have not won such wide popularity, owing to a difficulty to which, unfortunately, the publishers of his works have paid insufficient attention—the translation of the words. Translation of foreign songs is always a sore point; in Moussorgsky it is of enormous importance for the effect of the music. With him the word and the note are one, inseparable, indissolubly bound together, since the one has arisen solely from the other. Thus the translator ought to be not only a poet, but a fine musician, who would be able to set the words himself—a requirement not very easy to fulfil. In France only has this obtacle in the way of interpreting and popularizing Moussorgsky's songs been overcome with fair success. The latest translations especially, by d'Arcourt and Laloy, show remarkable prosodical and musical skill. Hitherto the problem of translation has been handled worst in Germany, where the translators have been men with a good knowledge of music, but incapable of writing good verses, or vice versa. Hence all printed translations of the words of Moussorgsky's songs have been hitherto found unsuitable for practical use or for the concert hall, and the songs of the composer of *Boris Godounov* have had no chance of appealing to the hearts of Germans. But it is to be hoped that new versions, of which some have appeared and others are expected, will soon bring about a decided change in this respect.

*   *   *

When we survey the fate of Moussorgsky's works, we are possessed with the consoling certainty that every genius has its own time; Nature brings forth nothing that is superfluous, and no healthy creative force can be lost. After Moussorgsky's death his works took forty years to conquer the world; but though their triumphal progress might be retarded, it was never completely checked. Now these works, at first derided and despised, then neglected and forgotten, have become a precious possession of the whole world of art and are recognized as such without contradiction.

Their fate, like that of their great author, is for all future time a solemn warning to the artistic and moral conscience of mankind.

APPENDICES

CHRONOLOGICAL LIST OF THE WORKS OF M. P. MOUSSORGSKY

1. "Porte-Ensigne Polka (Ensign's Polka)," for piano, composed 1852, published by Bernard (at the composer's expense?) at Petersburg. MS. lost.

2. *Han d'Islande,* opera taken from Victor Hugo's romance, begun at Petersburg in 1856. No trace of the music.

3. *"Souvenir d'enfance,"* for piano, composed October 16 (old style), [1] 1857, bears the dedication *"à mon ami Nicholas Obolensky";* published by Bessel, 1911 (V. Karatigin's edition). MS. in the Public Library at Petersburg.

4. "Tell me, star, where art thou?" song with piano accompaniment, composed 1857, dedicated to I. L. Grünberg, the singer, published by Bessel, 1911 (Karatigin). Words by an unknown author (Moussorgsky?); German words by Lippold, French words by Calvocoressi (1921); MS. at Paris, in the Conservatoire Library.

5. "A Happy Hour," a "Capriccio" for voice and piano, words by Koltzov, composed 1858, dedicated to V. Y. Sakharin; published by Bessel in Paris, 1923; French words by Laloy; Paris MS. [2]

6. "Ah, only tell me why!" for voice and piano, composed July 31, 1858, dedicated to Sinaide A. Burtzeva; A. Pushkin is

---

[1] All the dates are the old style, in use in Russia till 1918.

[2] Moussorgsky's MS. collection of songs, *Years of my Youth,* comprising seventeen original songs, and an arrangement of an Italian romance by Gordigiani as a duet, which the French musical critic Malherbe discovered in 1909, is referred to generally as the Paris Manuscript. After Charles Malherbe's death it became the property of the library of the Paris Conservatoire (1911). Further details of the MS. are to be found in the *Bulletin français de la S. I. M.* (Imperial Musical Society), 1909, No. 5, and in the *Russian Musical News,* 1909, Nos. 13, 14; see also the Prague musical journal, *Der Auftakt,* 1925, No. 3.

given as the author of the words, but no such poem is found in his works; published in 1867 by Johannson; new edition, 1898, by Belaiev (Leipzig), with French words by Sergennois. Paris MS. [1]

7. "Sadly rustle the leaves," for voice and piano (a "musical story"), words much altered from a poem by Pleshtcheiev, composed 1858, dedicated to M. O. Mikeshin, published, 1911, by Bessel (Karatigin); German words by Lippold, French by Laloy; Paris MS.

8. Scherzo in B flat major, for orchestra, composed 1858, dedicated to A. S. Goussakovsky; first performed, 1860, at a symphony concert of the Russian Musical Society; published by Bessel, 1883 (edited by Rimsky-Korsakov).

9. Scherzo in C sharp minor, for piano, composed November 25, 1858, dedicated to Liubov M. Bube; published by Bessel, 1911 (Karatigin). The MS. is in the collection of the *Russian Musical News* (N. F. Findeisen). Arranged for orchestra by V. A. Senilov, 1917.

10. "A Child's Jest" (Scherzo), for piano, composed 1859 (autumn), according to Stassov; the MS. is dated May 28, 1860; published 1873 by Bernard (?); new edition in the eighties by Belaiev (*Two Piano Pieces by M. Moussorgsky*, No. 1). See under "Intermezzo"; MS. in the possession of M. D. Calvocoressi.

11. *"Impromptu passionné,"* for piano, composed October 1, 1859, dedicated to Nadeshda Petrovna Opotchinina; published, 1911, by Bessel (Karatigin); MS. in the Public Library at Petersburg.

12. *Schamyl's March,* for chorus, tenor and bass solo, and orchestra (?), composed probably in autumn 1859, dedicated to A. P. Arseniev; unpublished; MS. in the possession of V. I. Belsky.

---

[1] The new edition of seven songs (Nos. 6, 33, 36, 39, 41, 43, 45 in this list) published by Belaiev has no German words. In the collected edition of Moussorgsky's songs brought out by Bessel in 1922 (Breitkopf & Härtel) they have German words (impracticable) by A. Scholz. A new edition of the collected songs with new German words by Heinrich Möller is being brought out by Bessel (Breitkopf & Härtel).

13. "I have castles to spare," for voice and piano, words by Kolt-
    zov, composed 1860, dedicated to P. T. Borispaletz; published
    in Paris by Bessel, 1923; French words by Laloy; Paris
    MS. [1]

14. "What mean the words of love?" for voice and piano, words by
    Amossov, composed 1860, dedicated to Marie V. Shilovskaia;
    published by Bessel, 1923; French words by Laloy; Paris
    MS.

15. Sonata in C major (*Allegro*) for piano duet, uncompleted,
    composed December 8, 1860; unpublished; MS. in the posses-
    sion of N. A. Rimsky-Korsakov's heirs.

16. *Œdipus,* music to Sophocles' tragedy; all that is in existence
    is a chorus for male and female voices; composed 1860–1,
    dedicated to M. A. Balakirev, and the same year performed
    for the first time at a concert given by K. N. Liadov; pub-
    lished, 1883 (full score), by Bessel (edited by Rimsky-Kor-
    sakov); new edition (piano score), no Russian words, only
    German (Lippold) and French (d'Arcourt); MS. in the Pub-
    lic Library at Petersburg.

17. "*Alla Marcia Notturna,*" for orchestra, "scored" May 14, 1861;
    unpublished; MS. in the Public Library at Petersburg.

18. "Intermezzo *in modo classico,*" for orchestra, composed in the
    winter of 1861, scored 1867, dedicated to A. P. Borodin;
    published by Bessel, 1883 (re-orchestrated by Rimsky-Korsa-
    kov); arranged for piano duet by Tchesnov: another arrange-
    ment for piano, published by Belaiev under the title "Inter-
    mezzo" (*Two Piano Pieces by M. Moussorgsky,* No. 2); see
    also "A Child's Jest" (No. 10 in this list); MSS. of the origi-
    nal score, dated July 12, 1862, and of a piano arrangement
    are in the Public Library at Petersburg.

19. "King Saul," for voice and piano, words from Byron's *Hebrew
    Melodies,* Russian translation by N. A. Koslov, much altered
    by Moussorgsky, composed 1863, dedicated to Alexander Pe-
    trovitch Opotchinin; published, 1871, by Bessel, new edition
    (Rimsky-Korsakov) 1908; orchestral edition by A. K. Gla-
    zounov; a completely different version of the piece is "King

---

[1] The complete edition of the songs in the Paris MS., first published by
Bessel (Paris), 1923, has no German words.

Saul Before the Battle," in the Paris MS.; published, 1923, by Bessel, with French words by Laloy.

20. "The Harper's Song," from Goethe's *Wilhelm Meister, "An die Türen will ich schleichen,"* for voice and piano, composed August 13, 1863, dedicated to A. P. Opotchinin, Russian translation by an unknown author (Moussorgsky?); published, 1911, by Bessel (Karatigin), with the original German words, and French words by Laloy.

21. "We parted coldly," for voice and piano, composed August 15, 1863, dedicated to N. P. Opotchinina; words by Kourotchkin; published, 1923, by Bessel in Paris; French translation by Laloy; Paris MS.

22. *Salambo (The Libyan),* opera in four acts and seven tableaux, from Flaubert's novel *(Salammbô).* Of this there exist:

"Song of the Balearic Islander," composed August 1864, published, 1923, by Bessel in Paris, Paris MS., French words by Laloy; another MS. of the first sixteen bars is in the Public Library at Petersburg;

Second Scene of Act II, composed December 15, 1863, unpublished, MS. in the Public Library at Petersburg;

Salambo's Prayer (first scene of the second tableau of Act II), published, 1911, by Bessel in piano score (Karatigin), 1915 in full score, orchestrated by V. A. Senilov;

First Scene of Act III; the MS. in the Public Library at Petersburg bears the two dates; begun July 23, 1864 and ended November 10, 1864; unpublished;

First Scene of Act IV; the MS., dated November 26, 1864, is in the Public Library at Petersburg; unpublished;

Female Chorus ("The Priestesses comfort Salambo and robe her in wedding garments") from the second scene of Act IV, composed February 8, 1866; published by Bessel (full score), orchestrated by Rimsky-Korsakov, 1884; new edition (piano score) 1909, with German words by Lippold and French by d'Arcourt; MS. in the possession of V. V. Yastrebtzev.

23. "The tempest rages," for voice and piano, words by Koltzov, composed March 28, 1864, dedicated to V. A. Loginov; pub-

lished by Bessel, 1911 (Karatigin); German words by Lippold, French by Laloy; Paris MS.

24. "Night," a "Fantasy," for voice and piano, words by Pushkin (much altered), composed April 10, 1864, dedicated to N. P. Opotchinina; published by Bessel, 1871; new edition in 1908 (Rimsky-Korsakov), with German words by A. Bernhard and French by M. D. Calvocoressi; MS. (incomplete) in the Public Library at Petersburg; Rimsky-Korsakov's version for orchestra is fitted to Pushkin's original words; the Paris MS. contains a very different version of the piece, published by Bessel, 1923, with French words by Laloy.

25. "Kallistrat," for voice and piano (orchestra?), words by Nekrassov, composed May 22, 1864, dedicated to Alexander P. Opotchinin; published by Bessel, 1883 (Rimsky-Korsakov); new edition, 1908, with German words by A. Bernhard, and French by Calvocoressi; the Paris MS. contains an entirely different version, published by Bessel, 1923, with French words by Laloy.

26. *"Ogni sabbato avrete il lume acceso"; canto popolare toscano, musica di Gordigiani, l'arrangemento a due voce di Modesto Moussorgsky, l'arrangemento è dedicato al signor Vold. Grotscii* (Grodsky?), *anno 1864, San Petroburgo;* unpublished; Paris MS.

27. "Prayer," for voice and piano, words by Lermontov, composed February 2, 1865, dedicated to the composer's mother; published by Bessel, 1923; Paris MS.

28. *Recollections of Childhood,* two piano pieces, No. 1, "Nanny and I"; No. 2, "The First Punishment (Nanny shuts me up in a dark room)"; composed 1865; dedicated to the memory of his mother; published, 1911, by Bessel, edited by Karatigin, who has added thirteen bars to the unfinished second piece; MS. in the Public Library at Petersburg.

29. *"Duma* (Reverie)," for piano, composed June 22, 1865, on a theme by V. Loginov, and dedicated to him; published by Bessel, 1911 (Karatigin); MS. in the Public Library at Petersburg.

30. "The Outcast (The Lost Soul)," essay in recitative for voice and piano, words by Iv. G. M. (?), composed July 5, 1865;

published by Bessel, 1923, with French words by Laloy;
Paris MS.

31. *"La Capricieuse,"* for piano, on a theme by Count L. Heyden,
composed July 26, 1865; unpublished; MS. in the Public Library at Petersburg.

32. "Cradle-song," from the drama *The Voivode* by Ostrovsky,
composed September 5, 1865; dedicated to the memory of his
mother; published by Bessel, 1871; new edition 1908, with
French words by Calvocoressi and German by A. Bernhard:
orchestral edition by Rimsky-Korsakov. The Paris MS. contains a longer version, which was published by Bessel, 1923,
with French words by Laloy. The other MS. is in the Public
Library at Petersburg.

33. "Fair Sávishna," for voice and piano, words by Moussorgsky,
composed 1865, dedicated to César Cui; published, 1867, by
Johannson; new edition, 1898, by Belaiev, with French words
by Sergennois. C. Cui presented the MS. to the library of
the Nikolai Cadet School at Petersburg (formerly the
Guards' Cadet Academy); it is dated September 2, 1866 (?).

34. "Why do thine eyes," for voice and piano, words by Pleshtcheiev, composed January 1866, dedicated to A. V. A. (?);
published by Bessel, with French words by Laloy; Paris MS.

35. *"Ich wollt', meine Liebe ergösse sich,"* by Heinrich Heine, for
voice and piano, composed April 16, 1866, dedicated to N. P.
Opotchinina; published, 1911, by Bessel (Karatigin), French
words by Calvocoressi; MS. in the Public Library at Petersburg.

36. "Gopak," for voice and piano, words by Shevtchenko (from
the play *The Haidamaks*), in a Russian translation by Mey,
August 31, 1866; dedicated to N. A. Rimsky-Korsakov; orchestrated by Moussorgsky, 1868; published, 1867, by Johannson; new edition, 1898, by Belaiev, with French words
by Sergennois (orchestrated by Rimsky-Korsakov); MS. in
the possession of N. A. Rimsky-Korsakov's heirs. (Compare
36a.)

37. "Yarema's Song," for voice and piano, words by Shevtchenko
(from *The Haidamaks*); in Russian translation by Mey;

composed 1866; in 1879 completely rewritten in the song "On the Dnieper"; see No. 84 of this list.

38. *The Destruction of Sennacherib,* for full chorus and orchestra, words from Byron's *Hebrew Melodies,* composed January 29, 1867, dedicated to M. A. Balakirev; first performance February 1867, at a concert of the Free School of Music, given by Balakirev; new version, with a new middle part, winter of 1873–4; published by Belaiev, 1893, scored afresh by Rimsky-Korsakov, with French words by Ruelle; the MSS. of both versions are in the Public Library at Petersburg.

39. "Hebrew Song," for voice and piano, words by Mey, composed June 12, 1867, dedicated to Filaret P. Moussorgsky and his wife; published by Johannson, 1868; new edition, 1898, by Belaiev, with French words by Sergennois; MS. in the Public Library at Petersburg.

40. "The Magpie," a musical jest, for voice and piano, words by Pushkin (two poems put together), composed August 26, 1867, dedicated to the two Opotchinins (Alexander Petrovitch and Nadeshda Petrovna); published by Bessel, 1871; new edition (Rimsky-Korsakov) in 1908, with German words by A. Bernhard and French by Calvocoressi; MS. in the Public Library at Petersburg.

41. "The Seminarist," for voice and piano, words by Moussorgsky, composed September 27, 1867, dedicated to L. D. Shestakova; printed by Rahter at Leipzig in 1870 (for the composer); new edition in 1908 by Belaiev, with French words by d'Arcourt; MS. in the Public Library at Petersburg.

42. "The Ragmuffin (The Street-urchin)," for voice and piano, words by Moussorgsky, composed December 19, 1867, dedicated to V. V. Stassov; published by Bessel, 1871; new edition (Rimsky-Korsakov) 1908, with German words by A. Bernhard and French by Calvocoressi; MS. in the Public Library at Petersburg.

43. "The Goat," a "society story," for voice and piano, words by Moussorgsky, composed December 23, 1867, dedicated to A. P. Borodin; published, 1868, by Johannson; new edition, 1898, by Belaiev, with French words by Sergennois; MS. in the Public Library at Petersburg.

44. "By the Don a garden blooms," for voice and piano, words by Koltzov (shortened and altered), composed December 1867; published by Bessel, 1883 (Rimsky-Korsakov); new edition, 1908, with German words by A. Bernhard and French by Calvocoressi; MS. in the possession of V. V. Yastrebtzev.

45. "The Banquet," a story for voice and piano, words by Koltzov, composed 1867, dedicated to L. I. Shestakova; published by Johannson, 1868; new edition, 1898, by Belaiev, with French words by Sergennois.

46. "Gathering Mushrooms," for voice and piano, words by Mey, composed 1867, dedicated to Prof. V. V. Nikolsky; published by Johannson, 1868; new edition in 1898 by Belaiev, with French words by Sergennois (arranged for orchestra by Rimsky-Korsakov).

47. "The Classic," a musical pamphlet, for voice and piano, words by Moussorgsky, composed 1867; dedicated to N. P. Opotchinina; published by Bernard, 1870, for the composer, afterwards by Bessel; new edition 1908 (Rimsky-Korsakov), with German words by A. Bernhard and French by Calvocoressi.

48. *Midsummer Eve on the Bare Mountain,* or *The Witches,* a symphonic poem for piano and orchestra—see *Mlada* and *A Night on the Bare Mountain* (Nos. 62 and 92 in this list); MS. in the Public Library at Petersburg. [1]

49. *The Marriage,* an attempt at dramatic music in prose, the first four scenes of Gogol's comedy of that name, composed from June 11 to July 8, 1868, dedicated to V. V. Stassov; published by Bessel, 1908 (Rimsky-Korsakov); orchestration left uncompleted by Rimsky-Korsakov owing to his death; scored by Hauk (in Petersburg) and M. Ravel (in Paris); first performance in Petersburg (with piano), March 19, 1909;

[1] In 1867 also come the following arrangements of Beethoven's quartets for piano solo, intended for the "Opotchinin Saturdays":

1. *Andante* from the Quartet in C major, Op. 59, No. 3; dated April 9, 1867; dedicated to A. F. Goussakovsky.
2. Scherzo from the Quartet in F major, Op. 135; August 3, 1867.
3. *Andante* (*Lento*) from the Quartet in F major, Op. 135; August 3, 1867; dedicated to N. P. Opotchinina.
4. Scherzo from the Quartet in E minor, Op. 59, No. 2; August 5, 1867.
5. Quartet in C sharp minor, Op. 131—fragments; 1867. The MSS. of these (except No. 1) are in the Public Library at Petersburg.

with Hauk's orchestration, in the Musical Drama Theatre, October 13, 1917; first performance in Paris, April 1923; MS. in the Public Library at Petersburg.

50. "The Orphan," for voice and piano, words by Moussorgsky, composed April 1868; published by Bessel, 1871; new edition 1908 (Rimsky-Korsakov), with German words by A. Bernhard and French by Calvocoressi; MS. in the Public Library at Petersburg.

51. "Child's Song," for voice and piano, words by Mey, composed April 1868; published by Bessel, 1871; new edition (Rimsky-Korsakov) 1908, with German words by A. Bernhard and French by Calvocoressi; MS. in the Public Library at Petersburg.

52. "Child and Nurse (Niania and I)," for voice and piano, words by Moussorgsky, composed April 26, 1868; included as No. 1 in the series *The Nursery* (see Nos. 56–9, also 64 and 65, in this list).

53. "Yeromoushka's Cradle-song," for voice and piano, words by Nekrassov, composed March 16, 1868; published by Bessel, 1871; new edition 1908 (Rimsky-Korsakov), with French words by Calvocoressi and German by A. Bernhard; MS. in the Public Library at Petersburg.

54. *Boris Godounov,* an opera (musical folk-drama) in four acts, with a prologue, after Pushkin and Karamzin; the original version was composed 1868–70, then revised, till 1872; first performance in this form January 24, 1874; piano score published by Bessel, 1875; twice revised by Rimsky-Korsakov: the first time (in 1896) it was much shortened, the second time (1908) nearly all the omitted passages were restored, but the order of the two last tableaux was changed; first performance of Rimsky-Korsakov's version in the autumn of 1896, at Petersburg; first performance in German, at Breslau, October 29, 1923. The edition of 1908 had German (Lippold), French (Laloy), English, and Italian words; the original piano edition of 1875 was republished by Bessel in 1924 with German (translator not known) and French (M. Delines and Laloy) words; the MSS. of the original version (unpublished) and the original piano edition are in the Pub-

lic Library at Petersburg, except the scene in the monastery cell, which is in the possession of N. A. Rimsky-Korsakov's heirs; the original score of the work is in the library of the (formerly Imperial) Marie Theatre at Petersburg.

55. "The Peep-show" ("The Penny Gaff"), a musical satire for voice and piano, composed June 15, 1870, dedicated to V. V. Stassov, words by Moussorgsky; published by Bessel, 1871; new edition (Rimsky-Korsakov) 1908, with German words by A. Bernhard and French by Calvocoressi; MS. in the Public Library at Petersburg.

56. "In the Corner," second number of *The Nursery*, for voice and piano, words by Moussorgsky, composed 1870, dedicated to Victor Hartmann; published by Bessel, 1872; for later editions see No. 65 of this list.

57. "The Beetle," third number of *The Nursery*, for voice and piano, words by Moussorgsky, composed 1870, dedicated to V. V. Stassov; published by Bessel, 1872; for later editions see No. 65.

58. "With the Doll," fourth number of *The Nursery*, for voice and piano, words by Moussorgsky, composed 1870, dedicated to Tania and Goga Moussorgsky (his brother Filaret's children); published by Bessel, 1872; for later editions see No. 65.

59. "Going to Sleep," fifth number of *The Nursery*, words by Moussorgsky, composed 1870, dedicated to Sasha Cui (son of the composer), published by Bessel, 1872; for later editions see No. 65.

60. *Bobil (The Tramp)*, plan of an opera that went no further, drawn up in 1870; sketches for it used for *Khovanstchina*.

61. "Evening Song," for voice and piano, words by Pleshtcheiev (?), composed March 15, 1871, dedicated to Mme S. V. Serbina, published by Bessel, 1912 (Karatigin), with German words by Lippold and French by Mme S. G. Karatigin; MS. in the Public Library at Petersburg.

62. *Mlada*, ballet-opera, was to have been composed by Moussorgsky, Rimsky-Korsakov, Borodin, and Cui together on the scenario of Gedeonov, manager of the Imperial Theatre; Moussorgsky used for it his *Midsummer Eve on the Bare Mountain* (see No. 48) and fragments of *Salambo* and *Œdi-*

pus; he composed a new "Procession of Slav Princes" (February 26, 1872), which in 1880 he orchestrated for a concert of the Imperial Russian Musical Society; the piece was afterwards known as:

63. "Turkish March," published, 1883, by Bessel, as scored by Rimsky-Korsakov; the "Turkish" trio was composed in 1880, when Moussorgsky intended to use the piece as accompaniment to a tableau vivant, "The Capture of Kars" (part of a projected gala performance to celebrate Alexander II's twenty-five years of reign).

64. "Murr, the Cat (Naughty Puss)," a child's *scena,* for voice and piano, words by Moussorgsky, composed August 15, 1872; the MS. is in the collection of the *Russian Musical News* (N. F. Findeisen): for other dates, see next number.

65. "A Ride on the Hobby-horse," children's *scena,* for voice and piano, words by Moussorgsky, composed September 14, 1872; this and the preceding number originally bore the same title; they were dedicated to D. V. Stassov and his wife and were first published in 1883 by Bessel (Rimsky-Korsakov); when the new edition of *The Nursery* appeared, in 1908 (Rimsky-Korsakov), they were inserted as No. 6 ("The Hobby-horse") and No. 7 ("Naughty Puss") in the series.

66. *Khovanstchina (The Princes Khovansky),* musical folk-drama in five acts (six tableaux), libretto by Moussorgsky (from an edition of V. V. Stassov's), composed from 1872 to 1880; published by Bessel, 1883, in Rimsky-Korsakov's version; the very first performance of the work in this form took place November 1886, at Petersburg (by the Musical and Dramatic Union in the Kononov Hall); the first production in the Marie Theatre at Petersburg, on November 7, 1911 (!); the original MS. is in the Public Library at Petersburg, except some parts (variants) of the fourth act, which are in the possession of the Golenishtchev-Kutúsov family; different parts of the MS. bear dedications to various persons; the singers M. I. Feodorova and D. M. Leonova, Count Arseny Golenishtchev-Kutúsov, Countess Olga Golenishtchev-Kutúsov; in 1913 was the first performance in Paris, in a new version by Igor Stravinsky and M. Ravel; the performance

in 1923 in Paris returned to Rimsky-Korsakov's version; first German performance in Frankfurt am Main, February 19, 1924; in 1924 appeared (published by Bessel) the piano edition of Rimsky-Korsakov's version, with German text by E. Fritzheim, French by d'Arcourt, English by Rosa Newmarch.

67. "The Hill of Nettles" ("The Crab"), "an impossible story," for voice and piano, words by Moussorgsky; unfinished, begun August 10, 1874; MS. in the Public Library at Petersburg, unpublished.

68. *Pictures at an Exhibition,* ten piano pieces, composed in 1874 (finished on June 22), dedicated to V. V. Stassov, in memory of V. Hartmann; published by Bessel, 1886 (Rimsky-Korsakov); arrangement for orchestra by Toushmalov (incomplete), published by Bessel and Leonardi (Paris); an orchestral arrangement by M. Ravel (1922) is in the possession of the conductor S. Koussevitzky, in MS.; the original MS. is in the Public Library at Petersburg.

69. "Ballad" ("Forgotten"), for voice and piano, words by Count A. Golenishtchev-Kutúsov, composed autumn 1874, dedicated to the painter V. V. Verestchagin; published, 1887, by Gutheil in Moscow, with French words by d'Arcourt.

70. *Joshua (Jesus Navinus),* for full chorus and soli (mezzo-soprano and baritone) and orchestra; a version of a chorus from *Salambo,* heard in 1874–5, written out July 2, 1877, dedicated to Mme N. N. Rimsky-Korsakov; published by Bessel, 1883 (scored by Rimsky-Korsakov), new edition (Rimsky-Korsakov), 1908, with German words by Lippold and French by d'Arcourt.

71. *Without Sunlight,* a cycle of six songs with piano accompaniment, words by Count A. Golenishtchev-Kutúsov; composed 1874, published the same year by Bessel; new edition 1908 (Rimsky-Korsakov), with German words by A. Bernhard and French by Calvocoressi.

72. *Songs and Dances of Death,* a cycle of songs with piano accompaniment, words by Count A. Golenishtchev-Kutúsov. No. 1, "Trepak," composed February 17, 1875, dedicated to the singer O. A. Petrov; No. 2, "Death's Cradle-song," composed April 14, 1875, dedicated to Mme A. I. Vorobieva-Petrova;

404

No. 3, "Serenade," composed May 11, 1875, dedicated to L. I. Shestakova; No. 4, "Field-Marshall Death," composed June 5, 1877; dedicated to Count A. Golenishtchev-Kutúsov; published by Bessel in 1882 (Rimsky-Korsakov); new edition in 1908, with German words by A. Bernhard and French by Calvocoressi. Nos. 1 and 2 were arranged for orchestra by A. K. Glazounov, Nos. 3 and 4 by Rimsky-Korsakov. MS. in the Public Library at Petersburg.

73. "Cruel Death (An Epitaph)," for voice and piano, words by Moussorgsky, unfinished, composed in 1875 (?), on the death of N. P. Opotchinina; published by Bessel, 1912 (Karatigin added the last twelve bars); French words by Calvocoressi, German by Lippold; the MS. is in the collection of the *Russian Musical News* (Findeisen), a variant in the Public Library at Petersburg.

74. "The Sphinx," for voice and piano; words by Moussorgsky, composed December 21, 1875; dedicated to Marie Kostiurina (Feodorova after her marriage); published, 1911, by Bessel (Karatigin), with German words by Lippold and French by Calvocoressi; the MS. belongs to A. A. Makarov.

75. *The Fair at Sorótchintzy,* a comic opera, after Gogol, in three acts; words by Moussorgsky; unfinished, begun in 1875; some numbers were published by Bernard in the composer's lifetime; new edition of separate numbers (Karatigin), 1912, by Bessel; first performance as an opera with spoken dialogue, in the version by I. Saknovsky and Mardshanov in Moscow at the Free Theatre, October 8, 1913; completed as as an opera by C. Cui and performed for the first time in this version October 13, 1917, in the Music and Drama Theatre at Petersburg; performed for the first time at Monte Carlo, March 27, 1923, in an entirely new version by N. Tcherepnin; first German performance at Breslau, May 6, 1925. The piano scores of Cui's version, with French text by Laloy, and Tcherepnin's, with German words by H. Möller and French by Laloy, were published by Bessel, 1924. The MS. is mostly in the possession of V. Bessel; some scenes are in the Public Library at Petersburg.

76. "Not like the lightning did misfortune strike (Misfortune)," for voice and piano, words by Count A. Tolstoy, composed March 5, 1877, dedicated to F. A. Vanliarsky; published, 1882 (Rimsky-Korsakov), by Bessel; new edition 1908, with French words by Calvocoressi and German by A. Bernhard; MS. in the Public Library at Petersburg.

77. "A soul soars through the heavenly fields (The Spirit in Heaven)," for voice and piano, composed March 9, 1877; the other dates as for No. 76.

78. "Minstrel's Song," for voice and piano, composed March 20, 1877; the other dates as for No. 76.

79. "At last 'tis over," for voice and piano, composed March 21, 1877; dedicated to Countess O. A. Golenishtchev-Kutúsov; the other dates as for No. 76.

80. "A Vision," for voice and piano, words by Count A. Golenishtchev-Kutúsov, composed April 8, 1877, dedicated to Elizabeth A. Gulevitch; the other dates as for No. 76.

81. "Master Haughty (Arrogance)," for voice and piano, words by Count A. Tolstoy, composed May 15–16, 1877, dedicated to A. E. Paltchikov; the other dates as for No. 76.

82. "The Wanderer," for voice and piano, words by Pleshtcheiev, composed 1878 (?), published, 1882, by Bessel (Rimsky-Korsakov); new edition 1908, with German words by A. Bernhard and French by Calvocoressi; MS. in the Public Library at Petersburg.

83. "Mephisto's Song in Auerbach's Cellar (The Song of the Flea)," words by Goethe, in Strugovstchikov's Russian translation, composed 1879, dedicated to the singer D. M. Leonova; published, 1883, by Bessel (Rimsky-Korsakov); new edition 1908, with the original German words, and French words by Calvocoressi.

84. "On the Dnieper," for voice and piano, words by Shevtchenko (from *The Haidamaks*), a new version of "Yarema's Song," composed December 23, 1879 (cf. No. 37); other dates unknown.[1]

---

[1] This song is included in the collected edition of Moussorgsky's songs brought out by Bessel (Breitkopf & Härtel) in 1922.

406

85. "On the South Coast of the Crimea," [1] capriccio for piano, composed 1879, published, 1880, by Bernard, new edition by Jürgenson in Moscow.

86. "On the South Coast of the Crimea (Goursouf)," [1] composed 1879, appeared 1880 in the musical journal *The Novelist;* new edition by Jürgenson.

87. "*Méditation,*" a short piece for piano, [1] composed 1880, published by Jürgenson.

88. "*Une Larme* (A Tear)," [1] for piano, composed 1880, published by Jürgenson.

89. "*La Couturière* (The Dressmaker)," [1] scherzino for piano, composed 1880, published by Jürgenson; new edition by Belaiev.

90. "*Au village* (In the Village)," for piano, composed 1880, published by Jürgenson, dedicated to I. F. Gorbounov.

91. Four Russian Folk-songs, arranged for male chorus, unaccompanied (1880 ?), published by Jürgenson at Moscow in the collection *Dumsky Krushok (Duma Union).*

92. *A Night on the Bare Mountain,* fantasia for orchestra; the final arrangement of this piece was made by Rimsky-Korsakov, and published by Bessel, 1886; the version is dedicated to V. V. Stassov; cf. No. 48 and No. 62 of this list.

93. *Pougatchovstchina,* title of an opera, of which only the sketch of a Kirghiz melody has been found; this was Moussorgsky's last plan for future compositions.

ADDENDUM

36a. "Oh, you drunken beast" (literally, "You drunken old heathcock") from the *Adventures of Pakhomitch,* for contralto and piano, words by Moussorgsky, composed September 22, 1866; dedicated to Vladimir Vassilievitch Nikolsky, who left the MS. in 1925 to the Public Library at Petersburg. It is to be published (in a photographic facsimile) by the Russian State Publishing Office.

In the Public Library at Petersburg there is also the MS. of

---

[1] The piano pieces Nos. 85–90 on the list were included by Bessel (Breitkopf & Härtel) in a collected edition of Moussorgsky's piano pieces.

a Don Cossack song, "set" by Moussorgsky, and "arranged" for full military band by Rimsky-Korsakov (the words come down from the sixteenth century). There are also in the Library many sketches of numerous foreign folk-songs written down by Moussorgsky (Burman, Caucasian, Persian, and Little Russian melodies, a dervish's song, songs of the Old Believers).

LIST OF LITERATURE RELATING
TO MOUSSORGSKY

BASKIN, W. S.: *M. P. Moussorgsky,* Moscow, 1887.

CUI, CÉSAR: *"Boris Godounov,"* St. Petersburg *News (Peterburg-skia Vedomosty),* 1874, No. 33.

—*The Russian Romance,* Petersburg, 1896.

—"Passages from my Memoirs," Petersburg, *Imperial Theatre Annual, 1899–1900.*

FINDEISEN, N. F.: "Moussorgsky's Youth," Petersburg, *Imperial Theatre Annual, 1906.*

—*"The Fair at Sorótchintzy,"* Russian *Musical News (Russkaia Musikalnaia Gazeta),* 1916, No. 11.

—*V. V. Bessel, a Sketch of his Life and Influence,* Petersburg, 1909.

GLEBOV, IGOR: *Symphonic Studies* ("M. P. Moussorgsky"), Petersburg, 1922.

YASTREBTZEV, V. V.: *My Recollections of N. A. Rimsky-Korsakov,* in two parts, Petersburg, 1917.

KARATIGIN, V. V.: *"Salambo,* by M. P. Moussorgsky"; in the journal *Apollo,* Petersburg, 1909, No. 2.

—"In Memory of Moussorgsky," ib., 1911, No. 4.

—*"Khovanstchina* and its authors," in the journal *The Musical Contemporary (Musikalny Sovremennik),* Petersburg, 1917, Nos. 5 and 6.

—*"The Fair at Sorótchintzy,"* ib.

—"In Moussorgsky's Home," ib.

—*Moussorgsky and Chaliapin,* Petersburg, 1922.

KERSIN, A.: *M. P. Moussorgsky,* Moscow, 1906.

KOMAROVA, VARVARA: "Childish Memories of Great Men," *Musical Contemporary,* 1917, Nos. 5 and 6.

LAROCHE, A. C.: *"Boris Godounov,* by Moussorgsky," Petersburg, in the paper *Golos (The Voice),* 1874, Nos. 29 and 44.

LEONOVA, D. M.: "Recollections," Petersburg, in the *Historical Messenger (Istoritchesky Vestnik),* 1891.

LUBIMOV, S. V.: *The Princes Kostrov. Documents on their family history. The Moussorgskys. An essay at tracing their pedigree.* Pskov, 1916.

MOUSSORGSKY, M. P.: Letters to N. A. Rimsky-Korsakov, *Russian Musical News,* 1909, No. 17.

—Letters to A. N. and N. N. Purgold, ib., 1911, Nos. 8 and 9.

—Two letters to N. A. Rimsky-Korsakov and A. N. Mollas, ib., 1911, No. 13.

—*Letters to V. V. Stassov,* published by N. F. Findeisen, Petersburg, 1916.

—Letters to L. I. Shestakova, *Musical Contemporary,* 1917, Nos. 5 and 6.

—"Autobiography," ib.

RIMSKY-KORSAKOV, N. A.: *My Musical Life* (1844–1906), Petersburg, 1909 (English translation by Judah A. Joffe, New York, Knopf, 1923).

RIMSKY-KORSAKOV, A. N. (junior): *"Boris Godounov* by M. P. Moussorgsky," *Musical Contemporary,* 1917, Nos. 5 and 6.

RUSSIAN MUSICAL NEWS: "Material for a Family History of Moussorgsky," 1911, No. 10.

SHESTAKOVA, L. I.: "Recollections of M. P. Moussorgsky," *Imperial Theatre Annual, 1893–4,* 2nd supplement, Petersburg.

STASSOV, V. V.: "M. P. Moussorgsky," Petersburg, in the *European Messenger (Yevropeisky Vestnik),* 1881, Nos. 5 and 6 (also in Vol. III of his collected works, Petersburg, 1894).

—*Essay on M. P. Moussorgsky,* Moscow, 1922 (reprinted).

TRIFONOV, V. N.: "Moussorgsky," *European Messenger,* 1893.

FRENCH

D'ALHEIM, PIERRE: *Moussorgsky,* Paris, 1896.

—*Sept Conférences sur Moussorgsky et enquête,* Paris, 1896.

BELLAIGUE, C.: *Impressions musicales et littéraires,* Paris, 1900.

410

—*Études musicales,* 2nd series *("Un Grand Musicien réaliste: Moussorgsky"),* Paris, 1901.

CALVOCORESSI, M. D.: *Moussorgsky,* 3rd edition, Paris, 1921. German revised edition by Carl Seelig, Vienna, 1921, published by E. P. Tal.

CUI, CÉSAR: *La Musique en Russie,* Paris, 1880.

DEBUSSY, CLAUDE: *"Moussorgsky,"* Revue *Blanche,* Paris, 1901 (April 15, June 1).

GODET, ROBERT: *"Les Deux Boris,"* La Revue musicale, Paris, 1922, No. 6.

KOECHLIN, CH.: *" 'Le Mariage,' Comédie musicale de Moussorgsky,"* La Revue musicale, 1923, No. 7.

OLENINE D'ALHEIM, MARIE: *Les Legs de Moussorgsky,* Paris, 1908.

LALO, PIERRE: Articles in the *Temps,* Paris, 1901 (April 18, June 19, July 5).

SCHLÖZER, BORIS: *" 'La Foire de Sorotschinzy' de Moussorgsky,"* La Revue musicale, 1923, No. 9.

VUILLERMOZ, E.: *"La Khowanchtchina,"* La Revue musicale, 1923, No. 7.

GERMAN

HANDSCHIN, S.: *"Mussorgski," Neujahrsblatt der Allgemeinen Musikgesellschaft,* Zurich, 1924.

LEONTEV, A. VON: *"Mussorgski, eine Erinnerung," Neue Züricher Zeitung,* 1923, No. 892.

LEPEL, FELIX VON: *"War Modest P. Mussorgski ein verwildertes Genie?"* Berlin, *Signale für die musikalische Welt,* 1923, Nos. 22–5.

RIESEMANN, O. VON: *"Die Oper in Russland,"* Berlin, *Die Musik,* 1906–7, Nos. 13–15.

—*"Les Legs de Moussorgsky,"* Berlin, *Signale für die musikalische Welt,* 1908, Nos. 36–9.

—*"Eine Neue Oper von Mussorgski,"* Berlin, *Die Musik,* 1922–3, No. 7.

—*"Jahre der Jugend von Mussorgski"* (the Paris manuscript), Prague, *Auftakt,* 1924, No. 3.

WOLFURT, KURT VON: *"Das Problem Mussorgski-Rimski-Korssakow,"* Berlin, *Die Musik,* 1925, April.

ENGLISH

GODET, ROBERT: "The True and the False Boris," London, *The Chesterian*, 1922, No. 23 (New Series).
—"The Death of Moussorgsky," ib., 1922, No. 27.
SWANN, ALFRED I: "The Three Styles of Moussorgsky," ib.

ITALIAN

DAMERINI, ADELMO: *"Boris Godunoff" di M. Mussorgski*, Milan.

DUTCH

POLS, ANDRÉ: *Mussorgski*, Amsterdam, 1925.

412

INDEX

INDEX

417

A CATALOGUE OF SELECTED DOVER BOOKS
IN ALL FIELDS OF INTEREST

A CATALOGUE OF SELECTED DOVER BOOKS
IN ALL FIELDS OF INTEREST

AMERICA'S OLD MASTERS, James T. Flexner. Four men emerged unexpectedly from provincial 18th century America to leadership in European art: Benjamin West, J. S. Copley, C. R. Peale, Gilbert Stuart. Brilliant coverage of lives and contributions. Revised, 1967 edition. 69 plates. 365pp. of text.

21806-6 Paperbound $2.75

FIRST FLOWERS OF OUR WILDERNESS: AMERICAN PAINTING, THE COLONIAL PERIOD, James T. Flexner. Painters, and regional painting traditions from earliest Colonial times up to the emergence of Copley, West and Peale Sr., Foster, Gustavus Hesselius, Feke, John Smibert and many anonymous painters in the primitive manner. Engaging presentation, with 162 illustrations. xxii + 368pp.

22180-6 Paperbound $3.50

THE LIGHT OF DISTANT SKIES: AMERICAN PAINTING, 1760-1835, James T. Flexner. The great generation of early American painters goes to Europe to learn and to teach: West, Copley, Gilbert Stuart and others. Allston, Trumbull, Morse; also contemporary American painters—primitives, derivatives, academics—who remained in America. 102 illustrations. xiii + 306pp. 22179-2 Paperbound $3.00

A HISTORY OF THE RISE AND PROGRESS OF THE ARTS OF DESIGN IN THE UNITED STATES, William Dunlap. Much the richest mine of information on early American painters, sculptors, architects, engravers, miniaturists, etc. The only source of information for scores of artists, the major primary source for many others. Unabridged reprint of rare original 1834 edition, with new introduction by James T. Flexner, and 394 new illustrations. Edited by Rita Weiss. 6⅝ x 9⅝.

21695-0, 21696-9, 21697-7 Three volumes, Paperbound $13.50

EPOCHS OF CHINESE AND JAPANESE ART, Ernest F. Fenollosa. From primitive Chinese art to the 20th century, thorough history, explanation of every important art period and form, including Japanese woodcuts; main stress on China and Japan, but Tibet, Korea also included. Still unexcelled for its detailed, rich coverage of cultural background, aesthetic elements, diffusion studies, particularly of the historical period. 2nd, 1913 edition. 242 illustrations. lii + 439pp. of text.

20364-6, 20365-4 Two volumes, Paperbound $5.00

THE GENTLE ART OF MAKING ENEMIES, James A. M. Whistler. Greatest wit of his day deflates Oscar Wilde, Ruskin, Swinburne; strikes back at inane critics, exhibitions, art journalism; aesthetics of impressionist revolution in most striking form. Highly readable classic by great painter. Reproduction of edition designed by Whistler. Introduction by Alfred Werner. xxxvi + 334pp.

21875-9 Paperbound $2.25

THE ARCHITECTURE OF COUNTRY HOUSES, Andrew J. Downing. Together with Vaux's *Villas and Cottages* this is the basic book for Hudson River Gothic architecture of the middle Victorian period. Full, sound discussions of general aspects of housing, architecture, style, decoration, furnishing, together with scores of detailed house plans, illustrations of specific buildings, accompanied by full text. Perhaps the most influential single American architectural book. 1850 edition. Introduction by J. Stewart Johnson. 321 figures, 34 architectural designs. xvi + 560pp.
22003-6 Paperbound $3.50

LOST EXAMPLES OF COLONIAL ARCHITECTURE, John Mead Howells. Full-page photographs of buildings that have disappeared or been so altered as to be denatured, including many designed by major early American architects. 245 plates. xvii + 248pp. 7⅞ x 10¾. 21143-6 Paperbound $3.00

DOMESTIC ARCHITECTURE OF THE AMERICAN COLONIES AND OF THE EARLY REPUBLIC, Fiske Kimball. Foremost architect and restorer of Williamsburg and Monticello covers nearly 200 homes between 1620-1825. Architectural details, construction, style features, special fixtures, floor plans, etc. Generally considered finest work in its area. 219 illustrations of houses, doorways, windows, capital mantels. xx + 314pp. 7⅞ x 10¾. 21743-4 Paperbound $3.50

EARLY AMERICAN ROOMS: 1650-1858, edited by Russell Hawes Kettell. Tour of 12 rooms, each representative of a different era in American history and each furnished, decorated, designed and occupied in the style of the era. 72 plans and elevations, 8-page color section, etc., show fabrics, wall papers, arrangements, etc. Full descriptive text. xvii + 200pp. of text. 8⅜ x 11¼.
21633-0 Paperbound $4.00

THE FITZWILLIAM VIRGINAL BOOK, edited by J. Fuller Maitland and W. B. Squire. Full modern printing of famous early 17th-century ms. volume of 300 works by Morley, Byrd, Bull, Gibbons, etc. For piano or other modern keyboard instrument; easy to read format. xxxvi + 938pp. 8⅜ x 11.
21068-5, 21069-3 Two volumes, Paperbound $8.00

HARPSICHORD MUSIC, Johann Sebastian Bach. Bach Gesellschaft edition. A rich selection of Bach's masterpieces for the harpsichord: the six English Suites, six French Suites, the six Partitas (Clavierübung part I), the Goldberg Variations (Clavierübung part IV), the fifteen Two-Part Inventions and the fifteen Three-Part Sinfonias. Clearly reproduced on large sheets with ample margins; eminently playable. vi + 312pp. 8⅛ x 11. 22360-4 Paperbound $5.00

THE MUSIC OF BACH: AN INTRODUCTION, Charles Sanford Terry. A fine, nontechnical introduction to Bach's music, both instrumental and vocal. Covers organ music, chamber music, passion music, other types. Analyzes themes, developments, innovations. x + 114pp. 21075-8 Paperbound $1.25

BEETHOVEN AND HIS NINE SYMPHONIES, Sir George Grove. Noted British musicologist provides best history, analysis, commentary on symphonies. Very thorough, rigorously accurate; necessary to both advanced student and amateur music lover. 436 musical passages. vii + 407 pp. 20334-4 Paperbound $2.25

A HISTORY OF COSTUME, Carl Köhler. Definitive history, based on surviving pieces of clothing primarily, and paintings, statues, etc. secondarily. Highly readable text, supplemented by 594 illustrations of costumes of the ancient Mediterranean peoples, Greece and Rome, the Teutonic prehistoric period; costumes of the Middle Ages, Renaissance, Baroque, 18th and 19th centuries. Clear, measured patterns are provided for many clothing articles. Approach is practical throughout. Enlarged by Emma von Sichart. 464pp.   21030-8 Paperbound $3.00

ORIENTAL RUGS, ANTIQUE AND MODERN, Walter A. Hawley. A complete and authoritative treatise on the Oriental rug—where they are made, by whom and how, designs and symbols, characteristics in detail of the six major groups, how to distinguish them and how to buy them. Detailed technical data is provided on periods, weaves, warps, wefts, textures, sides, ends and knots, although no technical background is required for an understanding. 11 color plates, 80 halftones, 4 maps. vi + 320pp. 6⅛ x 9⅛.   22366-3 Paperbound $5.00

TEN BOOKS ON ARCHITECTURE, Vitruvius. By any standards the most important book on architecture ever written. Early Roman discussion of aesthetics of building, construction methods, orders, sites, and every other aspect of architecture has inspired, instructed architecture for about 2,000 years. Stands behind Palladio, Michelangelo, Bramante, Wren, countless others. Definitive Morris H. Morgan translation. 68 illustrations. xii + 331pp.   20645-9 Paperbound $2.50

THE FOUR BOOKS OF ARCHITECTURE, Andrea Palladio. Translated into every major Western European language in the two centuries following its publication in 1570, this has been one of the most influential books in the history of architecture. Complete reprint of the 1738 Isaac Ware edition. New introduction by Adolf Placzek, Columbia Univ. 216 plates. xxii + 110pp. of text. 9½ x 12¾.
                                21308-0 Clothbound $10.00

STICKS AND STONES: A STUDY OF AMERICAN ARCHITECTURE AND CIVILIZATION, Lewis Mumford.One of the great classics of American cultural history. American architecture from the medieval-inspired earliest forms to the early 20th century; evolution of structure and style, and reciprocal influences on environment. 21 photographic illustrations. 238pp.   20202-X Paperbound $2.00

THE AMERICAN BUILDER'S COMPANION, Asher Benjamin. The most widely used early 19th century architectural style and source book, for colonial up into Greek Revival periods. Extensive development of geometry of carpentering, construction of sashes, frames, doors, stairs; plans and elevations of domestic and other buildings. Hundreds of thousands of houses were built according to this book, now invaluable to historians, architects, restorers, etc. 1827 edition. 59 plates. 114pp. 7⅞ x 10¾.
                                22236-5 Paperbound $3.00

DUTCH HOUSES IN THE HUDSON VALLEY BEFORE 1776, Helen Wilkinson Reynolds. The standard survey of the Dutch colonial house and outbuildings, with constructional features, decoration, and local history associated with individual homesteads. Introduction by Franklin D. Roosevelt. Map. 150 illustrations. 469pp. 6⅝ x 9¼.   21469-9 Paperbound $3.50

CATALOGUE OF DOVER BOOKS

MATHEMATICAL PUZZLES FOR BEGINNERS AND ENTHUSIASTS, Geoffrey Mott-Smith.
189 puzzles from easy to difficult—involving arithmetic, logic, algebra, properties
of digits, probability, etc.—for enjoyment and mental stimulus. Explanation of
mathematical principles behind the puzzles. 135 illustrations. viii + 248pp.
20198-8 Paperbound $1.25

PAPER FOLDING FOR BEGINNERS, William D. Murray and Francis J. Rigney. Easiest
book on the market, clearest instructions on making interesting, beautiful origami.
Sail boats, cups, roosters, frogs that move legs, bonbon boxes, standing birds, etc.
40 projects; more than 275 diagrams and photographs. 94pp.
20713-7 Paperbound $1.00

TRICKS AND GAMES ON THE POOL TABLE, Fred Herrmann. 79 tricks and games—
some solitaires, some for two or more players, some competitive games—to entertain
you between formal games. Mystifying shots and throws, unusual caroms, tricks
involving such props as cork, coins, a hat, etc. Formerly *Fun on the Pool Table*.
77 figures. 95pp. 21814-7 Paperbound $1.00

HAND SHADOWS TO BE THROWN UPON THE WALL: A SERIES OF NOVEL AND
AMUSING FIGURES FORMED BY THE HAND, Henry Bursill. Delightful picturebook
from great-grandfather's day shows how to make 18 different hand shadows: a bird
that flies, duck that quacks, dog that wags his tail, camel, goose, deer, boy, turtle,
etc. Only book of its sort. vi + 33pp. 6½ x 9¼. 21779-5 Paperbound $1.00

WHITTLING AND WOODCARVING, E. J. Tangerman. 18th printing of best book on
market. "If you can cut a potato you can carve" toys and puzzles, chains, chessmen,
caricatures, masks, frames, woodcut blocks, surface patterns, much more. Information
on tools, woods, techniques. Also goes into serious wood sculpture from Middle
Ages to present, East and West. 464 photos, figures. x + 293pp.
20965-2 Paperbound $2.00

HISTORY OF PHILOSOPHY, Julián Marías. Possibly the clearest, most easily followed,
best planned, most useful one-volume history of philosophy on the market; neither
skimpy nor overfull. Full details on system of every major philosopher and dozens
of less important thinkers from pre-Socratics up to Existentialism and later. Strong
on many European figures usually omitted. Has gone through dozens of editions in
Europe. 1966 edition, translated by Stanley Appelbaum and Clarence Strowbridge.
xviii + 505pp. 21739-6 Paperbound $2.75

YOGA: A SCIENTIFIC EVALUATION, Kovoor T. Behanan. Scientific but non-technical
study of physiological results of yoga exercises; done under auspices of Yale U.
Relations to Indian thought, to psychoanalysis, etc. 16 photos. xxiii + 270pp.
20505-3 Paperbound $2.50

Prices subject to change without notice.
Available at your book dealer or write for free catalogue to Dept. GI, Dover
Publications, Inc., 180 Varick St., N. Y., N. Y. 10014. Dover publishes more than
150 books each year on science, elementary and advanced mathematics, biology,
music, art, literary history, social sciences and other areas.